READINGS IN .... OCIOLOGY

Contemporary Political

READINGS IN CONTEMPORARY POLITICAL SOCIOLOGY

Edited by

Kate Nash

BLACKWELL
Publishers

Copyright © Blackwell Publishers Ltd 2000; editorial introductions and
arrangement copyright © Kate Nash 2000

First published 2000

Transferred to digital print 2004

2 4 6 8 10 9 7 5 3 1

Blackwell Publishers Inc.
350 Main Street
Malden, Massachusetts 02148
USA

Blackwell Publishers Ltd
108 Cowley Road
Oxford OX4 1JF
UK

Library of Congress Cataloging-in-Publication Data

Readings in contemporary political sociology / edited by Kate Nash.
    p.   cm.
    Includes bibliographical references and index.
    ISBN 0–631–21363–5 (hardbound : alk. paper). — ISBN
0–631–21364–3 (pbk.: alk. paper)
    1. Political sociology.   I. Nash, Kate, 1958– .
JA76.R4   1999
306.2 — dc21   99–16940
                                                              CIP

British Library Cataloguing in Publication Data

A CIP catalogue record for this book is available from the British Library.

Typeset in 10½ on 12 pt Sabon
by Best-set Typesetter Ltd, Hong Kong
Printed and bound in Great Britain by Marston Book Services Limited, Oxford

This book is printed on acid-free paper.

CONTENTS

CONTRIBUTORS

Arjun Appadurai is professor of anthropology and South Asian languages and civilization at the University of Chicago. He has recently published *Modernity at Large*, an elaboration of his influential ideas on cultural globalization.

Zygmunt Bauman is emeritus professor at the universities of Leeds and Warsaw. He has written and published widely in social theory, including, most recently, *Globalization* and a new edition of *Culture as Praxis*. Some of his essays on the relation between sociology and postmodernity are collected in *Intimations of Postmodernity*.

Craig Calhoun is professor of sociology at New York University. His interests are in critical social theory, identity, and difference. His publications in this field include *Social Theory and the Politics of Identity* and *Critical Social Theory*.

William E. Connolly is professor in the Department of Political Science at Johns Hopkins University. He has published widely on postmodernism, politics, and democratic theory, including *Identity/Difference* and *The Ethos of Pluralization*.

Mario Diani is professor of sociology at the University of Strathclyde, Glasgow. He has recently published *Green Networks*, and a comprehensive overview of social movement studies called *Social Movements* with Donatella Della Porta.

Michel Foucault was self-designated Professor of the History of Systems of Thought at the Collège de France in Paris from 1970 until his death

in 1984. The influence of his extensive writings on sociology and political theory cannot be over-estimated. They include *Discipline and
Punish*, three volumes of *The History of Sexuality*, and essays on gov-
ernmentality collected in *The Foucault Effect*.

Anthony Giddens is director of the London School of Economics. One
of the most prolific and influential sociologists working today, he has
published on virtually every topic in social theory. Recently, in such
books as *Beyond Left and Right* and *The Third Way*, he has focused
explicitly on politics.

Jürgen Habermas is professor emeritus of philosophy at the University
of Frankfurt. Well-known as a philosopher and social theorist of the
Frankfurt School, his sociological study *The Structural Transformation
of the Public Sphere* is linked to his interventions in debates on German
and European politics. Some of these are now collected in *A Berlin
Republic*.

Stuart Hall recently retired as professor of sociology at the Open
University. His work spans a lifetime of commitment to radical thought
and he has been a key figure in the formation of cultural studies as an
academic discipline. A selection of his writings and interviews, called
Stuart Hall: Critical Dialogues in Cultural Studies, has recently been
published.

David Harvey is professor of geography at Johns Hopkins University.
His book, *The Condition of Postmodernity*, is one of the most
influential re-statements of Marxism in recent times.

David Held is professor of politics and sociology at the Open University. His recent publications on globalization and democracy include
Democracy and the Global Order and *Global Transformations*, co-
authored with Anthony McGrew, David Goldblatt, and Jonathan
Perraton.

Chantal Mouffe is senior research fellow at the Centre for the Study of
Democracy of the University of Westminster, London and a member of
the Collège Internationale de Philosophie in Paris. An influential figure
in academic post-Marxism, she co-wrote *Hegemony and Socialist
Strategy* with Ernesto Laclau. Some of her more recent essays on
democratic theory are collected in *The Return of the Political*.

Carole Pateman is professor of political science at the University of
California, Los Angeles. An influential writer in democratic theory as

well as feminism, some of her most important feminist essays are collected in *The Disorder of Women*.

Maurice Roche is senior lecturer in sociology at the University of Sheffield. He has written widely on citizenship in contemporary society, most notably in *Rethinking Citizenship*.

Yasemin Nuhoğlu Soysal is lecturer in sociology at the University of Essex. Her interests in citizenship, identity, and migration are addressed in her book on post-national citizenship, *Limits of Citizenship*.

Sidney Tarrow is Maxwell Upson Professor of Government at Cornell University. He has carried out extensive research into historical and contemporary social movements, especially in Italy and France, and has recently published the second edition of his overview of social movement studies, *Power in Movement*.

Malcolm Waters is professor of sociology at the University of Tasmania. He has published widely on issues in contemporary political sociology, including *Postmodernization* with Stephen Crook and Jan Pakulski, *Globalization*, and *The Death of Class* with Jan Pakulski.

PREFACE

This reader is a collection of articles and extracts from books which have contributed significantly to a re-thinking of political sociology in the past two decades. Traditionally, political sociology has been concerned with the relations between society and the state. It may be distinguished in this respect from political science, which takes politics much more directly as its object of study and which is therefore more concerned with government and the state as such. It is less easily distinguished from political theory. Both political sociology and political theory are concerned with the empirical study of politics and also with conceptual definitions and analyses. Both disciplines have, therefore, been engaged in questioning the definition of politics on which traditional sociology and political science have been based. It is perhaps true to say that political theory is somewhat more concerned with normative questions than political sociology; certainly, this is the case where it shades into political philosophy. A number of the pieces collected here have also been extremely influential for those working in political theory, especially those in parts IV and V on citizenship and democracy.

Traditional political sociology takes the modern nation-state as the center of political activity. It is concerned above all with the relations between class, as the main dimension of stratification in modern societies, and politics. Power is seen as exercised by the state, which enjoys either a legitimate or an ideological monopoly of the use of force, depending on the theoretical perspective. The question for Marxists is the extent to which the state is determined by the class interests of the bourgeoisie, the owners of the means of production, and to what extent bureaucrats and politicians exercise independent control over the organization of social relations. The answer varies, but it is axiomatic for the Marxist approach that economic relations play a crucial part in politics. For those inspired more by Weberian sociology, in which the state is seen as influencing society independently of social and economic interests, questions concern the way in which class interests have been represented in the political process by major political parties, how democracy actually works, and how the modern state gains and maintains legitimacy. In the new political sociology, attention shifts from formal politics at the level of the nation-state, and its relationship to class, to politics as an inherent possibility in all social relations. The state remains important, but it is displaced as the center of political activity. The emphasis in new political sociology is on the contestation of social relations in culture: in everyday life, media representations, and institutional practices. Changes in the state may follow as a result of cultural contestation, and state practices may themselves be contested, but politics is not confined to the activities of political parties, interest groups lobbying politicians nor the agenda-setting of bureaucrats and elites. The state is not set against society as the realm of politics: politics is a potential in social life itself.

The redefinition of politics in new political sociology is a result of both empirical and theoretical changes. Theoretically, it depends on a re-conceptualization of power. The most influential theorist in this respect is undoubtedly Michel Foucault, for whom power is not dependent on institutions, nor possessed by a social group or class. Power is seen as productive of subjectivity, or identity. It is exercised in practices which, since the eighteenth century, have been closely related to the means by which knowledge is collected and used. For Foucault, the construction of subjectivity is at the same time subjection: to classification, surveillance, and normalization. Although Foucault himself gave little attention to politics in his work – he was more interested in the ethics of the individual self – a very different definition of politics results from this understanding of power. Politics involves the contestation of subjection or, alternatively, the repression of a confrontation in which subjection is contested. It is, therefore, a possibility in any social relation and may take place in any social context. These themes are addressed by Foucault in chapter 1.

The wider definition of politics developed in post-structuralism is closely related to what has been called the "cultural turn" in sociology. In its most general sense, this simply means that sociology is now more concerned with meaning and the interpretation that social actors give events and practices than with structure and the causes of social behavior. Sociologists may be said to have moved closer to the way in which anthropologists see society as cultural, as involving a particular way of life. However, this is somewhat misleading in that the "cultural turn" in sociology coincides with the "postmodern turn." Even though not all those who participate in the former are happy to be categorized as contributing to the latter, sociologists tend to share a view of culture in advanced capitalist societies as fragmented, unstable, fluid, and fast-changing. These are all characteristics taken to be defining of post-modern culture. They are not well captured by the anthropological view of culture which implies that ways of life are fixed and enduring. The understanding of culture exemplified in new political sociology is better seen as involving disparate and diverse signifying practices which do not necessarily form an easily identifiable, bounded totality, "a society."

This characterization of culture, and the prominent place of post-structuralism in redefining concepts of power and politics, mean that it is appropriate to think of new political sociology as participating in the "postmodern turn." This links it to the re-thinking which has been going on in all the disciplines of the social sciences and humanities to a greater or lesser extent in recent years. In relation to the study of politics it is important for two main reasons. First, politics may be seen as cultural. Where social life is based on signification, the manipulation of symbols is itself political. Politics in this sense involves the contestation of meanings, the repression of certain possibilities, and the realization of others. Secondly, if culture is taken to be unstable and fluid, cultural politics is the principle of social change. People no longer follow traditional ways, and social structures are taken to be insufficiently fixed to do any more than constrain their activities in flexible and indeterminate ways. Social life is endlessly being remade through the lifestyle choices, value judgments, and changing definitions of self-interest which individuals and groups bring to bear upon it. In this respect, not only is politics a potentiality in every aspect of social life, it is arguably also increasingly important. It is the continual contestation and re-formation of social identities and institutions in cultural politics which make possible the reproduction of relatively stable but fluid forms of contemporary social life.

Empirical changes have contributed to the change in focus of political sociology by decentering the state as the center of political activity. There are two main changes in this respect. First, processes of globalization have drawn attention to the reduced autonomy of the state. Given, however, that its dependence on socio-economic relations was an issue in traditional political sociology, this would not be sufficient in itself to require a re-thinking of the field. More importantly, such processes have called into question the very idea of society as a bounded entity, uncovering the traditional sociological assumption that a "society" is equivalent to the bounded territory of a nation-state. Once the extent to which economic activities, groups of people, ideas, media images, and so on cut across territorial borders is acknowledged, it is more difficult to think in terms of "British society" or "American society." Furthermore, global processes call into question the scope of political decisions. If people are affected by processes which the nation-

state cannot control, questions arise concerning where and how decisions about those processes should be made. Politics at the level of the
nation-state may be seen as quite irrelevant to such matters as environmental pollution, for example, which is not contained within the
borders of any single country. In fact, the growth of international political agreements and institutions, such as the UN, NATO, GATT, and so
on, means that the sovereignty of the nation-state is now shared to an
unprecedented extent. Furthermore, although the most powerful states
continue to play an important role in international relations, transnational political actors are also important: multinational corporations,
non-governmental organizations such as Oxfam and Amnesty International, and transnational social movements are now also players in
global politics.

This brings us to the second main dimension of change: the substantial increase in the activities of social movements since the 1960s.
Movements such as feminism, the environmental movement, the lesbian
and gay movement, and others are clearly engaged in changing identities, redefining taken-for-granted situations and events and creating new
lifestyles. All these activities must be considered political in the widest
sense of the term. They are difficult to see, however, within the terms
of traditional political sociology. Social movements do address the state;
in particular they are engaged in contesting the terms of citizenship as
it has been established in Western liberal democracies. However, to deal
with them only under this aspect of their activities is to neglect what
makes them social movements as such, rather than, say, interest groups
or political parties. Furthermore, social movements have politicized
identities, relations, and activities other than those of class and the labor
movement which was so prominent in the nineteenth and early twentieth centuries. As such, they are not easily encompassed in the traditional
model of political sociology in which politics is related to class and political organizations are organized around class interests.

To deal with politics in relation to processes of globalization and
social movements, the wider definitions of power and politics, which
tend to guide those working in contemporary political sociology, are
more appropriate. Not all those who have written the pieces collected
in this reader would agree that a paradigm shift in political sociology
is necessary or desirable. However, they all take seriously the idea that
important changes in contemporary social and political life are taking
place for which sociology needs to develop new tools and concepts. In
this respect, they have all contributed to the re-thinking of political
sociology represented in this volume.

The first part, on changing definitions of power and politics, is the
only one exclusively concerned with theoretical considerations. The
other parts, on globalization, social movements, citizenship, and democ-

racy, all contain pieces on the substantive area of study; most of the chapters combine empirical analyses with conceptual work. At the beginning of each part, the reader will find an introduction to the pieces collected there, summarizing and explaining concepts in order to help students unfamiliar with the literature to understand the main points of each chapter. The introductions also provide contextual background to the pieces where it is needed and make links and comparisons, cross-referencing ideas and topics in different chapters.

I would like to thank David Owen, Anna Marie-Smith, and Neil Wash-bourne for their help in putting this collection together. The source of each chapter is given in full at the foot of each chapter's opening page. An ellipsis in square brackets has been used whenever material has been omitted from the original [. . .]. Any other small changes also appear in square brackets. The editor and publishers wish to thank copyright holders for permission to use copyright material.

PART I POWER AND POLITICS

Introduction

New definitions of power and politics are the subject of part I. We begin with an article by Foucault (chapter 1), first published toward the end of his life, in which he reflects on his previous work in terms of the concepts of power and subjectivity. In this chapter he gives what is probably the most precise account of his understanding of power and politics to appear anywhere in his extensive writings.

Foucault suggests here that we begin to study power by looking at resistance, by which he means the anti-authority struggles of social movements. In particular he thinks social movements are engaged in struggles against the imposition of identity. The construction of subjectivity by those who tell us the "truth" of who we are – psychologists, doctors, criminologists, and others engaged in the "human sciences" – is at the same time a subjection to the power they exercise, according to Foucault. He argues that in contemporary society this exercise of power as the imposition of identity is increasingly resisted. Furthermore, since power is not a thing, nor a substance, the only way in which it can be identified is when it is exercised by some people over others. A display of resistance to power therefore provides an important indicator of its existence.

Foucault provides a number of definitions in chapter 1, which refine the understanding of power developed in his previous work. Most significantly, he states that power is only exercised over free subjects. He distinguishes it from violence in this respect, which works directly on the body, forcing it into submission. Power works rather on actions such that there must be a range of alternatives which the individual might have realized had it not been exercised. By definition, power depends on freedom which "supports it" and which means that wherever there is power there is always the possibility of resistance. Foucault also makes a useful distinction between power and domination. Where power has been consolidated into domination, resistance remains possible, but it becomes much more difficult. Domination means that all social relations and institutions are locked into a particular form, so that rather than multiple, small-scale struggles over power, there is either immobility or else the massive convulsions of attempted revolutions. Foucault does not give an example of domination, but he might well have had in mind totalitarian societies like the former communist societies of Eastern Europe.

Finally, there is another definition of power in chapter 1: power exercised in "government." Foucault argues that in contemporary societies power is increasingly rationalized, linked to communication and to the production of individual capacities for work. Furthermore, it is increasingly centralized under the auspices of the state. Foucault sees the state as having an extremely important role in controlling the exercise of power in contemporary societies. However, it is important to note that this is not because the state possesses power; nor is it a matter of the *legitimate* exercise of power, for Foucault. It is rather that, since the sixteenth century, the state has increasingly integrated practices of power developed in other social spaces in order to promote the well-being of the population and the wealth of the nation. It is this form of power as "government" that Foucault sees as particularly effective in contemporary society, and which he understands social movements to be resisting in the name of individual freedom to define one's own identity.

The extract from Zygmunt Bauman's book *Intimations of Postmodernity* (chapter 2) is part of a continuing project on his part to rework sociology, initially developed to study modern societies, to make it more relevant to the changing times. He sees postmodernity as the accentuation of certain features of modernity, features which – necessarily – escaped modern attempts at control. Postmodernity is marked by pluralism, contingency, instability, and fluidity and, in order to study them, sociology must develop new theoretical tools. Bauman's objections to the principal concepts of modern sociology as being inadequate for the study of contemporary social life may be summed up in three points. First, he sees the functionalist idea of society as a self-reproducing system as inappropriate. In postmodernity, social order is contingent and random; social organization does not tend toward the reproduction of a stable system. Social life is not like a biological organism, as functionalist sociologists would have us believe. Secondly, the idea of progress on which much of modern thought was based must also be dismissed. Where social order is like a kaleidoscope, emerging and disappearing without any particular line of development, society should not be seen as having a clear direction at all. Thirdly, the idea of social structure is inadequate in so far as social life in postmodernity is radically underdetermined. Far from causing social forms and events, as functionalists suppose, social structure is itself in a continual process of construction and reconstruction.

Bauman suggests several concepts which he takes to be more relevant to postmodernity than those of mainstream sociology. "Sociality" refers to the way in which social reality is continually being constructed and reconstructed so that social structures emerge as patterns from apparently random events, only to dissolve once again into randomness when new structures emerge. "Habitat" indicates the territory within which individuals move. It provides constraints and resources within which social agents maneuver to produce changes in their environment. If we think of social life as like a theater, habitat includes the theater itself and also a play based on improvisation in which actors are continually making changes as they give their performances. In fact, on this metaphor, we should actually see the actors as rebuilding the theater, and its surroundings too, as they act! "Self-constitution" describes the process by which social agents are continually remaking themselves through their choices in an under-structured world. To continue the metaphor, they change their parts while they are on stage. Bauman suggests the term "self-assembly" to denote the continuing and inconclusive nature of this activity.

Bauman makes clear the centrality of politics in postmodernity, as well as the way in which it differs from modern politics. He argues that the state has been weakened by processes of globalization and also, from below, by nationalism. It has responded by devolving power to separate agencies, thus fragmenting and weakening itself still further. An example would be the way in which member countries of the European Union have devolved power to the regional level in response to the EU emphasis on "subsidiarity" (which means that rule should be carried out at the most local level possible for any particular issue). As a result, Bauman argues that political claims are no longer readily addressed to the state. In postmodernity, political issues are more likely to be taken up in social life as matters of "self-reflexivity" – the search for certainty in a world in which certainty is ended which has the effect of constructing the self around chosen forms of knowledge and ways of life. Bauman is extremely pessimistic about the fragmentation of society into "tribal communities" created around symbols of collective identity and involving attempts to secure safety in an environment perceived as full of risks. Such fragmentation reduces the possibility of progressive politics addressed to the state still further since the solidarity between different groups which would be necessary to bring about changes in legislation and social policy cannot be sustained for long. Although Bauman is positive about postmodernity in so far as he sees it as increasing individual autonomy, he is pessimistic in seeing this as combined with an increase in inequality and in the repression of those who do not enjoy the extensive choices of individualized, consumer society.

Inequality is the theme of chapter 3 by Malcolm Waters. Here he deals with the question of class and new forms of inequality which are not easily seen in terms of occupation. He proposes an adaptation of what he calls the "class-theoretic template" of orthodox sociology. This combines four levels of analysis: class is seen as a socio-economic structure, as descriptive of social groups, as determining of behavior and attitudes, and as giving rise to collective identities with the potential for radical social transformation. Waters argues that it is no longer tenable to think of this model in terms of *class*, given social changes which have brought about new forms of inequalities and identities, though he maintains that the four levels of analysis are still useful. Changes which have made class irrelevant as a sociological category include the construction of the welfare state in the post-war period, the separation of ownership and control of the means of production, the growth in numbers of technical and professional "service industry" workers, and extensive migration from previously colonized countries to the West. At the same time, feminist studies of gender and studies of "race" and ethnicity following decolonization have brought dimensions of stratification excluded by the "class-theoretic template" to sociologists' attention. Women's position in patriarchal societies and the inequalities and conflicts associated with racialized ethnic groups are implicated in socio-economic stratification but they are also separate from it. Class is therefore an inadequate concept for their analysis.

Waters suggests that class has been historically significant since the nineteenth century, though in two rather different social formations. In the nineteenth century, "economic-class society" involved a sharp distinction between "workers" and "bosses" and a high level of antagonism and conflict which could be seen across society. From 1900 this gave way to what he calls "oganized-class society" in which these relations between classes were highly regulated by the state. In the past twenty-five years, however, Waters suggests that advanced capitalist societies are better seen as becoming "status-conventional societies" in which stratification is based on culture rather than on socio-economic structure. Inequalities are produced around symbolic values such as educational credentials, the ability to consume, and value-based status groupings. Political identities no longer follow class lines – exemplified by the way in which political parties now depend on instrumental and "floating voters" rather than loyal supporters.

Like Bauman, Waters sees contemporary society as highly individualized. Identities are reflexively self-composed from the multiple status groups to which an individual may subscribe. Perhaps the most extreme example of this is the way in which even the ascribed identity of sex is now, to some extent at least, a matter of choice. Again like Bauman, however, Waters warns against the view that this "status bazaar" will mean a greater degree of equality. On the contrary, the weakening of the state and the fragmentation of social solidarity mean that inequalities are hard to address; the "casino" market takes precedence over more egalitarian forms of social organization. Furthermore, it is impossible to address such inequalities, Waters suggests, in terms of the "class-theoretic template" of modern sociology. It must be adapted to the new times in order to understand socioeconomic relations, groups, identities, and political activities as based in culture and as productive of the highly individualized actors of the postmodernizing world.

CHAPTER 1

The Subject and Power

Michel Foucault

WHY STUDY POWER: THE QUESTION OF THE SUBJECT[1]

The ideas which I would like to discuss here represent neither a theory nor a methodology.

I would like to say, first of all, what has been the goal of my work during the last twenty years. It has not been to analyze the phenomena of power, nor to elaborate the foundations of such an analysis.

My objective, instead, has been to create a history of the different modes by which, in our culture, human beings are made subjects. My work has dealt with three modes of objectification which transform human beings into subjects.

The first is the modes of inquiry which try to give themselves the status of sciences; for example, the objectivizing of the speaking subject in *grammaire générale*, philology, and linguistics. Or again, in this first mode, the objectivizing of the productive subject, the subject who labors, in the analysis of wealth and of economics. Or, a third example, the objectivizing of the sheer fact of being alive in natural history or biology.

In the second part of my work, I have studied the objectivizing of the subject in what I shall call "dividing practices." The subject is either divided inside himself or divided from others. This process objectivizes him. Examples are the mad and the sane, the sick and the healthy, the criminals and the "good boys."

This chapter is taken from *Michel Foucault: Beyond Structuralism and Hermeneutics*, edited by H. Dreyfus and P. Rabinow (London, Harvester Wheatsheaf, 1982), pp. 208–26. Reprinted by permission of Harvester Wheatsheaf.

Finally, I have sought to study – it is my current work – the way a human being turns him- or herself into a subject. For example, I have chosen the domain of sexuality – how men have learned to recognize themselves as subjects of "sexuality."

Thus it is not power, but the subject, which is the general theme of my research.

It is true that I became quite involved with the question of power. It soon appeared to me that, while the human subject is placed in relations of production and of signification, he is equally placed in power relations which are very complex. Now, it seemed to me that economic history and theory provided a good instrument for relations of production; that linguistics and semiotics offered instruments for studying relations of signification; but for power relations we had no tools of study. We had recourse only to ways of thinking about power based on legal models, that is: What legitimates power? Or we had recourse to ways of thinking about power based on institutional models, that is: What is the state?

It was therefore necessary to expand the dimensions of a definition of power if one wanted to use this definition in studying the objectivizing of the subject.

Do we need a theory of power? Since a theory assumes a prior objectification, it cannot be asserted as a basis for analytical work. But this analytical work cannot proceed without an ongoing conceptualization. And this conceptualization implies critical thought – a constant checking.

The first thing to check is what I should call the "conceptual needs." I mean that the conceptualization should not be founded on a theory of the object – the conceptualized object is not the single criterion of a good conceptualization. We have to know the historical conditions which motivate our conceptualization. We need a historical awareness of our present circumstance.

The second thing to check is the type of reality with which we are dealing.

A writer in a well-known French newspaper once expressed his surprise: 'Why is the notion of power raised by so many people today? Is it such an important subject? Is it so independent that it can be discussed without taking into account other problems?"

This writer's surprise amazes me. I feel skeptical about the assumption that this question has been raised for the first time in the twentieth century. Anyway, for us it is not only a theoretical question, but a part of our experience. I'd like to mention only two "pathological forms" – those two "diseases of power" – fascism and Stalinism. One of the numerous reasons why they are, for us, so puzzling, is that in spite of their historical uniqueness they are not quite original. They used and extended mechanisms already present in most other societies. More than that: in spite of their own internal madness, they used to a large extent the ideas and the devices of our political rationality.

What we need is a new economy of power relations – the word *economy* being used in its theoretical and practical sense. To put it in other words: since Kant, the role of philosophy is to prevent reason from going beyond the limits of what is given in experience; but from the same moment – that is, since the development of the modern state and the political management of society – the role of philosophy is also to keep watch over the excessive powers of political rationality. Which is a rather high expectation.

Everybody is aware of such banal facts. But the fact that they're banal does not mean they don't exist. What we have to do with banal facts is to discover – or try to discover – which specific and perhaps original problem is connected with them.

The relationship between rationalization and excesses of political power is evident. And we should not need to wait for bureaucracy or concentration camps to recognize the existence of such relations. But the problem is: What to do with such an evident fact?

Shall we try reason? To my mind, nothing would be more sterile. First, because the field has nothing to do with guilt or innocence. Second, because it is senseless to refer to reason as the contrary entity to nonreason. Lastly, because such a trial would trap us into playing the arbitrary and boring part of either the rationalist or the irrationalist.

Shall we investigate this kind of rationalism which seems to be specific to our modern culture and which originates in *Aufklärung*? I think that was the approach of some of the members of the Frankfurt School. My purpose, however, is not to start a discussion of their works, although they are most important and valuable. Rather, I would suggest another way of investigating the links between rationalization and power.

It may be wise not to take as a whole the rationalization of society or of culture, but to analyze such a process in several fields, each with reference to a fundamental experience: madness, illness, death, crime, sexuality, and so forth.

I think that the word *rationalization* is dangerous. What we have to do is analyze specific rationalities rather than always invoking the progress of rationalization in general.

Even if the *Aufklärung* has been a very important phase in our history and in the development of political technology, I think we have to refer to much more remote processes if we want to understand how we have been trapped in our own history.

I would like to suggest another way to go further toward a new economy of power relations, a way which is more empirical, more directly related to our present situation, and which implies more relations between theory and practice. It consists of taking the forms of resistance against different forms of power as a starting point. To use another metaphor, it consists of using this resistance as a chemical catalyst so as to bring to light power relations, locate their position, find out their point of application and the methods used. Rather than analyzing power from the point of view of its internal rationality, it consists of analyzing power relations through the antagonism of strategies.

For example, to find out what our society means by sanity, perhaps we should investigate what is happening in the field of insanity.

And what we mean by legality in the field of illegality.

And, in order to understand what power relations are about, perhaps we should investigate the forms of resistance and attempts made to dissociate these relations.

As a starting point, let us take a series of oppositions which have developed over the last few years: opposition to the power of men over women, of parents over children, of psychiatry over the mentally ill, of medicine over the population, of administration over the ways people live.

It is not enough to say that these are anti-authority struggles; we must try to define more precisely what they have in common.

1   They are "transversal" struggles; that is, they are not limited to one country. Of course, they develop more easily and to a greater extent in certain countries, but they are not confined to a particular political or economic form of government.
2   The aim of these struggles is the power effects as such. For example, the medical profession is not criticized primarily because it is a profit-making concern, but because it exercises an uncontrolled power over people's bodies, their health and their life and death.
3   These are "immediate" struggles for two reasons. In such struggles people criticize instances of power which are the closest to them, those which exercise their action on individuals. They do not look for the "chief enemy," but for the immediate enemy. Nor do they expect to find a solution to their problem at a future date (that is, liberations, revolutions, end of class struggle). In comparison with a theoretical scale of explanations or a revolutionary order which polarizes the historian, they are anarchistic struggles.

But these are not their most original points. The following seem to me to be more specific.

4   They are struggles which question the status of the individual: on the one hand, they assert the right to be different and they underline everything which makes individuals truly individual. On the other hand, they attack everything which separates the individual,

breaks his links with others, splits up community life, forces the individual back on himself and ties him to his own identity in a constraining way. These struggles are not exactly for or against the
"individual," but rather they are struggles against the "government
of individualization."

5 They are an opposition to the effects of power which are linked with
   knowledge, competence, and qualification: struggles against the
   privileges of knowledge. But they are also an opposition against
   secrecy, deformation, and mystifying representations imposed on
   people. There is nothing "scientistic" in this (that is, a dogmatic
   belief in the value of scientific knowledge), but neither is it a skeptical or relativistic refusal of all verified truth. What is questioned is
   the way in which knowledge circulates and functions, its relations
   to power. In short, the *régime du savoir*.

6 Finally, all these present struggles revolve around the question: Who
   are we? They are a refusal of these abstractions, of economic and
   ideological state violence which ignore who we are individually, and
   also a refusal of a scientific or administrative inquisition which determines who one is.

To sum up, the main objective of these struggles is to attack not so much
"such or such" an institution of power, or group, or elite, or class, but
rather a technique, a form of power.

This form of power applies itself to immediate everyday life which
categorizes the individual, marks him by his own individuality, attaches
him to his own identity, imposes a law of truth on him which he must
recognize and which others have to recognize in him. It is a form of
power which makes individuals subjects. There are two meanings of the
word *subject*: subject to someone else by control and dependence, and
tied to his own identity by a conscience or self-knowledge. Both meanings suggest a form of power which subjugates and makes subject to.

Generally, it can be said that there are three types of struggles: either
against forms of domination (ethnic, social, and religious); against forms
of exploitation which separate individuals from what they produce; or
against that which ties the individual to himself and submits him to
others in this way (struggles against subjection, against forms of subjectivity and submission).

I think that in history, you can find a lot of examples of these three
kinds of social struggles, either isolated from each other, or mixed
together. But even when they are mixed, one of them, most of the time,
prevails. For instance, in the feudal societies, the struggles against the
forms of ethnic or social domination were prevalent, even though economic exploitation could have been very important among the revolt's
causes.

In the nineteenth century, the struggle against exploitation came into the foreground.

And nowadays, the struggle against the forms of subjection – against the submission of subjectivity – is becoming more and more important, even though the struggles against forms of domination and exploitation have not disappeared. Quite the contrary.

I suspect that it is not the first time that our society has been confronted with this kind of struggle. All those movements which took place in the fifteenth and sixteenth centuries and which had the Reformation as their main expression and result should be analyzed as a great crisis of the Western experience of subjectivity and a revolt against the kind of religious and moral power which gave form, during the Middle Ages, to this subjectivity. The need to take a direct part in spiritual life, in the work of salvation, in the truth which lies in the Book – all that was a struggle for a new subjectivity.

I know what objections can be made. We can say that all types of subjection are derived phenomena, that they are merely the consequences of other economic and social processes: forces of production, class struggle, and ideological structures which determine the form of subjectivity.

It is certain that the mechanisms of subjection cannot be studied outside their relation to the mechanisms of exploitation and domination. But they do not merely constitute the "terminal" of more fundamental mechanisms. They entertain complex and circular relations with other forms.

The reason this kind of struggle tends to prevail in our society is due to the fact that since the sixteenth century, a new political form of power has been continuously developing. This new political structure, as everybody knows, is the state. But most of the time, the state is envisioned as a kind of political power which ignores individuals, looking only at the interests of the totality or, I should say, of a class or a group among the citizens.

That's quite true. But I'd like to underline the fact that the state's power (and that's one of the reasons for its strength) is both an individualizing and a totalizing form of power. Never, I think, in the history of human societies – even in the old Chinese society – has there been such a tricky combination in the same political structures of individualization techniques, and of totalization procedures.

This is due to the fact that the modern Western state has integrated in a new political shape, an old power technique which originated in Christian institutions. We can call this power technique the pastoral power.

First of all a few words about this pastoral power.

It has often been said that Christianity brought into being a code of ethics fundamentally different from that of the ancient world. Less emphasis is usually placed on the fact that it proposed and spread new power relations throughout the ancient world.

Christianity is the only religion which has organized itself as a Church. And as such, it postulates in principle that certain individuals can, by their religious quality, serve others not as princes, magistrates, prophets, fortune-tellers, benefactors, educationalists, and so on, but as pastors. However, this word designates a very special form of power.

1   It is a form of power whose ultimate aim is to assure individual salvation in the next world.
2   Pastoral power is not merely a form of power which commands; it must also be prepared to sacrifice itself for the life and salvation of the flock. Therefore, it is different from royal power, which demands a sacrifice from its subjects to save the throne.
3   It is a form of power which does not look after just the whole community, but each individual in particular, during his entire life.
4   Finally, this form of power cannot be exercised without knowing the inside of people's minds, without exploring their souls, without making them reveal their innermost secrets. It implies a knowledge of the conscience and an ability to direct it.

This form of power is salvation oriented (as opposed to political power). It is oblative (as opposed to the principle of sovereignty); it is individualizing (as opposed to legal power); it is coextensive and continuous with life; it is linked with a production of truth – the truth of the individual himself.

But all this is part of history, you will say; the pastorate has, if not disappeared, at least lost the main part of its efficiency.

This is true, but I think we should distinguish between two aspects of pastoral power – between the ecclesiastical institutionalization which has ceased or at least lost its vitality since the eighteenth century, and its function, which has spread and multiplied outside the ecclesiastical institution.

An important phenomenon took place around the eighteenth century – it was a new distribution, a new organization of this kind of individualizing power.

I don't think that we should consider the "modern state" as an entity which was developed above individuals, ignoring what they are and even their very existence, but on the contrary as a very sophisticated structure, in which individuals can be integrated, under one condition: that this individuality would be shaped in a new form, and submitted to a set of very specific patterns.

In a way, we can see the state as a modern matrix of individualization, or a new form of pastoral power.

A few more words about this new pastoral power.

1   We may observe a change in its objective. It was no longer a ques-
    tion of leading people to their salvation in the next world, but rather
    ensuring it in this world. And in this context, the word *salvation*
    takes on different meanings: health, well-being (that is, sufficient
    wealth, standard of living), security, protection against accidents.
    A series of "worldly" aims took the place of the religious aims of
    the traditional pastorate, all the more easily because the latter, for
    various reasons, had followed in an accessory way a certain number
    of these aims; we only have to think of the role of medicine and
    its welfare function assured for a long time by the Catholic and
    Protestant churches.
2   Concurrently the officials of pastoral power increased. Sometimes
    this form of power was exerted by state apparatus or, in any case,
    by a public institution such as the police. (We should not forget that
    in the eighteenth century the police force was not invented only for
    maintaining law and order, nor for assisting governments in their
    struggle against their enemies, but for assuring urban supplies,
    hygiene, health and standards considered necessary for handicrafts
    and commerce.) Sometimes the power was exercised by private
    ventures, welfare societies, benefactors and generally by philan-
    thropists. But ancient institutions, for example the family, were also
    mobilized at this time to take on pastoral functions. It was also
    exercised by complex structures such as medicine, which included
    private initiatives with the sale of services on market economy
    principles, but which also included public institutions such as
    hospitals.
3   Finally, the multiplication of the aims and agents of pastoral power
    focused the development of knowledge of man around two roles:
    one, globalizing and quantitative, concerning the population; the
    other, analytical, concerning the individual.

And this implies that power of a pastoral type, which over centuries –
for more than a millennium – had been linked to a defined religious institution, suddenly spread out into the whole social body; it found support
in a multitude of institutions. And, instead of a pastoral power and a
political power, more or less linked to each other, more or less rival, there
was an individualizing "tactic" which characterized a series of powers:
those of the family, medicine, psychiatry, education, and employers.

At the end of the eighteenth century Kant wrote, in a German newspaper – the *Berliner Monatschrift* – a short text. The title was *Was heisst
Aufklärung?* It was for a long time, and it is still, considered a work of
relatively small importance.

But I can't help finding it very interesting and puzzling because it was the first time a philosopher proposed as a philosophical task to investigate not only the metaphysical system or the foundations of scientific knowledge, but a historical event – a recent, even a contemporary event.

When in 1784 Kant asked, *Was heisst Aufklärung?*, he meant, What's going on just now? What's happening to us? What is this world, this period, this precise moment in which we are living?

Or in other words: What are we? as *Aufklärer*, as part of the Enlightenment? Compare this with the Cartesian question: Who am I? I, as a unique but universal and unhistorical subject? I, for Descartes is everyone, anywhere at any moment?

But Kant asks something else: What are we? in a very precise moment of history. Kant's question appears as an analysis of both us and our present.

I think that this aspect of philosophy took on more and more importance. Hegel, Nietzsche . . . .

The other aspect of "universal philosophy" didn't disappear. But the task of philosophy as a critical analysis of our world is something which is more and more important. Maybe the most certain of all philosophical problems is the problem of the present time, and of what we are, in this very moment.

Maybe the target nowadays is not to discover what we are, but to refuse what we are. We have to imagine and to build up what we could be to get rid of this kind of political "double bind," which is the simultaneous individualization and totalization of modern power structures.

The conclusion would be that the political, ethical, social, philosophical problem of our days is not to try to liberate the individual from the state, and from the state's institutions, but to liberate us both from the state and from the type of individualization which is linked to the state. We have to promote new forms of subjectivity through the refusal of this kind of individuality which has been imposed on us for several centuries.

HOW IS POWER EXERCISED?

For some people, asking questions about the "how" of power would limit them to describing its effects without ever relating those effects either to causes or to a basic nature. It would make this power a mysterious substance which they might hesitate to interrogate in itself, no doubt because they would prefer *not* to call it into question. By proceeding this way, which is never explicitly justified, they seem to suspect the presence of a kind of fatalism. But does not their very distrust indicate a presupposition that power is something which exists with three distinct qualities: its origin, its basic nature, and its manifestations?

If, for the time being, I grant a certain privileged position to the question of "how" it is not because I would wish to eliminate the questions of "what" and "why." Rather it is that I wish to present these questions in a different way; better still, to know if it is legitimate to imagine a power which unites in itself a what, a why, and a how. To put it bluntly, I would say that to begin the analysis with a "how" is to suggest that power as such does not exist. At the very least it is to ask oneself what contents one has in mind when using this all-embracing and reifying term; it is to suspect that an extremely complex configuration of realities is allowed to escape when one treads endlessly in the double question: What is power? and Where does power come from? The little question, What happens?, although flat and empirical, once it is scrutinized is seen to avoid accusing a metaphysics or an ontology of power of being fraudulent; rather it attempts a critical investigation into the thematics of power.

"How," not in the sense of "How does it manifest itself?" but "By what means is it exercised?" and "What happens when individuals exert (as they say) power over others?"

As far as this power is concerned, it is first necessary to distinguish that which is exerted over things and gives the ability to modify, use, consume, or destroy them – a power which stems from aptitudes directly inherent in the body or relayed by external instruments. Let us say that here it is a question of "capacity." On the other hand, what characterizes the power we are analyzing is that it brings into play relations between individuals (or between groups). For let us not deceive ourselves; if we speak of the structures or the mechanisms of power, it is only in so far as we suppose that certain persons exercise power over others. The term "power" designates relationships between partners (and by that I am not thinking of a zero-sum game, but simply, and for the moment staying in the most general terms, of an ensemble of actions which induce others and follow from one another).

It is necessary also to distinguish power relations from relationships of communication which transmit information by means of a language, a system of signs, or any other symbolic medium. No doubt communicating is always a certain way of acting upon another person or persons. But the production and circulation of elements of meaning can have as their objective or as their consequence certain results in the realm of power; the latter are not simply an aspect of the former. Whether or not they pass through systems of communication, power relations have a specific nature. Power relations, relationships of communication, objective capacities should not therefore be confused. This is not to say that there is a question of three separate domains. Nor that there is on one hand the field of things, of perfected technique, work, and the transformation of the real; on the other that of signs, communication, reciprocity, and the production of meaning; finally that of the domination of the means of constraint, of inequality and the action of men upon other men.[2] It is a question of three types of relationships which in fact always overlap one another, support one another reciprocally, and use each other mutually as means to an end. The application of objective capacities in their most elementary forms implies relationships of communication (whether in the form of previously acquired information or of shared work); it is tied also to power relations (whether they consist of obligatory tasks, of gestures imposed by tradition or apprenticeship, of subdivisions and the more or less obligatory distribution of labor). Relationships of communication imply finalized activities (even if only the correct putting into operation of elements of meaning) and, by virtue of modifying the field of information between partners, produce effects of power. They can scarcely be dissociated from activities brought to their final term, be they those which permit the exercise of this power (such as training techniques, processes of domination, the means by which obedience is obtained) or those which in order to develop their potential call upon relations of power (the division of labor and the hierarchy of tasks).

Of course the coordination between these three types of relationships is neither uniform nor constant. In a given society there is no general type of equilibrium between finalized activities, systems of communication, and power relations. Rather there are diverse forms, diverse places, diverse circumstances or occasions in which these interrelationships establish themselves according to a specific model. But there are also "blocks" in which the adjustment of abilities, the resources of communication, and power relations constitute regulated and concerted systems. Take for example an educational institution: the disposal of its space, the meticulous regulations which govern its internal life, the different activities which are organized there, the diverse persons who live there or meet one another, each with his own function, his well-defined character – all these things constitute a block of capacity–communication–power. The activity which ensures apprenticeship and the acquisition of aptitudes or types of behavior is developed there by means of a whole ensemble of regulated communications (lessons, questions and answers, orders, exhortations, coded signs of obedience, differentiation marks of the "value" of each person and of the levels of knowledge) and by the means of a whole series of power processes (enclosure, surveillance, reward and punishment, the pyramidal hierarchy).

These blocks, in which the putting into operation of technical capacities, the game of communications, and the relationships of power are adjusted to one another according to considered formulae, constitute what one might call, enlarging a little the sense of the word, disciplines.

The empirical analysis of certain disciplines as they have been historically constituted presents for this very reason a certain interest. This is so because the disciplines show, first, according to artificially clear and decanted systems, the manner in which systems of objective finality and systems of communication and power can be welded together. They also display different models of articulation, sometimes giving pre-eminence to power relations and obedience (as in those disciplines of a monastic or penitential type), sometimes to finalize activities (as in the disciplines of workshops or hospitals), sometimes to relationships of communication (as in the disciplines of apprenticeship), sometimes also to a saturation of the three types of relationship (as perhaps in military discipline, where a plethora of signs indicates, to the point of redundancy, tightly knit power relations calculated with care to produce a certain number of technical effects).

What is to be understood by the disciplining of societies in Europe since the eighteenth century is not, of course, that the individuals who are part of them become more and more obedient, nor that they set about assembling in barracks, schools, or prisons; rather that an increasingly better invigilated process of adjustment has been sought after – more and more rational and economic – between productive activities, resources of communication, and the play of power relations.

To approach the theme of power by an analysis of "how" is therefore to introduce several critical shifts in relation to the supposition of a fundamental power. It is to give oneself as the object of analysis power relations and not power itself – power relations which are distinct from objective abilities as well as from relations of communication. This is as much as saying that power relations can be grasped in the diversity of their logical sequence, their abilities, and their interrelationships.

What constitutes the specific nature of power?

The exercise of power is not simply a relationship between partners, individual or collective; it is a way in which certain actions modify others. Which is to say, of course, that something called Power, with or without a capital letter, which is assumed to exist universally in a concentrated or diffused form, does not exist. Power exists only when it is put into action, even if, of course, it is integrated into a disparate field of possibilities brought to bear upon permanent structures. This also means that power is not a function of consent. In itself it is not a renunciation of freedom, a transference of rights, the power of each and all delegated to a few (which does not prevent the possibility that consent may be a condition for the existence or the maintenance of power); the relationship of power can be the result of a prior or permanent consent, but it is not by nature the manifestation of a consensus.

Is this to say that one must seek the character proper to power relations in the violence which must have been its primitive form, its permanent secret and its last resource, that which in the final analysis appears as its real nature when it is forced to throw aside its mask and to show itself as it really is? In effect, what defines a relationship of power is that it is a mode of action which does not act directly and immediately on others. Instead it acts upon their actions: an action upon an action, on existing actions or on those which may arise in the present or the future. A relationship of violence acts upon a body or upon things; it forces, it bends, it breaks on the wheel, it destroys, or it closes the door on all possibilities. Its opposite pole can only be passivity, and if it comes up against any resistance it has no other option but to try to minimize it. On the other hand a power relationship can only be articulated on the basis of two elements which are each indispensable if it is really to be a power relationship: that "the other"(the one over whom power is exercised) be thoroughly recognized and maintained to the very end as a person who acts; and that, faced with a relationship of power, a whole field of responses, reactions, results, and possible inventions may open up.

Obviously the bringing into play of power relations does not exclude the use of violence any more than it does the obtaining of consent; no doubt the exercise of power can never do without one or the other, often both at the same time. But even though consensus and violence are the instruments or the results, they do not constitute the principle or the basic nature of power. The exercise of power can produce as much acceptance as may be wished for: it can pile up the dead and shelter itself behind whatever threats it can imagine. In itself the exercise of power is not violence; nor is it a consent which, implicitly, is renewable. It is a total structure of actions brought to bear upon possible actions; it incites, it induces, it seduces, it makes easier or more difficult; in the extreme it constrains or forbids absolutely; it is nevertheless always a way of acting upon an acting subject or acting subjects by virtue of their acting or being capable of action. A set of actions upon other actions.

Perhaps the equivocal nature of the term *conduct* is one of the best aids for coming to terms with the specificity of power relations. For to "conduct" is at the same time to "lead" others (according to mechanisms of coercion which are, to varying degrees, strict) and a way of behaving within a more or less open field of possibilities.[3] The exercise of power consists in guiding the possibility of conduct and putting in order the possible outcome. Basically power is less a confrontation between two adversaries or the linking of one to the other than a question of government. This word must be allowed the very broad meaning which it had in the sixteenth century. "Government" did not refer only to political structures or to the management of states; rather it designated the way in which the conduct of individuals or of groups might be directed: the government of children, of souls, of communities, of families, of the sick. It did not only cover the legitimately constituted forms of political or economic subjection, but also modes of action, more or less considered and calculated, which were destined to act upon the possibilities of action of other people. To govern, in this sense, is to structure the possible field of action of others. The relationship proper to power would not therefore be sought on the side of violence or of struggle, nor on that of voluntary linking (all of which can, at best, only be the instruments of power), but rather in the area of the singular mode of action, neither warlike nor juridical, which is government.

When one defines the exercise of power as a mode of action upon the actions of others, when one characterizes these actions by the government of men by other men – in the broadest sense of the term – one includes an important element: freedom. Power is exercised only over free subjects, and only in so far as they are free. By this we mean individual or collective subjects who are faced with a field of possibilities in which several ways of behaving, several reactions and diverse comportments may be realized. Where the determining factors saturate the whole there is no relationship of power; slavery is not a power relationship when man is in chains. (In this case it is a question of a physical relationship of constraint.) Consequently there is no face to face confrontation of power and freedom which is mutually exclusive (freedom disappears everywhere power is exercised), but a much more complicated interplay. In this game freedom may well appear as the condition for the exercise of power (at the same time its precondition, since freedom must exist for power to be exerted, and also its permanent support, since without the possibility of recalcitrance, power would be equivalent to a physical determination).

The relationship between power and freedom's refusal to submit cannot therefore be separated. The crucial problem of power is not that of voluntary servitude (how could we seek to be slaves?). At the very heart of the power relationship, and constantly provoking it, are the recalcitrance of the will and the intransigence of freedom. Rather than speaking of an essential freedom, it would be better to speak of an "agonism"[4] – of a relationship which is at the same time reciprocal incitation and struggle; less of a face-to-face confrontation which paralyzes both sides than a permanent provocation.

How is one to analyze the power relationship?

One can analyze such relationships, or rather I should say that it is perfectly legitimate to do so, by focusing on carefully defined institutions. The latter constitute a privileged point of observation, diversified, concentrated, put in order, and carried through to the highest point of their efficacity. It is here that, as a first approximation, one might expect to see the appearance of the form and logic of their elementary mechanisms. However, the analysis of power relations as one finds them in certain circumscribed institutions presents a certain number of problems. First, the fact that an important part of the mechanisms put into operation by an institution are designed to ensure its own preservation brings with it the risk of deciphering functions which are essentially reproductive, especially in power relations between institutions. Second, in analyzing power relations from the standpoint of institutions one lays oneself open to seeking the explanation and the origin of the former in the latter, that is to say finally, to explain power to power. Finally, in so far as institutions act essentially by bringing into play two elements, explicit or tacit regulations and an apparatus, one risks giving to one or the other an exaggerated privilege in the relations of power and hence to see in the latter only modulations of the law and of coercion.

This does not deny the importance of institutions on the establishment of power relations. Instead I wish to suggest that one must analyze institutions from the standpoint of power relations, rather than vice versa, and that the fundamental point of anchorage of the relationships, even if they are embodied and crystallized in an institution, is to be found outside the institution.

Let us come back to the definition of the exercise of power as a way in which certain actions may structure the field of other possible actions. What therefore would be proper to a relationship of power is that it be a mode of action upon actions. That is to say, power relations are rooted deep in the social nexus, not reconstituted "above" society as a supplementary structure whose radical effacement one could perhaps dream of. In any case, to live in society is to live in such a way that action upon other actions is possible – and in fact ongoing. A society without power relations can only be an abstraction. Which, be it said in passing, makes all the more politically necessary the analysis of power relations in a given society, their historical formation, the source of their strength or fragility, the conditions which are necessary to transform some or to abolish others. For to say that there cannot be a society without power relations is not to say either that those which are established are necessary, or, in any case, that power constitutes a fatality at the heart of societies, such that it cannot be undermined. Instead I would say that the analysis, elaboration, and bringing into question of power relations and the "agonism" between power relations and the intransitivity of freedom is a permanent political task inherent in all social existence.

Concretely the analysis of power relations demands that a certain number of points be established:

1 *The system of differentiations* which permits one to act upon the actions of others: differentiations determined by the law or by traditions of status and privilege; economic differences in the appropriation of riches and goods, shifts in the processes of production, linguistic or cultural differences, differences in know-how and competence, and so forth. Every relationship of power puts into operation differentiations which are at the same time its conditions and its results.

2 *The types of objectives* pursued by those who act upon the actions of others: the maintenance of privileges, the accumulation of profits, the bringing into operation of statutary authority, the exercise of a function or of a trade.

3 *The means of bringing power relations into being:* according to whether power is exercised by the threat of arms, by the effects of the word, by means of economic disparities, by more or less complex means of control, by systems of surveillance, with or without archives, according to rules which are or are not explicit, fixed or modifiable, with or without the technological means to put all these things into action.

4 *Forms of institutionalization:* these may mix traditional predispositions, legal structures, phenomena relating to custom or to fashion (such as one sees in the institution of the family); they can also take the form of an apparatus closed in upon itself, with its specific *loci*, its own regulations, its hierarchical structures which are carefully defined, a relative autonomy in its functioning (such as scholastic or military institutions); they can also form very complex systems endowed with multiple apparatuses, as in the case of the state, whose function is the taking of everything under its wing, the bringing into being of general surveillance, the principle of regulation and, to a certain extent also, the distribution of all power relations in a given social ensemble.

5 *The degrees of rationalization:* the bringing into play of power relations as action in a field of possibilities may be more or less elaborate in relation to the effectiveness of the instruments and the certainty of the results (greater or lesser technological refinements employed in the exercise of power) or again in proportion to the possible cost (be it the economic cost of the means brought into operation, or the cost in terms of reaction constituted by the resistance which is encountered). The exercise of power is not a naked fact, an institutional right, nor is it a structure which holds out or is smashed: it is elaborated, transformed, organized; it end-ows itself with processes which are more or less adjusted to the situation.

One sees why the analysis of power relations within a society cannot be reduced to the study of a series of institutions, not even to the study of all those institutions which would merit the name "political." Power relations are rooted in the system of social networks. This is not to say, however, that there is a primary and fundamental principle of power which dominates society down to the smallest detail; but, taking as point of departure the possibility of action upon the action of others (which is coextensive with every social relationship), multiple forms of individual disparity, of objectives, of the given application of power over ourselves or others, of, in varying degrees, partial or universal institutionalization, of more or less deliberate organization, one can define different forms of power. The forms and the specific situations of the government of men by one another in a given society are multiple; they are superimposed, they cross, impose their own limits, sometimes cancel one another out, sometimes reinforce one another. It is certain that in contemporary societies the state is not simply one of the forms or specific situations of the exercise of power – even if it is the most important – but that in a certain way all other forms of power relation must refer to it. But this is not because they are derived from it; it is rather because power relations have come more and more under state control (although this state control has not taken the same form in pedagogical, judicial, economic, or family systems). In referring here to the restricted sense of the word *government*, one could say that power relations have been progressively governmentalized, that is to say, elaborated, rationalized, and centralized in the form of, or under the auspices of, state institutions.

Relations of power and relations of strategy

The word *strategy* is currently employed in three ways. First, to designate the means employed to attain a certain end; it is a question of rationality functioning to arrive at an objective. Second, to designate the manner in which a partner in a certain game acts with regard to what he thinks should be the action of the others and what he considers the others think to be his own; it is the way in which one seeks to have the advantage over others. Third, to designate the procedures used in a situation of confrontation to deprive the opponent of his means of combat and to reduce him to giving up the struggle; it is a question therefore of the means destined to obtain victory. These three meanings come together in situations of confrontation – war or games – where the objective is to act upon an adversary in such a manner as to render the struggle impossible for him. So strategy is defined by the choice of winning solutions. But it must be borne in mind that this is a very special type of situation and that there are others in which the distinctions between the different senses of the word *strategy* must be maintained.

Referring to the first sense I have indicated, one may call power strategy the totality of the means put into operation to implement power effectively or to maintain it. One may also speak of a strategy proper to power relations in so far as they constitute modes of action upon possible action, the action of others. One can therefore interpret the mechanisms brought into play in power relations in terms of strategies. But most important is obviously the relationship between power relations and confrontation strategies. For, if it is true that at the heart of power relations and as a permanent condition of their existence there is an insubordination and a certain essential obstinacy on the part of the principles of freedom, then there is no relationship of power without the means of escape or possible flight. Every power relationship implies, at least *in potentia*, a strategy of struggle, in which the two forces are not superimposed, do not lose their specific nature, or do not finally become confused. Each constitutes for the other a kind of permanent limit, a point of possible reversal. A relationship of confrontation reaches its term, its final moment (and the victory of one of the two adversaries) when stable mechanisms replace the free play of antagonistic reactions. Through such mechanisms one can direct, in a fairly constant manner and with reasonable certainty, the conduct of others. For a relationship of confrontation, from the moment it is not a struggle to the death, the fixing of a power relationship becomes a target – at one and the same time its fulfillment and its suspension. And in return the strategy of struggle also constitutes a frontier for the relationship of power, the line at which, instead of manipulating and inducing actions in a calculated manner, one must be content with reacting to them after the event. It would not be possible for power relations to exist without points of insubordination which, by definition, are means of escape. Accordingly, every intensification, every extension of power relations to make the insubordinate submit can only result in the limits of power. The latter reaches its final term either in a type of action which reduces the other to total impotence (in which case victory over the adversary replaces the exercise of power) or by a confrontation with those whom one governs and their transformation into adversaries. Which is to say that every strategy of confrontation dreams of becoming a relationship of power and every relationship of power leans toward the idea that, if it follows its own line of development and comes up against direct confrontation, it may become the winning strategy.

In effect, between a relationship of power and strategy of struggle there is a reciprocal appeal, a perpetual linking and a perpetual reversal. At every moment the relationship of power may become a confrontation between two adversaries. Equally, the relationship between adversaries in society may, at every moment, give place to the putting into operation of mechanisms of power. The consequence of this instability is the ability to decipher the same events and the same transformations either from inside the history of struggle or from the standpoint of the power relationships. The interpretations which result will not consist of the same elements of meaning or the same links or the same types of intelligibility, although they refer to the same historical fabric and each of the two analyses must have reference to the other. In fact it is precisely the disparities between the two readings which make visible those fundamental phenomena of "domination" which are present in a large number of human societies.

Domination is in fact a general structure of power whose ramifications and consequences can sometimes be found descending to the most incalcitrant fibers of society. But at the same time it is a strategic situation more or less taken for granted and consolidated by means of a long-term confrontation between adversaries. It can certainly happen that the fact of domination may only be the transcription of a mechanism of power resulting from confrontation and its consequences (a political structure stemming from invasion); it may also be that a relationship of struggle between two adversaries is the result of power relations with the conflicts and cleavages which ensue. But what makes the domination of a group, a caste, or a class, together with the resistance and revolts which that domination comes up against, a central phenomenon in the history of societies is that they manifest in a massive and universalizing form, at the level of the whole social body, the locking together of power relations with relations of strategy and the results proceeding from their interaction.

NOTES

1 "Why Study Power: the Question of the Subject" was written in English by Michel Foucault; "How is Power Exercised?" was translated from the French by Leslie Sawyer.
2 When Habermas distinguishes between domination, communication, and finalized activity, I do not think that he sees in them three separate domains, but rather three "transcendentals."
3 Foucault is playing on the double meaning in French of the verb *conduire* – to lead or to drive, and *se conduire* – to behave or conduct oneself, whence *la conduite*, conduct or behavior (*Translator's note*).
4 Foucault's neologism is based on the Greek ἀγώνισμα meaning "a combat." The term would hence imply a physical contest in which the opponents develop a strategy of reaction and of mutual taunting, as in a wrestling match (*Translator's note*).

CHAPTER 2

A Sociological Theory of Postmodernity

Zygmunt Bauman

I propose that:

(1)   The term *postmodernity* renders accurately the defining traits of the social condition that emerged throughout the affluent countries of Europe and of European descent in the course of the twentieth century, and took its present shape in the second half of that century. The term is accurate as it draws attention to the continuity and discontinuity as two faces of the intricate relationship between the present social condition and the formation that preceded and gestated it. It brings into relief the intimate, genetic bond that ties the new, postmodern social condition to *modernity* – the social formation that emerged in the same part of the world in the course of the seventeenth century, and took its final shape, later to be sedimented in the sociological models of modern society (or models of society created by modern sociology), during the nineteenth century; while at the same time indicating the passing of certain crucial characteristics in whose absence one can no longer adequately describe the social condition as modern in the sense given to the concept by orthodox (modern) social theory.

(2)   Postmodernity may be interpreted as fully developed modernity taking a full measure of the anticipated consequences of its historical work; as modernity that acknowledged the effects it was producing throughout its history, yet producing inadvertently, rarely conscious of its own responsibility, by default rather than design, as by-products often perceived as waste. Postmodernity may be conceived of as modernity con-

This chapter is taken from *Intimations of Postmodernity* by Zygmunt Bauman (London, Routledge, 1992), pp. 187–204. Reprinted by permission of Routledge.

scious of its true nature – *modernity for itself*. The most conspicuous features of the postmodern condition: institutionalized pluralism, variety, contingency and ambivalence – have been all turned out by modern society in ever increasing volumes; yet they were seen as signs of failure rather than success, as evidence of the unsufficiency of efforts so far, at a time when the institutions of modernity, faithfully replicated by the modern mentality, struggled for *universality, homogeneity, monotony* and *clarity*. The postmodern condition can be therefore described, on the one hand, as modernity emancipated from false consciousness; on the other, as a new type of social condition marked by the overt institutionalization of the characteristics which modernity – in its designs and managerial practices – set about to eliminate and, failing that, tried to conceal.

(3) The twin differences that set the postmodern condition apart from modern society are profound and seminal enough to justify (indeed, to call for) a separate sociological theory of postmodernity that would break decisively with the concepts and metaphors of the models of modernity and lift itself out of the mental frame in which they had been conceived. This need arises from the fact that (their notorious disagreements notwithstanding), the extant models of modernity articulated a shared vision of modern history as a *movement with a direction* – and differed solely in the selection of the ultimate destination or the organizing principle of the process, be it universalization, rationalization or systemization. None of those principles can be upheld (at least not in the radical form typical of the orthodox social theory) in the light of postmodern experience. Neither can the very master-metaphor that underlies them be sustained: that of the process with a pointer.

(4) Postmodernity is not a transitory departure from the "normal state" of modernity; neither is it a diseased state of modernity, an ailment likely to be rectified, a case of "modernity in crisis". It is, instead, a self-reproducing, pragmatically self-sustainable and logically self-contained social condition defined by *distinctive features of its own*. A theory of postmodernity therefore cannot be a modified theory of modernity, a theory of modernity with a set of negative markers. An adequate theory of postmodernity may be only constructed in a cognitive space organized by a different set of assumptions; it needs its own vocabulary. The degree of emancipation from the concepts and issues spawned by the discourse of modernity ought to serve as a measure of the adequacy of such a theory.

CONDITIONS OF THEORETICAL EMANCIPATION

What the theory of postmodernity must discard in the first place is the assumption of an *"organismic"*, equilibrated social totality it purports to model in Parsons-like style: the vision of a "principally co-ordinated" and enclosed totality (a) with a degree of cohesiveness, (b) equilibrated or marked by an overwhelming tendency to equilibration, (c) unified by an internally coherent value syndrome and a core authority able to promote and enforce it and (d) defining its elements in terms of the function they perform in that process of equilibration or the reproduction of the equilibrated state. The sought theory must assume instead that the social condition it intends to model is essentially and perpetually *unequilibrated*: composed of elements with a degree of autonomy large enough to justify the view of totality as a kaleidoscopic – momentary and contingent – outcome of interaction. The orderly, structured nature of totality cannot be taken for granted; nor can its pseudo-representational construction be seen as the purpose of theoretical activity. The randomness of the global outcome of uncoordinated activities cannot be treated as a departure from the pattern which the totality strives to maintain; any pattern that may temporarily emerge out of the random movements of autonomous agents is as haphazard and unmotivated as the one that could emerge in its place or the one bound to replace it, if also for a time only. All order that can be found is a local, emergent and transitory phenomenon; its nature can be best grasped by a metaphor of a whirlpool appearing in the flow of a river, retaining its shape only for a relatively brief period and only at the expense of incessant metabolism and constant renewal of content.

The theory of postmodernity must be free of the metaphor of progress that informed all competing theories of modern society. With the totality dissipated into a series of randomly emerging, shifting and evanescent islands of order, its temporal record cannot be linearly represented. Perpetual local transformations do not add up so as to prompt (much less to assure) in effect an increased homogeneity, rationality or organic systemness of the whole. The postmodern condition is a site of constant mobility and change, but no clear direction of development. The image of Brownian movement offers an apt metaphor for this aspect of postmodernity: each momentary state is neither a necessary effect of the preceding state nor the sufficient cause of the next one. The postmodern condition is both *undetermined* and *undetermining*. It "unbinds" time; weakens the constraining impact of the past and effectively prevents colonization of the future.

Similarly, the theory of postmodernity would do well if it disposed of concepts like *system* in its orthodox, organismic sense (or, for that matter, *society*), suggestive of a sovereign totality logically prior to its parts, a totality bestowing meaning on its parts, a totality whose welfare or perpetuation all smaller (and, by definition, subordinate) units serve; in short, a totality assumed to define, and be practically capable of defining, the meanings of individual actions and agencies that compose it. A sociology geared to the conditions of postmodernity ought to replace the category of *society* with that of *sociality*; a category that tries to convey the processual modality of social reality, the dialectical play of randomness and pattern (or, from the agent's point of view, of freedom and dependence); and a category that refuses to take the structured character of the process for granted – which treats instead all found structures as emergent accomplishments.

With their field of vision organized around the focal point of system-like, resourceful and meaning-bestowing totality, sociological theories of modernity (which conceived of themselves as sociological theories *tout court*) concentrated on the vehicles of homogenization and conflict-resolution in a relentless search for a solution to the "Hobbesian problem". This cognitive perspective (shared with the one realistic referent of the concept of "society" – the national state, the only totality in history able seriously to entertain the ambition of contrived, artificially sustained and managed monotony and homogeneity) a priori disqualified any "uncertified" agency; unpatterned and unregulated spontaneity of the autonomous agent was pre-defined as a destabilizing and, indeed, anti-social factor marked for taming and extinction in the continuous struggle for societal survival. By the same token, prime importance was assigned to the mechanisms and weapons of order-promotion and pattern-maintenance: the state and the legitimation of its authority, power, socialization, culture, ideology, etc. – all selected for the role they played in the promotion of pattern, monotony, predictability and thus also manageability of conduct.

A sociological theory of postmodernity is bound to reverse the structure of the cognitive field. The focus must be now on agency; more correctly, on the *habitat* in which agency operates and which it produces in the course of operation. As it offers the agency the sum total of resources for all possible action as well as the field inside which the action-orienting and action-oriented relevancies may be plotted, the habitat is the territory inside which both freedom and dependency of the agency are constituted (and, indeed, perceived as such). Unlike the system-like totalities of modern social theory, habitat neither determines the conduct of the agents nor defines its meaning; it is no more (but no less either) than the setting in which both action and meaning-assignment are *possible*. Its own identity is as under-determined and motile, as emergent and transitory, as those of the actions and their meanings that form it.

There is one crucial area, though, in which the habitat performs a determining (systematizing, patterning) role: it sets the agenda for the "business of life" through supplying the inventory of ends and the pool of means. The way in which the ends and means are supplied also determines the meaning of the "business of life": the nature of the tasks all agencies confront and have to take up in one form or another. In so far as the ends are offered as potentially alluring rather than obligatory, and rely for their choice on their own seductiveness rather than the supporting power of coercion, the "business of life" splits into a series of choices. The series is not pre-structured, or is pre-structured only feebly and above all inconclusively. For this reason the choices through which the life of the agent is construed and sustained is best seen (as it tends to be seen by the agents themselves) as adding up to the process of *self-constitution*. To underline the graduated and ultimately inconclusive nature of the process, self-constitution is best viewed as *self-assembly*.

I propose that sociality, habitat, self-constitution and self-assembly should occupy in the sociological theory of postmodernity the central place that the orthodoxy of modern social theory had reserved for the categories of society, normative group (like class or community), socialization and control.

MAIN TENETS OF THE THEORY OF POSTMODERNITY

(1) Under the postmodern condition, habitat is a *complex system*. According to contemporary mathematics, complex systems differ from mechanical systems (those assumed by the orthodox, modern theory of society) in two crucial respects. First, they are unpredictable; second, they are not controlled by statistically significant factors (the circumstance demonstrated by the mathematical proof of the famous "butterfly effect"). The consequences of these two distinctive features of complex systems are truly revolutionary in relation to the received wisdom of sociology. The "systemness" of the postmodern habitat no longer lends itself to the organismic metaphor, which means that agencies active within the habitat cannot be assessed in terms of functionality or dysfunctionality. The successive states of the habitat appear to be unmotivated and free from constraints of deterministic logic. And the most formidable research strategy modern sociology had developed – statistical analysis – is of no use in exploring the dynamics of social phenomena and evaluating the probabilities of their future development. Significance and numbers have parted ways. Statistically insignificant phenomena may prove to be decisive, and their decisive role cannot be grasped in advance.

(2) The postmodern habitat is a complex (non-mechanical) system for two closely related reasons. First, there is no "goal setting" agency with overall managing and co-ordinating capacities or ambitions – one whose presence would provide a vantage point from which the aggregate of effective agents appears as a "totality" with a determined structure of relevances; a totality which one can think of as an *organization*.

Second, the habitat is populated by a great number of agencies, most of them single-purpose, some of them small, some big, but none large enough to subsume or otherwise determine the behaviour of the others. Focusing on a single purpose considerably enhances the effectiveness of each agency in the field of its own operation, but prevents each area of the habitat from being controlled from a single source, as the field of operation of any agency never exhausts the whole area the action is affecting. Operating in different fields yet zeroing in on shared areas, agencies are *partly* dependent on each other, but the lines of dependence cannot be fixed and thus their actions (and consequences) remain staunchly under-determined, that is autonomous.

(3) Autonomy means that agents are only partly, if at all, constrained in their pursuit of whatever they have institutionalized as their purpose. To a large extent, they are free to pursue the purpose to the best of their mastery over resources and managerial capacity. They are free (and tend) to view the rest of the habitat shared with other agents as a collection of opportunities and "problems" to be resolved or removed. Opportunity is what increases output in the pursuit of purpose, problems are what threatens the decrease or a halt of production. In ideal circumstances (maximization of opportunities and minimization of problems) each agent would tend to go in the pursuit of their purpose as far as resources would allow; the availability of resources is the only reason for action they need and thus the sufficient guarantee of the action's reasonability. The possible impact on other agents' opportunities is not automatically re-forged into the limitation of the agent's own output. The many products of purpose-pursuing activities of numerous partly interdependent but relatively autonomous agents must yet find, *ex post facto*, their relevance, utility and demand-securing attractiveness. The products are bound to be created in volumes exceeding the pre-existing demand motivated by already articulated problems. They are still to seek their place and meaning as well as the problems that they may claim to be able to resolve.

(4) For every agency, the habitat in which its action is inscribed appears therefore strikingly different from the confined space of its own autonomic, purpose-subordinated pursuits. It appears as a space of chaos and chronic *indeterminacy*, a territory subjected to rival and contradictory meaning-bestowing claims and hence perpetually *ambivalent*. All states the habitat may assume appear equally *contingent* (that is, they have no overwhelming reasons for being what they are, and they could be different if any of the participating agencies behaved differently). The heuristics of pragmatically useful "next moves" displaces, therefore, the search for algorithmic, certain knowledge of deterministic chains. The succession of states assumed by the relevant areas of the habitat no agency can interpret without including its own actions in the

explanation; agencies cannot meaningfully scan the situation "objectively", that is in such ways as allow them to eliminate, or bracket away, their own activity.

(5) The existential modality of the agents is therefore one of insufficient determination, inconclusiveness, motility and rootlessness. The identity of the agent is neither given nor authoritatively confirmed. It has to be construed, yet no design for the construction can be taken as prescribed or foolproof. The construction of identity consists of successive trials and errors. It lacks a benchmark against which its progress could be measured, and so it cannot be meaningfully described as "progressing". It is now the incessant (and non-linear) *activity* of self-constitution that makes the identity of the agent. In other words, the self-organization of the agents in terms of a *life-project* (a concept that assumes a long-term stability; a lasting identity of the habitat, in its duration transcending, or at least commensurate with, the longevity of human life) is displaced by the *process of self-constitution*. Unlike the life-project self-constitution has no destination point in reference to which it could be evaluated and monitored. It has no visible end; not even a stable direction. It is conducted inside a shifting (and, as we have seen before, unpredictable) constellation of mutually autonomous points of reference, and thus purposes guiding the self-constitution at one stage may soon lose their current authoritatively confirmed validity. Hence the self-assembly of the agency is not a cumulative process; self-constitution entails disassembling alongside the assembling, adoption of new elements as much as shedding of others, learning together with forgetting. The identity of the agency, much as it remains in a state of permanent change, cannot be therefore described as "developing". In the self-constitution of agencies, the "Brownian movement"-type spatial nature of the habitat is projected onto the time axis.

(6) The only visible aspect of continuity and of the cumulative effects of self-constitutive efforts is offered by the human body – seen as the sole constant factor among the protean and fickle identities: the material, tangible substratum, container, carrier and executor of all past, present and future identities. The self-constitutive efforts focus on keeping alive (and preferably enhancing) the *capacity* of the body for absorbing the input of sensuous impressions and producing a constant supply of publicly legible self-definitions. Hence the centrality of *body-cultivation* among the self-assembly concerns, and the acute atention devoted to everything "taken internally" (food, air, drugs, etc.) and to everything coming in touch with the skin – that interface between the agent and the rest of the habitat and the hotly contested frontier of the autonomously managed identity. In the postmodern habitat, DIY operations (jogging, dieting, slimming, etc.) replace and to a large extent displace the panoptical drill of modern factory, school or the barracks;

unlike their predecessors, however, they are not perceived as externally imposed, cumbersome and resented necessities, but as manifestos of the agent's freedom. Their heteronomy, once blatant through coercion, now hides behind seduction.

(7) As the process of self-constitution is not guided or monitored by a sovereign life-project designed in advance (such a life-project can only be imputed in retrospect, reconstructed out of a series of emergent episodes), it generates an acute demand for a substitute: a constant supply of orientation points that may guide successive moves. It is the other agencies (real or imagined) of the habitat who serve as such orientation points. Their impact on the process of self-constitution differs from that exercised by normative groups in that they neither monitor nor knowingly administer the acts of allegiance and the actions that follow it. From the vantage point of self-constituting agents, other agents can be metaphorically visualized as a randomly scattered set of free-standing and unguarded totemic poles which one can approach or abandon without applying for permission to enter or leave. The self-proclaimed allegiance to the selected agent (the act of selection itself) is accomplished through the adoption of *symbolic tokens* of belonging, and freedom of choice is limited solely by the availability and accessibility of such tokens.

(8) *Availability* of tokens for potential self-assembly depends on their *visibility*, much as it does on their material presence. Visibility in its turn depends on the perceived *utility* of symbolic tokens for the satisfactory outcome of self-construction; that is, on their ability to reassure the agent that the current results of self-assembly are indeed satisfactory. This reassurance is the substitute for the absent certainty, much as the orientation points with the attached symbolic tokens are collectively a substitute for pre-determined patterns for life-projects. The reassuring capacity of symbolic tokens rests on borrowed (ceded) authority; of *expertise*, or of *mass following*. Symbolic tokens are actively sought and adopted if their relevance is vouched for by the trusted authority of the expert, or by their previous or concurrent appropriation by a great number of other agents. These two variants of authority are in their turn fed by the insatiable thirst of the self-constituting agents for reassurance. Thus *freedom* of choice and *dependence* on external agents reinforce each other, and arise and grow together as products of the same process of self-assembly and of the constant demand for reliable orientation points which it cannot but generate.

(9) *Accessibility* of tokens for self-assembly varies from agent to agent, depending mostly on the resources that a given agent commands. Increasingly, the most strategic role among the resources is played by knowledge; the growth of individually appropriated knowledge widens the range of assembly patterns which can be realistically chosen.

Freedom of the agent, measured by the range of realistic choices, turns under the postmodern condition into the main dimension of inequality and thus becomes the main stake of the *redistributional* type of conflict that tends to arise from the dichotomy of privilege and deprivation; by the same token, access to knowledge – being the key to an extended freedom – turns into the major index of social standing. This circumstance increases the attractiveness of *information* among the symbolic tokens sought after for their reassuring potential. It also further enhances the authority of experts, trusted to be the repositories and sources of valid knowledge. Information becomes a major resource, and experts the crucial brokers of all self-assembly.

POSTMODERN POLITICS

Modern social theory could afford to separate theory from policy. Indeed, it made a virtue out of that historically circumscribed plausibility, and actively fought for the separation under the banner of value-free science. Keeping the separation watertight has turned into a most distinctive mark of modern theory of society. A theory of postmodernity cannot follow that pattern. Once the essential contingency and the absence of supra- or pre-agentic foundations of sociality and of the structured forms it sediments has been acknowledged, it becomes clear that the politics of agents lies at the core of the habitat's existence; indeed, it can be said to be its existential modality. All description of the postmodern habitat must include politics from the beginning. Politics cannot be kept outside the basic theoretical model as an epiphenomenon, a superstructural reflection or belatedly formed, intellectually processed derivative.

It could be argued (though the argument cannot be spelled out here) that the separation of theory and policy in modern *theory* could be sustained as long as there was, unchallenged or effectively immunized against challenge, a *practical* division between theoretical and political practice. The latter separation had its foundation in the activity of the modern national state, arguably the only social formation in history with pretensions to and ambitions of administering a global order, and of maintaining a total monopoly over rule-setting and rule-execution. Equally policy was to be the state's monopoly, and the procedure for its formulation had to be made separate and independent from the procedure legitimizing an acceptable theory and, more generally, intellectual work modelled after the latter procedure. The gradual, yet relentless erosion of the national state's monopoly (undermined simultaneously from above and from below, by transnational and subnational agencies, and weakened by the fissures in the historical marriage between nationalism and the state, none needing the other very strongly in their mature form) ended the plausibility of theoretical segregation.

With state resourcefulness and ambitions shrinking, responsibility (real or just claimed) for policy shifts away from the state or is actively shed on the state's own initiative. It is not taken over by another agent, though. It dissipates; it splits into a plethora of localized or partial policies pursued by localized or partial (mostly one issue) agencies. With that, vanishes the modern state's tendency to condensate and draw upon itself almost all social protest arising from unsatisfied redistributional demands and expectations – a quality that further enhanced the inclusive role of the state among societal agencies, at the same time rendering it vulnerable and exposed to frequent political crises (as conflicts fast turned into political protests). Under the postmodern condition grievances which in the past would cumulate into a collective political process and address themselves to the state, stay diffuse and translate into self-reflexivity of the agents, stimulating further dissipation of policies and autonomy of postmodern agencies (if they do cumulate for a time in the form of a one-issue pressure group, they bring together agents too heterogeneous in other respects to prevent the dissolution of the formation once the desired progress on the issue in question has been achieved; and even before that final outcome, the formation is unable to override the diversity of its supporters' interests and thus claim and secure their *total* allegiance and identification). One can speak, allegorically, of the "functionality of dissatisfaction" in a postmodern habitat.

Not all politics in postmodernity is unambiguously postmodern. Throughout the modern era, politics of *inequality* and hence of *redistribution* was by far the most dominant type of political conflict and conflict-management. With the advent of postmodernity it has been displaced from its dominant role, but remains (and in all probability will remain) a constant feature of the postmodern habitat. Indeed, there are no signs that the postmodern condition promises to alleviate the inequalities (and hence the redistributional conflicts) proliferating in modern society. Even such an eminently modern type of politics acquires in many cases a postmodern tinge, though. Redistributional vindications of our time are focused more often than not on the winning of *human rights* (a code name for the agent's autonomy, for that freedom of choice that constitutes the agency in the postmodern habitat) by categories of population heretofore denied them (this is the case of the emancipatory movements of oppressed ethnic minorities, of the black movement, of one important aspect of the feminist movement, much as of the recent rebellion against the "dictatorship over needs" practised by the communist regimes), rather than at the express redistribution of wealth, income and other consumable values by society at large. The most conspicuous social division under postmodern conditions is one between *seduction* and *repression*: between the choice and the lack of choice, between the capacity for self-constitution and the denial of such capacity, between autonomously conceived self-definitions and imposed categorizations experienced as constraining and incapacitating. The redistributional aims (or, more precisely, consequences) of the resulting struggle are mediated by the resistance against repression of human agency. One may as well reverse the above statement and propose that in its postmodern rendition conflicts bared their true nature, that of the drive toward freeing of human agency, which in modern times tended to be hidden behind ostensibly redistributional battles.

Alongside the survivals of the modern form of politics, however, specifically postmodern forms appear and gradually colonize the centre-field of the postmodern political process. Some of them are new; some others owe their new, distinctly postmodern quality to their recent expansion and greatly increased impact. The following are the most prominent among them (the named forms are not necessarily mutually exclusive; and some act at cross-purposes):

(1)   *Tribal politics.* This is a generic name for practices aimed at collectivization (supra-agentic confirmation) of the agents' self-constructing efforts. Tribal politics entails the creation of tribes as *imagined communities*. Unlike the premodern communities the modern powers set about uprooting, postmodern tribes exist in no other form but the symbolically manifested commitment of their members. They can rely on neither executive powers able to coerce their constituency into submission to the tribal rules (seldom do they have clearly codified rules to which submission could be demanded), nor on the strength of neighbourly bonds or intensity of reciprocal exchange (most tribes are de-territorialized, and communication between their members is hardly at any time more intense than the intercourse between members and non-members of the tribe). Postmodern tribes, are, therefore, constantly in *statu nascendi* rather than *essendi*, brought over again into being by repetitive symbolic rituals of the members but persisting no longer than these rituals' power of attraction (in which sense they are akin to Kant's *aesthetic communities* or Schmalenbach's *communions*). Allegiance is composed of the ritually manifested support for positive tribal tokens or equally symbolically demonstrated animosity to negative (anti-tribal) tokens. As the persistence of tribes relies solely on the deployment of the affective allegiance, one would expect an unprecedented condensation and intensity of emotive behaviour and a tendency to render the rituals as spectacular as possible – mainly through inflating their power to shock. Tribal rituals, as it were, compete for the scarce resource of public attention as the major (perhaps sole) resource of survival.

(2) *Politics of desire*. This entails actions aimed at establishing the relevance of certain types of conduct (tribal tokens) for the self-constitution of the agents. If the relevance is established, the promoted conduct grows in attractiveness, its declared purposes acquire *seductive* power, and the probability of their choice and active pursuit increases: promoted purposes turn into agents' needs. In the field of the politics of desire, agencies vie with each other for the scarce resource of individual and collective dreams of the good life. The overall effect of the politics of desire is heteronomy of choice supported by, and in its turn sustaining, the autonomy of the choosing agents.

(3) *Politics of fear*. This is, in a sense, a supplement (simultaneously a complement and a counterweight) of the politics of desire, aimed at drawing boundaries to heteronomy and staving off its potentially harmful effects. If the typical modern fears were related to the threat of totalitarianism perpetually ensconced in the project of rationalized and state-managed society (Orwell's "boot eternally trampling a human face", Weber's "cog in the machine" and "iron cage", etc.), postmodern fears arise from uncertainty as to the soundness and reliability of advice offered through the politics of desire. More often than not, diffuse fears crystallize in the form of a suspicion that the agencies promoting desire are (for the sake of self-interest) oblivious or negligent of the damaging effects of their proposals. In view of the centrality of body-cultivation in the activity of self-constitution, the damage most feared is one that can result in poisoning or maiming the body through penetration or contact with the skin (the most massive panics have focused recently on incidents like mad cow disease, listeria in eggs, shrimps fed on poisonous algae, dumping of toxic waste – with the intensity of fear correlated to the importance of the body among the self-constituting concerns, rather than to the statistical significance of the event and extent of the damage).

The politics of fear strengthens the position of experts in the processes of self-constitution, while ostensibly questioning their competence. Each successive instance of the suspension of trust articulates a new area of the habitat as problematic and thus leads to a call for more experts and more expertise.

(4) *Politics of certainty*. This entails the vehement search for social confirmation of choice, in the face of the irredeemable pluralism of the patterns on offer and acute awareness that each formula of self-constitution, however carefully selected and tightly embraced, is ultimately one of the many, and always "until further notice". Production and distribution of certainty is the defining function and the source of power of the experts. As the pronouncements of the experts can be seldom put to the test by the recipients of their services, for most agents certainty about the soundness of their choices can be plausibly enter-

tained only in the form of *trust*. The politics of certainty consists there-fore mainly in the production and manipulation of trust; conversely, "lying", "letting down", "going back on one's words", "covering up" the unseemly deeds or just withholding information, betrayal of trust, abuse of privileged access to the facts of the case – all emerge as major threats to the already precarious and vulnerable self-identity of post-modern agents. Trustworthiness, credibility and perceived sincerity become major criteria by which merchants of certainty – experts, poli-ticians, sellers of self-assembly identity kits – are judged, approved or rejected.

On all four stages on which the postmodern political game is played, the agent's initiative meets socially produced and sustained offers. Offers potentially available exceed as a rule the absorbing capacity of the agent. On the other hand, the reassuring potential of such offers as are in the end chosen rests almost fully on the perceived superiority of such offers over their competitors. This is, emphatically, a *perceived* superiority. Its attractiveness relies on a greater volume of allocated trust. What is per-ceived as superiority (in the case of marketed utilities, life-styles or political teams alike) is the visible amount of *public attention* the offer in question seems to enjoy. Postmodern politics is mostly about the re-allocation of attention. Public attention is the most important – coveted and struggled for – among the scarce commodities in the focus of politi-cal struggle.

POSTMODERN ETHICS

Like politics, ethics is an indispensable part of a sociological theory of postmodernity pretending to any degree of completeness. The descrip-tion of modern society could leave ethical problems aside or ascribe to them but a marginal place, in view of the fact that the moral regulation of conduct was to a large extent subsumed under the legislative and law-enforcing activity of global societal institutions, while whatever remained unregulated in such a way was "privatized" or perceived (and treated) as residual and marked for extinction in the course of full mod-ernization. This condition does not hold anymore; ethical discourse is not institutionally pre-empted and hence its conduct and resolution (or irresolution) must be an organic part of any theoretical model of postmodernity.

Again, not all ethical issues found in a postmodern habitat are new. Most importantly, the possibly extemporal issues of the orthodox ethics – the rules binding short-distance, face-to-face intercourse between moral agents under conditions of physical and moral proximity – remain presently as much alive and poignant as ever before. In no way are they postmodern; as a matter of fact, they are not modern either. (On the whole, modernity contributed little, if anything, to the enrichment of moral problematics. Its role boiled down to the substitution of legal for moral regulation and the exemption of a wide and growing sector of human actions from moral evaluation.)

The distinctly postmodern ethical problematic arises primarily from two crucial features of the postmodern condition: *pluralism* of authority, and the centrality of *choice* in the self-constitution of postmodern agents.

(1)   Pluralism of authority, or rather the absence of an authority with globalizing ambitions, has a twofold effect. First, it rules out the setting of binding norms each agency must (or could be reasonably expected to) obey. Agencies may be guided by their own purposes, paying in principle as little attention to other factors (also to the interests of other agencies) as they can afford, given their resources and degree of independence. "Non-contractual bases of contract", devoid of institutional power support, are thereby considerably weakened. If unmotivated by the limits of the agency's own resources, any constraint upon the agency's action has to be negotiated afresh. Rules emerge mostly as reactions to strife and consequences of ensuing negotiations; still, the already negotiated rules remain by and large precarious and under-determined, while the needs of new rules – to regulate previously unanticipated contentious issues – keep proliferating. This is why the *problem* of rules stays in the focus of public agenda and is unlikely to be conclusively resolved. In the absence of "principal coordination" the negotiation of rules assumes a distinctly *ethical* character: at stake are the principles of non-utilitarian self-constraint of autonomous agencies – and both non-utility and autonomy define *moral* action as distinct from either self-interested or legally prescribed conduct. Second, pluralism of authorities is conducive to the resumption by the agents of moral responsibility that tended to be neutralized, rescinded or ceded away as long as the agencies remained subordinated to a unified, quasi-monopolistic legislating authority. On the one hand, the agents face now point-blank the consequences of their actions. On the other, they face the evident ambiguity and controversiality of the purposes which actions were to serve, and thus the need to justify argumentatively the values that inform their activity. Purposes can no longer be substantiated *monologically*; having become perforce subjects of a *dialogue*, they must now refer to principles wide enough to command authority of the sort that belongs solely to ethical values.

(2)   The enhanced autonomy of the agent has similarly a twofold ethical consequence. First – in as far as the centre of gravity shifts decisively from heteronomous control to self-determination, and autonomy turns into the defining trait of postmodern agents – self-monitoring, self-reflection and self-evaluation become principal activities of the agents,

indeed the mechanisms synonymical with their self-constitution. In the absence of a universal model for self-improvement, or of a clear-cut hierarchy of models, the most excruciating choices agents face are between life-purposes and values, not between the means serving the already set, uncontroversial ends. Supra-individual criteria of propriety in the form of technical precepts of instrumental rationality do not suffice. This circumstance, again, is potentially propitious to the sharpening up of moral self-awareness: only ethical principles may offer such criteria of value-assessment and value-choice as are at the same time supra-individual (carry an authority admittedly superior to that of individual self-preservation), and fit to be used without surrendering the agent's autonomy. Hence the typically postmodern heightened interest in ethical debate and increased attractiveness of the agencies claiming expertise in moral values (e.g. the revival of religious and quasi-religious movements). Second, with the autonomy of all and any agents accepted as a principle and institutionalized in the life-process composed of an unending series of choices, the limits of the agent whose autonomy is to be observed and preserved turn into a most closely guarded and hotly contested frontier. Along this borderline new issues arise which can be settled only through an ethical debate. Is the flow and the outcome of self-constitution to be tested before the agents right to autonomy is confirmed? If so, what are the standards by which success or failure are to be judged (what about the autonomy of young and still younger children, of the indigent, of parents raising their children in unusual ways, of people choosing bizarre life-styles, of people indulging in abnormal means of intoxication, people engaging in idiosyncratic sexual activities, individuals pronounced mentally handicapped)? And, how far are the autonomous powers of the agent to extend and at what point is their limit to be drawn (remember the notoriously inconclusive contest between "life" and "choice" principles of the abortion debate)?

All in all, in the postmodern context agents are constantly faced with moral issues and obliged to choose between equally well founded (or equally unfounded) ethical precepts. The choice always means the assumption of responsibility, and for this reason bears the character of a moral act. Under the postmodern condition, the agent is perforce not just an actor and decision-maker, but a *moral subject*. The performance of life-functions demands also that the agent be a morally *competent* subject.

SOCIOLOGY IN THE POSTMODERN CONTEXT

The strategies of any systematic study are bound to be resonant with the conception of its object. Orthodox sociology was resonant with the theoretical model of the modern society. It was for that reason that the proper accounting for the self-reflexive propensities of human actors proved to be so spectacularly difficult. Deliberately or against its declared wishes, sociology tended to marginalize or explain away self-reflexivity as rule-following, function-performing or at best sedimentation of institutionalized learning; in each case, as an epiphenomenon of social totality, understood ultimately as "legitimate authority" capable of "principally coordinating" social space. As long as the self-reflexivity of actors remained reduced to the subjective perception of obedience to impersonal rules, it did not need to be treated seriously; it rarely came under scrutiny as an independent variable, much less as a principal condition of all sociality and its institutionalized sedimentations.

Never flawless, this strategy becomes singularly inadequate under the postmodern condition. The postmodern habitat is indeed an incessant flow of reflexivity; the sociality responsible for all its structured yet fugitive forms, their interaction and their succession, is a discursive activity, an activity of interpretation and reinterpretation, of interpretation fed back into the interpreted condition only to trigger off further interpretative efforts. To be effectively and consequentially present in a postmodern habitat sociology must conceive of itself as a participant (perhaps better informed, more systematic, more rule-conscious, yet nevertheless a participant) of this never ending, self-reflexive process of reinterpretation and devise its strategy accordingly. In practice, this will mean in all probability, replacing the ambitions of the judge of "common beliefs", healer of prejudices and umpire of truth with those of a clarifier of interpretative rules and facilitator of communication; this will amount to the replacement of the dream of the legislator with the practice of an interpreter.

Acknowledgements

The ideas sketched in this [chapter] have been inspired or stimulated by readings and debates far too numerous for all the intellectual debts to be listed. And yet some, the most generous (even when unknowing), creditors must be named. They are: Benedict Anderson, Mikhail Bakhtin, Pierre Bourdieu, Anthony Giddens, Erving Goffman, Agnes Heller, Michel Maffesoli, Stefan Morawski, Alan Touraine. And, of course, Georg Simmel, who started it all.

CHAPTER 3

Inequality after Class

Malcolm Waters

The debate about the salience of class is back on the sociological agenda. At least five journals of international scope and repute have recently hosted debates on the issue.[1] These debates have introduced a body of new evidence and new arguments on the declining social and political relevance of class and on the increasingly problematic nature of class-based explanations of social inequalities and conflicts. Even such pioneers of class analysis as Lipset (Clark and Lipset, 1991; Clark et al., 1993) and contemporary sympathizers (e.g. Emmison and Western, 1990; Crompton, 1993) admit to problems and inadequacies that can no longer be glossed over. Two major new books have been published that canvas and take positions in the debate (Lee and Turner, 1996; Pakulski and Waters, 1996). This chapter therefore seeks to provide an alternative to what might be called the class manifesto.[2] It outlines the patterns of inequality that sociology needs to theorize, assuming that class is dead. However, it does not call for the class tradition to be ditched but rather seeks to apply the general methodological approach of class theory and analysis to the contemporary formation.

Class theory has arguably always been central to sociological analysis. One of the discipline's main claims has been to an expertise in demonstrating the ways in which the underlying realities of class can structure behaviour, opportunities, attitudes, living conditions and lifestyles. In an important sense sociology has been about the relationship between class structure and the Lebenswelt. Given this success it is appropriate to take class theory as the template for theorizing about

This chapter is taken from *Sociology after Postmodernism*, edited by D. Owen (London, Sage, 1997), pp. 23–39. Reprinted by permission of Sage Publications Ltd.

whatever might succeed it. The class-theoretic template, of which Marxist class theory is the best known example, embraces the following four propositions.

1 The proposition of *economism*. It views class as a fundamentally socioeconomic phenomenon. Class refers often to differential ownership of property, especially of productive or capital property with an accumulation potential. It can also refer to differential market capacity, especially labour-market capacity. Such economic phenomena as property or markets are held to be fundamental structuring or organizing principles in societal arrangements.

2 The proposition of *groupness*. Classes are held to be more than statistical aggregates or taxonomic categories. They are real features of social structure having detectable boundaries that set up the main lines of cleavage in society. So deep and fundamental are these cleavages that they are the enduring bases for conflict, struggle, possible exploitation and distributional contestation.

3 The proposition of *behavioural and cultural linkage*. Class membership is also claimed causally to be connected to consciousness, identity and action outside the arena of economic production. It determines values and norms, political preferences, lifestyle choices, child-rearing practices, opportunities for physical and mental health, access to educational opportunity, patterns of marriage, occupational inheritance, income, and so on. This linkage legitimizes the continuing salience of class analysis.

4 The proposition of *transformational capacity*. Classes are important collective actors in the economic and political fields. They have latent access to resources that can hold entire societies in thrall and, in so far as they consciously struggle against other classes, they can transform the general set of social arrangements of which they are a part. Class struggle therefore generates the dynamic thrust that energizes society – classes are collective actors that can make history.

Figure 3.1 summarizes these propositions. It draws two distinctions about the ways in which sociologists use the concept of class: first, between class as a generative or determining factor in social life and class as a set of categories for describing society; and secondly, between class as an objective condition of human existence and class as a subjective component of experience and consciousness. Intersecting these distinctions gives up the four aspects of class on which sociological debates focus. Sociologists variously identify class as an abstract structure of positions, as a formation that sets up a hierarchy of economic categories, as communities of common interest and culture, and as collective political actors. The propositions establish theoretical linkages

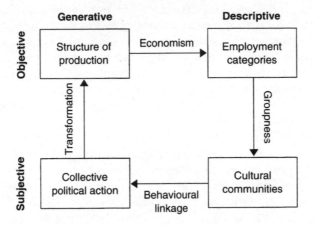

Figure 3.1 *Aspects of the sociology of class*

between these four: economism specifies that the main divisions in society are aspects of the economic structure; groupness specifies that these economic categories will develop into identifiable social entities; behavioural linkage specifies that this will determine their norms, attitudes and political behaviour; and transformation argues that class-based political action will lead to reform of the fundamental underlying structure.

EMERGENT FEATURES OF THE STRATIFICATION SYSTEM

Economically determined class has typically been regarded as the predominant feature of the capitalist system since it emerged to disrupt the feudal order of estates. However, many observers now identify as salient three emergent features of the stratification system that previously could be regarded as either reducible to or repressed by class. These three features are: power and domination; conventional status as expressed in lifestyles and value-commitments; and ascribed status memberships, particularly those specified by structures of gender, race and ethnicity.

Domination

A key feature of the development of industrial societies in the twentieth century has been an expansion of state activity. This development impacts radically on the stratification system. First, the state provides access to social resources and rewards that are autonomous relative to processes of production. Whatever social strata are generated by state employment and state benefits, they are not economic classes in the sense of being sourced in processes of production. Secondly, state action can modify social arrangements built around production processes so that economic areas previously defined as private and autonomous become subject to state control and regulation. States can regulate labour and commodities markets; they can intervene to provide capital infrastructure; and they can sponsor corporatist relations between employers and employees (Offe, 1984).

Where state activity intrudes into the economic sphere it provides the basis for a political restructuring of stratification arrangements. A bureaucratic-political elite controls the distribution of state resources and establishes consumption privileges on this basis – improved access to salaries, travel, working conditions, pension schemes, and so on. Below this a less autonomous and less privileged public service category of workers nevertheless enjoys a relatively high level of material security. The receipt of socioeconomic protection creates membership of a third and lower stratum of dependent citizens whose social location is entirely contingent on state activity. These are the recipients of welfare benefits, unemployment insurance, pensions, and so on. They include the structurally unemployed and underemployed, the physically and mentally disabled, female heads of households, and the aged. Membership in the dependent underclass is stable and reproducing. This is especially true where membership intersects with age, gender, race or ethnicity.

It is also possible to mount an argument that even in the private sector, the critical stratifying feature is rather more to do with the distribution of domination than the distribution of ownership. The principal issue here is the "separation of ownership from control" in which in functions of capital are increasingly performed by managers while stockholders merely own the corporation in a legal sense. Actual capitalists thus disappear from the production process and therefore, it might be argued, class relations cannot be understood merely in terms of property ownership (Berle and Means, 1932/1967; Burnham, 1941). Below the senior managerial level, increases in the scale and specialization of organizations can generate imperatives for coordination. A key characteristic of contemporary capitalism is its hierarchical and bureaucratic organization. In other words, organized capitalism offers a stable basis for the formation of intermediate strata defined by their access to domination. Dahrendorf (1959) offers what is perhaps the most influential account of contemporary stratification in terms of domination, although, like many others, he insists on continuing to use the term "class" for the groups that he identifies. He observes that capitalist societies are composed of a wide range of complex organizations, not only production enterprises but also distribution enterprises, state bureaucracies, political parties, churches, voluntary associations and trade unions (1959: 157–209). Each of these organizations is made up of specialized activities that must be coordinated in the direction of organizational goals. This is a functional imperative for complex organizations, so that each will include people who give commands and people who respond to them. These authority groups are the basis for "class" formation. But the "classes" are intra-organizational rather than societal. This allows Dahrendorf to conceive of multiple lines of authority-based divisions intersecting with one another and thereby to mount a conflict-based theory of social cohesion.

Conventional status

Conventional status is another possible contender in the contest to be at the centre of stratification arrangements. Here status must be understood in Weberian terms, that is as a coherent and shared lifestyle that consists of consumption patterns, forms of social intercourse, marital practices, associational memberships and shared value-commitments. Status differentiation can therefore be based on formal education, hereditary prestige, or occupational prestige. An argument in favour of conventional status would suggest that status groups can form across class divisions. Status groups can prevent the formation of classes because they monopolize privilege and thus prevent the mobilization of property or skills in order to gain access to it.

If one accepts that occupations are ranked by processes specified neither by production nor by a legal order, then they must be ranked or evaluated in terms of negotiation between human beings. Indeed, on such an argument, power-groups and classes can be reduced to conventional "socioeconomic status":

> The occupational structure in modern industrial society not only constitutes an important foundation for the main dimensions of social stratification but also serves as the connecting link between different institutions and spheres of inequality . . . The hierarchy of prestige strata and the hierarchy of economic classes have their roots in the occupational structure; so does the hierarchy of political power and authority, for political authority in modern society is largely exercised as a full-time occupation. (Blau and Duncan, 1967: 6–7)

Educational credentials are an important component in formulations of socioeconomic status. Larson (1977) shows that the original basis for credentialism was the establishment of medicine, and later law and academia, formally as professions as a response to the burgeoning specialization and monetarization of the market and to the growth of state bureaucracies engaged in its reproduction. Here, credentials found an important function in commodifying service provision by standardizing professional practices as well as by arranging pricing structures in relation to them in a fee-for-service system. However, the rise of credentialism in the twentieth century is the outcome of efforts by employed occupational groups, seeking to imitate the success of free professionals in monopolizing closure in the market. A similar argument, developed by Perkin (1989), shows how the professional principle progressively evicts the class principle.

On a reading of twentieth century developments that emphasizes status and credentials, the middle occupations can be seen as highly successful in their monopolizing activities. Indeed one of the central problems for recent class theory has been how to explain the emergence of the "new middle class" (Abercrombie and Urry, 1983). The post-war rise in numbers of professional and technical workers has been little short of spectacular, so that in most industrial societies they constitute about 20 per cent of the labour force. They have been variously interpreted by class theorists as a new ruling class (Bell, 1973), a "service class" (Goldthorpe, 1982), a "new petty bourgeoisie" (Poulantzas, 1974), a "new working class" (Mallet, 1975), a contradictory class (Wright, 1982), "expert classes" (Wright, 1985), a "new middle class" (Johnson, 1972), a "professional-managerial class" (Ehrenreich and Ehrenreich, 1979), or simply as a "new class" (Konrad and Szelenyi, 1979).

Class theory and class analysis have always found difficulty in specifying a class location for professional and technical workers. This is because, in class terms, their locations are highly diverse. They exhibit a wide range of relationships to the state, for example from state employment through state-authorized monopoly and state licensing to formal independence. Their organizational location is also diverse, encompassing participation in both large-scale state or private sector bureaucratic systems and small-scale partnerships, and incorporating various relationships to the system of authority including hierarchical, specialist-staff, collegial and consultancy relationships. Finally, particular individual workers have differential locations in authority and reward systems.

Ascribed status: ethnicity and patriarchy

The class paradigm has also found difficulty in accommodating the ascribed statuses of ethnicity, race and gender. Its principal coping strategy has been to assert that they are unimportant, irrelevant, irrational or non-existent and that economic class is the only significant structuring principle for society. In so far as it has done so it has constituted an ideology of white male supremacism. Historically, gender has exhibited far more pronounced inequalities of power and material rewards as well as offering more extreme examples of exploitation and brutal coercion than those occurring between classes. It is also arguable that in the public sphere the extremes of discrimination that have occurred between races as well as the passionate and bloody conflicts that continue to take place between ethnic groups far outweigh any supposed division and struggle between classes.

In treating ethnicity and race the class paradigm has always taken its lead from its intellectual ancestors. Marx viewed ethnic groups as "national left-overs" and "fanatic partisans of the counter-revolution" that threatened to divide the working class and thwart its historical mission (Parkin, 1979: 31). Equally, Weber theorized ethnic group formation as a form of irrational action that ran counter to the technical rationalization of modern bureaucracies and markets. In a sense, the development of the state that is outlined above conspired in this view. Originally an expression of nationality, the nation-state operated to suppress national minorities and sought to assimilate the entire population it controlled to the project of a national cultural community. Because sub-state nationalities were rendered invisible, sociologists often treated them as if they were unreal, as if they were only "imagined communities" (Anderson, 1983) relative to the structural realities of class.

Such a view is increasingly difficult to maintain. Three historical developments mean that race and ethnicity are now prominent features of the social topography. First, the previously colonized societies of the "South" have managed to re-establish self-government, albeit in a form shaped by the Northern colonizers. Part of the ideology that supported this shift was an attempt to establish that racism was an unethical and irrational form of behaviour by claiming that inequalities of race far outweighed those of class. Secondly, one of the emerging features of the contemporary world is mass migration motivated by relative economic disadvantage. Flows from ex-colonies into colonizing societies and from Eastern and Southern Europe into Western Europe have radically altered the ethnic mix in societies previously claimed to be ethnically homogeneous and these ethnic cleavages are now too apparent to be ignored. Thirdly, during the past quarter of a century the state has gone through a series of crises that have weakened its powers allowing the re-emergence of previously repressed national minorities. Nowhere is this more apparent than in the ex-socialist states of Eastern Europe and the ex-USSR where ethnic resurgence now threatens fragile political and economic arrangements but is also apparent in Western capitalist societies.

If sociology turned a blind eye to ethnicity then it must have turned two to gender. Gender inequalities and exploitations were obscured by the "naturalism" of sex-role theory and the triumphalism of a modernization theory that stressed the adaptive superiority of the nuclear family. In one sense the class paradigm can be regarded as less than culpable because one of its claims was that class processes transpired largely in the public sphere, and because women were excluded from employment and politics they were irrelevant to class processes. This was a widespread view found, for example, in Parsons: "The separation of the sex roles in our society is such as . . . to remove women from the kind of occupational status which is important for the determination of the status of the family" (1954: 80); in Giddens: "Given that women still have to await their liberation from the family, it remains the case in the capitalist societies that female workers are largely peripheral to the class system" (1973: 288); and Parkin: "for the majority of women . . . the allocation of social and economic rewards is determined primarily by the position of their families – and, in particular, that of the male head" (1979: 14–15). In a famous article, Goldthorpe (1983) asserted that he would continue to measure the class of any woman by classifying the occupation of her conjugal partner because household income was largely determined by the male partner, because women's labour force participation was intermittent, and because women's sociopolitical attitudes could be predicted more accurately by their partner's occupation than by their own, even if they were themselves employed.

Such a position is certainly no longer tenable. Female participation in the employment sphere is now at a higher level, is more stable and more influential than it has ever been. Patriarchy has been transformed into a "public patriarchy" (Walby, 1990) or "extended viriarchy" (Waters, 1989). This development raises a fundamental problem. It suggests that the class paradigm might have been wrong in claiming preeminence as a structuring principle. The development of a class structure was only possible in so far as it was based on a domestic division of labour that allowed men exclusively to construct a public sphere. In these terms we must consider the possibility that gender is primordial as *the* structural principle and that class is merely contingent. Certainly one could make a more convincing case that gender has always structured society than one could for class.

A REVISIONIST HISTORY OF CLASS

The continuing salience and the return to prominence of political domination, conventional status and ascribed status as principles of stratification suggest that an undifferentiated history of capitalism as the extended reproduction of class might have less to offer than a periodized framework. Within such a framework each period can be conceptualized as reflecting the predominance of one or more stratificational principles. Nineteenth century Britain, for example, might be viewed as a close approximation to the class-theoretic template set out in the early part of this chapter. This section rehearses an alternative history (built on Waters, 1994, 1995a; Pakulski and Waters, 1996) in which stratification can be conceptualized as exhibiting radically different features from those outlined in the class model.

On this argument, the term "class society" must be restricted to the particular configuration in which collective actors determined by production relations struggle within that arena for control of the system of property ownership. Employment relations or labour market position may continue to have salience in determining social rewards in periods during which this configuration is not central. However, in many, if not most instances these will be mediated by factors other than property ownership, including organizational position, skills and credentials, the social worth of value-commitments, the social construction of ascribed statuses, and patterns of political domination (see e.g. Mann, 1993).

In summary, the stratification order of capitalist societies might be traced as a succession of three periods roughly periodized into the nineteenth century, the first three-quarters of the twentieth century, and the contemporary period. In highly formalized and abstracted terms they may be described as economic-class society, organized-class society and status-conventional society.

Economic-class society is arranged into patterns of domination and struggle between interest groups that emerge from the economic realm. In the familiar terms of Marx, the classes will be property owners and sellers of labour power but they could be conceptualized as employers and employees. The dominant class can control the state and maintain itself as a ruling class either by capturing its apparatuses or by rendering them weak. In so far as the subordinate class undertakes collective action it will be rebellious or revolutionary in character, aimed at dislodging this ruling class by the abolition of private property. Culture is divided to match class divisions, into dominant and subordinate ideologies and into high and low cultures.

In terms of the four cells identified in figure 3.1, class society exhibits the following characteristics.

1 The social structure consists in a radically unequal distribution of property between capitalists and workers that enables the former to exploit the latter. Capital property is largely owned privately and familially rather than by the state and is inherited dynastically.

2 The social formation consists of a series of closed communities operating within the confines of a weak or liberal state that are divided by a central rift marked by antagonism, exploitation, struggle and

conflict. Classes stand in a functional relationship with patriarchy in which each serves to reproduce the other. The family is the main site for class reproduction.

3 Class societies are characterized by bounded subcultures. Capitalist class families legitimate their capital accumulation and its inheritance by reference to such dominant ideologies as Protestant thrift, divine election and puritan temperament. These show that the ruling class is entitled to its privileges because it has earned them and God recognizes the fact. Working-class cultures typically absorb such cultural imposts in expressions of deference, although radicalization is also possible especially where an alternative religious ideology can promote it.

4 Working-class political action is militant, ideological and occasionally revolutionary. It involves a close association between industrial organization and action and political organization and action. It expresses a deep sense of injury, pain and exploitation in an active hostility to "the bosses". Ruling-class political action involves the suppression and repression of working-class organizational vehicles and attempts to seduce working-class commitments within the rubrics of patriotism and paternalism.

Organized-class society is defined by a political or state sphere. The state is typically dominated by a single unified bloc, a political-bureaucratic elite, that exercises power over one or more subordinated masses. These blocs may be factionalized horizontally into formally opposed parties. The elite will comprise either a party leadership or a corporatized leadership integrating party leaders with the leaders of other organized interest groups, including economic and cultural ones. The elite uses the coercive power of the state to regulate economic and culture. The state can dominate the economy by redistribution or by the conversion of private into public property, although this need not be a complete accomplishment. Classes, in turn, reorganize themselves in national-political rather than industrial terms by establishing links with milieu parties. Meanwhile, the cultural realm can be unified under the state umbrella or under the aegis of state-sponsored monopolies. It can thus be turned into an industrialized or mass culture.[3]

Again, we can examine the contents of the four cells provided by the model given in figure 3.1 for organized-class systems.

(1) In organized-class society property is still distributed unequally but the sharp break between ownership and non-ownership disappears in favour of a gradient that, over time, progressively becomes less steep. An important element in this redistribution is the intervention of states in property ownership. Under the aegis of socialist, communist or fascist ideologies states can appropriate the means of production on behalf of

the working class. In other societies property ownership can be reorganized by the formation of shareholder corporations that tend to separate ownership from control and to facilitate the dispersal of the former. The key role in market participation is the occupation. What many sociologists now call classes are in fact groups of similar occupations effecting an unreliable closure against external recruitment and battling to climb the ladder of consumption privileges. The critical contexts for occupational advancement are the hierarchies of authority and responsibility established in state agencies and corporations. It is here that mobility barriers are erected and that participants strive for sufficient income to reproduce their standing by providing adequate educations for their offspring.

(2) In organized-class society, the nation-state orchestrates national class formation by incorporating its organizational forms into national compacts. Here "organized classes" are the political expression of occupational groupings but they are far more unstable than their predecessors. This is because education has become a critical vehicle for socioeconomic reproduction. Positions expand to a much wider variety and diversity especially in what is often called the "new middle class" and the allocation of persons to positions occurs at least as much in terms of individual ability and good fortune and the capacity of schools to develop talent as it does on family background. Patriarchy experiences some reorganization as women re-enter the public sphere if only in stereotypical roles and subordinated positions.

(3) Organized-class societies, especially in their corporatized and welfare versions, transform cultural orientations. Class cultures become more differentiated, profligate and indulgent at the top and the bottom although regulative and privatized in the middle. Nationally organized political ideologies match this development: social democracy favours a redistribution of consumption possibilities to the bottom; liberalism favours rewards for hard work in the middle; and conservatism the maintenance of privilege at the top. However, these political-ideological meta-narratives do not penetrate everyday meaning systems, social norms, consumption patterns and images very deeply. Their impact on lifeworlds is limited to a handful of committed and ideologically conscious activists and intellectuals. Such class ideologies function mainly as elite political formulae.

(4) Social classes take a new lease on life despite market fragmentation and a progressing division of labour. The political-organizational super-structures of class, trade unions and parties take over the dominant social-structuring role. Within the political programmes and platforms of these self-declared class bodies, class issues and interests are articulated, elaborated and disseminated. So class ideologies are constructed as totalizing packages combining specific social values with

general strategies of implementation. Socialism, liberalism and conservatism became associated with broad class interests because of their deployment as the political formulae of the major parties. Popular identifications, outlooks and interests are increasingly organized by the political activism and ideological appeals of these national class bodies. They reflect these packages rather than people's work and life experiences. The working classes are closely identified with support for social democratic parties; the "middle classes" are defined in terms of political programmes of the liberal-conservative parties and allegiances to liberal-conservative ideological packages. Even rightist extremism acquires class overtones as fascist parties appeal to petit bourgeois, antimodernist, anti-industrial sentiments. Modern industrial classes are thus reconstituted as "imagined communities," powerful abstractions occupying a central place in individual and collective identifications. This reconstitution of classes involves not only an organizational articulation of class, where the organizations become the real class actors, but also the development of uniform class symbolism, iconography and the dissemination of class identities and discourses.

In *status-conventional society* stratification is sourced in the cultural sphere. The strata are lifestyle and/or value-based status configurations. They can form around differentiated patterns of value-commitment, identity, belief, symbolic meaning, taste, opinion or consumption. Because of the ephemeral and fragile nature of these resources, a stratification system based on conventional status communities appears as a shifting mosaic that can destabilize economics and politics. The state is weakened because it cannot rely on mass support, and the economy is weakened (in its societal effectivity) because of the critical importance of symbolic values. Each order is deconcentrated by a prevailing orientation to values and utilities that are established conventionally rather than by reference to collective interests.

(1) In status-conventional society the redistribution of property that begins in organized-class society continues, especially in the context of privatization. More importantly the character of property changes so that it is much less easy to accumulate and monopolize. Intellectual property becomes more important relative to material property and the economy of intellectual and aesthetic signs is highly fluid and competitive (Lash and Urry, 1994). Education becomes a chancey mediator of socioeconomic reproduction. Under these conditions markets become casinos. Each individual is his or her own market player, needing to make educational and occupational career decisions in contexts that defy parental advance planning. Social rewards depend on performance, although the markets will not necessarily evaluate performance on a just calculus.

(2) The reproductive lineaments of class disappear. In a globalized world of symbolic currents the nation-state can no longer orchestrate

class groupings because it has been beaten into submission by irresolv-able problems and besieged by entitlement claimants who stand outside the old organized classes. The central site for reproduction is now the mobile, biographically self-composing individual. Moreover the stress on individual performance and capacity and on individual selection of lifestyle and value-commitment means that patriarchy becomes suscep-tible to feminist opposition.

(3)   Status-conventional societies experience simultaneous cultural homogenization and fragmentation. They homogenize at the level of material culture and milieu emphasizing consumption, especially sym-bolic consumption, but fragment at the level of lifestyles and value-commitments as these issues become redefined as matters of election and choice. Each of these developments spells the dissolution of class subcultures.

(4)   At the political level, status-conventional society is marked by class and partisan disalignment, declining partisanship and party trust, the appearance of "third parties", especially of the left-libertarian type and a growing tide of "new politics", "issue politics" and "life politics" (Dalton, 1988; Kitschelt, 1989; Giddens, 1991). With the decline of class organizations and the ideological packages that these organizations promote, the organized quasi-communities of class fade. The new politi-cal configurations promote the elaboration of new value-commitments that themselves become the focuses of differentiation and inequality.

POSTCLASS SOCIETY

This historical-phase model suggests that the stratification system might be moving into a culturalist or *status-conventional* phase. Figure 3.2 is a rejigging of figure 3.1 that outlines a status-theoretic template to replace the class-theoretic one. It shows that a historical transforma-tion from economic-class society to organized-class society to status-conventional society is not only an issue of socioeconomic stratification but one of wide-ranging societal transformation. The argument offered here is therefore a development of the general theoretical effort that focuses on postindustrialization (Bell, 1973), detraditionalization and reflexive modernization (Giddens, 1991; Beck, 1992; Beck et al., 1994), postmodernization (Lyotard, 1984; Harvey, 1989; Crook et al, 1992), societal disorganization (Offe, 1985; Lash and Urry, 1987, 1994) and globalization (Featherstone, 1990; Robertson, 1992; Waters, 1995b).

We can now theorize this transformation more formally. The early part of this chapter disaggregates class theory into four propositions that can be used to explain the substantive aspects of class. We can

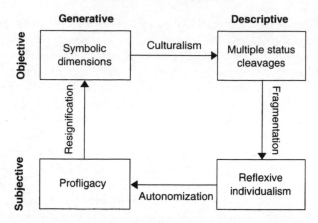

Figure 3.2 *Aspects of a sociology of status-conventional society*

follow a similar procedure in theorizing status-conventional society. The four propositions that class theory makes are: economism; groupness; behavioural linkage; and transformative capacity. A status-conventional theory would offer the following parallel propositions.

- The proposition of *culturalism*. Status-conventional stratification is primarily a cultural phenomenon. It is based on subscription to lifestyles that form around consumption patterns, information flows, cognitive agreements, aesthetic preferences and value-commitments. Material and power phenomena are reducible to these symbolically manifested lifestyle phenomena.

- The proposition of *fragmentation*. Conventional statuses, like classes, are real phenomena. However they consist of a virtually infinite overlap of associations and identifications that are shifting and unstable. Status-conventional society is a fluid matrix of fragile formations that cycle and multiply within a globalized field.

- The proposition of *autonomization*. The subjective orientation and behaviour of any individual or aggregate of individuals is very difficult to predict by virtue of stratificational location. There is no central cleavage or single dimension along which preferences can be ordered. Such attributes as political preference, access to educational opportunity, patterns of marriage and income are self-referential rather than externally constrained.

- The proposition of *resignification* based on subjective interests. The stratification process is continuously fluid. Its openness allows a constant respecification and invention of preferences and symbolic dimensions that provide for continuous regeneration. The source of novelty is a process of restless subjective choice that seeks to gratify churning and unrepressed emotions that include anxiety and aggression as well as desire.

Figure 3.2 also outlines the substantive status-conventional parallels to figure 3.1. It shows that the propositions can specify the possible phenomena that sociologists might seek to theorize and analyse. The starting point is the top left cell which indicates that the objective-generative phenomena in which we should be interested arc "symbolic dimensions." These are socially subscribed scales or networks of symbols that can provide focuses for identification and preference. They are broadly similar to the phenomena that Appadurai (1990) refers to as "scapes" (ethnoscapes, theoscapes, finanscapes etc.) in his analysis of cultural globalization. These symbolic dimensions include some of the "economic" phenomena traditionally associated with class, including socioeconomic status, but in a symbolized form. So "occupation" is now critical not in terms of its capacity to put one in a relationship of exploitation but because it is a badge of status, an indicator of one's importance and of one's capacity to consume. Alongside these we can place ascribed-status membership dimensions that have now become value-infused, symbolicized and reflexive (ethnicity, religion, education, race, gender and sexual preference) plus consumption statuses (yuppie, trekkie, hacker, clothes-horse, punk, gothic, jogger, opera buff etc.) and value-commitment statuses (feminist, environmentalist, Zionist, redneck, right-to-lifer etc.). Identity is thus not linked either to property or to organizational position. Under conditions of advanced affluence, styles of consumption and commitment become socially salient as markers and delimitators.

The proposition of culturalism specifies that these symbolic dimensions will compete with each other in the field of social structure. This will produce the phenomenon of multiple status cleavages. The stratificational categories of status-conventional society are a complex mosaic of taste subcultures, "new associations", civic initiatives, ethnic and religious revolutionary groups, generational cohorts, community action groups, new social movements, gangs, alternative lifestyle colonies, alternative production organizations, educational alumni, racial brotherhoods, gender sisterhoods, tax rebels, fundamentalist and revivalist religious movements, internet discussion groups, purchasing co-ops, professional associations, and so on. Many are ephemeral, some are continuous and stable.

A key feature of these multiple status cleavages is that because they are specialized and intersecting, membership in any one does not necessarily contradict membership in any other. From the subjective point of view the proposition of fragmentation ensures that individuals apprehend the stratification system as a status bazaar. Individuals stand simultaneously as members of several status-groups and have the potential to be members of any others. Their identities are reflexively self-composed as they move between status groups. However, the fact of a status market does not imply an absolute voluntarism, and indeed the freedoms in most cases are relevant to exit from status groups rather than entry. Closure processes remain effective in status-conventional society.

The proposition of autonomization nevertheless allows individuals to be profligate in their behaviour. They will tend to spend their resources of time, energy, money, influence and power in the pursuit of symbolic attachments that tend to advance the interests, identities, values and commitments to which they subscribe and aspire. The very act of doing this will, by the proposition of resignification, tend to redefine and reorder the symbolic dimensions that reference the system. Indeed, a particular effect is the redefinition of some traditional status-membership dimensions, especially education, religion and ethnicity into a more ephemeral and conventional regime. So education becomes a marketplace for credentials, religion becomes a vehicle for handling this week's anxieties, and ethnicity is something one rediscovers through community action and involvement.

CONCLUSION

Postclass societies will remain internally differentiated in terms of access to economic resources, political power and prestige. Indeed it is possible to argue that an organized-class society in its late corporatist form can have the greatest potential to achieve a historically unique degree of egalitarianism and that postclass society will bring about an increase in inequality. Nor will the emergence of postclass society imply the end of social division and conflict. Non-class social divisions and non-class conflicts have survived class, even if overshadowed by it under conditions of industrial capitalism. The new divisions and conflicts that might emerge in postclass society may prove even more crippling and destabilizing than the old ones. Unlike many postindustrial visions of social change, this argument then does not imply progressive equalization and social harmony.

The sociology of class is already adjusting to these changing social conditions. Marxist class theory has all but disappeared and is influential only in the empiricist form developed by Wright and his associates (1982, 1985, 1989) that both accepts that class can be sourced in authority and credentials as much as in property and that the stratificational map can identify up to 12 different class locations. The other mainstream approach, what is often called "class analysis", is even more diffident in its defence of a sociology of class. It claims only to be a research programme within which different theories can be assessed empirically (Goldthorpe and Marshall, 1992: 382–3). Interestingly, it also insists, "that specific consideration should also be given to theories holding that class relations are in fact of diminishing importance for life-chances and social action or that other relations and attributes – defined, for example, by income or consumption, status, lifestyle, ethnicity or gender – are or are becoming, of greater consequence" (1992: 382). Class analysis appears to be adjusting to the fact that class can empirically explain very little, a mere 17 per cent of income (Halaby and Weakliem, 1993) and perhaps 10 per cent of voting behaviour (Franklin et al., 1992; Clark et al., 1993), and even here class is operationalized as occupation. People may identify with classes but only when prompted and only after they have identified with occupation, family role, national citizenship, gender, ethnicity, age, region of residence, and supporting a sports team, so that "the discursive salience of class is almost minimal" (Emmison and Western, 1990: 241).

If class then is a traditionalistic remnant in a postmodernizing world, the question remains of whether sociology can continue to make a central theoretical contribution if it abandons the concept of "class" on which it relied for a hundred years. The answer is that it indeed must abandon its insistence on the centrality of class if it is to survive. The most instructive recent sociological studies are those that emphasize the intersection of multiple status cleavages within a single local context. These tend to the view that patterns of oppression and exploitation can become extreme where the status cleavages reinforce one another or can be moderated where they run counter to one another. Phizacklea's study (1990) of gender and ethnicity in the British fashion industry is an example of the former while Kornblum's study (1974) of Chicago steelworkers represents the latter. As the above quotation from Goldthorpe and Marshall shows, empirical "class analysis" equally can accommodate stratificational multi-dimensionality so long as it does not continue to privilege class. However, the key task that remains is the development of a macro-theoretical paradigm that can match the brilliant capacity of Marx and Weber to theorize a new principle of social stratification. They managed to avoid the dangers of retrospection, to avoid theorizing classes as "new estates" and we too must seek likewise to seek to avoid theorizing emergent status-conventional arrangements as "new classes".

NOTES

1   *American Sociological Review*, 58 (1); *British Journal of Sociology*, 44 (2, 3); *International Journal of Urban and Regional Research*, 15 (1): *International Sociology*, 8 (3), 9 (2–3); *Sociology*, 24 (2), 26 (2–3), 28 (2–4).

2   This chapter is based on work done in the "Impact of Class" project being carried out at the University of Tasmania and the Research School of Social Sciences, Australian National University in conjunction with Jan Pakulski and Gary Marks. It draws on material co-authored with Pakulski and published as *The Death of Class* (London, Sage, 1996). Some of the ideas and a few of the words belong to him and I am grateful for his permission to publish this chapter under sole authorship.

3   This argument about organized-class society is similar to that taken by early Frankfurt School theorists (see, for example, the contributions in Arato and Gebhardt, 1978: part 1).

REFERENCES

Abercrombie, N. and Urry, J. (1983) *Capital, Labour and the Middle Classes*. London: Allen and Unwin.

Anderson, B. (1983) *Imagined Communities*. London: Verso.

Appadurai, A. (1990) "Disjuncture and difference in the global cultural economy," in M. Featherstone (ed.), *Global Culture*, pp. 295–310. London: Sage.

Arato, A. and Gebhardt, E. (1978) *The Essential Frankfurt School Reader*. New York: Urizon.

Beck, U. (1992) *Risk Society: Toward a New Modernity*. London: Sage.

Beck, U., Giddens, A. and Lash, S. (1994) *Reflexive Modernization*. Cambridge: Polity Press.

Bell, D. (1973) *The Coming of Post-industrial Society*. New York: Basic Books.

Berle, A. and Means, G. (1932/1967) *The Modern Corporation and Private Property*. New York: Harcourt.

Blau, P. and Duncan, O. (1967) *The American Occupational Structure*. New York: Wiley.

Burnham, J. (1941) *The Managerial Revolution*. New York: Doubleday.

Clark, T. and Lipset, S. (1991) "Are social classes dying?," *International Sociology*, 6 (4): 397–410.

Clark, T., Lipset, S. and Rempel, M. (1993) "The declining political significance of social class," *International Sociology*, 8 (3): 279–93.

Crompton, R. (1993) *Class and Stratification*. Cambridge: Polity Press.

Crook, S., Pakulski, J. and Waters, M. (1992) *Postmodernization*. London: Sage.

Dahrendorf, R. (1959) *Class and Class Conflict in Industrial Society*. London: Routledge.

Dalton, R. (1988) *Citizen Politics in Western Democracies*. Chatham: Chatham Publishers.

Ehrenreich, B. and Ehrenreich, J. (1979) "The professional-managerial class," in P. Walker (ed.), *Between Labour and Capital*, pp. 5–45. Boston: South End Press.

Emmison, M. and Western, M. (1990) "Social class and social identity: a comment on Marshall et al.," *Sociology*, 24 (2): 241–53.

Featherstone, M. (ed.) (1990) *Global Culture: Nationalism, Globalization and Modernity*. London: Sage.

Franklin, M., Mackie, T. and Valen, H. (1992) *Electoral Change: Responses to Evolving Social and Attitudinal Structures in Western Countries*. Cambridge: Cambridge University Press.

Giddens, A. (1973) *The Class Structure of Advanced Societies*. London: Hutchinson.

Giddens, A. (1991) *Modernity and Self-identity*. Cambridge: Polity Press.

Goldthorpe, J. (1982) "On the service class, its formation and future," in A. Giddens and G. Mackenzie (eds), *Social Class and the Division of Labour*, pp. 162–85. Cambridge: Cambridge University Press.

Goldthorpe, J. (1983) "Women and class analysis," *Sociology*, 17 (4): 465–88.

Goldthorpe, J. and Marshall, G. (1992) "The promising future of class analysis: a response to recent critiques," *Sociology*, 26 (3): 381–400.

Halaby, C. and Weakliem, D. (1993) "Ownership and authority in the earnings function," *American Sociological Review*, 58 (1): 16–30.

Harvey, D. (1989) *The Condition of Postmodernity*. Oxford: Basil Blackwell.

Johnson, T. (1972) *Professions and Power*. London: Macmillan.

Kitschelt, H. (1989) *The Logics of Party Formation*. Ithaca, NY: Cornell University Press.

Konrad, G. and Szelenyi, I. (1979) *Intellectuals on the Road to Class Power*. Brighton: Harvester Press.

Kornblum, W. (1974) *Blue Collar Community*. Chicago: University of Chicago Press.

Larson, M. (1977) *The Rise of Professionalism*. Berkeley, CA: California University Press.

Lash, S. and Urry, J. (1987) *The End of Organised Capitalism*. Cambridge: Polity Press.

Lash, S. and Urry, J. (1994) *Economies of Signs and Space*. London: Sage.

Lee, D. and Turner, B. (eds) (1996) *Conflicts about Class*. London: Longman.

Lyotard, J. (1984) *The Postmodern Condition*. Manchester: Manchester University Press.

Mallet, S. (1975) *The New Working Class*. Nottingham: Spokesman.

Mann, M. (1993) *The Sources of Social Power*, vol. 2. Cambridge: Cambridge University Press.

Offe, C. (1984) *Contradictions of the Welfare State*. London: Hutchinson.

Offe, C. (1985) *Disorganised Capitalism*. Cambridge/Cambridge, MA: Polity/MITP.

Pakulski, J. and Waters, M. (1996) *The Death of Class*. London: Sage.

Parkin, F. (1979) *Marxism and Class Theory*. London: Tavistock.

Parsons, T. (1954) *Essays in Sociological Theory*. Glencoe, IL: Free Press.

Perkin, H. (1989) *The Rise of Professional Society*. London: Routledge.

Phizacklea, A. (1990) *Unpacking the Fashion Industry: Gender, Racism and Class in Production*. London: Routledge.

Poulantzas, N. (1974) *Classes in Contemporary Capitalism*. London: Verso.

Robertson, R. (1992) *Globalization*. London: Sage.

Walby, S. (1990) *Theorizing Patriarchy*. Oxford: Basil Blackwell.

Waters, M. (1989) "Patriarchy and viriarchy," *Sociology*, 32 (2): 193–211.

Waters, M. (1994) "Succession in the stratification order: a contribution to the 'death of class' debate," *International Sociology*, 9 (3): 295–312.

Waters, M. (1995a) "The thesis of the loss of the perfect market," *British Journal of Sociology*, 46 (3): 409–28.

Waters, M. (1995b) *Globalization*. London: Routledge.

Wright, E. (1982) "Class boundaries in advanced capitalist societies," in A. Giddens and D. Held (eds), *Classes, Power and Conflict*, pp. 112–29. Berkeley, CA: California University Press.

Wright, E. (1985) *Classes*. London: Verso.

Wright, E. (ed.) (1989) *The Debate on Classes*. London: Verso.

PART II
GLOBALIZATION

Introduction

This part consists of four chapters, each dealing with globalization from a different perspective. The extract from David Harvey's *The Condition of Postmodernity*, which forms chapter 4, is written from an orthodox Marxist perspective in which globalization is seen as determined by economic change. The extract from Anthony Giddens's *Beyond Left and Right*, which forms chapter 5, represents a more widely accepted alternative view – that globalization has multiple causes. Furthermore, Giddens sees globalization as itself contributing to the profound changes underway in contemporary culture. For Harvey, the cultural changes associated with postmodernity are, like globalization, economically determined. Although Appadurai (chapter 6) describes himself as sympathetic to Marxism, his account of the "global cultural economy" is a good deal more complex than Harvey's. He is particularly concerned to draw out the way in which the many processes of globalization are interrelated, producing contradictory and uneven effects. Finally, the brief extract by Stuart Hall (chapter 7) is illustrative of these contradictory effects; he takes the Salman Rushdie affair as exemplary of the continuing reconstruction of identities in globalization.

In chapter 4, Harvey writes about the transition from Fordism to post-Fordism which he sees as currently taking place. For Harvey, globalization is one aspect of this fundamental economic shift in relations of production. Fordism, which can be dated from Henry Ford's introduction of high wages and secure employment in his automated car assembly plant in 1914, involved mass production, mass consumption, and the scientific management of workers to increase productivity. In politics, it was combined with Keynesianism in the post-war period: the state, business leaders, and unionized workers co-operated to ensure high wages, a welfare state to enable workers to spend those wages on consumer goods, so keeping consumption levels high, and state-guaranteed capital investment to ensure high levels of productivity. Since the late 1970s, however, Fordism–Keynesianism has proved too rigid for capitalists, who are now developing more flexible means of capital accumulation. As a result, society is moving toward post-Fordism, characterized by insecure employment or unemployment for the majority, a decline in manufacturing industry, the growth of service employment, and, in production, flexible specialization for niche markets. Globalization, particularly of financial capital, is one of the strategies adopted by capitalists to escape the rigidities of Fordism–Keynesianism, organized around nation-state regulation. Harvey sees it as successfully empowering capitalism in relation to a weakened state. From this point of view, the politics of Thatcherism and Reaganism was no more than a continuation of economic trends already underway. The power of unions was weakened by restrictive employment practices and high levels of unemployment, and slackening economic growth resulted in the withdrawal of the welfare state. In Harvey's view, while the state still has to regulate capitalist activities in the name of "national interests," realistically it has been reduced to an entrepreneurial role, acting to create a "good business climate" to attract and keep investment which may easily be moved to another country.

Harvey's analysis of the economic changes linked to globalization is relatively uncontroversial among sociologists. Many, however, would take issue with his view that they provide as complete an *explanation* for it as Harvey supposes. Chapter 5, by Anthony Giddens, provides an alternative view: that globalization involves many processes. These include the dynamism of capitalist expansion, but globalization cannot be reduced to it as its sole cause. Giddens sees globalization as the result of institutional processes inherent in modernity: capitalism, industrialism, state control of the means of violence and of information.

Giddens's main point in this chapter is that globalization contributes to the de-traditionalization of social life and the growth of reflexivity. We live, Giddens argues, in post-traditional societies in which taken-for-granted ways of life are continually disrupted. He prefers the term "post-traditional" to postmodern because contemporary societies are a continuation of changes already underway in modernity. He sees "postmodern" as indicating a sharp break with modernity which is historically unfounded. Globalization further contributes to de-traditionalization as cultural diversity is no longer geographically bounded as it was in modernity. Cultures are now in contact on a daily basis and this weakens traditional beliefs and practices still further. Individuals are continually faced with choices about how to live. Giddens is one of the principal exponents of the concept of "reflexivity," also used in this collection of readings by Bauman (chapter 2) and Waters (chapter 3). It involves the continuing reflection on action as a result of the many possibilities with which individuals are faced. However, it is important to note that "reflexivity" does not only involve ideas; it is also effective in practice, regularly re-ordering and redefining social activities.

For Giddens, reflexivity involves new forms of global politics which he calls "life politics." Where fate becomes a matter of choice, new concerns arise about what kind of world and what kind of lives we are creating for ourselves. Feminist politics, which have contributed to and which respond to changes in the family, are an example of life politics. Even nature is no longer considered to be outside the scope of our intervention, though we now know that it is not easily controlled. Ecological politics which attempt to deal with the manufactured uncertainty that continually results from our attempts to manage nature in various ways is another form of life politics.

Giddens does not address the issue here, but it is clear that life politics is not adequately dealt with by individual nation-states. Where it is a matter of "challenges that face collective humanity" rather than national problems, states may contribute to reflexive attempts to deal with specific issues, but they must be addressed internationally and transnationally. In fact, Giddens has elsewhere stated his sympathies with David Held's model of cosmopolitan global democracy outlined in chapter 16. It is clear that the global crises Giddens refers to in chapter 5 require political structures of the kind Held details there.

Arjun Appadurai, in chapter 6, deals extensively with a feature of globalization mentioned in Giddens's chapter. It is mistaken to think of globalization as producing homogeneity across the world: it is lived in different ways in different localities. In particular, Appadurai stresses the "disjunctive," contradictory effects of global flows. The world order is no longer well represented by the centre–periphery model previously dominant in the sociology of development. The inter-relation of global flows produces unpredictable, random configurations not easily recognized in these terms.

In chapter 6, Appadurai develops his extremely influential idea of global "scapes" to enable an understanding of global flows of people, money, technology, images, and ideas across the territorial boundaries of nation-states. "Scapes" should be understood by analogy to landscapes; the form they take depends on the position of the viewer. They are not purely objective; nor are they subjective, since they take place in the real world. They are perspectival, differing according to the different points of view of those who act within the horizons they construct. Social actors here include nation-states, social movements, and transnational corporations as well as individuals. Finally, Appadurai develops an analysis of the state in relation to global scapes. Across the world, he argues, states are attempting to consolidate their power by allying themselves with nations, while nations are, in turn, attempting to do the same by capturing states. This process involves conflicts between existing states and sub-national groups, like the Basques, and also between states and transnational diasporas, like the Kurds. States are now in a contradictory position, as Appadurai sees it: they must open their borders to global flows, but they also attempt to control their own populations. China is a good example, attempting to balance greater openness to capital, markets, and new technology with continued resistance to ideas of democratization.

Chapter 7 by Stuart Hall provides a good example of the contradictory processes of globalization in relation to cultural identities. He compares two prominent responses to the pluralization of the West that has followed the post-war migration from previously colonized countries. Fundamentalist groups attempt to restore fractured and uncertain identities with an aggressive reassertion of tradition. Muslim revivalism is the most highly publicized fundamentalism, but we should also see right-wing xenophobic movements in this light too, Hall argues. Alternatively, other members of diasporas respond with an acceptance of hybridity, dealing creatively with the experience of being "translated" across the cultures within which they find themselves situated. Importantly, however, both responses attempt to deal with the challenge to identities which results from continual cultural confrontation (also mentioned in chapter 5 by Giddens). In this respect they are both attempts to deal with the challenges of diaspora, which simply means the dispersion of people with a common history and cultural background. The Salman Rushdie affair outlined by Hall is an excellent example of the clash between "tradition" and "translation." Although Iran has called off the death threat imposed by the Ayatollah Khomeini and Rushdie was able to come out of hiding in 1998, Hall's analysis of the underlying issues remains as pertinent as ever. This chapter may usefully be compared with chapter 17, where William Connolly makes a somewhat similar analysis of Christian and postmodern identities in relation to democratization.

CHAPTER 4

From Fordism to
Flexible Accumulation

David Harvey

In retrospect, it seems there were signs of serious problems within Fordism as early as the mid-1960s. By then, the West European and Japanese recoveries were complete, their internal markets saturated, and the drive to create export markets for their surplus output had to begin. And this occurred at the very moment when the success of Fordist rationalization meant the relative displacement of more and more workers from manufacturing. The consequent slackening of effective demand was offset in the United States by the war on poverty and the war in Vietnam. But declining corporate productivity and profitability after 1966 meant the beginnings of a fiscal problem in the United States that would not go away except at the price of an acceleration in inflation, which began to undermine the role of the dollar as a stable international reserve currency. The formation of the Eurodollar market, and the credit crunch of 1966–7, were indeed prescient signals of the United States' diminished power to regulate the international financial system. It was at about this time too that import substitution policies in many Third World countries (particularly Latin America), coupled with the first big push by multinationals into offshore manufacturing (particularly in South-East Asia), brought a wave of competitive Fordist industrialization to entirely new environments, where the social contract with labour was either weakly enforced or non-existent. International competition thereafter intensified as Western Europe and Japan, joined by a whole host of newly industrializing countries, challenged United States hegemony within Fordism to the point where the Bretton Woods agree-

This chapter is an edited extract from *The Condition of Postmodernity* by David Harvey (Oxford, Blackwell, 1989), pp. 141–72. Reprinted by permission of Blackwell Publishers.

ment cracked and the dollar was devalued. Floating and often highly
volatile exchange rates thereafter replaced the fixed exchange rates of
the postwar boom.

More generally, the period from 1965 to 1973 was one in which the
inability of Fordism and Keynesianism to contain the inherent contradictions of capitalism became more and more apparent. On the surface,
these difficulties could best be captured by one word: rigidity. There
were problems with the rigidity of long-term and large-scale fixed
capital investments in mass-production systems that precluded much
flexibility of design and presumed stable growth in invariant consumer
markets. There were problems of rigidities in labour markets, labour
allocation, and in labour contracts (especially in the so-called "monopoly" sector). And any attempt to overcome these rigidities ran into
the seemingly immovable force of deeply entrenched working-class
power – hence the strike waves and labour disruptions of the period
1968–72. The rigidities of state commitments also became more serious
as entitlement programmes (social security, pension rights, etc.) grew
under pressure to keep legitimacy at a time when rigidities in production restricted any expansion in the fiscal basis for state expenditures.
The only tool of flexible response lay in monetary policy, in the capacity to print money at whatever rate appeared necessary to keep the
economy stable. And so began the inflationary wave that was eventually to sink the postwar boom. Behind all these specific rigidities lay a
rather unwieldy and seemingly fixed configuration of political power
and reciprocal relations that bound big labour, big capital, and big government into what increasingly appeared as a dysfunctional embrace of
such narrowly defined vested interests as to undermine rather than
secure capital accumulation.

[. . .]

The sharp recession of 1973, exacerbated by the oil shock, evidently
shook the capitalist world out of the suffocating torpor of "stagflation"
(stagnant output of goods and high inflation of prices), and set in motion
a whole set of processes that undermined the Fordist compromise. The
1970s and 1980s have consequently been a troubled period of economic
restructuring and social and political readjustment. In the social space
created by all this flux and uncertainty, a series of novel experiments in
the realms of industrial organization as well as in political and social
life have begun to take shape. These experiments may represent the
early stirrings of the passage to an entirely new regime of accumulation,
coupled with a quite different system of political and social regulation.

Flexible accumulation, as I shall tentatively call it, is marked by a
direct confrontation with the rigidities of Fordism. It rests on flexibility
with respect to labour processes, labour markets, products, and patterns
of consumption. It is characterized by the emergence of entirely new

sectors of production, new ways of providing financial services, new markets, and, above all, greatly intensified rates of commercial, techno-logical, and organizational innovation. It has entrained rapid shifts in the patterning of uneven development, both between sectors and between geographical regions, giving rise, for example, to a vast surge in so-called "service-sector" employment as well as to entirely new industrial ensem-bles in hitherto underdeveloped regions (such as the "Third Italy", Flanders, the various silicon valleys and glens, to say nothing of the vast profusion of activities in newly industrializing countries). It has also entailed a new round of what I shall call "time–space compression" in the capitalist world – the time horizons of both private and public decision-making have shrunk, while satellite communication and declin-ing transport costs have made it increasingly possible to spread those decisions immediately over an ever wider and variegated space.

These enhanced powers of flexibility and mobility have allowed employers to exert stronger pressures of labour control on a workforce in any case weakened by two savage bouts of deflation, that saw un-employment rise to unprecedented postwar levels in advanced capital-ist countries (save, perhaps, Japan). Organized labour was undercut by the reconstruction of foci of flexible accumulation in regions lacking previous industrial traditions, and by the importation back into the older centres of the regressive norms and practices established in these new areas. Flexible accumulation appears to imply relatively high levels of "structural" (as opposed to "frictional") unemployment, rapid destruction and reconstruction of skills, modest (if any) gains in the real wage and the rollback of trade union power – one of the political pillars of the Fordist regime.

The labour market has, for example, undergone a radical restructur-ing. Faced with strong market volatility, heightened competition, and narrowing profit margins, employers have taken advantage of weakened union power and the pools of surplus (unemployed or underemployed) labourers to push for much more flexible work regimes and labour con-tracts. It is hard to get a clear overall picture, because the very purpose of such flexibility is to satisfy the often highly specific needs of each firm. Even for regular employers, systems such as "nine-day fortnights", or work schedules that average a forty-hour week over the year but oblige the employee to work much longer at periods of peak demand, and compensate with shorter hours at periods of slack, are becoming much more common. But more important has been the apparent move away from regular employment toward increasing reliance upon part-time, temporary or sub-contracted work arrangements.

The result is a labour market structure of the sort depicted in [. . .] the Institute of Personnel Management's *Flexible Patterns of Work* (1986). The *core* – a steadily shrinking group according to accounts

emanating from both sides of the Atlantic – is made up of employees "with full time, permanent status and is central to the long term future of the organization". Enjoying greater job security, good promotion and re-skilling prospects, and relatively generous pension, insurance, and other fringe benefit rights, this group is nevertheless expected to be adaptable, flexible, and if necessary geographically mobile. The potential costs of laying off core employees in time of difficulty may, however, lead a company to sub-contract even high level functions (varying from design to advertising and financial management), leaving the core group of managers relatively small. The *periphery* encompasses two rather different sub-groups. The first consists of "full-time employees with skills that are readily available in the labour market, such as clerical, secretarial, routine and lesser skilled manual work". With less access to career opportunities, this group tends to be characterized by high labour turnover "which makes work force reductions relatively easy by natural wastage." The second peripheral group "provides even greater numerical flexibility and includes part-timers, casuals, fixed term contract staff, temporaries, sub-contractors and public subsidy trainees, with even less job security than the first peripheral group". [. . .]
  [. . .]
  The transformation in labour market structure has been paralleled by equally important shifts in industrial organization. Organized sub-contracting, for example, opens up opportunities for small business formation, and in some instances permits older systems of domestic, artisanal, familial (patriarchal), and paternalistic ("godfather", "guv'nor" or even mafia-like) labour systems to revive and flourish as centrepieces rather than as appendages of the production system. The revival of "sweatshop" forms of production in cities such as New York and Los Angeles, Paris and London, became a matter for commentary in the mid-1970s and has proliferated rather than shrunk during the 1980s. The rapid growth of "black", "informal", or "underground" economies has also been documented throughout the advanced capitalist world, leading some to suggest that there is a growing convergence between "third world" and advanced capitalist labour systems. Yet the rise of new and the revival of older forms of industrial organization (often dominated by new immigrant groups in large cities, such as the Filipinos, South Koreans, Vietnamese, and Taiwanese in Los Angeles, or the Bangladeshis and Indians in East London) represents rather different things in different places. Sometimes it indicates the emergence of new survival strategies for the unemployed or wholly discriminated against (such as Haitian immigrants in Miami or New York), while in others it is more simply immigrant groups looking for an entry into a capitalist system, organized tax-dodging, or the attraction of high profit

from illegal trade that lies at its basis. But in all such cases, the effect is to transform the mode of labour control and employment.

Working-class forms of organization (such as the trade unions), for example, depended heavily upon the massing of workers within the factory for their viability, and find it peculiarly difficult to gain any purchase within family and domestic labour systems. Paternalistic systems are dangerous territories for labour organizing because they are more likely to corrupt union power (if it is present) than union power is likely to liberate employees from "godfather" domination and paternalistic welfarism. Indeed, one of the signal advantages of embracing such ancient forms of labour process and of petty-capitalist production is that they undermine working-class organization and transform the objective basis for class struggle. Class consciousness no longer derives from the straight class relation between capital and labour, and moves onto a much more confused terrain of interfamilial conflicts and fights for power within a kinship or clan-like system of hierarchically ordered social relations. Struggling against capitalist exploitation in the factory is very different from struggling against a father or uncle who organizes family labour into a highly disciplined and competitive sweatshop that works to order for multinational capital.

The effects are doubly obvious when we consider the transformed role of women in production and labour markets. Not only do the new labour market structures make it much easier to exploit the labour power of women on a part-time basis, and so to substitute lower-paid female labour for that of more highly paid and less easily laid-off core male workers, but the revival of sub-contracting and domestic and family labour systems permits a resurgence of patriarchal practices and homeworking. This revival parallels the enhanced capacity of multinational capital to take Fordist mass-production systems abroad, and there to exploit extremely vulnerable women's labour power under conditions of extremely low pay and negligible job security (see Nash and Fernandez-Kelly, 1983). The Maquiladora programme that allows US managers and capital ownership to remain north of the Mexican border, while locating factories employing mainly young women south of the border, is a particularly dramatic example of a practice that has become widespread in many of the less developed and newly industrializing countries (the Philippines, South Korea, Brazil, etc.). The transition to flexible accumulation has in fact been marked by a revolution (by no means progressive) in the role of women in labour markets and labour processes during a period when the women's movement has fought for both greater awareness and improved conditions for what is now more than 40 per cent of the labour force in many of the advanced capitalist countries.

[. . .]

The economies of scale sought under Fordist mass production have, it seems, been countered by an increasing capacity to manufacture a variety of goods cheaply in small batches. Economies of scope have beaten out economies of scale. By 1983, for example, *Fortune* reported that "seventy-five per cent of all machine parts today are produced in batches of fifty or less." Fordist enterprises could, of course, adopt the new technologies and labour processes (a practice dubbed "neo-Fordist" by some), but in many instances competitive pressures and the struggle for better labour control led either to the rise of entirely new industrial forms or to the integration of Fordism with a whole network of sub-contracting and "outsourcing" to give greater flexibility in the face of heightened competition and greater risk. Small-batch production and sub-contracting certainly had the virtues of bypassing the rigidities of the Fordist system and satisfying a far greater range of market needs, including quick-changing ones.

Such flexible production systems have permitted, and to some degree depended upon, an acceleration in the pace of product innovation together with the exploration of highly specialized and small-scale market niches. Under conditions of recession and heightened competition, the drive to explore such possibilities became fundamental to survival. Turnover time – always one of the keys to capitalist profitability – stood to be reduced dramatically by deployment of the new technologies in production (automation, robots) and new organizational forms (such as the "just-in-time" inventory-flows delivery system, which cuts down radically on stocks required to keep production flow going). But accelerating turnover time in production would have been useless unless the turnover time in consumption was also reduced. The half-life of a typical Fordist product was, for example, from five to seven years, but flexible accumulation has more than cut that in half in certain sectors (such as textile and clothing industries), while in others – such as the so-called "thoughtware" industries (e.g. video games and computer software programmes) – the half-life is down to less than eighteen months. Flexible accumulation has been accompanied on the consumption side, therefore, by a much greater attention to quick-changing fashions and the mobilization of all the artifices of need inducement and cultural transformation that this implies. The relatively stable aesthetic of Fordist modernism has given way to all the ferment, instability, and fleeting qualities of a postmodernist aesthetic that celebrates difference, ephemerality, spectacle, fashion, and the commodification of cultural forms.

These shifts on the consumption side, coupled with changes in production, information gathering and financing, seem to underly a remarkable proportionate surge in service employment since the early 1970s. To some degree, this trend could be detected much earlier, perhaps as a consequence of rapid increases in efficiency in much of manufacturing industry through Fordist rationalization and of the evident difficulty of making similar productivity gains in service provision. But the rapid contraction in manufacturing employment after 1972 has highlighted a rapid growth of service employment, not so much in retailing, distribution, transportation, and personal services (which have remained fairly stable or even lost ground), as in producer services, finance, insurance, and real estate, and certain other sectors such as health and education (see Walker, 1985; also Novelle and Stanback, 1984; Daniels, 1985). [. . .]

[. . .]

What this suggests is that the tension that has always prevailed within capitalism between monopoly and competition, between centralization and decentralization of economic power, is being worked out in fundamentally new ways. This does not necessarily imply, however, that capitalism is becoming more "disorganized" as Offe (1985) and Lash and Urry (1987) suggest. For what is most interesting about the current situation is the way in which capitalism is becoming ever more tightly organized *through* dispersal, geographical mobility, and flexible responses in labour markets, labour processes, and consumer markets, all accompanied by hefty doses of institutional, product, and technological innovation.

The tighter organization and imploding centralization have in fact been achieved by two parallel developments of the greatest importance. First, accurate and up-to-date information is now a very highly valued commodity. Access to, and control over, information, coupled with a strong capacity for instant data analysis, have become essential to the centralized co-ordination of far-flung corporate interests. The capacity for instantaneous response to changes in exchange rates, fashions and tastes, and moves by competitors is more essential to corporate survival than it ever was under Fordism. The emphasis on information has also spawned a wide array of highly specialized business services and consultancies capable of providing up-to-the-minute information on market trends and the kind of instant data analyses useful in corporate decision-making. It has also created a situation in which vast profits stand to be made on the basis of privileged access to information, particularly in financial and currency markets (witness the proliferating "insider trading" scandals of the 1980s that struck both New York and London). But this is, in a sense, only the illegal tip of an iceberg where privileged access to information of any sort (such as scientific and technical know-how, government policies, and political shifts) becomes an essential aspect of successful and profitable decision-making.

Access to scientific and technical know-how has always been important in the competitive struggle, but here, too, we can see a renewal of interest and emphasis, because in a world of quick-changing tastes and needs and flexible production systems (as opposed to the relatively stable world of standardized Fordism), access to the latest technique, the latest product, the latest scientific discovery implies the possibility of seizing an important competitive advantage. Knowledge itself becomes a key commodity, to be produced and sold to the highest bidder, under conditions that are themselves increasingly organized on a competitive basis. Universities and research institutes compete fiercely for personnel as well as for being first in patenting new scientific discoveries (whoever gets first to the antidote for the Aids virus will surely profit handsomely, as the agreement reached between US researchers and France's Pasteur Institute over the sharing of information and royalties clearly recognized). Organized knowledge production has expanded remarkably over the past few decades, at the same time as it has been increasingly put upon a commercial basis (witness the uncomfortable transitions in many university systems in the advanced capitalist world from guardianship of knowledge and wisdom to ancillary production of knowledge for corporate capital). The celebrated Stanford Silicon Valley or the MIT – Boston Route 128 "high-tech" industry connections are configurations that are quite new and special to the era of flexible accumulation (even though, as David Noble points out in *America by design*, many US universities were set up and promoted by corporate capital from their very inception).

[. . .]

The second development – and this has been far more important than the first – was the complete reorganization of the global financial system and the emergence of greatly enhanced powers of financial coordination. Again, there has been a dual movement, on the one hand towards the formation of financial conglomerates and brokers of extraordinary global power, and, on the other hand, a rapid proliferation and decentralization of financial activities and flows through the creation of entirely new financial instruments and markets. [. . .] The formation of a global stock market, of global commodity (even debt) futures markets, of currency and interest rate swaps, together with an accelerated geographical mobility of funds, meant, for the first time, the formation of a single world market for money and credit supply.

The structure of this global financial system is now so complicated that it surpasses most people's understanding. The boundaries between distinctive functions like banking, brokerage, financial services, housing finance, consumer credit, and the like have become increasingly porous at the same time as new markets in commodity, stock, currency, or debt futures have sprung up, discounting time future into time present in baffling ways. Computerization and electronic communications have pressed home the significance of instantaneous international coordination of financial flows. "Banking", said *The Financial Times* (8

May 1987), "is rapidly becoming indifferent to the constraints of time, place and currency." It is now the case that "an English buyer can get a Japanese mortgage, an American can tap his New York bank account through a cash machine in Hong Kong and a Japanese investor can buy shares in a London-based Scandinavian bank whose stock is denominated in sterling, dollars, Deutsche Marks and Swiss francs." This "bewildering" world of high finance encloses an equally bewildering variety of cross-cutting activities, in which banks borrow massively short-term from other banks, insurance companies and pension funds assemble such vast pools of investment funds as to function as dominant "market makers", while industrial, merchant, and landed capital become so integrated into financial operations and structures that it becomes increasingly difficult to tell where commercial and industrial interests begin and strictly financial interests end.

[...]

Awash with liquidity, and perturbed by an indebtedness that has spiralled out of control since 1973, the world's financial system has, however, eluded any collective control on the part of even the most powerful advanced capitalist states. The formation of the so-called "Eurodollar" financial market out of surplus US dollars in the mid-1960s is symptomatic of the problem. Quite uncontrolled by any national government, this market in "stateless" money expanded from $50 billion in 1973 to nearly $2 *trillion* by 1987, thus approaching the size of the money aggregates within the United States. The volume of Eurodollars increased at a rate of around 25 per cent per year in the 1970s, compared to a 10 per cent increase in money supply within the USA and a 4 per cent growth rate in the volume of foreign trade. The debt of third world countries likewise mushroomed out of control. It does not take much imagination to see that such imbalances portend severe stresses and strains within the global capitalist system. Prophets of doom (like the Wall Street investment banker Felix Rohatyn) now abound, and even *The Economist* and the *Wall Street Journal* sounded sombre warnings of impending financial disaster well before the stock market crash of October 1987.

The new financial systems put into place since 1972 have changed the balance of forces at work in global capitalism, giving much more autonomy to the banking and financial system relative to corporate, state, and personal financing. Flexible accumulation evidently looks more to finance capital as its co-ordinating power than did Fordism. This means that the potentiality for the formation of independent and autonomous monetary and financial crises is much greater than before, even though the financial system is better able to spread risks over a broader front and shift funds rapidly from failing to profitable enterprises, regions, and sectors. Much of the flux, instability, and gyrating can be directly attributed to this enhanced capacity to switch capital flows around in ways that seem almost oblivious of the constraints of time and space that normally pin down material activities of production and consumption.

The increasing powers of co-ordination lodged within the world's financial system have emerged to some degree at the expense of the power of the nation state to control capital flow and, hence, its own fiscal and monetary policy. The breakdown, in 1971, of the Bretton Woods agreement to fix the price of gold and the convertibility of the dollar was an acknowledgement that the United States no longer had the power to control world fiscal and monetary policy singlehandedly. The adoption of a flexible exchange rate system in 1973 (in response to massive speculative currency movements against the dollar) signalled the complete abolition of Bretton Woods. Since that time all nation states have been at the mercy of financial disciplining, either through the effects of capital flow (witness the turnaround in French socialist government policy in the face of strong capital flight after 1981), or by direct institutional disciplining. Britain's concession under a Labour government to austerity measures dictated by the International Monetary Fund in order to gain access to credit in 1976 was a simple acknowledgement of external financial power over internal politics (there was more to matters, evidently, than a simple conspiracy of the "gnomes of Zurich" that had been so castigated by the Wilson government of the decade before). There had, of course, always been a delicate balance between financial and state powers under capitalism, but the breakdown of Fordism – Keynesianism evidently meant a shift toward the empowerment of finance capital *vis-à-vis* the nation state.

[. . .]

Some of the power shifts since 1972 within the global political economy of advanced capitalism have been truly remarkable. United States dependence on foreign trade (historically always rather small – in the range of 4–5 per cent of gross domestic product) doubled in the period 1973–80. Imports from developing countries increased almost tenfold, and foreign imports (particularly from Japan) surged to claim a major share of US markets in areas as diverse as silicon chips, televisions and videos, numerically controlled machine tools, shoes, textiles and cars. The balance of payments in goods and services for the United States rapidly moved that country from a net global creditor to the status of the world's largest debtor. Meanwhile the financial power of Japan grew, turning Tokyo into one of the world's most important financial centres (topping New York for the first time in 1987) simply because of the vast quantities of surplus funds controlled by the Japanese banks. The latter displaced the Americans as the largest holders of international assets in 1985, and by 1987 held $1.4 trillion compared with the $630 billion held by Americans. The four largest banks in the world (in asset terms) are now Japanese.

These shifts have been accompanied and in part ushered in by the rise of an aggressive neo-conservatism in North America and much of Western Europe. The electoral victories of Thatcher (1979) and Reagan (1980) are often viewed as a distinctive rupture in the politics of the postwar period. I understand them more as consolidations of what was already under way throughout much of the 1970s.

[. . .]

To the degree that heightened international competition under conditions of flagging growth forced all states to become more "entrepreneurial" and concerned to maintain a favourable business climate, so the power of organized labour and of other social movements had to be curbed. Though the politics of resistance may have varied – with tangible results, as Therborn's (1984) comparative study of European states shows – austerity, fiscal retrenchment, and erosion of the social compromise between big labour and big government became watchwords in every state in the advanced capitalist world. Although, therefore, states retain considerable power to intervene in labour contracts, what Jessop (1982, 1983) calls "the accumulation strategy" of each capitalist nation state has become more strictly circumscribed.

On the reverse side of the coin, governments ideologically committed to non-intervention and fiscal conservatism have been forced by events to be more rather than less interventionist. Laying aside the degree to which the evident insecurities of flexible accumulation create a climate conducive to authoritarianism of the Thatcher–Reagan type, financial instability and the massive problems of internal and external indebtedness have forced periodic interventions in unstable financial markets. The deployment of Federal Reserve power to ameliorate the Mexican debt crisis of 1982, and the US Treasury's agreement to broker what might amount to a $20 billion write-off of Mexican debt held by US banks in 1987, are two examples of this new kind of interventionism in international markets. The decision to nationalize the failing Continental Illinois Bank in 1984, and the massive outlays of the US Federal Deposit and Insurance Corporation (FDIC) to absorb the rising costs of bank failure, and the similar drain on the resources of the Federal Savings and Loan Insurance Corporation that required a $10 billion recapitalization effort in 1987 to guard against the fact that some 20 per cent of the nation's 3,100 thrift institutions were technically insolvent, illustrates the scale of the problem (the estimated bail-out required to deal with the savings and loan crisis stood at $50 to $100 billion by September 1988). So exercised did William Isaacs, Chairman of the FDIC, become that he felt obliged to warn the American Bankers Association as early as October 1987 that the USA "might be headed towards nationalization of banking", if they could not stem their losses. Operations in international currency markets to stabilize exchange rates come no cheaper – the New York Federal Reserve reported spending more than $4 billion in the two months after the stock market crash of October 1987 to keep the dollar exchange rate relatively orderly, and the Bank of England sold £24 billion in 1987 in order to keep the British pound from rising too fast and too far. The role of the state as a lender or operator of last resort has, evidently, become more rather than less crucial.

But, by the same token, we now see that it is also possible for nation states (South Africa, Peru, Brazil, etc.) to default on their international financial obligations, forcing inter-state negotiations on debt repayments. It is also, I suspect, no accident that the first economic summit between the major capitalist powers occurred in 1975, and that the pursuit of international co-ordinations – either through the IMF or through the pursuit of collective agreements to intervene in currency markets – has intensified ever since, becoming even more emphatic in the wake of the 1987 stock market crash. There has been, in short, a struggle to win back for the collectivity of capitalist states some of the power they have individually lost over the past two decades. This trend was institutionalized in 1982, when the IMF and the World Bank were designated as the central authority for exercising the collective power of capitalist nation states over international financial negotiations. Such power is usually deployed to force curbs on public expenditure, cuts in real wages, and austerity in fiscal and monetary policy, to the point of provoking a wave of so-called "IMF riots" from São Paulo to Kingston, Jamaica, and from Peru to the Sudan and Egypt since 1976 (see Walton, 1987, for a complete list).

There are many other signs of continuity rather than rupture with the Fordist era. The massive government deficits in the United States, mainly attributable to defence, have been fundamental to whatever economic growth there has been in world capitalism in the 1980s, suggesting that Keynesian practices are by no means dead. Neither does the commitment to "free-market" competition and deregulation entirely fit with the wave of mergers, corporate consolidations, and the extraordinary growth of interlinkages between supposedly rival firms of different national origin. Arenas of conflict between the nation state and trans-national capital have, however, opened up, undermining the easy accommodation between big capital and big government so typical of the Fordist era. The state is now in a much more problematic position. It is called upon to regulate the activities of corporate capital in the national interest at the same time as it is forced, also in the national interest, to create a "good business climate" to act as an inducement to trans-national and global finance capital, and to deter (by means other than exchange controls) capital flight to greener and more profitable pastures.

While the history may have varied substantially from one country to another, there is strong evidence that the modalities and targets of, as well as the capacity for, state intervention have changed substantially since 1972 throughout the capitalist world, no matter what the ideological complexion of the government in power (the recent experience of the French and Spanish socialists further helps substantiate the point). This does not mean, however, that state interventionism has generally diminished, for in some respects – particularly regarding labour control – state intervention is more crucial now than it ever was.

This brings us, finally, to the even thornier problem of the ways in which norms, habits, and political and cultural attitudes have shifted since 1970, and the degree to which such shifts integrate with the transition from Fordism to flexible accumulation. Since the political success of neo-conservatism can hardly be attributed to its overall economic achievements (its strong negatives of high unemployment, weak growth, rapid dislocation, and spiralling indebtedness are offset only by control of inflation), several commentators have attributed its rise to a general shift from the collective norms and values, that were hegemonic at least in working-class organizations and other social movements of the 1950s and 1960s, towards a much more competitive individualism as the central value in an entrepreneurial culture that has penetrated many walks of life. This heightened competition (in labour markets as well as amongst entrepreneurs) has, of course, proved destructive and ruinous to some, yet it has undeniably generated a burst of energy that many, even on the left, compare favourably with the stifling orthodoxy and bureaucracy of state control and monopolistic corporate power. It has also permitted substantial redistributions of income to be achieved, which have advantaged, for the most part, the already privileged. Entrepreneurialism now characterizes not only business action, but realms of life as diverse as urban governance, the growth of informal sector production, labour market organization, research and development, and it has even reached into the nether corners of academic, literary, and artistic life.

While the roots of this transition are evidently deep and complicated, their consistency with a transition from Fordism to flexible accumulation is reasonably clear even if the direction (if any) of causality is not. To begin with, the more flexible motion of capital emphasizes the new, the fleeting, the ephemeral, the fugitive, and the contingent in modern life, rather than the more solid values implanted under Fordism. To the degree that collective action was thereby made more difficult – and it was indeed a central aim of the drive for enhanced labour control to render it thus – so rampant individualism fits into place as a necessary, though not a sufficient, condition for the transition from Fordism to flexible accumulation. It was, after all, mainly through the burst of new business formation, innovation, and entrepreneurialism that many of the new systems of production were put into place. But, as Simmel (1978) long ago suggested, it is also at such times of fragmentation and economic insecurity that the desire for stable values leads to a heightened emphasis upon the authority of basic institutions – the family, religion, the state. And there is abundant evidence of a revival of support for such institutions and the values they represent throughout the Western world since about 1970. Such connections are, at least, plausible, and they ought, therefore, to be given more careful scrutiny. The immediate task at hand is to outline an interpretation of the roots of such a major transition in capitalism's dominant regime of accumulation.

REFERENCES

Daniels, P. (1985) *Service Industries: a Geographical Appraisal*. London.
Institute of Personnel Management (1986) *Flexible Patterns of Work*. London.
Jessop, B. (1982) *The Capitalist State*. Oxford.
Jessop, B. (1983) "Accumulation strategies, state forms, and hegemonic projects," *Kapitalistate*, 10 (11): 89–110.
Lash, S. and Urry, J. (1987) *The End of Disorganized Capitalism*. Oxford.
Nash, J. and Fernandez-Kelly, P. (1983) *Women, Men and the International Division of Labor*. Albany, NY.
Noyelle, T. and Stanback, T. (1984) *The Economic Transformation of American Cities*. Totowa, NJ.
Offe, C. (1985) *Disorganized Capitalism*. Oxford.
Simmel, G. (1978) *The Philosophy of Money*. London.
Therborn, G. (1984) *Why Some People are More Unemployed than Others*. London.
Walker, R. A. (1985) "Is there a service economy? The changing capitalist division of labour," *Science and Society*, 49: 42–83.
Walton, J. (1987) "Urban protest and the global political economy: the IMF riots," in M. P. Smith and J. R. Feagin (eds), *The Capitalist City*. Oxford.

CHAPTER 5

The Social Revolutions of our Time

Anthony Giddens

If the terms right and left no longer have the meaning they once did, and each political perspective is in its own way exhausted, it is because our relationship (as individuals and as humanity as a whole) to modern social development has shifted. We live today in a world of manufactured uncertainty, where risk differs sharply from earlier periods in the development of modern institutions. This is partly a matter of scope. Some risks now are "high-consequence" risks – the dangers they represent potentially affect everyone, or large numbers of people, across the face of the globe. Equally important, however, is the contrast in their origins. Manufactured uncertainty refers to risks created by the very developments the Enlightenment inspired – our conscious intrusion into our own history and our interventions into nature.

The high-consequence risks which face us in the present day, and many other risk environments of a less extensive sort, are social in origin. The risks associated with global warming, the punctured ozone layer, large-scale pollution or desertification are the result of human activities. They go along with a diversity of other humanly produced risks, such as that of large-scale war, the disruption of the global economy, the over-population of the planet, or "techno-epidemics" – illnesses generated by technological influences, such as those producing pollution of air, water or food.

In some areas of human activity, of course, levels of security are higher than they used to be. Thus journeys that could once be under-

This chapter is an edited extract from *Beyond Left and Right: the Future of Radical Politics* by Anthony Giddens (Cambridge, Polity Press, 1994), pp. 78–103. Reprinted by permission of Blackwell Publishers and Stanford University Press.

taken by only the most intrepid of explorers, in the face of numerous
hazards, can now be made by anyone (with the ability to pay) in comfort
and relative safety. But new uncertainties also open up almost everywhere. The uncertainties inherent in high-consequence risks are perhaps
particularly worrying, because we have little or no way of "testing them
out". We cannot learn from them and move on, because if things go
wrong the results are likely to be cataclysmic. With these we are con-
demned to grapple for the indefinite future. We can suspect that the
correct strategies have been pursued only when certain events do not
happen, rather than when others do; and for a long while all we shall
be able to say effectively is: so far, so good.[1]

High-consequence risks are at some distance from our individual
lives. Urgent though they may in fact be, in most matters of everyday
life they seem remote. Our daily actions are nevertheless thoroughly
infected by manufactured uncertainties of a less inclusive kind. For on
an individual or collective, as well as a global, level the accumulation
of reflexively ordered knowledge creates open and problematic futures
which we have, as it were, to "work on" as we go along in the present.
As we do so, we influence processes of change, but full control of them
chronically eludes our grasp.

[. . .]

SIMPLE AND REFLEXIVE MODERNIZATION

The creation of a world of manufactured uncertainty is the result of the
long-term development of the industrial order. Yet for a long while its
characteristics were suppressed by the dominance of simple modernization. In such modernization, capitalist or industrial evolution seems a
predictable process, even if understood in a revolutionary way in the
manner of Marx. Science and the technological advances associated
with it are generally accepted as embodying claims to authoritative
truth; while industrial growth has a clear "direction".

Reflexive modernization responds to different circumstances. It has
its origins in profound social changes [. . .]: the impact of globalization;
changes happening in everyday and personal life; and the emergence of
a post-traditional society. These influences flow from Western modernity, but now affect the world as a whole – and they refract back to
start to reshape modernization at its points of origin.

The current period of globalization is not simply a continuation of
the expansion of capitalism and of the West. If one wanted to fix its
specific point of origin, it would be the first successful broadcast transmission made via satellite. From this time onwards, instantaneous electronic communication across the globe is not only possible, but almost

immediately begins to enter the lives of many millions. Not only can everyone now see the same images at the same time; instantaneous global communication penetrates the tissue of everyday experience and starts to restructure it – although becoming restructured in turn, as a continuous process.

Globalization is not the same as the development of a "world system", and it is not just "out there" – to do with very large-scale influences. It is also an "in here" phenomenon, directly bound up with the circumstances of local life. We shouldn't think of globalization as a unitary process tending in a single direction, but as a complex set of changes with mixed and quite often contradictory outcomes. Globalization implies the idea of a world community, but does not produce it; such a community is signalled as much by the globalization of "bads" as by integrative influences.

Globalizing influences are fracturing as well as unifying, create new forms of stratification, and often produce opposing consequences in different regions or localities. These events and changes no longer pass just from the West to the rest. Thus the industrial development of the East is directly bound up with the deindustrialization of the older industries in the heart of the core countries in the global order. Two areas that exist directly alongside one another, or groups living in close proximity, may be caught up in quite different globalizing systems, producing bizarre physical juxtapositions. The sweatshop worker may be just across the street from a wealthy financial centre.

On the cultural level, globalization tends to produce cultural diasporas. Communities of taste, habit and belief frequently become detached from place and from the confines of the nation also. Diasporic cultural traits are quite often standardizing, and as such influenced by mass advertising and cultural commodification. Styles of dress, from suits to blue jeans, taste in music, films or even religion take on global dimensions. Cultural diasporas are no longer carried solely through the physical movement of peoples and their cultures, important though this still is. Even – and perhaps sometimes particularly – in situations of poverty people become involved in diasporic cultural interchanges. As elsewhere in globalizing processes, however, there is not a one-way movement toward cultural homogeneity. Globalization leads also to an insistence on diversity, a search to recover lost local traditions, and an emphasis on local cultural identity – seen in a renewal of local nationalisms and ethnicities.

Globalizing influences tend to evacuate out local contexts of action, which have to be reflexively reordered by those affected – although those reorderings also, conversely, affect globalization as well. Major changes therefore occur in the very warp and weave of everyday life, affecting even the constitution of our personal identities. The self becomes a reflexive project and, increasingly, the body also. Individuals cannot rest content with an identity that is simply handed down, inherited, or built on a traditional status. A person's identity has in large part to be discovered, constructed, actively sustained. Like the self, the body is no longer accepted as "fate", as the physical baggage that comes along with the self. We have more and more to decide not just who to be, and how to act, but how to look to the outside world.

The growth in food disorders is a negative index of the advance of these developments on the level of everyday life. Anorexia, bulimia and other food pathologies still tend to be concentrated in First World countries, but are now also starting to appear in Third World societies too. In many parts of the world people starve for no fault of their own, but because they live in conditions of extreme poverty. Their emaciated bodies bear witness to the intensity of global inequalities. The shrunken body of the anorexic looks physically identical, but reflects very different social and material circumstances. The anorexic is "starving to death in a sea of abundance". Anorexia happens in a world where, for very large numbers of people, for the first time in history, copious quantities of food are available, well beyond what is necessary to meet basic nutritional needs.[2]

Anorexia and bulimia do not come only from a Western emphasis on slimness, but from the fact that eating habits are formed in terms of a diversity of choices about foodstuffs. There is a close and obvious association here with globalization. The invention of container transport and new ways of the freezing of foods – innovations dating from only a few decades ago – meant that foods could be stored for long periods and shipped all over the world. Since that date, all those living in more affluent countries and regions have been on a diet; that is to say, they have to make active decisions about how and what to eat, in respect of foodstuffs available more or less all the year. Deciding what to eat is also deciding "how to be" in respect of the body – and for individuals subject to specific social tensions, particularly young women, the iron self-discipline of anorexia results.[3]

Anorexia is a defensive reaction to the effects of manufactured uncertainty on everyday life. Our day-to-day lives, one can say, have become experimental in a manner which parellels the "grand experiment" of modernity as a whole. In many situations of social life we cannot choose but to choose among alternatives – even if we should choose to remain "traditional". "Everyday experiments" become an intrinsic part of our daily activities, in contexts in which information coming from a diversity of sources – local knowledge, tradition, science and mass communications – must in some way be made sense of and utilized. Tradition more and more must be contemplated, defended, sifted through, in relation to the awareness that there exists a variety of other ways of doing things.

The experimental character of daily life, it is important to see, is constitutive. How we tackle the decisions that have to be made in the course of our actions helps structure the very institutions we are reacting to. Nowhere is this more obvious than in the field of personal relations. Individuals have to decide today not only when and whom to marry, but whether to marry at all. "Having a child" need not any longer have anything to do with marriage, and is a precious and difficult decision for both men and women, far from the circumstances of the past when such a thing, in many situations, seemed more or less natural. One even has to settle what one's "sexuality" is, as well as grasp what "relationships" are and how they might best be constructed. All these things are not decisions made about given contexts of action; they help define and reshape, in a mobile way, what those contexts are and become.

The evacuation of local contexts of action – the "disembedding" of activities – can be understood as implying processes of intensified detraditionalization. We are the first generation to live in a thoroughly post-traditional society, a term that is in many ways preferable to "postmodern". A post-traditional society is not a national society – we are speaking here of a global cosmopolitan order. Nor is it a society in which traditions cease to exist; in many respects there are impulses, or pressures, toward the sustaining or the recovery of traditions. It is a society, however, in which tradition changes its status. In the context of a globalizing, cosmopolitan order, traditions are constantly brought into contact with one another and forced to "declare themselves".

The modern social order came into being in the context of a break with the past. The "two great revolutions" which initiated the modern period each in their way were detraditionalizing forces. The spread of capitalistic production uprooted many local communities and dissolved many local customs and practices. The universalizing codes of democracy treat political constitutions as having to be made, not as inherited from the past. Yet the stabilizing of simple modernization depended also on the remoulding of tradition. New traditions were invented, such as those of nationalism and renewed forms of religion. Other traditional traits, such as those affecting gender and the family, became recast during the late eighteenth and the nineteenth centuries.

The world marked by simple modernization was a culturally diverse one. Its cultural diversity, however, depended in a substantial way on the continuance of geographical segregation. This was true even within the developed countries. Working-class communities associated with certain types of industry, for example, came into being only after the industrial revolution, but often established their own local traditions. Today we see these traditions breaking down again, or becoming altered, almost everywhere.

At a time of thoroughgoing detraditionalization, those who hold to traditions have to ask themselves, and are asked by others, why. Globalization here intersects with active struggles and confrontations. Thus feminist movements have challenged traditional conceptions of, and practices involved with, gender. They have sought to bring into public discourse that which remained latent in gender traditions. "Femininity" is an open matter; and now masculinity, for so long something taken for granted, has been opened to scrutiny.

The profound influence of detraditionalizing influences explains why the concept and the existence of fundamentalism have become so important. The fundamentalist, as I have said, is someone who seeks to defend tradition in the traditional way – in circumstances where that defence has become intrinsically problematic. Fundamentalism's "insistence" on tradition and its emphasis on "purity" are only understandable in these terms.

The term fundamentalism was first applied, in a religious context, at about the turn of the century, to refer to a defence of Protestant orthodoxy against the encroachments of modern thought.[4] It has only come into wider usage over the past thirty years or so – something that expresses the very recency of the detraditionalizing forces to which it corresponds.

Fundamentalism is not a long-term reaction to modernity, as the quite recent nature of its development indicates. The defence of tradition only tends to take on the shrill tone it assumes today in the context of detraditionalization, globalization and diasporic cultural interchanges. The point about fundamentalism is not its defence of tradition as such, but the manner of its defence in relation to a world of interrogation and dialogue. Defending tradition in the traditional way means asserting its ritual truth in circumstances in which it is beleaguered. Refusing the discursive engagements which a world of cosmopolitan communication tends to enforce, fundamentalism is protecting a *principle* as much as a set of particular doctrines. This is why fundamentalist positions can arise even in religions (like Hinduism and Buddhism) which have hitherto been very ecumenical and tolerant of other beliefs.

If this view is correct, the concept of fundamentalism should not be applied only to the area of religion. Fundamentalisms – defending tradition in the traditional way – can arise in any basic domain of social life subject to detraditionalization. These include ethnic relations, nationalism, gender and the family. Religious fundamentalisms, as is well known, tend to overlap with these other contexts. A Protestant fundamentalist, for example, is likely to have strong beliefs about the need to preserve "traditional" forms of the nation, family and so forth. Yet the fact that the notion of fundamentalism can be applied so widely has nothing directly to do with the spill-over of religious beliefs into these fields. It comes from the fact that these are all contexts occupied by tradition, but which are now becoming discursively forced into the open.

Detraditionalization not only affects the social world, but influences, as it is influenced by, the transformation of nature. Tradition, like nature, used to be an "external" context of social life, something that was given and largely unchallengeable. The end of nature – as the natural – coincides with the end of tradition – as the traditional.

Social reflexivity is both condition and outcome of a post-traditional society. Decisions have to be taken on the basis of a more or less continuous reflection on the conditions of one's action. "Reflexivity" here refers to the use of information about the conditions of activity as a means of regularly reordering and redefining what that activity is. It concerns a universe of action where social observers are themselves socially observed; and it is today truly global in scope. Anyone who doubts that such is the case might do well to consider the changing status of anthropology. In the era of simple modernization, stamped by the dominance of the West, anthropology was the study of peoples who, by and large, did not answer back. An anthropologist would visit an alien culture; on his or her return, a monograph would be written and deposited in the library.

Such a situation no longer holds. In the depths of the jungle, anthropologists are likely to encounter native peoples who are familiar with some anthropological ideas or even texts. Ethnologies are used to interpret local cultures, reconstruct lost traditional skills and habits, and count as evidence in courts of law. Such phenomena are often important in power struggles. Thus the idea of the Australian "aboriginal" or the North American "Indian" was a Western one, but these constructs have been deployed by those to whom they refer to intervene in local and national politics – and even in disputes before international courts.

Revived or protected traditions, as we all know, can easily degenerate into kitsch – reflexive awareness of this ever-present possibility is actually one of the driving forces of fundamentalism. Thus the novelist Yukio Mishima made a celebrated, if futile, attempt to revive declining Samurai values and practices in postwar Japan. The endeavour, which culminated in his ritual suicide, seemed somewhat absurd to most Japanese, but had a certain dignity. One couldn't, probably, say the same of the inhabitants of Suya Mura, a Japanese village made famous (in Japan as well as elsewhere) by an anthropological study written by John Embree. Embree's wife revisited the area where she had carried out the fieldwork with her husband some fifty years earlier. She found that the villagers were less interested in reminiscing than in making use of her presence in their attempts to turn the municipality into a tourist spot – as "Japan's anthropological village".[5]

In a society of high reflexivity the regular appropriation of expertise – in all its many forms – tends to replace the guidance of tradition. This is by definition an energetic society, not a passive one. Even where they stick by traditions, or recreate them, individuals, groups and collectivities are more or less compelled to take an active stance toward the conditions of their existence. Not just social movements, but self-help groups of all kinds, are a distinctive feature of a post-traditional order – they may be purely local, but often have globalizing implications and participate in global diasporas.

STRUCTURAL CONSEQUENCES

The driving expansionism of capitalistic enterprise continues to fuel globalizing processes, as it has done in the past. Yet capitalism – as will be discussed further below – was never the sole influence on globalization, and today its impact across the world is more complex and many-sided than was previously the case.

With the fall of the Soviet Union and the redirection of economic growth mechanisms in China and other remaining Communist societies, there is a world capitalist economy in a more complete sense than ever before. However, that economy is much more thoroughly infused with reflexive mechanisms than it once was; and it is increasingly decentred, no matter what power Western states and agencies continue to hold over what was "the periphery". Socialist theorists of "the development of underdevelopment" had an easy target to blame for the ills of the world – the influence of capitalism. However critical one might still want to be of unfettered processes of capitalist enterprise, that target has now become much more elusive. Conspiracy-style theories of global disparities don't have the purchase they once seemed, to some observers at least, to have.

The global spread of the capitalist economy is a major influence on the difficulties of the welfare state in the affluent countries and very substantially affects class relations [. . .]. When not counterbalanced by other forces, capitalism retains its tendency to produce polarizations of income, both within and between different countries. Those states which are able to fund developed welfare systems are able to hold off this tendency with considerable success, but only at the cost of increasing social and fiscal strain.

Neoliberal interpretations of economic development insist that the paring down of welfare provisions is the necessary condition of competitiveness in a globalizing economy. According to such interpretations, either a Pareto-type effect pertains in economic growth processes in open economies, combined with "trickle down"; or widening inequalities are simply the price to be paid for competitiveness. Much hangs on whether or not such a view is correct, for it is the key argument advanced to insist that leftist thinkers have paid insufficient attention to supply-side considerations in their analysis of the "welfare state compromise".

[. . .] Here it is enough to note that widening economic inequalities within societies are not, certainly not necessarily, the condition of increasing overall prosperity. On the contrary, increasing equality can accompany fast economic growth, as measured by conventional indices, and very possibly may actively contribute to it. Thus in the Asian economies which have leaped to prominence over the past three or four decades, the incomes of lower-paid workers have grown both in absolute terms and relative to executives and entrepreneurs. South Korea and Taiwan, for example, have developed rapidly from the mid-1960s at the same time as the gap between rich and poor has narrowed; while in many African and Latin American countries, conversely, economic stagnation has been accompanied by a decline in the relative income of those at the bottom.

We have to be careful about what increasing equalization means here [. . .]. The successful Asian countries do not rely on Western-style welfare state mechanisms to create equalization, but instead provide means for poorer groups actively to improve their life circumstances. Because of their sheer numbers, poorer people in the aggregate have much greater resources than the rich. Moreover, in the Asian economies poorer people "save" by investing in others with whom they are closely linked, in family or friendship networks. The payoff of "investments" of this form is to be found in increased social solidarity – but these probably also have important implications for economic productivity. In societies where the gap between rich and poor is very large, such "investments" tend not to be made.

The globalizing of capitalist economic relations would seem on the face of things to leave large business corporations in a dominant position within the economies of states and in the world economy as a whole. And they do indeed wield great power, able as they are to move capital investments from place to place, often with scant regard to the impact on the lives of local populations affected. At the same time, the demonizing of the large corporations, so popular among some sections of the left at one time, does not make much sense now.

Globalizing influences tend to break down the formation of monopolies or oligopolies such as are often found within national economies. The celebrated propensity of capitalist production toward monopoly probably depended in fact on collaborative connections between the state and capital which are now being undermined. Like other organizations, the large companies face an economic environment hostile to fixed bureaucratic orders. It doesn't follow, as some have suggested, that the giant corporations are likely to become wholly dismembered, but it would be difficult to argue that present-day economic conditions are leading to an untramelled extension of their economic or social power.

The big companies influence new forms of social and economic regionalization, but they are not necessarily the main agents involved. Changing patterns of regionalization respond to wider aspects of glo-balization or, more accurately, to shifting relations of the local and global. As elsewhere, processes of regionalization are dialectical; many pre-existing local communities disintegrate or become substantially re-structured, but these self-same changes also promote local communal mobilization.

The combined effects of globalization and social reflexivity alter the character of stratification systems within the economically developed societies as well as elsewhere. Much has been made in the recent socio-logical literature of the consequences of the shrinking of blue-collar work and the concomitant rise in the proportions of people in white-collar and professional occupations – changes which intersect in a complex way with the widespread entry of women into the paid labour force. Such changes are undeniably of great importance, affecting as they do the class system and also the political life of modern societies; and these changes are themselves heavily affected by globalization.

Equally important, however, is the fact that the growth of social reflexivity produces forms of "double discrimination" affecting the underprivileged. To the effects of material deprivation are added a dis-qualification from reflexive incorporation in the wider social order. Exclusionary mechanisms here are normally both social and psycho-logical. In other words, they concern not only subjection to modes of power coming from the technical control of knowledge-based systems, but also attack the integrity of the self [. . .].

THE ADVENT OF LIFE POLITICS

The political outlook of the left – and therefore, in counter-reaction, the right – has always centred on a notion of emancipation. Emancipation means freedom, or rather freedoms of various kinds: freedom from tra-dition, from the shackles of the past; freedom from arbitrary power; and freedom from the constraints of material poverty or deprivation. Emancipatory politics is a politics of life chances. It is about enhancing autonomy of action.

Emancipatory politics obviously remains important to any radical political programme. It is joined today, however, by a series of concerns coming from the changes just described – from detraditionalization plus the disappearance of nature. These concerns raise issues of life politics. Life politics, and the disputes and struggles connected with it, are about how we should live in a world where everything that used to be natural (or traditional) now has in some sense to be chosen, or decided about.

Life politics is a politics of identity as well as of choice. One reason why debates between right and left have become so often unappealing to many of the lay population is that they simply don't address these new fields of action. It would be a basic error to see life politics as only a concern of the more affluent. In some respects, in fact, the contrary is true. Some of the poorest groups today (and not only in the developed societies) come up against problems of detraditionalization most sharply. Thus women are now leaving marriages in large numbers, and in conjunction with this assertion of autonomy are recasting their lives. Many, however, become part of the "new poor", especially if they are lone-parent heads of households. Cast down economically, they are also called on to pioneer new forms of domestic life and kin relations.

Life politics is not, or not only, a politics of the personal; the factors involved have become generic to many aspects of social life, including some of very wide span indeed. Ecological and feminist concerns are of major importance in life-political struggles, but they certainly do not exhaust them. Instead, thinking in life-political terms helps explain just why they have come to such prominence. They are reactions to, and engagements with, a world precisely where tradition is no longer traditional, and nature no longer natural.

Life politics also covers quite orthodox areas of political involvement: for example, work and economic activity. Like so many other areas of social life, work was until recently experienced by many as fate. Most men could expect to be in the paid labour force for much of their lives, while women were often confined to the domestic milieu. Protest against such "fate" was first of all mostly emancipatory in impulse. This was true of the union movement, dominated by men, which developed most strongly among manual workers, who more than anyone else experienced work as a given set of conditions, offering little autonomy of action. It was also true of the earlier forms of feminism.

In current times, even among more deprived groups, work is now rarely approached as fate (unemployment, perversely, more often is). There is a wide reflexive awareness that what counts as "work" is much more broadly defined than it used to be, and that work is a problematic and contested notion. Given changes in the class structure, fewer people automatically follow the occupations of their parents or those typical of homogeneous working communities. The involvement of large numbers of women in the labour force has made it clear that there are decisions to be made, and priorities allocated, not just in respect of trying to get one job rather than another, but as concerns what place work should have compared to other life values. Many other factors are also relevant. For example, the fact that many younger people spend years in higher education breaks the "natural" transition between school and work. Many students now roam the world before attempting to enter the labour market. And older people may do much the same at a later phase of their lives.

Life politics is about the challenges that face collective humanity, not just about how individuals should take decisions when confronted with many more options than they had before. It has been said by some that the ecological crisis is to us today what capitalistic crises were to earlier forms of industrialized society. There is something in this idea, but expressed in such a way it is not compelling. Capitalism, after all, has not been overcome, as the socialists hoped and anticipated; moreover, the ecological issues which perturb us cannot be understood as matters concerning only the environment. They are rather a signal, as well as an expression, of the centrality of life-political problems. They pose with particular force the questions we must face when "progress" has become sharply double-edged, when we have new responsibilities to future generations, and when there are ethical dilemmas that mechanisms of constant economic growth either cause us to put to one side or make us repress.

[. . .]

MANUFACTURED UNCERTAINTY AND GLOBAL RISK ENVIRONMENTS

There are four main contexts in which we confront high-consequence risks coming from the extension of manufactured uncertainty. Each corresponds, as I shall try to show, to an institutional dimension of modernity.

The first concerns the impact of modern social development on the world's ecosystems. Our relation to the environment has become problematic in several ways. The material resources needed to sustain human life, and in particular the way of life of the industrialized parts of the world, look likely to become threatened in the medium-term future. The original report of the Club of Rome emphasized threats to non-sustainable resources, but at the present time more stress tends to be laid by environmentalists on the world's capacity to dispose of wastes. The list of dangers is well known: the probable development of global warming, as a result of the production of the so-called "greenhouse gases"; the depletion of the ozone layer; destruction of the rain forests; desertification; and the poisoning of waters to a degree likely to inhibit the processes of regeneration they contain.

A second crisis concerns the development of poverty on a large scale – what has been described as the "holocaust of poverty". The statistics are not precise, but however they are calculated they disclose alarming levels of deprivation. Over 20 per cent of the world's population lives in conditions of absolute poverty, if such be defined as a situation where people cannot regularly meet their most basic subsistence needs.

The causes of global poverty are complex and the overall trend of change difficult to interpret. The days when global inequalities could simply be blamed on the spread of capitalism are certainly over, although there can be little doubt that capitalistic markets do often have a polarizing effect on distributions of wealth and income. It has also become evident that it is not always lack of economic development that brings about impoverishment, but sometimes such "development" itself. A way of life which may have been very modest in economic terms, but which was self-sustaining and organized through local tradition becomes broken up when a development project – dam, plantation or factory – is introduced.[6]

People thus affected are likely to find themselves in a situation of relative poverty even if their material standards of life are somewhat improved; they are pitchforked into a society for which they are ill-prepared and in which they are marginalized. Relative poverty is a notoriously more elusive notion than absolute deprivation – some argue that all poverty is relative, giving the concept thereby an elastic definition. Judged by the usual measures, at any rate, including official designations of poverty, millions of people in the richest societies are also poor.

A third source of crisis is the widespread existence of weapons of mass destruction, together with other situations in which collective violence looms as a possibility. The ending of the Cold War has lessened the possibility of a nuclear confrontation that could have destroyed much of human life on the earth; it has not removed that threat altogether. There may be as many as fifteen countries which possess nuclear weapons. The number has expanded since the days of the Cold War, as a result of the new nuclear nations which have emerged with the break-up of the Soviet Union. The proliferation of nuclear weapons is a likely prospect given the large number of "peaceful" reactors that exist capable of producing plutonium, and given the world trade that is carried on in the substance.

The problem of violence, how to lessen or prevent it, stands as one of the most difficult questions revealed by the disappearance of the superpower confrontation. As we all (reflexively) know, there is a new world order, but it looks almost as disturbing as the old. The problem is not just the accumulation of military hardware, but the exacerbation of local tensions in many different areas, tied in as they often are to nationalist, religious and ethnic divisions. It is evident in retrospect that the Cold War stand-off, overwhelmingly dangerous though it was, in some respects was a stabilizing force across many areas of the world.

In terms of scale, violence is above all a problem linked to the global military order; but it is of course also something that occurs in a multiplicity of more mundane situations. Male violence against women outside the context of war, for example, is a phenomenon of pervasive importance. If there is, as Marilyn French has claimed, a "war against women", it is not one confined to any particular part of the globe.[7]

A fourth source of global crisis concerns the large-scale repression of democratic rights "and the inability of increasing numbers of people to develop even a small part of their human potential".[8] Military rule seems to be on the decline. Yet as of 1993 there were still over fifty military regimes in different parts of the world. According to Amnesty International, people were imprisoned for matters of conscience – solely because of their religion, language or ethnic origin – in more than eighty countries across the globe.

There are close connections here with the previous categories. The Cold War kept in place a hypocritical dialogue of "democratic rights", during which time that concept became largely an empty one – a cloak for strategic superpower interests. Successive American governments made it clear that they would not tolerate regimes deemed incompatible with US interests – and others were actively destabilized where they were not seen to conform to these interests. The Soviet Union proclaimed its support for "democracy" just as loudly as its global opponent; at the same time it also pursued policies governed mainly by geopolitical concerns.

The disappearance of the Cold War has served to make it clear that there are basic structural factors in global society which make for a denial of democratic rights. The repression of democracy was not just a Cold War phenomenon, or even one of political authoritarianism. Many people are "unable to develop even a small part of their human potential" either because of enforced poverty or because of the restrictive nature of the circumstances in which they live.

The four sets of global "bads" distinguished above relate to different institutional dimensions of modern civilization, as indicated in my first diagram:

(Capitalism)	Economic polarization	Ecological threats	(Industrialism)
(Surveillance)	Denial of democratic rights	Threat of large-scale war	(Means of violence)

The global spread of modernity, as the left always stressed (and left and right now agree on this), was driven in large part by the dynamism of capitalist enterprise. The modern world, however, is not solely *capitalistic*; it has other structuring dimensions as well, as I have tried to show at some length in other works. These dimensions include *industrialism*, as a mode of production driving our changing relation to material nature; control of military power and the *means of violence*, and control of information, or *surveillance*, as a means of generating administrative power.

Along each of these dimensions – and in relation to each of the four risk environments – the question that must be posed by political radicalism is: what alternative sociopolitical forms could potentially exist? [. . .] [see my second diagram]:

(Capitalism)	Post-scarcity economy	Humanized nature	(Industrialism)
(Surveillance)	Dialogic democracy	Negotiated power	(Means of violence)

(1) The notion of a post-scarcity economy, in a certain version at any rate, was a prominent idea within some versions of Marxism. It was long derided, in fact, as utopian by those concerned to advance the more "realistic" economic option of the directive control of the economy. Now things have reversed themselves. The idea of subjecting economic life to central direction has lost its radical credentials. The concept of a post-scarcity economy, by contrast [. . .] is no longer wholly utopian. Like the other political possibilities described here, it can be approached with an attitude of *utopian realism*; it has utopian features, yet is not unrealistic because it corresponds to observable trends.

The Marxist idea of a post-scarcity society was a vision of an era of universal abundance, in which scarcity would effectively disappear. In this guise it is indeed purely utopian and offers no purchase at all on a global situation where the conservation of resources, rather than their unlimited development, is what is called for. As I use it [. . .] the concept of post-scarcity means something different; it refers to a situation, or more accurately a complex of situations, in which economic growth is no longer of overriding importance.

Post-scarcity doesn't mean the absence of scarcity – there will in any case always be "positional" goods. Tendencies toward a post-scarcity economy emerge where accumulation processes are widely seen to *threaten or destroy valued ways of life*; where accumulation becomes manifestly *counterproductive in its own terms*, that is, where there is "overdevelopment" leading to suboptimal economic, social or cultural consequences; and where in the domains of life politics individuals or groups take lifestyle decisions that *limit, or actively go against, maximizing economic returns.*

The attempt to counter economic inequality has been closely associated in the developed societies with the rise of the welfare state, the core concern of socialism turned defensive. [. . .] However, such a discussion [. . .] cannot take place in isolation from wider problems of global poverty.

(2)   The humanization of nature comprises ecology, but ecological issues have to be approached in the manner suggested by the analysis of detraditionalization. Nature has come to an end in a parallel way to tradition. The point at which the denaturing of nature effectively ended our "natural environment" cannot be fixed in an exact way; but somewhere over the last century or so the age-old relation between human beings and nature was broken through and reversed. Instead of being concerned above all with what nature could do to us, we have now to worry about what we have done to nature.

To confront the problem of the humanization of nature means beginning from the existence of "plastic nature" – nature as incorporated within a post-traditional order. Decisions about what to conserve, or to strive to recover, can rarely be decided by reference to what exists independently of human beings. Questions of resource depletion and environmental damage can sometimes be analysed in terms of how far they deviate from natural cycles of regeneration. In other respects, however – in respect of tradition as well as nature – conservation (or renewal, rebuilding) has to address the problem of how to accommodate to and interpret the past with respect to various projected futures.

(3)   Large-scale warfare today threatens the environment in just as devastating a way as more pacific forms of technology. It was not always so; here there is a connection between industrialization and the waging of war. Industrialized weapons technologies are capable of destroying vast areas of landscape or polluting the atmosphere of the earth as a whole. Even quite a limited nuclear exchange might create the conditions of a "nuclear winter" – as with other high-consequence risks, no one really knows how likely this is. Other forms of industrial weaponry, such as chemical weapons, can be massively polluting. And who knows what another ten, twenty or a hundred years of further weapons development might bring?

If violence means the use of physical force to achieve one's ends, it is of course an everyday occurrence, not something linked only to military power or war. A normative political theory of violence cannot concern itself only with peace, or at any rate must generalize beyond a hypothetical situation of the absence of war. In today's world [. . .] there is a new relation between violence, on the one hand, and the possibility of dialogic communication on the other; and this relation applies in principle to all forms of violence, from domestic violence to war.

(4) Could there ever be a social order free from violence? The idea, of course, is utopian. Yet the possibility of actively reducing levels of violence, in social domains ranging from the personal right through to the most global, is quite realistic – and, as in other areas of high-consequence risk, is surely necessary if humanity is to survive the dangerous period that now looms. The obverse of the use of force is negotiated power, a phenomenon which stands close to democracy. Democratization is bound up with the surveillance capacities of states and other organizations in the late modern world – the fourth dimension of modern institutions noted above. [. . .]

NOTES

1 John Sours, *Starving to Death in a Sea of Objects* (New York, Aronson, 1981).
2 Susie Orbach, *Hunger Strike* (London, Faber, 1986).
3 Anthony Giddens, *Modernity and Self-identity* (Cambridge, Polity Press, 1991), ch. 3.
4 For the most comprehensive study, see Martin E. Marty and R. Scott Appelby, *The Fundamentalism Project* (3 vols, Chicago, Chicago University Press, 1993).
5 This and many other examples are described in John Knight, "Globalisation and new ethnographic localities," *Journal of the Anthropological Society of Oxford*, vol. 3, 1992.
6 Paul Ekins, *A New World Order* (London, Routledge, 1992).
7 Marilyn French, *The War against Women* (London, Penguin, 1992).
8 Ekins, *A New World Order*, p. 1.

CHAPTER 6

Disjuncture and Difference in the Global Cultural Economy

Arjun Appadurai

The central problem of today's global interactions is the tension between cultural homogenization and cultural heterogenization. A vast array of empirical facts could be brought to bear on the side of the "homogenization" argument, and much of it has come from the left end of the spectrum of media studies (Schiller, 1976; Hamelink, 1983; Mattelart, 1983), and some from other, less appealing, perspectives (Gans, 1985; Iyer, 1988). Most often, the homogenization argument subspeciates into either an argument about Americanization, or an argument about "commoditization," and very often the two arguments are closely linked. What these arguments fail to consider is that at least as rapidly as forces from various metropolises are brought into new societies they tend to become indigenized in one or other way: this is true of music and housing styles as much as it is true of science and terrorism, spectacles and constitutions. The dynamics of such indigenization have just begun to be explored in a sophisticated manner (Barber, 1987; Hannerz, 1987, 1989; Feld, 1988; Ivy, 1988; Nicoll, 1989; Yoshimoto, 1989), and much more needs to be done. But it is worth noticing that for the people of Irian Jaya, Indonesianization may be more worrisome than Americanization, as Japanization may be for Koreans, Indianization for Sri Lankans, Vietnamization for the Cambodians, Russianization for the people of Soviet Armenia and the Baltic Republics. Such a list of alternative fears to Americanization could be greatly expanded, but it is not a shapeless inventory: for polities of smaller scale, there is always a fear of cultural absorption by polities of larger scale, especially those

This chapter is taken from *Global Culture: Nationalism, Globalization and Modernity*, edited by M. Featherstone (London, Sage, 1990), pp. 295–310. Reprinted by permission of Sage Publications Ltd.

that are near by. One man's imagined community (Anderson, 1983) is another man's political prison.

This scalar dynamic, which has widespread global manifestations, is also tied to the relationship between nations and states, to which I shall return later in this [chapter]. For the moment let us note that the simplification of these many forces (and fears) of homogenization can also be exploited by nation-states in relation to their own minorities, by posing global commoditization (or capitalism, or some other such external enemy) as more "real" than the threat of its own hegemonic strategies.

The new global cultural economy has to be understood as a complex, overlapping, disjunctive order, which cannot any longer be understood in terms of existing center–periphery models (even those that might account for multiple centers and peripheries). Nor is it susceptible to simple models of push and pull (in terms of migration theory) or of surpluses and deficits (as in traditional models of balance of trade), or of consumers and producers (as in most neo-Marxist theories of development). Even the most complex and flexible theories of global development which have come out of the Marxist tradition (Amin, 1980; Mandel, 1978; Wallerstein, 1974; Wolf, 1982) are inadequately quirky, and they have not come to terms with what Lash and Urry (1987) have recently called "disorganized capitalism." The complexity of the current global economy has to do with certain fundamental disjunctures between economy, culture and politics which we have barely begun to theorize.[1]

I propose that an elementary framework for exploring such disjunctures is to look at the relationship between five dimensions of global cultural flow which can be termed: (a) ethnoscapes; (b) mediascapes; (c) technoscapes; (d) finanscapes; and (e) ideoscapes.[2] I use terms with the common suffix scape to indicate first of all that these are not objectively given relations which look the same from every angle of vision, but rather that they are deeply perspectival constructs, inflected very much by the historical, linguistic and political situatedness of different sorts of actors: nation-states, multinationals, diasporic communities, as well as sub-national groupings and movements (whether religious, political or economic), and even intimate face-to-face groups, such as villages, neighborhoods and families. Indeed, the individual actor is the last locus of this perspectival set of landscapes, for these landscapes are eventually navigated by agents who both experience and constitute larger formations, in part by their own sense of what these landscapes offer. These landscapes thus are the building blocks of what, extending Benedict Anderson, I would like to call "imagined worlds," that is, the multiple worlds which are constituted by the historically situated imaginations of persons and groups spread around the globe (Appadurai, 1989). An important fact of the world we live in today is that many persons on the globe live in such imagined "worlds" and not just in imagined communities, and thus are able to contest and sometimes even subvert the "imagined worlds" of the official mind and of the entrepreneurial mentality that surround them. The suffix scape also allows us to point to the fluid, irregular shapes of these landscapes, shapes which characterize international capital as deeply as they do international clothing styles.

By *ethnoscape*, I mean the landscape of persons who constitute the shifting world in which we live: tourists, immigrants, refugees, exiles, guestworkers and other moving groups and persons constitute an essential feature of the world, and appear to affect the politics of and between nations to a hitherto unprecedented degree. This is not to say that there are not anywhere relatively stable communities and networks, of kinship, of friendship, of work and of leisure, as well as of birth, residence and other filiative forms. But it is to say that the warp of these stabilities is everywhere shot through with the woof of human motion, as more persons and groups deal with the realities of having to move, or the fantasies of wanting to move. What is more, both these realities as well as these fantasies now function on larger scales, as men and women from villages in India think not just of moving to Poona or Madras, but of moving to Dubai and Houston, and refugees from Sri Lanka find themselves in South India as well as in Canada, just as the Hmong are driven to London as well as to Philadelphia. And as international capital shifts its needs, as production and technology generate different needs, as nation-states shift their policies on refugee populations, these moving groups can never afford to let their imaginations rest too long, even if they wished to.

By *technoscape*, I mean the global configuration, also ever fluid, of technology, and of the fact that technology, both high and low, both mechanical and informational, now moves at high speeds across various kinds of previously impervious boundaries. Many countries now are the roots of multinational enterprise: a huge steel complex in Libya may involve interests from India, China, Russia and Japan, providing different components of new technological configurations. The odd distribution of technologies, and thus the peculiarities of these technoscapes, are increasingly driven not by any obvious economies of scale, of political control, or of market rationality, but of increasingly complex relationships between money flows, political possibilities and the availability of both low and highly-skilled labor. So, while India exports waiters and chauffeurs to Dubai and Sharjah, it also exports software engineers to the United States (indentured briefly to Tata-Burroughs or the World Bank), then laundered through the State Department to become wealthy "resident aliens," who are in turn objects of seductive messages to invest their money and know-how in federal and state projects in India. The global economy can still be described in terms of traditional "indicators" (as the World Bank continues to do) and studied in terms of traditional comparisons (as in Project Link at the University of Pennsylvania), but the complicated technoscapes (and the shifting ethnoscapes), which underlie these "indicators" and "comparisons" are further out of the reach of the "queen of the social sciences" than ever before. How is one to make a meaningful comparison of wages in Japan and the United States, or of real estate costs in New York and Tokyo, without taking sophisticated account of the very complex fiscal and investment flows that link the two economies through a global grid of currency speculation and capital transfer?

Thus it is useful to speak as well of *finanscapes*, since the disposition of global capital is now a more mysterious, rapid and difficult landscape to follow than ever before, as currency markets, national stock exchanges, and commodity speculations move mega-monies through national turnstiles at blinding speed, with vast absolute implications for small differences in percentage points and time units. But the critical point is that the global relationship between ethnoscapes, technoscapes and finanscapes is deeply disjunctive and profoundly unpredictable, since each of these landscapes is subject to its own constraints and incentives (some political, some informational and some technoenvironmental), at the same time as each acts as a constraint and a parameter for movements in the other. Thus, even an elementary model of global political economy must take into account the shifting relationship between perspectives on human movement, technological flow, and financial transfers, which can accommodate their deeply disjunctive relationships with one another.

Built upon these disjunctures (which hardly form a simple, mechanical global "infrastructure" in any case) are what I have called "mediascapes" and "ideoscapes," though the latter two are closely related landscapes of images. *Mediascapes* refer both to the distribution of the electronic capabilities to produce and disseminate information (newspapers, magazines, television stations, film production studios, etc.), which are now available to a growing number of private and public interests throughout the world; and to the images of the world created by these media. These images of the world involve many complicated inflections, depending on their mode (documentary or entertainment), their hardware (electronic or pre-electronic), their audiences (local, national or transnational) and the interests of those who own and control them. What is most important about these mediascapes is that they provide (especially in their television, film and cassette forms) large and complex repertoires of images, narratives and ethnoscapes to viewers throughout the world, in which the world of commodities and the world of "news" and politics are profoundly mixed. What this means is that many audiences throughout the world experience the media themselves as a complicated and interconnected repertoire of print, celluloid, electronic screens and billboards. The lines between the "realistic" and the fictional landscapes they see are blurred, so that the further away these audiences are from the direct experiences of metropolitan life, the more likely they are to construct "imagined worlds" which are chimerical, aesthetic, even fantastic objects, particularly if assessed by the criteria of some other perspective, some other "imagined world."

Mediascapes, whether produced by private or state interests, tend to be image-centered, narrative-based accounts of strips of reality, and what they offer to those who experience and transform them is a series of elements (such as characters, plots and textual forms) out of which scripts can be formed of imagined lives, their own as well as those of others living in other places. These scripts can and do get disaggregated into complex sets of metaphors by which people live (Lakoff and Johnson, 1980) as they help to constitute narratives of the "other" and proto-narratives of possible lives, fantasies which could become prologemena to the desire for acquisition and movement.

Ideoscapes are also concatenations of images, but they are often directly political and frequently have to do with the ideologies of states and the counter-ideologies of movements explicitly oriented to capturing states power or a piece of it. These ideoscapes are composed of elements of the Enlightenment world-view, which consists of a concatenation of ideas, terms and images, including "freedom," "welfare," "rights," "sovereignty," "representation" and the master-term "democracy." The master-narrative of the Enlightenment (and its many variants in England, France and the United States) was constructed with a certain internal logic and presupposed a certain relationship between reading, representation and the public sphere (for the dynamics of this process in the early history of the United States, see Warner, 1990). But their diaspora across the world, especially since the nineteenth century, has loosened the internal coherence which held these terms and images together in a Euro-American master-narrative, and provided instead a loosely structured synopticon of politics, in which different nation-states, as part of their evolution, have organized their political cultures around different "keywords" (Williams, 1976).

As a result of the differential diaspora of these keywords, the political narratives that govern communication between elites and followings in different parts of the world involve problems of both a semantic and a pragmatic nature: semantic to the extent that words (and their lexical equivalents) require careful translation from context to context in their global movements; and pragmatic to the extent that the use of these words by political actors and their audiences may be subject to very different sets of contextual conventions that mediate their translation into public politics. Such conventions are not only matters of the nature of political rhetoric (viz. what does the aging Chinese leadership mean when it refers to the dangers of hooliganism? What does the South Korean leadership mean when it speaks of "discipline" as the key to democratic industrial growth?).

These conventions also involve the far more subtle question of what sets of communicative genres are valued in what way (newspapers versus cinema, for example) and what sorts of pragmatic genre conventions govern the collective "readings" of different kinds of text. So, while an Indian audience may be attentive to the resonances of a political speech in terms of some keywords and phrases reminiscent of Hindi cinema, a Korean audience may respond to the subtle codings of Buddhist or neo-Confucian rhetorical strategy encoded in a political document. The very relationship of reading to hearing and seeing may vary in important ways that determine the morphology of these different ideoscapes as they shape themselves in different national and transnational contexts. This globally variable synaesthesia has hardly even been noted, but it demands urgent analysis. Thus "democracy" has clearly become a master-term, with powerful echoes from Haiti and Poland to the Soviet Union and China, but it sits at the center of a variety of ideoscapes (composed of distinctive pragmatic configurations of rough "translations" of other central terms from the vocabulary of the Enlightenment). This creates ever new terminological kaleidoscopes, as states (and the groups that seek to capture them) seek to pacify populations whose own ethnoscapes are in motion, and whose mediascapes may create severe problems for the ideoscapes with which they are presented. The fluidity of ideoscapes is complicated in particular by the growing diasporas (both voluntary and involuntary) of intellectuals who continuously inject new meaning-streams into the discourse of democracy in different parts of the world.

This extended terminological discussion of the five terms I have coined sets the basis for a tentative formulation about the conditions under which current global flows occur: *they occur in and through the growing disjunctures between ethnoscapes, technoscapes, finanscapes, mediascapes and ideoscapes.* This formulation, the core of my model of global cultural flow, needs some explanation. First, people, machinery, money, images, and ideas now follow increasingly non-isomorphic paths: of course, at all periods in human history, there have been some disjunctures between the flows of these things, but the sheer speed, scale and volume of each of these flows is now so great that the disjunctures have become central to the politics of global culture. The Japanese are notoriously hospitable to ideas and are stereotyped as inclined to export (all) and import (some) goods, but they are also notoriously closed to immigration, like the Swiss, the Swedes and the Saudis. Yet the Swiss and Saudis accept populations of guestworkers, thus creating labor diasporas of Turks, Italians and other circum-mediterranean groups. Some such guestworker groups maintain continuous contact with their home-nations, like the Turks, but others, like high-level South Asian migrants tend to desire lives in their new homes, raising anew the problem of reproduction in a deterritorialized context.

Deterritorialization, in general, is one of the central forces of the modern world, since it brings laboring populations into the lower class sectors and spaces of relatively wealthy societies, while sometimes creating exaggerated and intensified senses of criticism or attachment to politics in the home-state. Deterritorialization, whether of Hindus, Sikhs, Palestinians or Ukranians, is now at the core of a variety of global fundamentalisms, including Islamic and Hindu fundamentalism. In the Hindu case, for example, it is clear that the overseas movement of Indians has been exploited by a variety of interests both within and outside India to create a complicated network of finances and religious identifications, in which the problems of cultural reproduction for Hindus abroad has become tied to the politics of Hindu fundamentalism at home.

At the same time, deterritorialization creates new markets for film companies, art impressarios and travel agencies, who thrive on the need of the deterritorialized population for contact with its homeland. Naturally, these invented homelands, which constitute the mediascapes of deterritorialized groups, can often become sufficiently fantastic and one-sided that they provide the material for new ideoscapes in which ethnic conflicts can begin to erupt. The creation of "Khalistan," an invented homeland of the deterritorialized Sikh population of England, Canada and the United States, is one example of the bloody potential in such mediascapes, as they interact with the "internal colonialisms" (Hechter, 1974) of the nation-state. The West Bank, Namibia and Eritrea are other theaters for the enactment of the bloody negotiation between existing nation-states and various deterritorialized groupings.

The idea of deterritorialization may also be applied to money and finance, as money managers seek the best markets for their investments, independent of national boundaries. In turn, these movements of monies are the basis of new kinds of conflict, as Los Angelenos worry about the Japanese buying up their city, and people in Bombay worry about the rich Arabs from the Gulf States who have not only transformed the price of mangoes in Bombay, but have also substantially altered the profile of hotels, restaurants and other services in the eyes of the local population, just as they continue to do in London. Yet, most residents of Bombay are ambivalent about the Arab presence there, for the flip side of their presence is the absence of friends and kinsmen earning big money in the Middle East and bringing back both money and luxury commodities to Bombay and other cities in India. Such commodities transform consumer taste in these cities, and also often end up smuggled through air and sea ports and peddled in the gray markets of Bombay's streets. In these gray markets, some members of Bombay's middle-classes and of its lumpenproletariat can buy some of these goods, ranging from cartons of Marlboro cigarettes, to Old Spice shaving cream and tapes of Madonna. Similarly gray routes, often subsidized by the moonlighting activities of sailors, diplomats, and airline stewardesses who get to move in and out of the country regularly, keep the gray markets of Bombay, Madras and Calcutta filled with goods not only from the West, but also from the Middle East, Hong Kong and Singapore.

It is this fertile ground of deterritorialization, in which money, commodities and persons are involved in ceaselessly chasing each other around the world, that the mediascapes and ideoscapes of the modern world find their fractured and fragmented counterpart. For the ideas and images produced by mass media often are only partial guides to the goods and experiences that deterritorialized populations transfer to one another. In Mira Nair's brilliant film, *India Cabaret*, we see the multiple loops of this fractured deterritorialization as young women, barely competent in Bombay's metropolitan glitz, come to seek their fortunes as cabaret dancers and prostitutes in Bombay, entertaining men in clubs with dance formats derived wholly from the prurient dance sequences of Hindi films. These scenes cater in turn to ideas about Western and foreign women and their "looseness," while they provide tawdry career alibis for these women. Some of these women come from Kerala, where cabaret clubs and the pornographic film industry have blossomed, partly in response to the purses and tastes of Keralites returned from the Middle East, where their diasporic lives away from women distort their very sense of what the relations between men and women might be. These tragedies of displacement could certainly be replayed in a more detailed analysis of the relations between the Japanese and German sex tours to Thailand and the tragedies of the sex trade in Bangkok, and in other similar loops which tie together fantasies about the other, the conveniences and seductions of travel, the economics of global trade and the brutal mobility fantasies that dominate gender politics in many parts of Asia and the world at large.

While far more could be said about the cultural politics of deterritorialization and the larger sociology of displacement that it expresses, it is appropriate at this juncture to bring in the role of the nation-state in the disjunctive global economy of culture today. The relationship between states and nations is everywhere an embattled one. It is possible to say that in many societies, the nation and the state have become one another's projects. That is, while nations (or more properly groups with ideas about nationhood) seek to capture or co-opt states and state power, states simultaneously seek to capture and monopolize ideas about nationhood (Baruah, 1986; Chatterjee, 1986; Nandy, 1989). In general, separatist, transnational movements, including those which have included terror in their methods, exemplify nations in search of states: Sikhs, Tamil Sri Lankans, Basques, Moros, Quebecois, each of these represent imagined communities which seek to create states of their own or carve pieces out of existing states. States, on the other hand, are everywhere seeking to monopolize the moral resources of community, either by flatly claiming perfect coevality between nation and state, or by systematically museumizing and representing all the groups, within them in a variety of heritage politics that seems remarkably uniform throughout the world (Herzfeld, 1982; Handler, 1988; McQueen, 1988). Here, national and international mediascapes are exploited by nation-states to pacify separatists or even the potential fissiparousness of all ideas of difference. Typically, contemporary nation-states do this by exercising taxonomical control over difference; by creating various kinds of international spectacle to domesticate difference; and by seducing small groups with the fantasy of self-display on some sort of global or cosmopolitan stage. One important new feature of global cultural politics, tied to the disjunctive relationships between the various landscapes discussed earlier, is that state and nation are at each's throats, and the hyphen that links them is now less an icon of conjuncture than an index of disjuncture. This disjunctive relationship between nation and state has two levels: at the level of any given nation-state, it means that there is a battle of the imagination, with state and nation seeking to cannibalize one another. Here is the seed-bed of brutal separatisms, majoritarianisms that seem to have appeared from nowhere, and micro-identities that have become political projects within the nation-state. At another level, this disjunctive relationship is deeply entangled with the global disjunctures discussed throughout this [chapter]: ideas of nationhood appear to be steadily increasing in scale and regularly crossing existing state boundaries: sometimes, as with the Kurds, because previous identities stretched across vast national spaces, or, as with the Tamils in Sri Lanka, the dormant threads of a transnational diaspora have been activated to ignite the micro-politics of a nation-state.

In discussing the cultural politics that have subverted the hyphen that links the nation to the state, it is especially important not to forget its mooring in the irregularities that now characterize "disorganized capital" (Lash and Urry, 1987; Kothari, 1989). It is because labor, finance and technology are now so widely separated that the volatilities that underlie movements for nationhood (as large as transnational Islam on the one hand, or as small as the movement of the Gurkhas for a separate state in the North-East of India) grind against the vulnerabilities which characterize the relationships between states. States find themselves pressed to stay "open" by the forces of media, technology, and travel which had fueled consumerism throughout the world and have increased the craving, even in the non-Western world, for new commodities and spectacles. On the other hand, these very cravings can become caught up in new ethnoscapes, mediascapes, and eventually, ideoscapes, such as "democracy" in China, that the state cannot tolerate as threats to its own control over ideas of nationhood and "peoplehood." States throughout the world are under siege, especially where contests over the ideoscapes of democracy are fierce and fundamental, and where there are radical disjunctures between ideoscapes and technoscapes (as in the case of very small countries that lack contemporary technologies of production and information); or between ideoscapes and finanscapes (as in countries, such as Mexico or Brazil where international lending influences national politics to a very large degree); or between ideoscapes and ethoscapes (as in Beirut, where diasporic, local and translocal filiations are suicidally at battle); or between ideoscapes and mediascapes (as in many countries in the Middle East and Asia) where the lifestyles represented on both national and international TV and cinema completely overwhelm and undermine the rhetoric of national politics: in the Indian case, the myth of the law-breaking hero has emerged to mediate this naked struggle between the pieties and the realities of Indian politics, which has grown increasingly brutalized and corrupt (Vachani, 1989).

The transnational movement of the martial arts, particularly through Asia, as mediated by the Hollywood and Hong Kong film industries (Zarilli, 1995) is a rich illustration of the ways in which long-standing martial arts traditions, reformulated to meet the fantasies of contemporary (sometimes lumpen) youth populations, create new cultures of masculinity and violence, which are in turn the fuel for increased violence in national and international politics. Such violence is in turn the spur to an increasingly rapid and amoral arms trade which penetrates the entire world. The world-wide spread of the AK-47 and the Uzi, in films, in corporate and state security, in terror, and in police and military activity, is a reminder that apparently simple technical uniformities often conceal an increasingly complex set of loops, linking images of violence to aspirations for community in some "imagined world."

Returning then to the ethnoscapes with which I began, the central paradox of ethnic politics in today's world is that primordia (whether of language or skin color or neighborhood or of kinship) have become globalized. That is, sentiments, whose greatest force is in their ability to ignite intimacy into a political sentiment and turn locality into a staging ground for identity, have become spread over vast and irregular spaces, as groups move, yet stay linked to one another through sophisticated media capabilities. This is not to deny that such primordia are often the product of invented traditions (Hobsbawm and Ranger, 1983) or retrospective affiliations, but to emphasize that because of the disjunctive and unstable interplay of commerce, media, national policies and consumer fantasies, ethnicity, once a genie contained in the bottle of some sort of locality (however large) has now become a global force, forever slipping in and through the cracks between states and borders.

But the relationship between the cultural and economic levels of this new set of global disjunctures is not a simple one-way street in which the terms of global cultural politics are set wholly by, or confined wholly within, the vicissitudes of international flows of technology, labor and finance, demanding only a modest modification of existing neo-Marxist models of uneven development and state-formation. There is a deeper change, itself driven by the disjunctures between all the landscapes I have discussed, and constituted by their continuously fluid and uncertain interplay, which concerns the relationship between production and consumption in today's global economy. Here I begin with Marx's famous (and often mined) view of the fetishism of the commodity, and suggest that this fetishism has been replaced in the world at large (now seeing the world as one, large, interactive system, composed of many complex sub-systems) by two mutually supportive descendants, the first of which I call production fetishism, and the second of which I call the fetishism of the consumer.

By *production fetishism* I mean an illusion created by contemporary transnational production loci, which masks translocal capital, transnational earning-flows, global management and often faraway workers (engaged in various kinds of high-tech putting out operations) in the idiom and spectacle of local (sometimes even worker) control, national productivity and territorial sovereignty. To the extent that various kinds of Free Trade Zone have become the models for production at large, especially of high-tech commodities, production has itself become a fetish, masking not social relations as such, but the relations of production, which are increasingly transnational. The locality (both in the sense of the local factory or site of production and in the extended sense of the nation-state) becomes a fetish which disguises the globally dispersed forces that actually drive the production process. This generates alienation (in Marx's sense) twice intensified, for its social sense is now compounded by a complicated spatial dynamic which is increasingly global.

As for the *fetishism of the consumer*, I mean to indicate here that the consumer has been transformed, through commodity flows (and the mediascapes, especially of advertising, that accompany them) into a sign, both in Baudrillard's sense of a simulacrum which only asymptotically approaches the form of a real social agent; and in the sense of a mask for the real seat of agency, which is not the consumer but the producer and the many forces that constitute production. Global advertising is the key technology for the world-wide dissemination of a plethora of creative, and culturally well-chosen, ideas of consumer agency. These images of agency are increasingly distortions of a world of merchandising so subtle that the consumer is consistently helped to believe that he or she is an actor, where in fact he or she is at best a chooser.

The globalization of culture is not the same as its homogenization, but globalization involves the use of a variety of instruments of homogenization (armaments, advertising techniques, language hegemonies, clothing styles and the like), which are absorbed into local political and cultural economies, only to be repatriated as heterogeneous dialogues of national sovereignty, free enterprise, fundamentalism, etc. in which the state plays an increasingly delicate role: too much openness to global flows and the nation-state is threatened by revolt – the China syndrome; too little, and the state exits the international stage, as Burma, Albania and North Korea, in various ways have done. In general, the state has become the arbiter of this *repatriation of difference* (in the form of goods, signs, slogans, styles, etc.). But this repatriation or export of the designs and commodities of difference continuously exacerbates the "internal" politics of majoritarianism and homogenization, which is most frequently played out in debates over heritage.

Thus the central feature of global culture today is the politics of the mutual effort of sameness and difference to cannibalize one another and thus to proclaim their succesful hijacking of the twin Enlightenment ideas of the triumphantly universal and the resiliently particular. This mutual cannibalization shows its ugly face in riots, in refugee-flows, in state-sponsored torture and in ethnocide (with or without state support). Its brighter side is in the expansion of many individual horizons of hope and fantasy, in the global spread of oral rehydration therapy and other low-tech instruments of well-being, in the susceptibility even of South Africa to the force of global opinion, in the inability of the Polish state to repress its own working-classes, and in the growth of a wide range of progressive, transnational alliances. Examples of both sorts could be multiplied. The critical point is that both sides of the coin of global cultural process today are products of the infinitely varied mutual contest of sameness and difference on a stage characterized by radical disjunctures between different sorts of global flows and the uncertain landscapes created in and through these disjunctures.

NOTES

A longer version of this [chapter] appears in *Public Culture* 2 (2), Spring 1990. This longer version sets the present formulation in the context of global cultural traffic in earlier historical periods, and draws out some of its implications for the study of cultural forms more generally.

1   One major exception is Fredric Jameson, whose (1984) essay on the relationship between postmodernism and late capitalism has in many ways inspired this [chapter]. However, the debate between Jameson (1986) and Ahmad (1987) in *Social Text* shows that the creation of a globalizing Marxist narrative, in cultural matters, is difficult territory indeed. My own effort, in this context, is to begin a restructuring of the Marxist narrative (by stressing lags and disjunctures) that many Marxists might find abhorrent. Such a restructuring has to avoid the dangers of obliterating difference within the "third world," of eliding the social referent (as some French postmodernists seem inclined to do) and of retaining the narrative authority of the Marxist tradition, in favor of greater attention to global fragmentation, uncertainty and difference.
2   These ideas are argued more fully in *Modernity at Large: Cultural Dimensions of Globalization* (Minneapolis, University of Minnesota Press, 1996).

REFERENCES

Ahmad, A. (1987) "Jameson's rhetoric of otherness and the 'National Allegory,'" *Social Text*, 17: 3–25.

Amin, S. (1980) *Class and Nation: Historically and in the Current Crisis*. New York and London: Monthly Review.

Anderson, B. (1983) *Imagined Communities: Reflections on the Origin and Spread of Nationalism*. London: Verso.

Appadurai, A. (1989) "Global ethnoscapes: notes and queries for a transnational anthropology," in R. G. Fox (ed.), *Interventions: Anthropology of the Present*.

Barber, K. (1987) "Popular arts in Africa," *African Studies Review*, 30 (3).

Baruah, S. (1986) "Immigration, ethnic conflict and political turmoil, Assam 1979–1985," *Asian Survey*, 26 (11).

Chatterjee, P. (1986) *Nationalist Thought and the Colonial World: a Derivative Discourse*. London: Zed Books.

Feld, S. (1988) "Notes on world beat," *Public Culture*, 1 (1): 31–7.

Gans, Eric (1985) *The End of Culture: Toward a Generative Anthropology*. Berkeley, CA: University of California.

Hamelink, C. (1983) *Cultural Autonomy in Global Communications*. New York: Longman.

Handler, R. (1988) *Nationalism and the Politics of Culture in Quebec*. Madison: University of Wisconsin.

Hannerz, U. (1987) "The world in creolization," *Africa*, 57 (4): 546–59.

Hannerz, U. (1989) "Notes on the global ecumene," *Public Culture*, 1 (2): 66–75.

Hecheter, M. (1974) *Internal Colonialism: the Celtic Fringe in British National Development, 1536–1966*. Berkeley and Los Angeles: University of California.

Herzfeld, M. (1982) *Ours Once More: Folklore, Ideology and the Making of Modern Greece*. Austin: University of Texas.

Hobsbawm, E. and Ranger, T. (eds) (1983) *The Invention of Tradition*. New York: Columbia University Press.

Ivy, M. (1988) "Tradition and difference in the Japanese mass media," *Public Culture*, 1 (1): 21–9.

Iyer, P. (1988) *Video Night in Kathmandu*. New York: Knopf.

Jameson, F. (1984) "Postmodernism, or the cultural logic of late capitalism," *New Left Review*, 146 (July–August): 53–92.

Jameson, F. (1986) "Third World literature in the era of multi-national capitalism," *Social Text*, 15 (Fall): 65–88.

Kothari, R. (1989) *State Against Democracy: in Search of Humane Governance*. New York: New Horizons.

Lakoff, G. and Johnson M. (1980) *Metaphors We Live By*. Chicago and London: University of Chicago.

Lash, S. and Urry, J. (1987) *The End of Organized Capitalism*. Madison: University of Wisconsin.

McQueen, H. (1988) "The Australian stamp: image, design and ideology," *Arena*, 84 (Spring): 78–96.

Mandel, E. (1978) *Late Capitalism*. London: Verso.

Mattelart, A. (1983) *Transnationals and Third World: the Struggle for Culture*. South Hadley, MA: Bergin and Garvey.

Nandy, A. (1989) "The political culture of the Indian state," *Daedalus*, 118 (4): 1–26.

Nicoll, F. (1989) "My trip to Alice," *Criticism, Heresy and Interpretation (CHAI)*, 3: 21–32.

Schiller, H. (1976) *Communication and Cultural Domination*. White Plains, NY: International Arts and Sciences.

Vachani, L. (1989) "Narrative, pleasure and ideology in the Hindi film: an analysis of the outsider formula," MA thesis, The Annenberg School of Communication, The University of Pennsylvania.

Wallerstein, I. (1974) *The Modern World-System*, 2 vol. New York and London: Academic Press.

Warner, M. (1990) *The Letters of the Republic: Publication and the Public Sphere*. Cambridge, MA: Harvard.

Williams, R. (1976) *Keywords*. New York: Oxford.

Wolf, E. (1982) *Europe and the People without History*. Berkeley, CA: University of California.

Yoshimoto, M. (1989) "The postmodern and mass images in Japan," *Public Culture*, 1 (2): 8–25.

Zarilli, P. (1995) "Repositioning the body: an Indian martial art and its pan-Asian publics," in C. A. Breckenridge (ed.), *Consuming Modernity: Public Cultures in a South Asian World*. Minneapolis: University of Minnesota Press.

CHAPTER 7

The Question of Cultural Identity

Stuart Hall

"THE REST" IN "THE WEST"

[. . .] After World War II, the decolonizing European powers thought they could pull out of their colonial spheres of influence, leaving the consequences of imperialism behind them. But global interdependence now works both ways. The movements of Western styles, images, commodities and consumer identities outwards has been matched by a momentous movement of peoples from the peripheries to the centre in one of the largest and most sustained periods of "unplanned" migration in recent history. Driven by poverty, drought, famine, economic undevelopment and crop failure, civil war and political unrest, regional conflict and arbitrary changes of political regime, the accumulating foreign indebtedness of their governments to Western banks, very large numbers of the poorer peoples of the globe have taken the "message" of global consumerism at face value, and moved toward the places where "the goodies" come from and where the chances of survival are higher. In the era of global communications, the West is only a one-way airline charter ticket away.

There have been continuous, large-scale, legal and "illegal" migrations into the US from many poor countries of Latin America, and the Caribbean basin (Cuba, Haiti, Puerto Rico, the Dominican Republic, the islands of the British Caribbean), as well as substantial numbers of "economic migrants" and political refugees from South-East Asia and the Far East – Chinese, Koreans, Vietnamese, Cambodians, Indians,

This chapter is an edited extract from *Modernity and its Futures*, edited by S. Hall, D. Held, and A. McGrew (Oxford, Blackwell, 1992), pp. 306–14. Reprinted by permission of Blackwell Publishers.

Pakistanis, Japanese. Canada has a substantial minority Caribbean population. One consequence is a dramatic shift in the "ethnic mix" of the US population – the first since the mass migrations of the early part of this century. In 1980, one in every five Americans came from an African-American, Asian-American or American-Indian background. In 1990, the figure was one in four. In many major cities (including Los Angeles, San Francisco, New York, Chicago, and Miami), whites are now a minority. In the 1980s, the population of California grew by 5.6 million, 43 per cent of which were people of colour – that is, including Hispanics and Asians, as well as African-Americans (compared to 33 per cent in 1980) – and one-fifth is foreign born. By 1995 one-third of American public school students are expected to be "non-white" (US Census, 1991, quoted in Platt, 1991).

Over the same period, there has been a parallel "migration" into Europe of Arabs from the Maghreb (Morocco, Algeria, Tunisia), and Africans from Senegal and Zaire into France and Belgium; of Turks and North Africans into Germany; of Asians from the ex-Dutch East and West Indies and Surinam into The Netherlands; of North Africans into Italy; and, of course, of people from the Caribbean and from India, Pakistan, Bangladesh, Kenya, Uganda and Sri Lanka into the UK. There are political refugees from Somalia, Ethiopia, the Sudan and Sri Lanka and other places in small numbers everywhere.

This formation of ethnic-minority "enclaves" within the nation-states of the West has led to a "pluralization" of national cultures and national identities.

THE DIALECTIC OF IDENTITIES

How has this situation played itself out in Britain in terms of identity? The first effect has been to contest the settled contours of national identity, and to expose its closures to the pressures of difference, "otherness" and cultural diversity. This is happening, to different degrees, in all the Western national cultures and as a consequence it has brought the whole issue of national identity and the cultural "centredness" of the West into the open.

> Older certainties and hierarchies of British identity have been called into question in a world of dissolving boundaries and disrupted continuities. In a country that it is now a container of African and Asian cultures, the sense of what it is to be British can never again have the old confidence and surety. Other sources of identity are no less fragile. What does it mean to be European in a continent coloured not only by the cultures of its former colonies, but also by American and now Japanese cultures? Is not

the very category of identity itself problematical? Is it at all possible, in global times, to regain a coherent and integral sense of identity? Continuity and historicity of identity are challenged by the immediacy and intensity of global cultural confrontations. The comforts of Tradition are fundamentally challenged by the imperative to forge a new self-interpretation based upon the responsibilities of cultural Translation. (Robins, 1991: 41)

Another effect has been to trigger a widening of the field of identities, and a proliferation of new identity-positions together with a degree of polarization amongst and between them. These developments constitute [. . .] the possibility that globalization might lead to a *strengthening* of local identities, or to the production of *new identities*.

The strengthening of local identities can be seen in the strong defensive reaction of those members of dominant ethnic groups who feel threatened by the presence of other cultures. In the UK, for example, such defensiveness has produced a revamped Englishness, an aggressive little Englandism, and a retreat to ethnic absolutism in an attempt to shore up the nation and rebuild "an identity that coheres, is unified and filters out threats in social experience" (Sennett, 1971: 15). This is often grounded in [. . .] "cultural racism", and is evident now in legitimate political parties of both Left and Right, and in more extremist political movements throughout Western Europe.

It is sometimes matched by a strategic retreat to more defensive identities amongst the minority communities themselves in response to the experience of cultural racism and exclusion. Such strategies include re-identification with cultures of origin (in the Caribbean, India, Bangladesh, Pakistan); the construction of strong counter-ethnicities – as in the symbolic identification of second-generation Afro-Caribbean youth, through the symbols and motifs of Rastafarianism, with their African origin and heritage; or the revival of cultural traditionalism, religious orthodoxy and political separatism, for example, amongst *some* sections of the Muslim community.

There is also some evidence of the third possible consequence of globalization – the production of *new* identities. A good example is those new identities which have emerged in the 1970s, grouped around the signifier "black," which in the British context provides a new focus of identification for *both* Afro-Caribbean and Asian communities. What these communities have in common, which they represent through taking on the "black" identity, is not that they are culturally, ethnically, linguistically or even physically the same, but that they are seen and treated as "the same" (i.e. non-white, "other") by the dominant culture. It is their exclusion which provides what Laclau and Mouffe [1985] call the common "axis of equivalence" of this new identity. However, despite the fact that efforts are made to give this "black" identity a single or unified content, it continues to exist as an identity *alongside a wide range of other differences*. Afro-Caribbean and Indian people continue to maintain different cultural traditions. "Black" is thus an example, not only of the *political* character of new identities – i.e. their *positional* and conjunctural character (their formation in and for specific times and places) – but also of the way identity and difference are inextricably articulated or knitted together in different identities, the one never wholly obliterating the other.

As a tentative conclusion it would appear then that globalization *does* have the effect of contesting and dislocating the centred and "closed" identities of a national culture. It does have a pluralizing impact on identities, producing a variety of possibilities and new positions of identification, and making identities more positional, more political, more plural and diverse; less fixed, unified or trans-historical. However, its general impact remains contradictory. Some identities gravitate toward what Robins (1991) calls "Tradition", attempting to restore their former purity and recover the unities and certainties which are felt as being lost. Others accept that identity is subject to the play of history, politics, representation and difference, so that they are unlikely ever again to be unitary or "pure"; and these consequently gravitate toward what Robins (following Homi Bhabha) calls "Translation".

[. . .]

Fundamentalism, Diaspora and Hybridity

Where identities are concerned, this oscillation between Tradition and Translation (which was briefly traced above in relation to Britain) is becoming more evident on a global canvas. Everywhere, cultural identities are emerging which are not fixed, but poised, *in transition*, between different positions; which draw on different cultural traditions at the same time; and which are the product of those complicated crossovers and cultural mixes which are increasingly common in a globalized world. It may be tempting to think of identity in the age of globalization as destined to end up in one place or another: either returning to its "roots" or disappearing through assimilation and homogenization. But this may be a false dilemma.

For there is another possibility: that of "Translation". This describes those identity formations which cut across and intersect natural frontiers, and which are composed of people who have been *dispersed* forever from their homelands. Such people retain strong links with their places of origin and their traditions, but they are without the illusion of a return to the past. They are obliged to come to terms with the new cultures they inhabit, without simply assimilating to them and losing their identities completely. They bear upon them the traces of the particular cultures, traditions, languages and histories by which they were shaped. The difference is that they are not and will never be *unified* in the old sense, because they are irrevocably the product of several interlocking histories and cultures, belong at one and the same time to several "homes" (and to no one particular "home"). People belonging to such *cultures of hybridity* have had to renounce the dream or ambition of rediscovering any kind of "lost" cultural purity, or ethnic absolutism. They are irrevocably *translated*. The word "translation", Salman Rushdie notes, "comes etymologically from the Latin for 'bearing across'". Migrant writers like him, who belong to two worlds at once, "having been borne across the world . . . are translated men" (Rushdie, 1991). They are the products of the new *diasporas* created by the post-colonial migrations. They must learn to inhabit at least two identities, to speak two cultural languages, to translate and negotiate between them. Cultures of hybridity are one of the distinctly novel types of identity produced in the era of late-modernity, and there are more and more examples of them to be discovered.

[. . .]

Some people argue that "hybridity" and syncretism – the fusion between different cultural traditions – is a powerful creative source, creating new forms that are more appropriate to late-modernity than the old, embattled national identities of the past. Others, however, argue that hybridity, with the indeterminacy, "double consciousness", and relativism it implies, also has its costs and dangers. Salman Rushdie's novel about migration, Islam, and the prophet Mohammed, *The Satanic Verses*, which its deep immersion in Islamic culture *and* its secular consciousness of the exiled "translated man", so offended the Iranian fundamentalists that they passed sentence of death on him for blasphemy. It also outraged many British Muslims. In defending his novel, Rushdie offered a strong and compelling defence of "hybridity".

> Standing at the centre of the novel is a group of characters most of whom are British Muslims, or not particularly religious persons of Muslim background, struggling with just the sort of great problems that have arisen to surround the book, problems of hybridization and ghettoization, of reconciling the old and the new. Those who oppose the novel most vociferously today are of the opinion that intermingling with different cultures will inevitably weaken and ruin their own. I am of the opposite opinion. *The Satanic Verses* celebrates hybridity, impurity, intermingling, the transformation that comes of new and unexpected combinations of human beings, cultures, ideas, politics, movies, songs. It rejoices in mongrelization and fears the absolutism of the Pure. *Mélange*, hotchpotch, a bit of this and a bit of that is *how newness enters the world*. It is the great pos-

sibility that mass migration gives the world, and I have tried to embrace it. *The Satanic Verses* is for change-by-fusion, change-by-conjoining. It is a love-song to our mongrel selves. (Rushdie, 1991: 394)

However, *The Satanic Verses* may well have become trapped between the irreconcilable forces of Tradition and Translation. [. . .]

[. . .]

On the other hand, there are equally powerful attempts to reconstruct purified identities, to restore coherence, "closure" and Tradition, in the face of hybridity and diversity. Two examples are the resurgence of nationalism in Eastern Europe and the rise of fundamentalism.

In an era when regional integration in the economic and political fields, and the breaking down of national sovereignty, are moving very rapidly in Western Europe, the collapse of the communist regimes in Eastern Europe and the break-up of the old Soviet Union have been followed by a powerful revival of ethnic nationalism, fuelled by ideas of both racial purity and religious orthodoxy. The ambition to create new, culturally and ethnically unified nation-states (which [. . .] never really existed in Western national cultures) was the driving force behind the break-away movements in the Baltic States of Estonia, Latvia and Lithuania, the disintegration of Yugoslavia and the move to independence of many former Soviet Republics, from Georgia, the Ukraine, Russia and Armenia to Kurdistan, Uzbekistan and the "Muslim" Asian republics of the old Soviet state. Much the same process has been taking place in the "nations" of Central Europe which were carved out of the disintegration of the Austro-Hungarian and Ottoman empires at the end of the First World War.

These new would-be "nations" try to construct states that are unified in both ethnic and religious terms, and to create political entities around homogeneous cultural identities. The problem is that they contain within their "borders" minorities who identify themselves with different cultures. Thus, for example, there are "ethnic" Russian minorities in the Baltic Republics and the Ukraine, ethnic Poles in Lithuania, an Armenian enclave (Nagorno-Karabakh) in Azerbaijan, Turkic-Christian minorities amongst the Russian majorities of Moldavia, and large numbers of Muslims in the southern republics of the old Soviet Union who share more, in cultural and religious terms, with their Middle-Eastern Islamic neighbours than with many of their "countrymen".

The other significant form of the revival of particularistic nationalism and ethnic and religious absolutism is, of course, the phenomenon of "fundamentalism". This is evident everywhere (for example, in the revived little-Englandism referred to earlier), though its most striking example is to be found in some Islamic states in the Middle East. Beginning with the Iranian Revolution, fundamentalist Islamic movements, which seek to create religious states in which the political principles of organization are aligned with the religious doctrines and laws of the *Koran*, have arisen in many, hitherto secular Islamic societies. In fact, this trend is difficult to interpret. Some analysts see it as a reaction to the "forced" character of Western modernization; certainly, Iranian fundamentalism was a direct response to the efforts of the Shah in the 1970s to adopt Western models and cultural values wholesale. Some interpret it as a response to being left out of "globalization". The reaffirmation of cultural "roots" and the return to orthodoxy has long been one of the most powerful sources of counter-identification amongst many Third World and post-colonial societies and regions (one thinks here of the roles of nationalism and national culture in the Indian, African and Asian independence movements). Others see the roots of Islamic fundamentalism in the failure of Islamic states to throw up successful and effective "modernizing" leaderships or secular, modern parties. In conditions of extensive poverty and relative economic under-development (fundamentalism is stronger in the poorer Islamic states of the region), a restoration of the Islamic faith is a powerful mobilizing and binding political and ideological force, especially where democratic traditions are weak.

The trend toward "global homogenization", then, is matched by a powerful revival of "ethnicity", sometimes of the more hybrid or symbolic varieties, but also frequently of the exclusive or "essentialist" varieties cited above. Bauman has referred to this "resurgence of ethnicity" as one of the main reasons why the more extreme, free-ranging or indeterminate versions of what happens to identity under the impact of the "global post-modern" requires serious qualification.

> The "resurgence of ethnicity" . . . puts in the forefront the unanticipated flourishing of ethnic loyalties inside national minorities. By the same token, it casts a shadow on what seems to be the deep cause of the phenomenon: the growing separation between the membership of body politic and ethnic membership (or more generally, cultural conformity) which removes much of its original attraction from the programme of cultural assimilation . . . Ethnicity has become one of the many categories or tokens, or "tribal poles", around which flexible and sanction-free communities are formed and in reference to which individual identities are constructed and asserted. There are now, therefore, [many] fewer centrifugal forces which once weakened ethnic integrity. There is instead a powerful demand for pronounced, though symbolic rather than institutionalized, ethnic distinctiveness. (Bauman, 1990: 167)

The resurgence of nationalism and other forms of particularism at the end of the twentieth century, alongside and intimately linked to globalization, is of course a remarkable reversal, a most unexpected turn of events. Nothing in the modernizing Englightenment perspectives or ideologies of the West – neither liberalism nor indeed Marxism, which for all its opposition to liberalism also saw capitalism as the unwitting agent of "modernity" – foresaw such an outcome.

Both liberalism and Marxism, in their different ways, implied that the attachment to the local and the particular would gradually give way to more universalistic and cosmopolitan or international values and identities; that nationalism and ethnicity were archaic forms of attachment – the sorts of thing which would be "melted away" by the revolutionizing force of modernity. According to these "metanarratives" of modernity, the irrational attachments to the local and the particular, to tradition and roots, to national myths and "imagined communities", would gradually be replaced by more rational and universalistic identities. Yet globalization seems to be producing neither simply the triumph of "the global" nor the persistence, in its old nationalistic form, of "the local". The displacements or distractions of globalization turn out to be more varied and more contradictory than either its protagonists or opponents suggest. However, this also suggests that, though powered in many ways by the West, globalization may turn out to be part of that slow and uneven but continuing story of the de-centring of the West.

REFERENCES

Bauman, Z. (1990) "Modernity and ambivalence," in M. Featherstone (ed.), *Global Culture: Nationalism, Globalization and Modernity*. London: Sage.
Laclau, E. and Mouffe, C. (1985) *Hegemony and Socialist Strategy*. London: Verso.
Platt, A. (1991) *Defending the Canon*. Ferdinand Braudel Centre and Institute of Global Studies, Binghampton, State University of New York.
Robins, K. (1991) "Tradition and translation: national culture in its global context," in J. Corner and S. Harvey (eds), *Enterprise and Heritage: Crosscurrents of National Culture*. London: Routledge.
Rushdie, S. (1991) *Imaginary Homelands*. London: Granta Books.
Sennett, R. (1971) *The Ideas of Disorder*. Harmondsworth: Penguin.

PART III SOCIAL MOVEMENTS AND THE POLITICIZATION OF THE SOCIAL

Introduction

The three chapters in this part are concerned with the study of social movements. Chapter 8 by Craig Calhoun looks at the issue of the novelty of "new" social movements, a widely debated topic in sociology in the past two decades. The historical understanding he develops has important implications for how we see movements, such as the civil rights movement, the women's movement, the environmental movement, the lesbian and gay movement, and others that emerged in the 1960s, in relation to what was assumed to be *the* social movement of modernity: the working-class labor movement. In chapter 9, Mario Diani discusses recent work on social movements, comparing the different traditions of study to arrive at an understanding of how they differ from other forms of collective action. Finally, in an extract from his book *Power in Movement*, Sidney Tarrow (chapter 10) looks at social movement activity in relation to globalization, considering how it might develop on the basis of changes that are already underway.

In chapter 8, Calhoun carefully investigates historical studies of social movements of the early nineteenth century, tracing their similarities to those movements which erupted on to the scene in the 1960s. Sociologists in the 1960s and 1970s tended to see social movements as an entirely new phenomenon, exhibiting a number of features which made them quite different from previous political groups and organizations. In fact, it was the labor movement, with its organized trade unions and political parties, which was taken to be the norm and which was, explicitly or implicitly, seen as the "old" social movement. Calhoun argues that sociologists were mistaken in this belief. He does so by comparing social movements in the early nineteenth and late twentieth century in terms of a number of features which sociologists have thought set new social movements apart. It was supposed that new social movements were different from the labor movement in the following ways: that they made limited but non-negotiable demands, rather than attempting to revolutionize society completely; that they engaged in the politicization of everyday life (in civil society) rather than addressing grievances to the state; that they did not mobilize along class lines; that they were organized in non-hierarchical and democratic ways intended to prefigure the social conditions that they sought to bring about; that they engaged in novel political tactics rather than going through conventional parliamentary channels; that they were not united by a single over-arching organization. In each case, Calhoun shows that the labor movement in the early nineteenth century was actually much more like the "new" social movements than has been supposed, while many other movements of the nineteenth century, including the women's, religious, and nationalist movements, also shared many of these features and were much more important than has generally been recognized.

Calhoun uses history to excellent effect to refine sociological understanding of social movements. However, his argument has wider consequences for sociological theory. Calhoun argues that it is no coincidence that social movements were overlooked for so long; their neglect is an example of sociology's bias in favor of studying rational, instrumental action. In so far as social movements other than the labor movement were studied before the 1960s, by functionalist sociologists, they tended to be seen as deviant, irrational responses to the strains of modern life. Resource Mobilization theorists, who began the study of social movements from a more sympathetic point of view in the 1970s, reacted to this approach by resolutely applying theories of rational choice to their activities. As Calhoun sees it, it was only with the development of New Social Movement theory that the cultural and aesthetic aspects of social movements began to be taken seriously. The formation of shifting collective identities and the importance of lifestyle choices to social movements began to be seen as objects of study for the first time. Calhoun's argument has a wider importance, therefore, in suggesting that sociologists should put culture at the center of their analyses, acknowledging the plurality of social movements and displacing what was previously taken to be *the* progressive movement of modernity, the working-class labor movement, as simply one among many.

Diani, in chapter 9, is more explicitly concerned with different theories of social movements that developed from the 1970s. He argues that there have been four main approaches: collective behavior, Resource Mobilization theory, the "political process" approach, and New Social Movement theory. The first is relatively little used now, while the second and third are often combined. They have been dominant in US sociology, while the fourth has come from Europe. Resource Mobilization theory and the "political process" approach have focused on social movement organizations and political opportunities offered by the state which affect social movement activities. New Social Movement theorists, on the other hand, tend to use the term "social movement" only to refer to those movements which do not engage in politics at the level of the state, but which contest cultural conflicts in civil society. Until recently, theories of social movements were seen as divided between these two, very different, traditions. Diani argues, however, that, as a result of conceptual and empirical work on both sides, they now have a good deal in common. Comparing the different approaches in an attempt to define what makes social movements different from other forms of collective action, including interest groups, political parties, and religious sects, Diani argues that they converge on a number of points.

First, social movements are seen as based on networks of informal interaction between organizations, groups, and individuals. A single organization is not a social movement; nor is a single protest event. Secondly, all approaches now see the construction of collective identity as an important aspect of social movement activity. Social movements are not united by rationally perceived interests; members are engaged in developing shared understandings of the world and who they are in relation to others. It is the recognition of the importance of collective identity on the part of all major social movement theorists which has done most to bring the different approaches together. It was always central to New Social Movement theory, but it has now been developed in the US-based tradition through the adoption of Goffman's concept of "framing." "Framing" involves the simplification of the world by coding it into readily grasped situations and experiences which enable us to make sense of it. Social movements frame events in such a way as to construct a collective identity for their members. Thirdly, social movements engage in collective action in social conflicts with other actors, including institutions and counter-movements. Those persuaded by Resource Mobilization theory and the "political process" approach continue to emphasize the importance of political conflicts at the level of the state, in comparison with those more influenced by New Social Movement theory who see cultural conflicts as most significant. However, Diani argues that this difference is not fundamental.

In chapter 10, Tarrow looks at transnational social movements from a "political process" perspective. He sees domestic social movements as engaged in contentious politics with elites in nation-states. *Transnational* social movements, on the other hand, engage with opponents – national or non-national – by organizing across national boundaries. Tarrow investigates the reasons put forward by sociologists and political scientists for the growth of transnational social movements:

increased speed in global communications; the weakening of states as a result of globalization; increased access to global resources on the part of social movements; the integration of international norms into domestic life (see chapter 13); the growth of international organizations and institutions (see chapter 16). However, Tarrow is skeptical about the immediate prospects of a flourishing global civil society in which transnational social movements would play an important part. Historically, there has long been a transnational dimension to many movements, including the labor movement, the women's movement, and the anti-slavery movement in the niñeteenth century; and there are currently some which may genuinely be described as transnational, such as Islamic fundamentalism, for example. Tarrow argues, however, that many transnational activities which are analyzed as exemplary of social movements are better seen in other ways.

To this end he discusses the cases of cross-border diffusion and transnational political exchange, arguing that these involve insufficiently integrated transnational networks in the first case and short-lived or episodic action in the second. Such activities are more significant, he suggests, for the construction of national social movements than for lasting transnational links across national borders. Tarrow also rejects the transnational advocacy networks of non-governmental organizations, often held to be the principal support for a global civil society, as candidates for the title of transnational social movement. He argues that they should be seen as networks rather than movements since they do not involve the same degree of collective solidarity, close interpersonal relations, and exposure to similar political opportunities that characterize domestic social movements. They are, however, closely linked to national social movements in that social movement activists often become involved in transnational advocacy networks; they may provide opportunities for resource-poor domestic movements; and they sometimes contribute to their growth. While Tarrow insists that transnational social movements are not yet a significant feature of global politics, he remains open to the possibility that globalization may be bringing about the conditions in which their growth becomes much more likely. In the final section of chapter 10, he poses a number of questions concerning the changes underway, inviting the reader to consider for themselves whether this is a real possibility.

CHAPTER 8

"New Social Movements" of the Early Nineteenth Century

Craig Calhoun

Sometime after 1968, analysts and participants began to speak of "new social movements" that worked outside formal institutional channels and emphasized lifestyle, ethical, or "identity" concerns rather than narrowly economic goals. A variety of examples informed the conceptualization. Alberto Melucci (1988: 247), for instance, cited feminism, the ecology movement or "greens," the peace movement, and the youth movement. Others added the gay movement, the animal rights movement, and the antiabortion and prochoice movements. These movements were allegedly new in issues, tactics, and constituencies. Above all, they were new by contrast to the labor movement, which was the paradigmatic "old" social movement, and to Marxism and socialism, which asserted that class was the central issue in politics and that a single political economic transformation would solve the whole range of social ills. They were new even by comparison with conventional liberalism with its assumption of fixed individual identities and interests. The new social movements thus challenged the conventional division of politics into left and right and broadened the definition of politics to include issues that had been considered outside the domain of political action (Scott, 1990).

These new social movements (NSMs) grew partly from the New Left and related student movements of the 1960s. The conceptualization of their novelty was part of the movements themselves as well as

This chapter is an edited extract from Craig Calhoun, "'New social movements' of the early nineteenth century," *Social Science History*, 17: 3 (Fall 1993), pp. 385–428. Copyright 1993, Duke University Press. All rights reserved. Reprinted with permission.

of the academic analyses that (primarily in Europe) took debate on these movements as an occasion to reform or reject Marxist theory and social democratic politics. The emphasis on novelty was extended to claims of epochal change when the NSMs were taken as signs of postindustrial or postmodern society. In this [chapter], however, I argue that the historical claim implicit in the idea of *new* social movements (as in the ideas of *post*modernism and *post*industrialism) is specious. I explore the major distinguishing characteristics attributed to NSMs in the recent literature and show that these fit very well the many movements that flourished in the late eighteenth and especially early nineteenth centuries. My point is not just negative, however; I do not suggest that we abandon the notion that NSMs are distinctive to the late twentieth century.

Abandoning the false historical claim enables us to understand better the whole modern history of social movements. This is so in three senses. First, as Tarrow (1989) has suggested, many of the characteristics described in the flourishing movements of the 1960s and after may stem from the newness of each movement rather than from novel features of the whole wave of movements. In other words, all movements in their nascent period – including the labor movement and social democracy – tend to fit certain aspects of the NSM model. Second, we are better prepared to analyze all social movements if we pay attention to the inherent plurality of their forms, contents, social bases, and meaning to participants and do not attempt to grasp them in terms of a single model defined by labor or revolutionary movements, or a single set of instrumental questions about mobilization. Within any historical period, at least in the modern era, we can identify a whole field of social movements shaped by their relationships to each other and appealing to different, though overlapping, potential participants. Of the various movements in such a field, we can fruitfully ask the kinds of questions pioneered by new social movement theory – about identity politics, the possibility of thinking of movements as ends in themselves, and so forth – and not just those of resource mobilization or Marxism. Third, if we abandon both the developmentalism that treats early nineteenth-century movements as either precursors to the later consolidation of labor and socialism or else as historical sidetracks, and the opposite refusal to look for macrohistorical patterns, we can begin to explore what factors determine whether (in specific settings) periods are characterized by proliferation or consolidation or expansion or contraction in the social movement field as a whole.

[. . .]

The key point is that it is misleading to compartmentalize religious movements, for example, apart from more stereotypically social or political ones. Religious movements may have political and economic agendas – particularly when politics is not seen as exclusively a matter of relations to the state. More basically, as E. P. Thompson (1968) showed clearly, religious and labor movements can influence each other, compete for adherents, and complemented each other in the lives of some participants; in short, they can be part of the same social movement field. Part of the problem is that much of the traditional analysis of social movements (and collective action more generally) has ignored or explicitly set aside questions of culture or the interpretation of meaning. This tends to deflect attention away from those movements concerned largely with values, norms, language, identities, and collective understandings – including those of movement participants themselves – and toward those that focus instrumentally on changing political or economic institutions. Social movement analysts have also often avoided addressing emotions, perhaps for fear of association with discredited accounts of mass psychology. For present purposes, it is better to see social movements as including all attempts to influence patterns of culture, social action, and relationships in ways that depend on the participation of large numbers of people in concerted and self-organized (as distinct from state-directed or institutionally mandated) collective action.

Both the wide range of recent social movements and the literature labeling them NSMs encourage such a broader view. Rather than dismissing NSM theory because of its historical misrepresentation, we should see the importance of the issues it raises for understanding social movements generally. "Identity politics" and similar concerns were never quite so much absent from the field of social movement activity – even in the heydays of liberal party politics or organized trade union struggle – as they were obscured from conventional academic observation. Particularly after 1848, just as socialism became more "scientific," so social scientists lost sight of the traditions of direct action, fluid and shifting collective identities, and communitarian and other attempts to overcome the means/ends division of more instrumental movement organization (Calhoun, 1989). The secularism of academics particularly and post-Enlightenment intellectuals generally may have made collective action based on religious and other more spiritual orientations appear of a different order from the "real" social movement of trade-union-based socialism or from liberal democracy. Nationalism was often treated as a regressive deviation rather than a modern form of social movement and identity formation. Early feminism attracted relatively little scholarly attention until later feminism prompted its rediscovery.

In short, one kind of movement – formally organized, instrumental action aimed at economic or institutionally political goals – was relatively new and ascendant through much of the late nineteenth and the twentieth centuries and has often been misidentified as simply a progressive tendency, the rational future of politics, or even insurgent politics. This pattern was particularly pronounced in Europe during the ascendancy of labor and social democracy, and it is what made America look exceptional. But nowhere were movement politics ever limited to this form. While America had relatively weak trade unions and socialist politics, it nurtured a relatively strong and open proliferation of the other sort of social movement, new social movements. This has been true throughout American history, and it is very marked in the early nineteenth-century period on which this [chapter] focuses. The flowering of movements in this period was, however, international (as I will illustrate with brief examples from France and Britain). Indeed, the social movement field of the early nineteenth century was inherently international, linking participants in different countries not only by communications but by a pattern of migration in which people literally moved from one country to another without leaving their movement contexts. Remember Marx's ties to German radicals in London and his writing for their newspaper in New York and recall the émigré intellectual ferment of Paris between 1830 and 1848 (Kramer, 1988). Migration to America – to join a socialist commune or to establish a religious community, for example – was a prominent feature of the era and often tied to movement participation. We have only to recall the travels of Tom Paine, however, to remind ourselves that the Atlantic crossing could be reversed.

[. . .]

DEFINING CHARACTERISTICS OF NEW SOCIAL MOVEMENTS

Throughout the early nineteenth century, communitarianism, temperance, and various dietary and lifestyle movements attracted hundreds of thousands of adherents in both Europe and America. Religious awakening, revitalization, and proliferation were major themes, as were anticlericalism and freethinking. Antislavery or abolitionist movements were often closely linked to religion but were autonomous from any particular religious organizations. Popular education was the object of struggle, with early success in America. Even after mid-century, the divergence between Europe and America should not be exaggerated. The nationalist discourse of the (northern) Union before and after the Civil War – including even "manifest destiny" – was not altogether different from the nationalist discourse of Giuseppe Mazzini and Young Europe or of Giuseppe Garibaldi. Nativism was recurrent throughout the nineteenth century, from the Know-Nothings through populism, and the racial, ethnic, and religious hostilities taken to an extreme by the Ku Klux Klan were not altogether different from the xenophobic side of nationalism. Ethnic and nationalist movements, moreover, were never as fully suppressed by class as Melucci (1989: 89–92) suggests but have ebbed and flowed throughout modernity. Women's and temperance movements renewed mobilizations dating from the eighteenth century.

The early nineteenth century was fertile ground for social movements as perhaps no other period was until the 1960s.[1] Indeed, direct ancestors of several of the movements that sparked the new social movement conceptualization in the 1960s and 1970s were part of the early nineteenth-century efflorescence. In the early nineteenth century too, the labor movement itself was a new social movement and not clearly first among equals, let alone hegemonic; the idea that a class-based movement might claim to be all encompassing was not widespread. If we ignore the claim that they apply distinctively to the late twentieth century, the core ideas of NSM theory offer a useful lens for looking at early nineteenth-century social movements. Specifically, I turn now to a list of the most widely cited distinguishing features of late twentieth-century NSMs.[2] Relying for the most part on brief examples, I show that each was a prominent concern or feature of early nineteenth-century social movements.

Identity, autonomy and self-realization

Compared with the largely instrumental and economistic goals of both the institutionalized labor movement and the European social democratic parties, NSMs have been crucially focused on "identity politics" (Aronowitz, 1992). Many of these movements themselves, however, have roots in the late eighteenth and early nineteenth centuries: modern feminist ideology is often traced to Mary Wollstonecraft, and the broader women's movement to the substantial concern with sexual equality and redefinition of gender in Owenite socialism (Taylor, 1983) and to the disproportionate participation of women in abolitionist, temperance, and other "moral crusades" of the early nineteenth century.

The tracing of roots, however, is not necessarily the identification of a linear, unidirectional process of development. Claiming an autonomous identity and a moral voice for women often took a different form in the early nineteenth century than in succeeding years. Indeed, Rendall has argued that the very assumptions of twentieth-century feminists about equality make it hard "to understand that the assertion of an 'equality in difference' could mean a radical step forward . . . Stress on the latent moral superiority of women could bring with it the basis

for a new confidence, a new energy, a new assertion of women's potential power" (1985a: 3). This is more easily recognized in the frame of
reference established by the NSMs (and much recent poststructuralist
and feminist theory) than in that of the classical liberalism or universalism informing the assumptions to which Rendall refers. The words
of the Owenite Catherine Barmby, "Woman and man are two in variety
and one in equality" (quoted in Rendall 1985b: 308), no longer sound
so unfamiliar. Early nineteenth-century women argued from a claim to
morally – and publicly – relevant difference not again so clearly formulated until the final quarter of the twentieth century. "As it is the
Divine Will that the two sexes *together* shall constitute humanity, so I
believe it to be the Divine intention that the influence and exertion of
the two sexes *combined* shall be necessary to the complete success of
any human institution, or any branch of such institution" (Agnes Davis
Pochin 1855, quoted in Rendall 1985b: 312). Not only was there a
claim that the different qualities of men and women were complementary (as the broader culture also asserted, though with more bias); there
was a claim to moral authority grounded within the domestic sphere,
which was in the early nineteenth century becoming increasingly
separated from the public sphere. "Within that primarily domestic
world, women could and did create a culture which was not entirely an
imposed one, which contained within it the possibilities of assertion
. . . That assertion could become the assertion of autonomy" (Rendall
1985a: 3). The very claim to distinct and possibly autonomous identity
in the domestic sphere ironically became the basis for public claims. As
Mary Ryan (1990, 1992) has shown, from 1830 to 1860 there was a
rapid increase in the public life of the American citizenry. This was not
just a matter of one public growing more active, but of a proliferation
of multiple publics. Some of these were autonomously female and constituted themselves in terms of distinct claims to identity not altogether
unrelated to those by which the male-dominated public spheres sought
to exclude women.

Not only was moral authority claimed for distinctive female identities; gender relations were directly a focus of concern. By no means
all of the social movements of the early nineteenth century oriented
their action to the public sphere, and still less to organized politics.
Withdrawal from mainstream society in order to reconstitute human
relations was a central theme of the communitarian movements of the
era and of the often millenarian religious movements with which they
sometimes overlapped (see below). Robert Owen's communitarian
vision may have turned on a Lockean vision of essential human sameness and malleability, but this was certainly not so for Charles Fourier's
notion of phalansteries composed of 1,620 individuals in order to

represent all possible combinations of the essential and distinctive passions of each sex. Gender relations were also an important concern of the New England transcendentalists, innovatively treated as a social movement by Anne Rose. "Alienated by a culture built of fear," she writes, "the Transcendentalists took steps to establish social relations allowing freedom, growth, justice, and love" (1981: 93). Communitarian experiments like Brook Farm were designed simultaneously to foster individual self-fulfillment and equitable, nurturant social relationships.

In a very different vein, what was the focus of early nineteenth-century nationalism if not identity? "Nations are individualities with particular talents," wrote Fichte (quoted by Meinecke, 1970: 89). At least through the 'springtime of nations" that collided with the mid-century crisis, nationalism was conceived substantially as a liberal and inclusive doctrine, not as the reactionary, exclusionary one it would in many cases become. This "nationalist internationalism" (Walicki, 1982) of figures like Mazzini maintained that all true nationalities had rights to autonomous self-expression and indeed cast itself as the defender of liberty against empire (a theme that has never entirely disappeared). Not unlike more recent movements that focused on the legitimation of identities, nationalism grew in part because of the rise of the modern state and the ideology of rights that became a crucial part of its legitimation apparatus and a continual opening for new claims. Nationality, despite nationalism's own ideology, was never simply a given identity, inherited unproblematically from the past, but always a construction and a claim within a field of identities. Not only did nationalist movements claim autonomy for specific peoples against others (for example, for Hungarians against the Austrian-dominated empire, or briefly for Texans against both Mexico and the United States) they also claimed a primacy for national identity over class, region, dialect, gender, and other subsidiary identities.

Last but not least in this connection, we need to recognize how profoundly early workers' movements were engaged in a politics of identity. Marx and numerous activists offered the claim that the common identity of *worker* should take primacy over a diversity of craft, region, ethnic, and other identities. Yet this strong version of the claim to working-class identity was seldom if ever realized, and certainly not in the early nineteenth century. What were achieved were more mediated versions of working-class solidarity in which primary identification with a craft or local group became the means of forging a discourse or movement based on national (or international) class identities. This mediated understanding of class membership is quite different from the categorical Marxist notion of individuals equivalently constituted as members of the working class. Yet it is the fluidity of possible workers' identities that stands out in the historiography of the early nineteenth century.

Defense rather than offense

The "old social movement" was utopian and sought to remake the whole of society through overcoming existing relations of domination and exploitation, theorists claim. NSMs, in contrast, defend specific spheres of life; their demands are more limited in scope but are also less negotiable. Here NSM theory points valuably to the importance of the defense of specific lifeworlds and its link to nonnegotiable demands, but through a sharply misleading historical opposition.

The underlying idea is that socialism was a comprehensive utopian project. [. . .] New social movements arose out of this "exhaustion of utopian energies" and embodied a too-often neoconservative focus on defense of endangered ways of life (Habermas, 1990: ch. 2). But this seems exactly backward. The labor movement has been as defensive in much of its struggle as any NSM and has hardly always been committed to a thorough restructuring of society. For most of its history the traditional left was normally suspicious of utopian energies, though these occasionally erupted anyway. The "traditional left," indeed, was formed in the consolidation and institutionalization of a "post-utopian" movement in the late nineteenth century; this replaced the earlier efflorescence of more utopian movements and earned the appellation *traditional* by resisting the challenge of new movements not just in the 1960s but in the early twentieth century and recurrently. Indeed, much of the new left (like the NSMs more generally) can be understood as an attempt to recover the utopian energies of the early nineteenth century.[3] Rooted in the attachments of everyday life and specific communities, these movements were often radical and even utopian in what they sought.

[. . .]

Just as the common saying suggests that "the best defense is a good offense," so it is hard to distinguish defensive from offensive moments in the nineteenth-century communal movement. Indeed, these often appear as two sides of the same utopian ideology. Utopian visions were often rooted in (or derived part of their appeal from) religious traditions and/or images of the recently vanished golden age of craftsmen and small farmers. At the same time, they stood in tension or confrontation with many of the tendencies and characteristics of contemporary society. The line was not sharply drawn between withdrawing from this world to prepare for the next or to protect a purer life, and withdrawing in order to constitute an example that might transform social relations more generally. It is important to see the ways in which early nineteenth-century social movements were rooted in problems and attachments of everyday life and the defense of valued ways of life; it is crucial not to imagine that this made them intrinsically conservative or deprived them of utopian energies. Roots made many movements radical, even when they did not offer comprehensive plans for societal restructuring.

Politicization of everyday life

Central to the importance of identity politics and defensive orientations is the argument that NSMs are distinctive in politicizing everyday life rather than focusing on the large-scale systems of state and economy. Where the postwar consensus consecrated overall economic growth, distributive gains, and various forms of legal protections as the basic social issues that the political process was to address (Offe, 1985: 824), the NSMs brought forward a variety of other issues grounded in aspects of personal or everyday life: sexuality, abuse of women, student rights, protection of the environment.

[. . .]

Compared with the postwar consensus, a politicization of everyday life certainly began in the 1960s, but this was not a reversal of long-standing consensus about the proper boundaries of the political. On the contrary, the modern era is shaped by a certain oscillation between politicization and depoliticization of everyday life. In the late nineteenth and early twentieth centuries, as well as in the early nineteenth century, social movements brought a range of new phenomena into the public (if not always the political) realm. Indeed, the early labor movements themselves aimed crucially to politicize aspects of everyday life formerly (and by their opponents) not considered properly political. Temperance, abolitionism, campaigns for popular education, and perhaps above all early women's movements sought public recognition or action with regard to grievances their detractors considered clearly outside the realm of legitimate state action (Evans and Boyte, 1986: ch. 3). They were moral crusades in almost exactly the same way as the NSMs are in Klaus Eder's (1985) description. For parts of the women's movement this was sometimes a source of contradiction: women had to protest in public and thereby politicize the issue of protecting the female sphere of the private household (Rendall, 1985a; see also Ryan, 1992). The contradictions have reappeared in the current period, as, for example, when Phyllis Schlafley simultaneously maintained that a woman's proper (and ideally protected) place is in the home but suggested that she herself ought to be appointed to the Supreme Court. In the case of women's movements, the struggle to politicize aspects of everyday life – and the contradictions around it – continued right through the nineteenth and early twentieth centuries. It recurred also in the temperance/prohibition and civil rights movements. The latter, indeed, is almost a quintessential case, with the proprietors of segregated restaurants, for example, arguing that their decisions about whom to serve were purely private matters, beyond the legitimate reach of the state.

[. . .]

Non-class or middle-class mobilization

A central link between NSM theory and the notion of a postindustrial or postmodern society is the idea that political economic identities have lost their salience and are being replaced by a mixture of ascriptive identities (like race or gender) and personally chosen or expressive identities (like sexual orientation or identification with various lifestyle communities). NSMs, accordingly, neither appeal to nor mobilize predominantly on class lines.

[. . .]

If class bases were ever central determinants of mobilization patterns, it was in late nineteenth- and early twentieth-century Europe. Before that, class was seldom the self-applied label or the basis even of workers' mobilization. Was Chartism strictly a class movement? Though its ideology increasingly focused on class, its demands included issues with appeal to most of the range of people excluded from suffrage and effective citizenship rights in early nineteenth-century Britain (Jones, 1984; Thompson, 1986). Indeed, its admixture of members of the industrial working class with artisans, outworkers, and other presaged the fault lines of its eventual demise. Similarly, it has been shown fairly conclusively that class-based analyses fail to explain who manned and who attacked barricades in Paris in 1848 (Traugott, 1985). Even more basically, it has been argued that republicanism was the central ideological focus of the early nineteenth-century struggles in France and that class bases mattered mainly as the underpinnings of different visions of the republic (Aminzade, 1993). The point is not that class was irrelevant but that the early nineteenth-century struggles most often taken as paradigmatic of class-based political movements – Chartism, the revolution of 1848 – were political movements internally differentiated by the appeal of their ideology to different groups of workers, shopkeepers, and others.

In America, too, republicanism was a central rhetoric of political and even economic struggle. In his study of Cincinnati workers, Ross (1985) sees an effort to forge and preserve a "republican world" only giving way to an alternative, more economically and class based form of struggles in the 1840s. This was only partly because Cincinnati was more egalitarian and socially integrated than East Coast cities. Wilentz's study of New York also shows the centrality of republican visions into the 1820s. Even after the crucial shifts of 1828–29, the Working Men's movement involved an attempt to push Jacksonian democracy further than the well-connected attorney's and party functionaries of Tammany Hall. The new radicals were shaped by old Adamsite political visions and by new social movements like Owenite socialism and a mixture of feminism, deism, and Jacobinism brought forward by Frances Wright (Wilentz, 1984: ch. 5). These radicals were journeyman artisans and small master mechanics but also disaffected elites; their appeals were as apt to be agrarian as focused on the transformation of urban classes. In the words of Thomas Skidmore, the program was to end social oppression and political force "till there shall be no lenders, no borrowers; no landlords, no tenants; no masters, no journeymen; no Wealth, no Want" (quoted in Wilentz, 1984: 187). This was a vision that would appeal less, no doubt, to elites than to those they oppressed or exploited, but it was not a vision narrowly focused on any specific class (see Evans and Boyte, 1986: ch. 4).

The communitarian visions that predominated in the movements of the era generally minimized class divisions. They offered a new kind of social relations – egalitarian and cooperative – to replace the old; they expected the beneficiaries of the old system to resist most, but they argued that the benefit of the new order would flow to everyone. Class variation figured as a source of variable discontent and interest; class-specific patterns of association (working together, living in the same neighborhoods, intermarrying) led to mobilization partly on class lines, but this did not make these class movements. This was, after all, precisely the complaint of Marx and Engels about Owenism; they could praise its communitarianism (particularly where family was concerned) but had to attack its neglect – or denial – of class struggle (see, for example, 1976 [1848]: pt. 3).

[. . .]

Self-exemplification

One of the most striking features of the paradigmatic NSMs has been their insistence that the organizational forms and styles of movement practice must exemplify the values the movement seeks to promulgate. This means, at the same time, that the movements are ends in themselves. Relatedly, many NSMs are committed to direct democracy and a nonhierarchical structure, substantially lacking in role differentiation, and resistant to involvement of professional movement staff.

Many versions of the modern women's movement thus eschew complete identification with instrumental goals – changing legislation, achieving equal job opportunity, and other concerns. They focus also on constructing the movement itself as a nurturant, protected space for women. The emphasis on self-exemplification and noninstrumentality is indeed a contrast to much of the history of the organized labor movement. Many socialist and especially communist parties have institutionalized internal hierarchies and decision-making structures deeply at odds with their professed pursuit of nonhierarchical, nonoppressive social arrangements. But what could be a better example of making a "work-object" (in Melucci's 1989 phrase) of a social movement's own organizational forms than the communal movement(s) of the 1840s? Charles Lane, influenced by Fourier, was a veteran of several communal experiments from the anarchist Fruitlands to the Shakers; he praised celibacy and like values in 1843:

> The human beings in whom the Eternal Spirit has ascended from low animal delights or mere human affections, to a state of spiritual chastity and intuition, are in themselves a divine atmosphere, they *are* superior circumstances, and are constant in endeavoring to create, as well as to modify, all other conditions, so that these also shall more and more conduce to the like consciousness in others. Hence our perseverance in efforts to attain simplicity in diet, plain garments, pure bathing, unsullied dwellings, open conduct, gentle behavior, kindly sympathies, serene minds. These and several other particulars needful to the true end of man's residence on earth, may be designated Family Life ... The Family, in its highest, divinest sense, is therefore our true position, our sacred earthly destiny. (quoted by Rose, 1981: 201)

End and means are very much the same.

Communal groups were not an isolated aspect of early nineteenth-century society; they were closely linked to prominent religious currents, leading philosophies, and the working-class movement. They were, nonetheless, distinctive in the extremes to which they took antihierarchical ideology. Most other movements of the period admitted of clearer leadership structures. Still, direct democracy was a regulative norm for many, including several branches of the workers' movement, radical republicans, and socialists. Marx himself joined in the advocacy of immediate rights of recall over legislators who voted against the wishes of their constituents – a key issue in the relations of the 1848 Paris political clubs to the assembly (Amann, 1975) – and proposed limited terms and other measures designed to minimize the development of a leadership too autonomous from the masses.

Unconventional means

New social movements depart from conventional parliamentary and electoral politics, taking recourse to direct action and novel tactics. As Tarrow (1989) has remarked, however, this description confuses two senses of *new*: the characteristics of all movements when they are new, and the characteristics of a putatively new sort of movement.

It is indeed generally true that any movement of or on behalf of those excluded from conventional politics starts out with a need to attract attention; movement activity is not just an instrumental attempt to achieve movement goals, but a means of recruitment and continuing mobilization of participants. Each new movement may also experiment with new ways to outwit authorities either in getting its message across or in causing enough disruption to extract concessions or gain power. In this way, each movement may add to a repertoire of collective action (in Tilly's 1978 phrase) that is available to subsequent movements.

In another sense, *unconventional* is defined not by novelty *per se* but by movement outside the normal routines of politics. All forms of direct action thus are unconventional, even when – like barricade fighting in Paris – they have 200 years of tradition behind them. What defines unconventional action in the political realm is mainly the attempt to circumvent the routines of elections and lobbying, whether by marching on Washington, occupying an office, or bombing the prime minister's residence. Unconventional means in this sense are particularly likely in a movement of people who have few resources other than their public actions. One of the key developments of late nineteenth- and early twentieth-century democratic politics in Europe and societies of European settlement was the institutionalization of strong norms of conventional politics, organized primarily through political parties. This drew more than one branch of the socialist movement into the orbit of conventional politics.

Direct action was, by contrast, central to the social movements of the early to mid-nineteenth century. Revolution still seemed to be a possibility in most European countries, which gave an added punch to all forms of public protest and threatened real civil disturbance. In the French revolution of 1848, the predominant radical factions espoused a red republicanism that traced its ancestry to the 1789 revolution and called on the direct action of the people as its main means. Pierre-Joseph Proudhon was the theorist of this politics, and its defeat in 1848 helped to discredit it in academic circles. Though partially sidelined, it hardly ceased to move activists, however, as the subsequent histories of syndicalism and anarchism reveal. With Georges-Eugène Sorel as a bridging theorist, this tradition of direct action also influenced fascism (Calhoun, 1988). Without comparably revolutionary aims, a variety of early (and later) labor activists chose direct action both to dramatiz and immediately to achieve their ends. The Luddites of early nineteenth-century England are only the most famous. Of course, restrictions on the franchise denied most of them access to the parliamentary system.

If Luddites made a virtue of necessity by direct action, Owenite socialism – and utopian socialists and communitarians generally – rejected conventional politics on principle. E. P. Thompson complains that "Owen simply had a vacant place in his mind where most men have political responses" (1968: 786). This may be, and it is also true that Robert Owen identified with elites and was not shy about approaching those in political power and trying to persuade them of the merits of his social system. Nonetheless, many of his followers had deep convictions against organizing for the pursuit of political power or the disruption of the political system. They attempted to teach by example and exposition and tried to create their own self-organizing sphere of life (Harrison, 1969). The recurrent half-aesthetic, half-political romantic movements from Blake and Shelley to Ruskin, Morris, and the arts and crafts movement similarly disdained conventional politics and were determined to carry on their work outside that tawdry sphere. Henry David Thoreau's advocacy of civil disobedience typified the emphasis on purity of conscience. His celebrated essay on the subject stemmed from his individual opposition to the draft, but the theme of direct action by the morally responsible individual tied together Thoreau's retreat to Walden and early effort to teach by striking example and his later more manifestly political and even violent common cause with John Brown (McWilliams, 1973: 290–300).

Purity and freedom from corruption were not the only reasons for direct action. At least as important was the sense that organized politics and public discourse were resistant or too slow to respond. Sheer practical expedient led abolitionists to provide material assistance to runaway slaves, for example. While most early protemperance ministers stuck to lectures and essay contests, a direct action wing eventually took to saloon smashing (Rorabaugh 1979). In both cases, tensions between advocates of direct action (who also generally demanded a more complete abolition or abstinence) and adherents of more conventional politics helped to split the movements. In both cases also, the disproportionate and publicly prominent participation of women was in itself an unconventional means of action (as was even more true of women's suffrage campaigns).

Partial and overlapping commitments

The claim of old social movements – the labor and socialist movements – was to be able, at least potentially, to handle all the public needs of their constituents. It was not necessary to belong to a variety of special issue groups, for example, if one belonged to a trade union and, either through it or directly, to the labor party. One might struggle within a social democratic party, or within a union, to see that one's specific interests were well attended to, but one made a primary commitment to that organization or at least that movement. The NSMs, by contrast, do not make the same claims on their members or offer the same potential to resolve a range of issues at once. They are not political parties or other organizations that accept the charge of prioritizing the range of issues that compete for public attention. They are affinity groups knit together not by superordinate logic but by a web of overlapping memberships, rather like the crosscutting social circles Georg Simmel (1903) thought essential to modern identity and social organization. One may thus combine feminism with pacifism and not be much moved by environmental concerns, and no organization will divert one's feminist and pacifist dollars or envelope licking to environmentalist uses. This is described sometimes as a consumerist orientation to political involvement, with a variety of movement products to choose from. The various movements are knit together into a field but not a superordinate umbrella organization.

So it was in the early nineteenth century: temperance, nationalism, craft struggle, communitarianism, abolitionism, free-thinking, and camp-meeting religion coexisted and sometimes shared adherents without ever joining under a common umbrella. Neither socialism nor liberalism were hegemonic movements before mid-century. Educational reform perhaps came close to being a common denominator in the early American movements (Walters, 1978: 210), but it linked others rather than encompassing them.

Though there was no overall umbrella, early nineteenth-century movements nonetheless combined to create a field of activity. Movement activists were joined into networks that crisscrossed specific movements, and the broader public recognized that there were many possible movements to consider. Sometimes these movements demanded near total devotion (as did, for example, most communal settlements, at least while one remained resident in the commune). On the other hand, multiple membership, either simultaneous or serial, was common. It has been argued, for example, that modern feminism was born from the activism of women in abolition and temperance movements. In the former case, the very large number of female activists were marginalized; women like Elizabeth Cady Stanton and Lucretia Mott were denied voting status and were relegated to a curtained balcony at the World Anti-Slavery Convention of 1840. After the Civil War, women made the temperance movement their own and gained experience that would translate crucially into suffrage campaigns (Evans and Boyte, 1986:

80–95). Similarly, the Second Great Awakening helped to spark the militant abolitionist movement, transcendentalists were influenced by other communalists (and antagonistic to evangelicals), feminists were drawn to several of the communitarian groups, some Chartists promoted temperance, and Wesleyan preachers found occasions to preach something like what would later be called the social gospel far too often for the comfort of the church hierarchy and sometimes wound up as trade-union leaders.

Sometimes the personal networks of movement activists quickly expanded to touch a range of others. Consider Mary Wollstonecraft (the pioneering feminist) and William Godwin (the anarchist political philosopher). Godwin claimed credit for "converting" Robert Owen from factory management to the task of developing his social system; they met on numerous occasions. The daughter of Wollstonecraft and Godwin, Mary, eloped with Percy Bysshe Shelley (a fan of her father's) and, while living with him and Lord Byron, wrote the story of Dr Frankenstein's monster. Byron of course died during his Romantic flirtation with Greek nationalism. Feminism, Owenite socialism, anarchism, nationalism, and Romanticism were thus linked in an intimate network.

The connections were not just intimate, though, but included public events and opportunities for those less involved to enter the movement field, learn its discourse, and choose among its protagonists. In April 1829, for example, in the midst of the Second Great Awakening, Robert Owen, the genius of New Lanark, journeyed to Cincinnati, Ohio, to debate [with] a prominent evangelical clergyman, Alexander Campbell of Bethany, Virginia. The focus of the debate was on religion, with Owen out to demonstrate the superiority of rational unbelief and Campbell taking equally rationalist grounds to argue the merits of biblical Christianity [Owen and Campbell, 1829]. Interestingly, Owen was pushed to defend his doctrine of environmental determination against attacks by Campbell, who saw free will as essential to Christianity (a theme that was contradictory to predestination and that would become central to the evangelical upsurge of two years later). Thousands of people attended the eight days of lengthy and abstruse debate, shopping among millennial visions. [. . .]

[. . .]

This debate was a major event in its day, attracting widespread attention. A transcript (taken down in stenography by a former resident of New Harmony be then drawn to Christianity) was published with both debaters' approval and sold widely. Yet the event is hardly mentioned in accounts of either Owenite or Campbellite movements (nor in Ross's 1985 history of Cincinnati workers). It is as though later ideas about the relationship between socialism and religion, particularly evangelical protestant religion, have rendered the connection invisible by placing the two movements in separate fields. One figures as a precursor to modern socialism, the other to a mainline protestant sect and less directly to Mormonism. What could be more different? Yet, in the early nineteenth century, especially in America, such new social movements were not only numerous but occupied a vital common space and were often linked.

WHY DID NEW SOCIAL MOVEMENTS HAVE TO BE REDISCOVERED?

In both early nineteenth- and late twentieth-century America and Europe a lively range of social movements emerged, different in form, content, social bases, and meaning to their participants. These were linked in social movement fields of considerable similarity. The similarities go beyond those noted above through the lens of new social movement theory. They include, for example, a lively involvement with aesthetic production and reception. The 1960s student and kindred movements are all but inconceivable without folk and especially rock music; they also nurtured an aestheticizing of the self and a wide variety of engagements with aesthetic criteria for judging personal activity and social arrangements. Feminism has been distinctive for the extent to which aesthetic production of various sorts – literature, drama, music, graphic arts – has been tied into the movement. Part of the impetus behind the ecology movement is an aesthetic judgment about nature and about appropriate lifestyles that should not be collapsed into an altogether instrumental concern for saving the earth or ourselves from extinction. This reminds us of the Romantic view of nature, and Romanticism was both an aspect of many late eighteenth- and early nineteenth-century social movements and is in a sense one of those movements. A similar use of aesthetic criteria in judgments about the practical affairs of life was important to the communal movement of the early nineteenth century and to the Transcendentalists.

Of course aesthetics entered prominently into the social movement field at various other times – for example, in the era of high modernism. Nonetheless, mention of aesthetics points us toward part of the answer to a crucial question: why have the similarities between the social movement fields of the early nineteenth and late twentieth centuries not been more generally apparent to social theorists? An easy bit of the answer is simply that many social theorists know little history. It is also true that the concerns of both academic social theory and Marxism were shaped by the prominence of labor and socialist movements in the period of their origins. Variants of liberalism and conservatism dominated universities while Marxism became the dominant extra-academic radical theory, eclipsing the various utopian socialists, proponents of direct action, and other alternative social visions of the early nineteenth century. Thus, both in and out of academia, most theoretical orientations offered little insight into and attributed little contemporary significance to religious movements, nationalism, identity politics, gender difference, sexuality, and other concerns. Thus is so largely because they operate with a highly rationalized conception of human life and relatively fixed notion of interests. Thus aesthetic activity and inquiry and the range of issues raised by the NSMs were typically set apart from the "serious" issues that shaped theorists' largely instrumental inquiries into social movements.

[. . .]

The late nineteenth-century institutionalization of the labor/socialist movements and the response to them crystallized the notion of a division between sorts of movements. There was *the* social movement that was tied into the overall process of industrialization and social change, and there was the variety of false starts and short circuits that expressed human dreams and frustrations but had little to do with the overall course of social change. Rather than treating the different sorts of movements together, late nineteenth- and early twentieth-century social scientists compartmentalized them. The very field of social movement studies shows traces of this. Its roots lie on the one hand in sociopsychological studies of collective behavior (generally interpreted as deviant) and on the other in studies of the labor movement (analyzed broadly in liberal/Weberian or Marxian terms). This contributed to a tendency to conduct argument as though the joint activity of large numbers of people must either be shown to be instrumentally rational or be deemed irrational and explicable on sociopsychological criteria (see [. . .] the review in McAdam et al., 1988). [. . .]

[. . .]

The field of social movement research was transformed by the attempt to comprehend the civil rights movement and the antiwar and student movements of the 1960s (Oberschall, 1973; Tilly, 1978; Zald and McCarthy, 1979; McAdam et al., 1988). The range of movements studied and the perspectives employed were broadened, and emphasis was shifted from micropsychological to macrostructural and/or rational choice accounts. Leading approaches reproduced, however, the basic division between liberal (utilitarian, rational choice, and resource mobilization) and Marxist perspectives. Most theories saw movements either as challengers for state power or as contentious groups pursuing some other set of instrumental objectives. There was little recognition of how "the personal is political" or of how important political (or more generally macrostructural) results may stem from actions that are not explicitly political or instrumental in their self-understanding.[4] Such theories overcame the division of collective behavior from real politics, but they did not bring culture – or any rich understanding of democratic processes and civil society – to the foreground. This was done primarily by NSM theory.

NSM theory not only brought culture to the fore but challenged the sharp division between micro and macro, processual and structural accounts. In Cohen and Arato's words, "Contemporary collective actors see that the creation of identity involves social conflict around the reinterpretation of norms, the creation of new meanings, and a challenge to the social construction of the very boundaries between public, private, and political domains of action" (1992: 511). It is as important not to prejudge whether to apply a political process model of instrumentally rational interaction (Tilly, 1978; McAdam, 1982) as to avoid an assumption that collective behavior stems from psychological breakdown.

CONCLUSION: MODERNITY AND SOCIAL MOVEMENTS

For at least 200 years, under one label or another, the public has been opposed to the private; the economic to the aesthetic; the rationalist to the romantic; secularization to revival; and institutionalization to nascent movements intent on breaking free. These tensions lie behind recurrent ebbs and flows in movement organization, changing forms of movement activity, and recurrent proliferations of movements beyond any single narrative of a developing labor movement, socialism, or even democracy. This [chapter] does not trace a longer narrative or attempt to graph the ebbs and flows of different styles of movement. Its main contributions are limited to (a) showing how prominent new social movements were in the early nineteenth century and (b) suggesting that attention should be focused not simply on a supposed transition from old to new forms of movement, but on the interplay of different sorts of movements in a social movement field that was and is not only basic to modernity but internally diverse and international. By not confounding the variety of movement characteristics with a presumed unidirectional narrative we can better discern the variables that distinguish movements of varying age in terms of their extent and forms of organization, their relative emphasis on identity politics, their social bases, and orientations to action. These are themes to which we should be alert in the study of all social movements, and we should seek to explain their absence as well as their presence.

Attuned to the richness of the social movement field in the early nineteenth and late twentieth centuries, we may see on further investigation that the late nineteenth and early twentieth centuries were not so completely dominated by economistic organization as is commonly thought. Trade unions and social democracy competed with the Salvation Army and xenophobic nationalists nearly everywhere and with revivalist preachers in America and anti-Semites in much of Europe. Academic social scientists, however, failed to grant such other forms of movement attention proportionate to their popular appeal, while tending to expect the labor movement and mainstream party politics to grow ever stronger and more institutionalized.

If, however, it is also true, as I suggest, that the early nineteenth-century social movement field is in certain respects more similar to the late twentieth century than to the intervening years, we are faced with an interesting problem of historical explanation. The standard account of movement cycles proposed by Hirschman (1982) and Tarrow (1989) focuses primarily on shorter term phenomena: the way specific mobilizations exhaust participants' energies within a few months or years. Bur the mid-century shift in social movement activity was more than this. The struggles of many different varieties of people about the conditions and rewards of their work were increasingly joined in a single labor movement; their diverse ideologies were transformed, at least in part, into a continuum of more or less radical labor values from strong socialism to elitist unionism. Similarly, the so-called utopian socialisms faded in the face of Marxism, Fabianism, and other reform programs and social democracy. As Taylor (1983) has noted, this had striking implications for women, who had been included centrally, if asymmetrically, in Owenism but who found themselves marginalized in Marxist socialism, trade unionism, and social democratic parties. Underlying this specific instance was a general redefinition of private and public life that removed not only women but the concerns most closely identified with women – family, for example – from the public sphere, transforming political questions into merely personal concerns. It was this historically specific change – not some eternal tendency of patriarchy – that feminists later challenged with the slogan "the personal is political."

Phases of state and capitalist development were probably significant in all this (Hirsch, 1988; Tarrow, 1989). State elites may have become more unified and thus both better able to respond to movements and less likely to split between support and opposition. Certainly states developed better mechanisms for managing discontent (though these were hardly proof against the new, largely middle-class mobilizations of the 1960s). Not least of all, the franchise was extended, and in its wake electoral politics offered the chance to trade votes for various kinds of largely economic distributional benefits. At the same time, the institutional development of states created mechanisms for continual negotiation over some issues – notably labor and welfare concerns. This brought certain movement concerns permanently into the political arena while leaving others out.

The concentration of large parts of the population in industrial work may also have played a role, offering unions a fertile organizing base. Perhaps more basically, workers within capitalist production were in a position (unlike most of their predecessors) to bargain for increased shares of capitalist growth. They were not asking for the protection of old crafts or the communities attached to them. There was, thus, an increasing return to investment in economistic movement organizations once workers were asking for something that capitalists could give in monetary terms. Mature industrial capitalism also posed organizational challenges to the labor movement that pushed it toward large-scale, formally organized, institutional structures. Of course, the labor movement dominated in the movement field because of its success; its dominance was an achievement of struggle, not just an inheritance from background variables. Finally, we should not fail to consider the impact of delimited events as well as trends in underlying factors. The repression of the revolutions of 1848 and the American Civil War most visibly helped to bring the early nineteenth-century burgeoning of social movements to a close. The demographic effects of both – increased migration as well as massive killing – also may have reduced the probability of movement formation and proliferation and increased popular preference for institutionalized rather than riskier forms of collective action.

I will not try to offer even a similar ad hoc list of possible factors worth exploring in the attempt to explain the reopening of the social movement field in the 1960s (or at the turn of the century). Arguments about the shift from mass-production capitalism to smaller scale, more dispersed patterns of work; about the role of new media; and about the role of the state only scratch the surface of contending positions. Perhaps demographics were again crucial; perhaps rapid social change created a sense of new possibilities. Most basically, we need to consider the possibility that proliferation of NSMs is normal to modernity and not in need of special explanation because it violates the oppositions of left and right, cultural and social, public and private, aesthetic and instrumental that organize so much of our thought. The challenge may be to explain the relative paucity of NSMs in some periods or places. While rebellions, reforms, and other kinds of collective actions have certainly occurred throughout history, the modern era is in general distinctively characterized by a rich efflorescence of social movements. This is in part because it provides opportunities and capacities for mobilization lacking in many other epochs and settings. A proneness to various sorts of social movements, indeed, seems to be one of the features that links the distinctive history of Western modernity to the novel modernities being pioneered on the Indian subcontinent, in China, in Africa, and elsewhere.

It is a mistake thus to equate the mid-nineteenth- to mid-twentieth-century pattern simply with modernity. This helps, among other things, to nourish illusions about what it could mean to pass into postmodernity. The relative predominance of a single cluster of movements during this period is not necessarily either more typical than the proliferation of different movements both before and after it; indeed, it may be less so. The seeming dominance of labor and social democracy – whether in European actuality or only in the minds of social scientists – is historically specific and contingent. There never was *the* social movement of modernity. Rather, modernity was internally split and contested from the beginning – or perhaps I should say was "always already" the object of contending movements.

We need to constitute our theoretical notion of modernity not as a master narrative but in a way that reflects both its heterogeneity and contestation and that takes full account of the central place of social movements within it. If we are to discern a postmodernity, a change of tendency, or a trend, we need more clearly to know what we may be moving beyond. State power and capitalism have not been transcended; neither has competitive individualism passed away nor the world of merely instrumental relations become inherently more spiritual. Many of the grievances and dissatisfactions that drove the movements of the early nineteenth century remain. Likewise, the proliferation of new social movements should not be taken too quickly to spell the end of trade union activism or mainstream political and economic concerns as movement themes. The cycle may continue. In any case, modernity remains visible, in part, precisely in the shape of the movements challenging it and asking for more from it.

ACKNOWLEDGMENTS

Earlier versions of this [chapter] were presented in 1991 to the Social Science History Association, the Department of Sociology at the University of Oslo, and the Program in Comparative Study of Social Transformations at the

University of Michigan. The author is grateful for comments from members of each audience and also for research assistance from Cindy Hahamovitch.

Notes

1 In focusing on the early nineteenth century, I do not wish to argue that NSMs ceased to be prominent in the second half of the nineteenth century or the first half of the twentieth. On the contrary, some of the same NSMs maintained or returned to prominence – as, for example, the Women's Christian Temperance Union of the 1870s and 1880s succeeded the American Temperance Union of the 1830s and 1840s. The followers of W. K. Kellogg, promoter of abstinence and cold cereals in the early twentieth century, were not so different from those of Sylvester Graham, the "peristaltic persuader" and inventor of the Graham cracker in the 1830s (Nissenbaum, 1980). Many manifestations of antimodernism in late nineteenth- and early twentieth-century intellectual circles involve NSM activity (Lears, 1981). There is no ready index for assessing when movement activity is greater or lesser, so my impressionistic comparative judgment is open to challenge, though I think there can be little doubt that the early nineteenth century was particularly active.
2 This account is indebted to discussions with George Steinmetz; see also Steinmetz (1990).
3 Part of the confusion comes from failing to distinguish two senses of utopian. The programs of neocorporatist social democratic parties may be all encompassing and in that sense utopian, but they are eminently negotiable and not necessarily radical. Feminist calls for an end to all violence and discrimination against women are in a sense defensive but are also both radical and nonnegotiable, and in that sense utopian. In different ways, each utopian goal may be unreachable in the world as we know it, a shared sense of the term.
4 Trying to make sense of the New Left, Alvin Gouldner (1970: vii) contemplated the song "Light my Fire," recorded by Jim Morrison and The Doors. He saw it in two guises: "an ode to urban conflagration" sung during the Detroit riots, and a singing commercial for a Detroit carmaker. The question, in other words, was between political resistance and economic hegemony. What Gouldner missed, apparently, was the centrality of sex to the New Left as to so much of the rest of the new social movement ferment of the era (as of the early nineteenth century).

References

Amann, Peter (1975) *Revolution and Mass Democracy: the Paris Club Movement in 1848.* Princeton, NJ: Princeton University Press.
Aminzade, Ronald (1993) *Ballots and Barricades.* Princeton, NJ: Princeton University Press.

Aronowitz, Stanley (1992) *Identity Politics*. London: Routledge.

Calhoun, Craig (1988) "Populist politics, communications media, and large scale social integration," *Sociological Theory*, 6: 219–41.

Calhoun, Craig (1989) "Classical social theory and the French revolution of 1848," *Sociological Theory*, 7: 210–25.

Cohen, Jean and Arato, Andrew (1992) *Civil Society and Political Theory*. Cambridge, MA: MIT Press.

Eder, Klaus (1985) "The 'new social movements:' moral crusades, political pressure groups, or social movements?," *Social Research*, 52: 869–901.

Evans, Sara M. and Boyte, Harry C. (1986) *Free Spaces*. Chicago: University of Chicago Press.

Gouldner, Alvin (1970) *The Coming Crisis of Western Sociology*. Boston: Beacon Press.

Habermas, Jürgen (1990) *The New Conservatism: Cultural Criticism and the Historians' Debate*. Cambridge, MA: MIT Press.

Harrison, John F. C. (1969) *Quest for the New Moral World: Robert Owen and the Owenites in Britain and America*. New York: Scribners.

Hirsch, Joachim (1988) "The crisis of Fordism, transformations of the 'Keynesian' security state, and new social movements," *Research in Social Movements, Conflict and Change*, 10: 43–55.

Hirschman, Albert (1982) *Shifting Involvements*. Princeton, NJ: Princeton University Press.

Jones, Gareth Stedman (1984) *Languages of Class*. Cambridge: Cambridge University Press.

Kramer, L. (1988) *Threshold of a New World: Intellectuals and the Exile Experience in Paris, 1830–1848*. Ithaca, NY: Cornell University Press.

Lears, Jackson (1981) *No Place of Grace: Antimodernism and the Transformation of American Culture, 1880–1920*. New York: Pantheon.

McAdam, Doug (1982) *Political Process and the Development of Black Insurgency 1930–1970*. Chicago: University of Chicago Press.

McAdam, Doug, McCarthy, John D. and Zald, Mayer (1988) "Social movements," in N. J. Smelser (ed.), *Handbook of Sociology*. Newbury Park, CA: Sage.

McWilliams, Wilson Carey (1973) *The Idea of Fraternity in America*. Berkeley, CA: University of California Press.

Marx, Karl and Engels, Friedrich (1976 [1848]) *Manifesto of the Communist Party*, in Karl Marx/Frederick Engels, *Collected Works*, vol. 6, pp. 477–519. London: Lawrence and Wishart.

Meinecke, Friedrich (1970) *Cosmopolitanism and the National State*. Princeton, NJ: Princeton University Press.

Melucci, Alberto (1988) "Social movements and the democratization of everyday life," in J. Keane (ed.), *Civil Society and the State*, pp. 245–60. London: Verso.

Melucci, Alberto (1989) *Nomads of the Present: Social Movements and Individual Needs in Contemporary Society*. Philadelphia: Temple University Press.

Nissenbaum, Stephen (1980) *Sex, Diet, and Debility in Jacksonian America*. Greenwich, CT: Greenwood.

Oberschall, Anthony (1973) *Social Conflict and Social Movements.* Englewood Cliffs, NJ: Prentice-Hall.

Offe, Claus (1985) "New social movements: challenging the boundaries of institutional politics," *Social Research,* 52: 817–68.

Owen, Robert and Campbell, Alexander (1829) *Debate on the Evidences of Christianity Containing an Examination of the "Social System" and of All the Systems of Scepticism of Ancient and Modern Times,* 2 vols. Bethany, VA: Alexander Campbell.

Rendall, Jane (1985a) *The Origins of Modern Feminism: Women in Britain, France and the United States, 1780–1860.* Chicago: Lyceum.

Rendall, Jane (ed.) (1985b) *Equal or Different: Women's Politics, 1800–1914.* Oxford: Blackwell.

Rorabaugh, W. J. (1979) *The Alcoholic Republic: an American Tradition.* New York: Oxford University Press.

Rose, Anne (1981) *Transcendentalism as a Social Movement, 1830–1850.* New Haven, CT: Yale University Press.

Ross, Steven J. (1985) *Workers on the Edge: Work, Leisure and Politics in Industrializing Cincinnati, 1788–1890.* New York: Columbia University Press.

Ryan, Mary (1990) *Women in Public: Between Banners and Ballots.* Baltimore, MD: Johns Hopkins University Press.

Ryan, Mary (1992) "Gender and public access: women's politics in 19th century America," in C. Calhoun (ed.), *Habermas and the Public Sphere,* pp. 259–88. Cambridge, MA: MIT Press.

Scott, Alan (1990) *Ideology and the New Social Movements.* London: Unwin Hyman.

Simmel, G. (1903) "The metropolis and mental life," in D. N. Levine (ed.), *Georg Simmel on Individuality and Social Forms,* pp. 324–39. Chicago: University of Chicago Press.

Steinmetz, George (1990) "Beyond subjectivist and objectivist theories of conflict: Marxism, post-Marxism, and the new social movements," Wilder House Working paper no. 2, University of Chicago.

Steinmetz, George (1989) *Struggle, Politics and Reform: Collective Action, Social Movements and Cycles of Protest.* Ithaca, NY: Cornell University Press (Western Societies papers no. 21).

Taylor, Barbara (1983) *Eve and the New Jerusalem.* New York: Pantheon.

Thompson, Dorothy (1986) *Chartism.* New York: Pantheon.

Thompson, E. P. (1968) *The Making of the English Working Class,* rev. edn. Harmondsworth: Penguin.

Tilly, Charles (1978) *From Mobilization to Revolution.* Reading, MA: Addison–Wesley.

Traugott, Mark (1985) *Armies of the Poor: Determinants of Working-class Participation in the Parisian Insurrection of June 1848.* Princeton, NJ: Princeton University Press.

Walicki, Andrzej (1982) *Philosophy and Romantic Nationalism: the Case of Poland.* Oxford: Clarendon.

Walters, Ronald G. (1978) *American Reformers, 1815–1860.* New York: Hill and Wang.

Wilentz, Sean (1984) *Chants Democratic: New York City and the Rise of the American Working Class, 1788–1850*. New York: Oxford.

Zald, Mayer N. and McCarthy, John D. (eds) (1979) *The Dynamics of Social Movements*. Cambridge: Winthrop.

CHAPTER 9

The Concept of Social Movement

Mario Diani

Social movement studies have grown impressively in recent years (Rucht, 1990a,b). At the same time, efforts to merge originally distant approaches into a more comprehensive one have been made (e.g. Cohen, 1985; Klandermans et al., 1988; Scott, 1990; Eyerman and Jamison, 1990). Quite surprisingly, these attempts have largely passed over any discussion of the concept of "social movement". While several scholars have provided analytical definitions of it, we still lack, to my knowledge, a systematic comparison of these conceptualisations. This [chapter] aims to fill this gap, discussing the concept of social movement as it has been formulated by some influential contributors to the field since the 1960s.

Focusing on the conceptual level seems important to me, for a number of reasons. I share the view that, while concepts cannot be identified with theories, they are nevertheless the cornerstone of any theorising (see e.g. Sartori, 1984). Therefore, any effort to synthesise different approaches risks to be flawed, if little or no attention is paid to concept definition. This holds even more true for social movements studies. There, even an implicit, "empirical" agreement about the use of the term is largely missing. In fact, social and political phenomena as heterogeneous as revolutions, religious sects, political organisations, single-issue campaigns are all, on occasion, defined as social movements (see e.g. McAdam et al., 1988: 695). This terminological ambiguity entails, however, a loss of specificity and theoretical clarity. This is reflected in that many valuable analyses of social movements pay hardly any attention to the concept

This chapter is taken from *The Sociological Review*, 40 (1992), pp. 1–25. Reprinted by permission of The Editorial Board of The Sociological Review and Blackwell Publishers.

itself. They rather move immediately to more substantive questions, such as the factors which account for mobilization processes (e.g. Klandermans et al., 1988) or the difference between old and new movements (e.g. Dalton and Kuechler, 1990). This is perfectly legitimate, of course. Yet, one may sometimes feel that the same topics might be as successfully treated without mentioning "social movements" at all, adopting rather concepts such as "collective action", "social change", "social conflict" and the like.[1] The question therefore rises, what does "social movements" specifically refer to.

The absence of discussion concerning the concept of social movement has been usually attributed to the heterogeneity and incompatibility of the different approaches, which would make any synthesis impossible (e.g. Morris and Herring, 1987: 139). In contrast to this view, I argue that a common thread exists between the analyses of social movements, produced within otherwise very diverse intellectual traditions. My goal here is to highlight this linkage and to identify the elements that are common to the different "schools". These elements connote social movements as a specific social dynamic which is logically related to, yet distinct from, the ones mentioned above. It consists in a process whereby several different actors, be they individuals, informal groups and/or organisations, come to elaborate, through either joint action and/or communication, a shared definition of themselves as being part of the same side in a social conflict. By doing so, they provide meaning to otherwise unconnected protest events or symbolic antagonistic practices, and make explicit the emergence of specific conflicts and issues (see e.g. Melucci, 1989; Eyerman and Jamison, 1990). This dynamic is reflected in the definition of social movements as consisting in networks of informal interaction between a plurality of individuals, groups and/or organisations, engaged in a political and/or cultural conflict, on the basis of a shared collective identity.

The argument develops as follows. In the following section, some recent definitions proposed by leading figures in the field are introduced. Then, four sub-components of the concept are identified and discussed. In the next section, a more empirical issue is addressed. The capacity of the concept to differentiate social movements from related phenomena (such as parties and interest groups, coalitions, protest events) is assessed. Finally, it is shown how the proposed definition reflects recent developments in the field, and how it can contribute to identify a specific area of investigation for social movement research.

AN OVERVIEW

This discussion focuses on the views elaborated by Ralph Turner and Lewis Killian, John McCarthy and Mayer Zald, Charles Tilly, Alain

Touraine and Alberto Melucci. This group of scholars may be considered as representative of the four main trends within social movement analysis since the 1960s. These trends consist respectively of the most recent expansions of the "Collective Behaviour" perspective (Turner and Killian); the several approaches which have been subsumed, though with various qualifications, under the label of "Resource Mobilisation Theory" (RMT) (Zald and McCarthy); the "Political Process" perspective (Tilly); and the "New Social Movements" (NSMs) approach (Touraine, Melucci).[2] Whereas the first three have been particularly influential in the USA, the fourth has been mainly associated with European scholars, to the extent that some (Klandermans and Tarrow, 1988) have even talked of an "American" and a "European" approach to the study of social movements. As there are a number of excellent, recent reviews of the literature, a thorough examination of the different "schools" may be omitted [here] (see Morris and Herring, 1987; Klandermans and Tarrow, 1988; McAdam et al., 1988; Tarrow, 1988; Neidhardt and Rucht, 1990; Scott, 1990). However, some hints will be provided when discussing the single authors.

Turner and Killian (1987, but originally 1957) define social movements as a peculiar kind of collective behaviour, which is contrasted to "organizational" and "institutional" behaviour (1987: 4). In spite of these traits, however, collective behaviour cannot be consigned to lack of organisation or to irrational behaviour. On the contrary, as the theory of emergent norm suggests, collective behaviour represents merely a looser organisational principle (see also Neidhardt and Rucht, 1990). Turner and Killian define a social movement as:

> a collectivity acting with some continuity to promote or resist a change in the society or organisation of which it is part. As a collectivity a movement is a group with indefinite and shifting membership and with leadership whose position is determined more by informal response of adherents than by formal procedures for legitimising authority. (1987: 223)

Social movements "are not necessarily or typically coterminous with movement organisations, [even though these] carry out much of the movement work and frequently attempt to control and speak for movements" (Turner, 1981: 5).

RMT differs from Turner and Killian's and related collective behaviour approaches in that greater attention is paid to the role of organisational factors within social movements. Indeed, Zald and McCarthy define social movements in a way which is not far from Turner and Killian's, i.e. as "a set of opinions and beliefs which represents preferences for changing some elements of the social structure and/or reward distribution of a society. A countermovement is a set of opinions and beliefs in a population opposed to a social movement" (McCarthy and Zald, 1977: 1217–18). Yet, their greatest concern lies clearly with the conditions under which such beliefs are transformed into concrete action. From this perspective, both leaders with previous political experiences and strong, often professional, organisations are needed (McCarthy and Zald, 1973, 1977). Emphasis is also put on the conditions which facilitate the constitution of social movement organisations (SMOs), as well as on the dynamics of co-operation/competition between them (see also Zald and McCarthy, 1980). The existence of interactions within social movements is reflected in the notion of "social movement sectors" (McCarthy and Zald, 1977). According to this view, social movement organisations are not isolated actors; rather, they tend to interact with other organisations, even when they are not able to develop any sort of regular co-ordination; moreover, social movement constituencies often overlap in a significant way. A recent formulation of this perspective states that social movement sectors are "social movement activity largely oriented toward change that is achieved in the differentiated political arena . . . the configuration of social movements, the structure of antagonistic, competing and/or co-operating movements which in turn is part of a larger structure of action" (Garner and Zald, 1985: 120).

Instead of focusing on organisational resources, Tilly (1978) relates the emergence of social movements to a broader "political process," where excluded interests try to get access to the established polity. Tilly analyses this process from an historical perspective, periodising phases of intense contention within contemporary history and mapping shifts in the "repertoires" of collective action. In contrast to McCarthy and Zald, his emphasis is on the overall dynamics which determine social unrest and its characteristics, rather than on social movements as specific organised actors. This theoretical perspective is reflected in the definition of social movements as a:

> sustained series of interactions between power holders and persons successfully claiming to speak on behalf of a constituency lacking formal representation, in the course of which those persons make publicly visible demands for changes in the distribution or exercise of power, and back those demands with public demonstrations of support. (Tilly, 1984: 306)

Social movements are an organised, sustained, self-conscious challenge which implies shared identity among participants (Tilly, 1984: 303).

Both RMT and the "political process" approach analyse the "how" rather than the "why" (Melucci, 1989) of social movements. In other words, they focus on the conditions which facilitate or constrain the occurrence of conflicts, taking the existence of potential grievances for granted. In contrast, the NSM approach tries to relate social movements to large-scale structural and cultural changes. The most explicit advocate of this is Alain Touraine (1977, 1981, 1985). Touraine identifies social movements with the dominant conflict in a given society: "The social movement is the organised collective behaviour of a class actor struggling against his class adversary for the social control of historicity in a concrete community" (1981: 77). *Historicity* consists of the "overall system of meaning which sets dominant rules in a given society" (1981: 81). In industrial society, the core conflict opposed work to labour; in the "programmed society", technocrats to their adversaries. All the other conflicts which occur within a given society (e.g. conflicts for redistribution of resources) or during the transition from one society to another (e.g. the national conflicts) are subordinated to the core conflict, the only one where it is possible to talk of social movements. For other conflicts, labels such as submovements, communitarian movements, national movements would be more appropriate (Touraine, 1985).

As Touraine's analysis is both highly complex and well-known, I will focus on only two aspects which may be helpful in understanding his definition of social movements, even where one does not accept his broader theoretical framework. The first concerns the idea of a social movement as the "combination of a principle of identity, a principle of opposition and a principle of totality" (1981: 81), where social actors identify themselves, their social opponents and the stakes in a conflict. Such a combination or process of "identity formation" may, in fact, be detected in any aspect of social behaviour, but social movements are distinct in so far as the issue at stake refers, as we have seen, to the historicity, rather than to the "institutional decisions or organisational norms" in a society (1981: 81). The second aspect concerns the high differentiation of beliefs and orientations within social movements. Touraine's methodology of the "sociological intervention" is meant to provide a better reconstruction of these orientations as well as to help movement actions to achieve a better understanding of their own actions (Touraine, 1981: 139ff; Touraine et al., 1983a,b).

Alberto Melucci is not as interested as Touraine in singling out the new core conflict of contemporary post-industrial society, even though he agrees that these conflicts are more present today in the cultural and symbolic sphere. Rather, Melucci proposes a definition of social movements as a:

specific class of collective phenomena which contains three dimensions . . . [it] is a form of collective action which involves solidarity . . . [it] is engaged in conflict, and thus in opposition to an adversary who lays

claims on the same goods or values . . . [it] breaks the limits of compatibility of the system that it can tolerate without altering its structure.
(1989: 29)

According to Melucci, social movements are not coterminous with
"visible" political conflicts. In fact, public action is only one part of the
experience of social movements. Even when they are not engaged in
campaigns and mobilisations, social movements may still be active in
the sphere of cultural production. Some strongly culture-oriented movements may mobilise only occasionally in the political arena. Their activities largely develop in "movement areas", i.e. "networks of groups and
individuals sharing a conflictual culture and a collective identity"
(1985), "multiplicity of groups that are dispersed, fragmented and
submerged in everyday life, and which act as cultural laboratories"
(1989: 60).

A PROPOSAL FOR SYNTHESIS

The definitions introduced above emphasise at least four aspects of
social movement dynamics: (a) networks of informal interaction; (b)
shared beliefs and solidarity; (c) collective action on conflictual issues;
(d) action which displays largely outside the institutional sphere and the
routine procedures of social life.

Networks of informal interaction

The presence of informal interactions involving individuals, groups and
organisations is widely acknowledged. Even Touraine, who as we have
seen adopts a very peculiar definition, stresses the view of social movements as collective actors where organisations, individuals and groups
all play a role (e.g. 1981: 150). Even where the emphasis is put on a
"set of opinions and beliefs", as in the case of McCarthy and Zald, the
transformation of these ideas into action requires the interaction
between specific SMOs, constituents, adherents and bystander publics
(McCarthy and Zald, 1977: 1223). Interaction is further stressed in
notions such as "social movement sector" (SMS) or "micro mobilisation context", recently adopted by McCarthy and Zald in their reassess-
ment of the field (McAdam et al., 1988). Defined as "any small group
setting in which processes of collective attribution are combined with
rudimentary forms of organisation to produce mobilisation for collective action" (1988: 709), this concept greatly modifies the basically hierarchical conception of relationships between constituents and SMOs,

informal?

proposed by the RM theorists in their earlier formulations, forming a perspective more consistent with such notions as Melucci's "social movement area".

The characteristics of these networks may range from the very loose and dispersed links described by Gerlach and Hine (1970) in their seminal book, to the tightly clustered networks which facilitate adhesion to terrorist organisations (della Porta, 1988). Such networks promote the circulation of essential resources for action (information, expertise, material resources) as well as of broader systems of meaning. Thus, networks contribute both to creating the preconditions for mobilisation (which is what RMT has mostly emphasised) and to providing the proper setting for the elaboration of specific world-views and life-styles (as described by Melucci).

In spite of their different emphasis, these definitions agree in recognising the plurality of actors involved in social movements and the informality of the ties which link them to each other. A synthetic definition of this aspect of the concept of social movements therefore may run as follows: *A social movement is a network of informal interactions between a plurality of individuals, groups and/or organisations.*

Shared beliefs and solidarity

To be considered a social movement, an interacting collectivity requires a shared set of beliefs and a sense of belongingness. Respective authors refer to "a set of opinions and beliefs" (McCarthy and Zald); "solidarity" (Melucci); "identity" (Touraine, Melucci, Tilly). Turner and Killian emphasise the continuity of social movements, which relies upon "group identity" and "ideologies". Identity and ideology are defined here in the broad sense of the term, which makes them very close to sets of beliefs (Turner and Killian, 1987: 249ff and ch. 14 respectively). Collective identity[3] and solidarity can be considered synonymous in this context, in so far as it is hard to conceive of the former without the latter, i.e. of a sense of belongingness without sympathetic feelings, associated with the perception of a common fate to share (Melucci, 1984a). The case is different for the definition proposed by McCarthy and Zald. Their notion of social movements as "sets of opinions and beliefs" does not necessarily imply the presence of shared feelings of belongingness. However, their more recent work, and in particular the emphasis on the role of *"micro-mobilization contexts"* and *"frame alignment processes"* testify to their growing concern for the interactive processes of symbolic mediation which support individuals' commitment.[4]

Collective identity is both a matter of self- and external definition. Actors must define themselves as part of a broader movement and, at

the same time, be perceived as such, by those within the same movement, and by opponents and/or external observers.[5] In this sense, collective identity plays an essential role in defining the boundaries of a
social movement. Only those actors, sharing the same beliefs and
sense of belongingness, can be considered to be part of a social movement. However, "collective identity" does not imply homogeneity of
ideas and orientations within social movement networks. A wide spectrum of different conceptions may be present, and factional conflicts
may arise at any time. Therefore, the construction and preservation
of a movement's identity implies a continuous process of "realignment" (Snow et al., 1986) and "negotiation" (Melucci, 1989) between
movement actors.

The presence of shared beliefs and solidarities allows both actors and
observers to assign a common meaning to specific collective events
which otherwise could not be identified as part of a common process
(see also Oliver, 1989). It is through this "framing process" that the
presence of a distinct social actor becomes evident, as well as that of
related issues. Indeed, social movements condition and help constitute
new orientations on existing issues and also the rise of new public issues,
in so far as they contribute to "the existence of a vocabulary and an
opening of ideas and actions which in the past was either unknown or
unthinkable" (Gusfield, 1981: 325). The process of identity formation
cannot be separated from the process of symbolic redefinition of what
is both real and possible. Moreover, such collective identity may persist
even when public activities, demonstrations and the like are not taking
place, thus providing for some continuity to the movement over time
(Turner and Killian, 1987; Melucci, 1989).

Taking these qualifications into account, we can define the second
component of the concept of social movement as follows: *The boundaries of a social movement network are defined by the specific collective
identity shared by the actors involved in the interaction.*

Collective action on conflictual issues

Some of the views reviewed here put a specific emphasis on conflict as
a core component of the concept of social movement (Touraine,
Melucci, Tilly). Others emphasise that social movements define themselves with respect to processes of social change (Turner and Killian,
McCarthy and Zald). Even these latter, however, acknowledge that as
promoters or opponents of social change social movements become
involved in conflictual relations with other actors (institutions, counter-
movements, etc.). If there is at least broad agreement concerning the fact
that conflict is a distinctive feature of a social movement, the notion of
conflict is understood in very different ways by different scholars.

Touraine claims that "social movements" applies only to conflicts about historicity, while others use the term in a looser and more inclusive way. Melucci considers typical of social movements only those actions which challenge the mechanism of systemic domination, while American scholars tend to subsume under that heading any protest event, including those referring to negotiable issues. Finally, some authors consider as social movements networks of collective action which are exclusively or primarily oriented toward cultural and personal change (Melucci and Turner and Killian), while others focus on actors in the political sphere (Tilly, McCarthy and Zald).

On a closer look, however, many of these inconsistencies prove to be more apparent than real. We have already seen that, when analysing other types of conflicts than those concerning historicity, Touraine attaches different qualifications (e.g. nationalist, communitarian, cultural) to the label "movement". Along similar lines, Melucci differentiates between social movements, which operate at the systemic level, and other types of collective action. He speaks for instance of "conflictual action", meaning a kind of behaviour which implies collective identity and the presence of a conflict, yet which does not break the limits of compatibility of the system (Melucci, 1984b). In other words, both Touraine and Melucci use the term "social movement" to identify a specific category of phenomena within a broader category of "movements", whereas other scholars use the term to mean movements of any kind.

Another presumed source of inconsistency consists in conceptions which focus on political movements and those emphasising that social movements are also, and often mainly involved in cultural conflicts. Several authors (among them Gusfield, 1981; Melucci, 1989) maintain that the true bulk of social movement experience has to be found in the cultural sphere: what is challenged is not only the uneven distribution of power and/or economic goods, but socially shared meanings as well, that is the ways of defining and interpreting reality. Social movements tend to focus more and more on self-transformation. Conflicts arise in areas previously considered typical of the private sphere, involving problems of self-definition and challenges to the dominant life-styles, for example. The difference with those who insist on the political side of movements like McCarthy and Zald and Tilly is undeniable. Yet, this is a difference in emphasis rather than one concerning incompatible notions of what a social movement is. Indeed, the existence of cultural movements has never been denied either by Resource Mobilization theorists (Zald and Ash, 1966 speak of movements of "personal change") nor by proponents of the "political process" perspective (Tilly, 1984 mentions "religious movements").

The opportunity to include both cultural and political movements within the broader category of social movements brings us to the third component of the concept: *Social movement actors are engaged in political and/or cultural conflicts, meant to promote or oppose social change either at the systemic or non-systemic level.*

Action which primarily occurs outside the institutional sphere and the routine procedures of social life

Until the early 1970s debates on social movements were dominated by structural functionalists like Smelser (1962) who put a great emphasis on the non-institutionalised nature of their behaviour. Today, social movement scholars are more cautious on this point. The aspects of "collective effervescence" and "nascent state" which had been emphasised by some (e.g. Alberoni, 1984 but originally 1965) as a distinctive feature of social movements are now more closely associated with the phase of their emergence. From very different perspectives, it has been demonstrated that social movements continue even when collective effervescence is over, and that this is not immediately followed by institutionalisation (see e.g. Melucci, 1984a, 1989; Tarrow, 1989). There is actually a more complex pattern of interaction between non-institutional aspects and institutional ones, wherein social movements may either be an agent of change at the level of symbolic codes (as Melucci emphasises) or create new opportunities for interest intermediation (e.g. Nedelmann, 1984). Moreover, movements may also develop without going through a phase of "collective effervescence". In other words, collective identities may arise, that are strong enough to foster sustained collective action, yet that do not imply a "nascent state" (Diani, 1990b).

If the relationship between non-institutional behaviour and social movements is not strong enough to identify the former as a fundamental component of the latter, the same holds true for the idea that social movements may be distinguished from other political actors because of their adoption of "unusual" patterns of political behaviour. Several scholars maintain that the fundamental distinction between movements and other social political actors is to be found in the contrast between conventional styles of political participation (such as voting or lobbying political representatives) and public protest. However, while the recourse to public protest is undoubtedly a qualifying element of political movements, it plays only a marginal role in movements oriented to personal and cultural change. If one accepts, as I do, that even the latter may be subsumed under the concept of social movements, then there is no reason to introduce this specification in the definition of the concept.

Another widely shared assumption, as least in the more conventional version of the idea of social movements as "unusual" phenomena, is that organisations involved in social movements are basically loosely structured. While informality and looseness are essential properties of the system of interaction, the same is not necessarily true for the single units of the system. Even though many loosely structured organisations are actually part, possibly the dominant one, of social movement networks, they are by no means their only component. Indeed, the spectrum of SMOs is so wide and differentiated as to prevent any clear restriction of its boundaries: a key role in social movements may be played by such heterogeneous organisations as churches (e.g. in the black civil rights movement in America: McAdam, 1982); local branches of trade unions (e.g. in the peace movement in Britain: Byrne, 1988); neighbourhood solidarity organisations (e.g. in the British urban movements: Lowe, 1986). Moreover, the choice between a grassroots organisation or a bureaucratic lobby appears more and more frequently dependent upon tactical calculations by social movement actors (Zald, 1988: 35–6). Even collective behaviour theorists agree that a proper understanding of social movements requires principles from both collective and organisational behaviour (Turner and Killian, 1987: 230).

This discussion suggests that features such as the extra-institutional nature of social movements, the prevalence of violent or disruptive political protest and the loose structure of social movement organisations cannot really be taken as fundamental characteristics of a social movement. These may however be extremely useful in differentiating between types of movements, or between different phases in the life of a specific movement. Thus, the following synthetic definition of the concept of social movement can be put forward: *A social movement is a network of informal interactions between a plurality of individuals, groups and/or organizations, engaged in political or cultural conflict, on the basis of a shared collective identity.*

SOCIAL MOVEMENTS, ORGANISATIONS, POLITICAL EVENTS

The different traditions of social movement analysis I have discussed so far show some degree of compatibility. To be fair, this "immanent" consensus is sometimes only implicit in an author's formulation. In this reconstruction I have tried to emphasise the elements of continuity between different positions, rather than those of divergence – which are, by the way, the best known. The question is whether the effort to mediate between several distinct approaches is not detrimental to theoretical clarity. In this section I will discuss this point. I try in particular to show in what sense this particular definition of social movements helps to differentiate them from (a) political and social organisations like parties, interest groups or religious sects; (b) other informal networks of collective action such as political mobilisation campaigns and political coalitions.

Social movements vs. political or religious organisations

As we already noted in the previous section, social movements, political parties and interest groups are often compared under the assumption that they all embody different styles of political organisation (e.g. Wilson, 1973). At times, they are identified with religious sects and cults (e.g. Robbins, 1988). However, if our definition is correct, the difference between social movements and other political actors does not consist primarily of differences in organisational characteristics or patterns of behaviour, but on the fact that social movements are not organisations, not even of a peculiar kind (Tilly, 1988; Oliver, 1989). They are networks of interaction between different actors which may either include formal organisations or not, depending on shifting circumstances. As a consequence, a single organisation, whatever its dominant traits, is not a social movement. Of course it may be part of one, but the two are not identical, as the latter reflects a different, more structured organisational principle. Indeed, many influential scholars in the field keep using "social movement" to mean both networks of interaction and specific organisations: citizens' rights groups like Common Cause, environmental organisations like the Sierra Club, or even religious sects like Nichiren Shoshu (McAdam et al., 1988: 695). Yet, this overlap is a source of analytical confusion, in so far as it fosters the application to social movement analysis of concepts borrowed from organisational theory, that only partially fit the looser structure of social movements.[6] Talking of Common Cause or the Sierra Club or Nichiren Shoshu as "social movements" leads one to formulate concepts like "professional social movement" (McCarthy and Zald, 1973) or "single-organisation movements" (Turner and Killian, 1987: 369–70) to emphasise differences between these cases and the nature of social movements as informal networks (which as we have seen they all agree upon). But qualifying Common Cause as a "professional social movement" does not add very much to the understanding of it, that cannot be provided by concepts like "public interest group" (see, among others, Etzioni, 1985). Similarly, a religious organisation like Nichiren Shoshu or Hare Krishna may be conveniently analysed as a "sect". This concept takes into account the greater organisational rigidity and the more hierarchical structure that these organisations display by comparison with social movement networks (see Robbins, 1988: 150–5). In contrast, what both "public interest group" and "sect" do not really capture is the interaction processes through which actors with different identities and orientations come to elaborate a shared system of beliefs and a sense of belongingness, which exceeds by far the boundaries of any single group or organisation, while maintaining at the same time their specificity and distinctive traits.

If we accept that social movements are analytically different from SMOs we have also to redefine our notion of what is part and what is not part of a movement. Indeed, any organisation which fulfils the requirements I have pointed out (interactions with other actors, conflict and collective identity) may be considered part of a given movement. This may also hold for bureaucratic interest groups, and even political parties. The inclusion of political parties within social movements will surely raise many eyebrows and requires some qualification. By saying that political parties may be part of social movements I do not mean to suggest that "social movements" is a broader theoretical category of which several types of organizations (interest groups, community groups, political parties and so forth) represent as many sub-types. Far from it. Rather, I suggest that the features of the processes I have described as a social movement do not exclude that under certain and specific conditions some political party may feel itself as part of a movement and be recognised as such both by other actors in the movement and by the general public. This is likely to be the exception rather than the rule, and to be largely restricted to parties originated by social movements, such as the Green Parties (Kitschelt, 1989).

One could reasonably object that no matter how strong their identification with a movement, political parties actually perform specific functions at the level of interest representation and in this sense are different from social movements. That differences exist at the functional level is beyond question. Yet, the main peculiarity of social movements does not consist in their specific way of performing the function of interest representation. Of course, their networks of interaction favour the formulation of demands, the promotion of mobilisation campaigns and the elaboration and diffusion of beliefs and collective identities. These factors all, in turn, contribute to redefine the cultural and political setting in which the action of interest representation takes place. However, when we focus on the function of interest representation in strict terms, we do not look at the way "the movement" performs this function. We actually look at the way different specific SMOs perform these functions. Whether they decide or not to include participation into elections within their repertoire of action is dependent upon several factors including external opportunities, tactical and/or ideological considerations and their links to other actors in the movement. The mere fact that they decide to do so, however, will not automatically exclude them from the movement. Rather, they will be part of two different systems of action (the party system and the social movement system), where they will play different roles. The way such roles are actually shaped will constitute a crucial area of investigation (Kitschelt, 1989).

Social movements, protest events, coalitions

If social movements do not coincide with SMOs, they do not coincide with other types of informal interaction either. In other words, they differ from both loosely structured protest events and political coalitions. Under what conditions may a protest against the construction of a motorway run by informal citizens' action groups, a "wild-cat" strike for higher wages in a firm or a demonstration for better nursing facilities in a neighbourhood be considered part of a social movement? And when are they just simple isolated "protest events"? Some have suggested looking at the scope, dimension and length of campaigns (see e.g. Marwell and Oliver, 1984; Turner and Killian, 1987) in making this distinction. In broad terms, this is consistent with the notion of collective identity, as long and sustained campaigns will be more likely to create new specific identities among participants than sudden and brief protest outbursts or riots. However, there is also empirical evidence which casts doubt on the strength of this relation. Actually, the emergence of collective identity appears to be dependent on a plurality of factors.[7]

Even initiatives, which are apparently very specific, may thus be considered part of a social movement, provided they are interpreted in the light of a wider system of beliefs. This is possible if they develop in a context which is not only conducive to collective action in general terms, but where a realignment of frames (Snow et al., 1986) can occur. As we have seen in the previous section, the essential condition is that the sense of belongingness exceeds the length of the public activities and campaigns. Collective identity may thus either become a precondition for the creation of new and different identities (and consequently, of new and different social movements); or provide a persistent, though latent, basis for a new upsurge of mobilisation campaigns under the same heading. Social movements often persist even when they are not active on the public stage, and are rather going through a "latency" phase. Those countercultural movements which alternate sudden explosions of protest with long periods of latency may be analysed in this light, for example. In their case, collective identity provides the link between occasional outbursts which would be otherwise unexplainable (Melucci, 1984a, 1989).

A further argument for the discriminating capacity of the notion of collective identity comes from other examples of informal networks of collective action, such as coalitions (for an introduction and a definition: Hinckley, 1981: 4–6). These reveal some similarity with social movements, in so far as they imply the existence of a conflict and of a collective activity. However, the interaction and co-ordination between different actors occurs mostly on an instrumental level, as actors try to maximise their outcomes by establishing alliances to other actors. In contrast to what happens in social movements, interaction in coalitions does not foster the emergence of collective identities, nor does it imply necessarily any sort of continuity beyond the limits of the specific conflictual situation, let alone a global redefinition of the issues at stake.[8]

CONCLUSIONS

In this [chapter] I have tried to show that different approaches to the field share, in their definitions of "social movement", the emphasis on some specific dynamics. In particular, three basic components of social movements have been identified: networks of relations between a plurality of actors; collective identity; conflictual issues. In contrast, it has been denied that anti-institutional styles of political participation or anti-systemic attitudes may constitute a distinctive trait of the concept of social movements.

I would arge that this definition of social movements may constitute the bulk of a programme of research and theorising that adopt "social movements" as an analytical, rather than a merely evocative, concept. It may also contribute to the integration of different theoretical perspectives. During the 1970s, the resurgence of scholarly interest for social movements had focused either on the structural determinants of new conflicts (mostly in Europe) or on mobilisation processes (mostly in the USA). Emphasising the interplay between networks, identity and conflicts challenges some conventional wisdom inherited from these traditions. On the one hand, it challenges the idea that the study of social movements may be equated to the study of new social conflicts. While there is an obvious strong correlation between movements and conflicts, the concept proposed here accepts that, in principle, conflicts can arise even in the absence of social movements. How single, isolated conflicts may become a movement is a central matter for investigation. To this purpose, attention must necessarily be paid to social networks and processes of meaning construction. On the other hand, stressing the importance of social networks prevents one from confusing the analysis of "social movements" with the analysis of "social movement organisations" or "mobilisation processes". This also bears substantial implications in terms of research strategy. Only the study of the properties of interorganisational and interpersonal networks is, in this perspective, directly relevant to the analysis of social movements. In contrast, for example, the study of individuals' commitment to a specific movement organisation, albeit of obvious substantial interest, is not specific to social movement studies. Rather, it is more directly connected to the broader analysis of individuals' incentives to collective action and political participation.

I do not pretend that the view proposed here is absolutely original. I would rather argue that it reflects – and partially expands on – recent efforts toward theoretical integration in the field. To start with, many have recently argued for greater attention to be paid to the intermediate structures of collective action, i.e. the networks that link individuals, groups and SMOs active in the same, or related, conflicts (McAdam et al., 1988; Tarrow, 1988). This, in order to provide a proper link between "macro" explanations, focusing on structural changes and factors, and "micro" explanations, focusing on individual attitudes and behaviours. So far, research in this area has almost exclusively analysed the role of personal links in facilitating mobilisation (e.g. Klandermans et al., 1988). A more systematic investigation of the properties of these networks is needed, however, in order to assess their impact on a larger set of processes. These processes include how resources are put together and made available for action; the impact of the alliance and influence structure of social movements on their capacity to exert pressure on public authorities; the role of micro-mobilisation contexts, and in particular of the complex interpersonal bonds, which constitute the latent structure of social movements, in the elaboration of interpretative frames; and so forth (McAdam et al., 1988).

Recent research has also assigned special relevance to the role of collective identity. Scholars like Touraine (1981) and Melucci (1989) have revealed that this is not a datum, but a key problem for the study of collective action. As we already noticed in our previous discussion, the sense of belongingness to a movement must never be taken for granted. In contrast, collective identity is always the precarious and temporary outcome of a "bargaining" process between actors who embody quite different and heterogeneous beliefs. How do actors, who are broadly interested in similar issues, yet from different perspectives, come to think of themselves as part of a broader movement, while preserving their peculiarity? And how do they manage to maintain their collective identity, and eventually to adapt it to changes in the conflict, instead of splitting the movement in several factions and sects? Finally, how do movement identities react to shifts in dominant cultures in their environment? These and related questions become, if we take up this perspective, a central area of investigation.[9]

The growth of cultural conflicts has also been at the core of recent theorising. The inclusion of both socio-political and cultural movements within this definition differentiates it from others – like Tilly – who conceive of the existence of shared beliefs and solidarity mainly as a precondition to the occurrence of public action and political protest. In contrast, other theorists (e.g. Gusfield, 1981; Touraine, 1981; Melucci, 1989) suggest that the processes of meaning construction may also be regarded as the true essence of many conflicts in contemporary society. Of course, symbolic antagonism may often develop in parallel to political protest. Yet, the relationship between the two aspects is not necessarily in the sense of the former being a precondition of the latter. It may rather take different forms, which must become an object of careful investigation (for a recent example: Lumley, 1990).

Finally, the definition also changes the idea that social movements are necessarily anti-systemic actors. This leaves more room for the analysis of how social movements change over time, in aspects as different as the number and quality of actors involved in protest events; the cultural interpretations of the conflict; the issues at stake; the repertoires of action and the degrees of radicalisation (e.g. Tilly, 1978, 1984, 1988; Tarrow, 1989). What appears as a challenge to the system in the mounting phase of protest may be viewed as a reformist attempt in a longer historical perspective; periods when social conflict is globally intense may encourage social movements to adopt radical, disruptive strategies with a greater frequency than phases when conflicts are not so strong and public concern tends to address other, non-conflictual issues. For these reasons it seems advisable to select a very limited number of variables to define the notion of social movement, and to leave more specific connotations to the analysis of specific conflicts, cycles of protest or phases of deep underlying cultural strife.

ACKNOWLEDGEMENTS

This [chapter] has greatly benefited from comments from Jack Brand, Donatella della Porta, Ron Eyerman and two anonymous referees. A preliminary version has been discussed during the Annual Meeting of the Political Studies Association (University of Durham, April 1990). Joanna McPake, John Davis and Ron Eyerman have graciously helped with the language. Financial support from the European Consortium for Political Research and the Consiglio Nazionale delle Ricerche is also gratefully acknowledged.

NOTES

1   It is not by chance that one of the most popular debates among social movement scholars in recent years concerns the role of social networks in

facilitating individuals' mobilisation (e.g. Klandermans et al., 1988): an important contribution, but to a controversy originated by Mancur Olson's seminal work in a different theoretical (rational choice theory) and empirical (participation in trade unions and interest groups) context.

2   Many other scholars apart from Touraine and Melucci (mostly, but not exclusively, European) have played an important role in the debate on "new" social movements. Among them are Habermas, Offe, Castells (see for some discussion, Cohen, 1985; Misztal, 1988; Scott, 1990). They are not taken into account here because they focus almost exclusively on macrosocial dynamics and do not pay attention to the specificity of the concept. In the light of what follows, the remark might somewhat apply to Touraine as well. Yet he introduces as series of more specific definitions which are important to the development of the discussion here.

3   Pizzorno (1978) has been among the first to use this notion in order to challenge Olson's well-known hypothesis about the irrationality of collective action.

4   Snow and associates (Snow et al., 1986; Snow and Benford, 1988) use the concept of "frame alignment" (from Goffman's notion of *frames*) to identify those changes in individuals' sets of beliefs which account for their decisions to join collective action. Even though originally elaborated in the context of the analysis of individual mobilisation, the same notion may be usefully referred to the process whereby a broader collective identity is created.

5   See, among others, Touraine (1977), Turner (1981), Melucci (1989). The degree of inclusiveness or exclusiveness of such identifications is on the other hand subjected to shifting conditions (Zald and Ash, 1966).

6   As Pamela Oliver puts it: "all too often we speak of *movement* strategy, tactics, leadership, membership, recruitment, division of labour, success and failure – terms which strictly apply only to coherent decision-making entities (i.e., organisations or groups), not to crowds, collectivities, or whole social movements" (1989: 4).

7   Several protests were for instance promoted by nature protection associations in Italy during the 1960s and the 1970s. In absolute terms, they were probably more frequent than the protests against nuclear power which developed in a very restricted period in the late 1970s. Yet, the latter developed a specific collective identity and were perceived as a movements, while this was not so with the former, who have come to identify themselves as a part of the environmental movement only in the 1980s. The explanation may lie in the persistence, until the late 1970s, of attitudes of mistrust towards collective action within nature protection associations. These attitudes were not conducive to the formation of broader collective identities (Diani, 1990b).

8   Industrial action in countries like Italy, that have several competing trade unions, provides a good example of the point. The defence of workers' interests is usually undertaken by single organisations, which may or may not set up alliances, yet maintain basically their specific identities unchanged and give to these identities priority over the identification with a broader workers' movement. For several years after 1968, however, the drive

towards a redefinition of the concept of industrial action and of what was at stake in the conflict brought about a change in identities as well, whereby the sense of belongingness to the new workers' movement became more important than pre-existing loyalties to specific organisations (see Regalia et al., 1978).

9   For a broader, yet similar, perspective, see Morris and Herring (1987: 192ff).

REFERENCES

Alberoni, F. (1984) *Movement and Institution*. New York: Columbia University Press.

Byrne, P. (1988) *The Campaign for Nuclear Disarmament*. London: Croom Helm.

Cohen, J. L. (1985) "Strategy and identity: new theoretical paradigms and contemporary social movements," *Social Research*, 52: 663–716.

Dalton, R. and Kuechler, M. (eds) (1990) *Challenging the Political Order: New Social and Political Movements in Western Democracies*. Cambridge: Polity Press.

della Porta, D. (1988) "Recruitment processes in clandestine political organizations: Italian left-wing terrorism," in Klandermans et al., 1988.

Diani, M. (1990a) "The network structure of the Italian ecology movement," *Social Science Information*, 29: 5–31.

Diani, M. (1990b) "The Italian ecology movement: from radicalism to moderation," in Rudig, W. (ed.), *Green Politics 1. 1990*. Edinburgh: Edinburgh University Press.

Eder, K. (1985) "The 'new social movements': moral crusades, political pressure groups, or social movements?," *Social Research*, 52: 869–901.

Etzioni, A. (1985) "Special interest groups versus constituency representation," in Kriesberg, L. (ed.), *Research in Social Movement: Conflict and Change*, vol. 8. Greenwich, Conn.: JAI Press.

Eyerman, R. and Jamison, A. (1990) *Social Movements: a Cognitive Approach*. Cambridge: Polity Press.

Gamson, W. (1988) "Political discourse and collective action," in Klandermans et al., 1988.

Garner, R. and Zald, M. N. (1985) "The political economy of social movement sectors," in G. Suttles and M. N. Zald (eds), *The Challenge of Social Control*. Norwood, NJ: Ablex.

Gerlach, L. and Hine, V. (1970) *People, Power and Change*. Indianapolis: Bobbs-Merrill.

Gusfield, J. (1981) "Social movements and social change: perspectives of linearity and fluidity," in L. Kriesberg (ed.), *Research in Social Movements: Conflict and Change*, vol. 4. Greenwich, Conn.: JAI Press.

Hinckley, B. (1981) *Coalitions and Politics*. New York: Harcourt Brace Jovanovich.

Kitschelt, H. (1989) *The Logics of Party Formation: Ecological Politics in Belgium and West Germany*. Ithaca, NY: Cornell University Press.

Klandermans, B. (ed.) (1989) *Organizing for Change: Social Movement Organizations across Cultures*. Greenwich, Conn.: JAI Press.

Klandermans, B. and Tarrow, S. (1988) "Mobilization into social movements: synthesizing European and American approaches," in Klandermans et al., 1988.

Klandermans, B., Kriesi, H. and Tarrow, S. (eds) (1988) *From Structure to Action: Comparing Social Movement Research across Cultures*. Greenwich, Conn.: JAI Press.

Lowe, S. (1986) *Urban Social Movements: the City after Castells*. London: Macmillan.

Lumley, R. (1990) *States of Emergency: Cultures of Revolt in Italy from 1968 to 1978*. London: Verso.

McAdam, D. (1982) *Political Process and the Development of Black Insurgency, 1930–1970*. Chicago: University of Chicago Press.

McAdam, D., McCarthy, J. D. and Zald, M. N. (1988) "Social movements," in Smelser, N. J. (ed.), *Handbook of Sociology*. Beverly Hills/London: Sage.

McCarthy, J. D. and Zald, M. N. (1973) *The Trend of Social Movements in America: Professionalization and Resource Mobilization*. Morristown: General Learning Press.

McCarthy, J. D. and Zald, M. N. (1977) "Resource mobilization and social movements: a partial theory," *American Journal of Sociology*, 82: 1212–41.

Marwell, G. and Oliver, P. (1984) "Collective action theory and social movements research," in L. Kriesberg (ed.), *Research in Social Movements: Conflict and Change*, vol. 7. Greenwich, Conn.: JAI Press.

Melucci, A. (ed.) (1984a) *Altri codici: Aree di movimento nella metropoli*. Bologna: Il Mulino.

Melucci, A. (1984b) "Movimenti in un mondo di segni," in Melucci, A. 1984a.

Melucci, A. (1985) "The symbolic challenge of contemporary movements," *Social Research*, 52: 789–816.

Melucci, A. (1989) *Nomads of the Present*. London: Hutchinson Radius.

Misztal, B. (1988) "Social movements of the core and the periphery," *Australian and New Zealand Journal of Sociology*, 24: 65–82.

Morris, A. and Herring, C. (1987) "Theory and research in social movements: a critical review," *Annual Review of Political Science*, 2: 137–98.

Nedelmann, B. (1984) "New political movements and changes in processes of intermediation," *Social Science Information*, 23: 1029–48.

Neidhardt, F. and Rucht, D. (1990) "The analysis of social movements: the state of the art and some perspectives for further research," in Rucht, D. 1990a.

Oliver, P. (1989) "Bringing the crowd back in: the nonorganizational elements of social movements," in Kriesberg, L. (ed.), *Research in Social Movements: Conflict and Change*, vol. 11. Greenwich, Conn.: JAI Press.

Pizzorno, A. (1978) "Political exchange and collective identity in industrial conflict," in C. Crouch and A. Pizzorno (eds), *The Resurgence of Class Conflict in Western Europe since 1968*. London: Macmillan.

Regalia, I., Regini, M. and Reyneri, E. (1978) "Labour conflicts and industrial relations in Italy," in C. Crouch and A. Pizzorno (eds), *The Resurgence of Class Conflict in Western Europe since 1968*. London: Macmillan.

Robbins, T. (1988) *Cults, Converts and Charisma: the Sociology of New Religious Movements*. London: Sage.

Rucht, D. (ed.) (1990a) *Research in Social Movements: the State of the Art*. Boulder, CO: Westview Press.

Rucht, D. (1990b) "The strategies and action repertoires of new movements," in Dalton and Kuechler, 1990.

Sartori, G. (1984) "Guidelines for concept analysis," in Sartori, G. (ed.) *Social Science Concepts: a Systematic Analysis*. Beverly Hills/London: Sage.

Scott, A. (1990) *Ideology and the New Social Movements*. London: Unwin Hyman.

Smelser, N. J. (1962) *Theory of Collective Behaviour*. New York: The Free Press.

Snow, D. A. and Benford, R. D. (1988) "Ideology, frame resonance, and participant mobilization," in Klandermans et al., 1988.

Snow, D. A., Burke Rochford, E., Worden, S. K. and Benford, R. D. (1986) "Frame alignment processes, micromobilization, and movement participation," *American Sociological Review*, 51: 464–81.

Tarrow, S. (1983) "Struggling to reform: social movements and policy change during cycles of protest," *Western Societies Paper No. 15*. Ithaca, NY: Cornell University Press.

Tarrow, S. (1988) "National politics and collective action: recent theory and research in Western Europe and the USA," *Annual Review of Sociology*, 14: 421–40.

Tarrow, S. (1989) *Democracy and Disorder: Protest and Politics in Italy 1965–1975*. Oxford: Oxford University Press.

Tilly, C. (1978) *From Mobilization to Revolution*. Reading: Addison-Wesley.

Tilly, C. (1984) "Social movements and national politics," in C. Bright and S. Harding (eds), *State-making and Social Movements: Essays in History and Theory*. Ann Arbor: University of Michigan Press.

Tilly, C. (1988) "Social movements, old and new," in B. Misztal (ed.), *Research in Social Movements: Conflict and Change*, vol. 10. Greenwich, Conn.: JAI Press.

Touraine, A. (1977) *The Self-production of Society*. Chicago: University of Chicago Press.

Touraine, A. (1981) *The Voice and the Eye: an Analysis of Social Movements*. Cambridge: Cambridge University Press.

Touraine, A. (1985) "An introduction to the study of social movements," *Social Research*, 52: 749–88.

Touraine, A., Hegedus, Z., Dubet, F. and Wieviorka. M. (1983a) *Anti-nuclear Protest: the Opposition to Nuclear Power in France*. Cambridge: Cambridge University Press.

Touraine, A., Dubet, F., Wieviorka, M. and Strzelecki, J. (1983b) *Solidarity. The Analysis of a Social Movement: Poland 1980–1981*. Cambridge: Cambridge University Press.

Turner, R. (1981) "Collective behaviour and resource mobilization as approaches to social movements: issues and continuities," in L. Kriesberg (ed.), *Research in Social Movements: Conflicts and Change*, vol. 4. Greenwich, Conn.: JAI Press.

Turner, R. and Killian, L. (1987) *Collective Behaviour*. Englewood Cliffs, NJ: Prentice Hall.

Wilson, J. Q. (1973) *Political Organizations*. New York: Basic Books.

Zald, M. N. (1988) "The trajectory of the social movements in America," in B. Misztal (ed.), *Research in Social Movements: Conflict and Change*, vol. 10. Greenwich, Conn.: JAI Press.

Zald, M. N. and Ash, R. (1966) "Social movement organizations: growth, decay and change," *Social Forces*, 44: 327–41.

Zald, M. N. and McCarthy, J. D. (1980) "Social movement industries: competition and cooperation among movement organizations," in L. Kriesberg (ed.), *Research in Social Movements: Conflict and Change*, vol. 3. Greenwich, Conn.: JAI Press.

Zald, M. N. and McCarthy, J. D. (eds) (1987) *Social Movements in Organizational Society: Resource Mobilization, Conflict and Institutionalization*. New Brunswick, NJ: Transaction Books.

CHAPTER 10

Transnational Contention

Sidney Tarrow

On February 27, 1997, Louis Schweitzer, president of the ailing French auto firm Renault, announced the imminent closure of the company's plant in Vilvoorde, Belgium (*Le Soir*, February 28, 1997).[1] The first angry reaction to Renault's announcement came from Belgian prime minister, Jean-Luc Dehaene, and gave rise to accusations in the Flemish press of French "chauvinism" (*Le Monde*, March 5, 1997). Belgian ire rose when it became clear that the French government had been apprised of Renault's plan at least six weeks prior to its announcement and that the firm was hoping to use European Union (EU) structural funds to expand its plant in Valladolid, Spain, just as it closed Vilvoorde (*Le Monde*, March 6 and 8, 1997). The European Parliament expressed outrage at what some of its members called an "Anglo-Saxon" restructuring; even normally deadpan Commission President Jacques Santer called the decision "a serious blow to European confidence," urging the automaker's Belgian workers to sue the company for violating European labor law (*International Herald Tribune*, March 10, 1997). The unions promptly took the firm to court both in Belgium and, for good measure, in France.

But if Belgian and EU officials were ruffled by Renault's move, that was nothing compared with the reactions of Vilvoorde's workers. Almost immediately following the announcement of the closure, they occupied the plant, "kidnapped" a large number of cars due for

This chapter is an edited extract from *Power in Movement: Social Movements and Contentious Politics* by Sidney Tarrow (2nd edn, Cambridge, Cambridge University Press, 1998), pp. 176–95. Reprinted by permission of Cambridge University Press.

shipment, and began a series of public protests that would make Vilvoorde synonymous with a new term in the European political lexicon – "the Eurostrike." These actions quickly crossed the border, bringing a Vilvoorde "commando" into France and French Renault workers into Belgium to demonstrate alongside their Belgian colleagues. When the Belgian unions organized a mass demonstration in Brussels, they were joined by leaders of the French left and a large delegation of French Renault workers. As Schweitzer was hung in effigy and a giant wickerwork figure carried by the demonstrators made nazi salutes, Belgium's Christian Democratic union leader, Willy Peirens, told the crowd: "This is a signal of anger and indignation; a signal of solidarity against brutality" (Reuter's, March 17, 1997).

The joint pressure on the French government from Belgian politicians, the EU, and the French and Belgian demonstrators was too much for French Prime Minister Juppé; on March 20, he appeared on television to announce that 800,000 francs per worker would be disbursed for the measures of reconversion and accompaniment to the plant's closure (Le Monde, March 26, 1997). By July, with a new Socialist government in place in France and both French and Belgian courts finding in their favor, the workers agreed to the compensation package Renault was offering (Le Monde, April 6–7, 1997). But there was no joy in Vilvoorde; as one poster on the day the workers voted to accept the plant closing put it: "In America, they have Clinton, Johnny Cash, and Stevie Wonder; in Belgium, we have Dehaene, but neither cash nor wonder" (L'Humanité, June 22, 1997).

For students of social movements, episodes like the "Eurostrike" raise important questions. Alongside the familiar artifacts of social movement theory were three new aspects: first, the conflict pitted the private citizens of one country against a firm based in another; second, there was cooperation across boundaries between national social actors with a common interest; and, third, a supranational institution and European law were used to advance their claims.

But was the episode a transnational social movement? Or even the start of one? The Belgian workers made common cause with their counterparts in France, using international law and institutions to do so; but was their protest – in the definition [of social movement] employed in this study – *a collective challenge, based on common purposes and social solidarities, in sustained interaction with elites, opponents, and authorities?* Or was it rather a brief episode of political *exchange* between French and Belgian workers and Belgian and EU officials upset by the "American" tactics used by the French firm (Pizzorno, 1978)? Was this a stage in a growing spiral of transnational contention or merely an incident in the normal conflict between capital and labor that happened to cross national lines?

What can we learn from such episodes about the growth of transnational movements in parts of the world that are not – like western Europe – regulated by a network of supranational institutions? [. . .] "Western analysts," writes John McCarthy, "increasingly employ a common set of conceptual tools in making sense of the emergence and trajectories of social movements;" can we use these concepts to understand challengers in other parts of the world that "seek to influence transnational as well as national and sub-national authorities" (1997: 243)? These are the questions I raise in this chapter.

GLOBALIZATION AND TRANSNATIONAL SOCIAL MOVEMENTS

In northern Quebec, South America, and rural India, campaigns to stop dam construction have been mounted by coalitions of indigenous groups and non-governmental organizations from abroad; on the Mexican–United States border, Mexican and American environmental and workers' rights groups cooperate in the framework of the North American Free Trade Agreement (NAFTA); in eastern Europe before 1989, the Helsinki accords provided an international framework within which dissident groups organized; on the high seas, Greenpeace and other ecological groups oppose firms and governments that pollute the environment. However disparate, such episodes bring a transnational dimension to contentious politics.

Scholars have been quick to pick up on these events, often making generalizations based on a few spectacular – but perhaps unrepresentative – episodes. Some conclude that transnational collective action poses a challenge to the sovereignty of the national state (Cerny, 1995), while others talk only of "fading states" (Rudolf, 1997); some wonder if such movements are steps in the creation of a global civil society (Wapner, 1995, 1996), while others write of "a plurality of transnational spaces" (Rudolf, 1997: 2); some see globalization "disenfranchising societies" (Castells, 1997), while others already speak of "world society" (Meyer et al., 1996). As one scholar confidently puts it, "Movements are changing from fairly coherent national organizations into transnational networks, with highly fragmented and specialized nodes composed of organizations and less organized mobilizations, all of which are linked through new technologies of communication" (Garner, 1994: 431).

Transnational politics is of great importance at the turn of the new century (Risse, 1995). But our problem in this chapter is not to recognize or celebrate it, but to sort out the short-term and ephemeral connections across borders from the lasting and profound ones and to assess the opportunities and constraints on the formation of transnational

social movements. Only then can we begin to understand their implications for the future of contentious politics.

Three hypotheses surround the general thesis of transnational contention. The first is that the world economy is rapidly globalizing
along with its attendant system of communications; the second that
these changes open up enhanced possibilities for transnational collective
action; and the third that – knit together by international institutions and
transnational social movements – something resembling a transnational
civil society is developing. Let us review these themes before turning to the
processes of transnational contention that can be perceived today.

The sources of globalization

In the most popular version of the theory of transnational social movements, sometime around the end of World War II, and assisted by the
liberalization of international trade and the appearance of a new economic hegemon, a global economy began to develop. Its most basic
aspect, writes Kevin Robins, was a shift to a world "in which all aspects
of the economy – raw materials, labor information and transportation,
finance, distribution, marketing – are integrated or interdependent on a
global scale" (1995: 345).

Like that of many students of globalization, Robins's evocation of
a global economy is stronger on declaration than demonstration. When
Robert Wade carried out a careful statistical analysis of past and
present international investment, trade, and finance, he concluded that
"the world economy is more international than global:" "In the bigger
national economies, more than 80 percent of production is for domestic consumption and more than 80 percent of investment by domestic
investors. Companies are rooted in national home bases with national
regulatory regimes" (1996: 61).

Where Robins has hit on a truly new factor in the world economy
today is in pointing out that – in contrast to past periods of enhanced
international exchange – economic changes occur "on an almost instantaneous basis" (1995: 345). This takes us to the second element of the
globalization thesis: the appearance of public communication structures
that weave core and periphery of the world system closer together. This
growth is accelerated by decentralized and private communications
technologies, which provide individuals and groups with independent
means of communication, like fax machines, electronic mail, and cam-
corders (Ganley, 1992).

The expansion of worldwide markets and global communications
brings citizens of the north and west and those of the east and south
closer together, making the former more cosmopolitan and the latter
more aware of their inequality. The most spectacular expression of this

cognitive and physical integration is immigration from the east and south to the west and north, with the consequence that global cities have developed into microcosms "in which to observe the growing dualism between the world's rich and poor and the encounter of global cultures" (Castells, 1994; Robins, 1995: 345). But it has also made it possible for Western environmentalists and human rights and women's rights advocates to move in the opposite direction: speaking the same language and working toward the same goals as their counterparts in the Third World. In support of this trend, Jackie Smith points out that a slowly increasing proportion of transnational organizations now have their offices outside the industrial democracies (Smith, 1997: 49).

These structural changes have a cultural concomitant: that we live in a culturally more unified universe, one in which young people dress similarly, listen to the same music, and attend school systems built on the same models (Meyer et al., 1997). One result may be to "destroy the cultural isolation in which misunderstanding grows;" but another is to intensify perceptions of difference that "increase social antagonisms and promote social fragmentation" (O'Neil, 1993: 68). A third is to create perceived chains of economic and social impact between different parts of the globe, while a fourth is the mutual discovery of similar problems on the part of indigenous groups in formerly isolated areas (Brysk, 1994; Yashar, 1996). Groups as diverse as Andean Indians and northern European Lapps are now in contact across national borders.

There is an institutional concomitant to increased economic and communication flows. Since World War II, a dense network of international institutions, regimes, and intergovernmental and transnational contacts has knit together different parts of the world (Meyer et al., 1996). Consider the international human rights regime with Thomas Risse and colleagues: "Since World War II human rights have been increasingly regulated and specified in international regimes. The evolution of human rights regimes concentrates on the United Nations system complemented by regional arrangements." Alongside this formal regime is an informal "liberal club" of nations that identify themselves and are identified as a category of states from which others are excluded (Risse et al., 1999: 4). These international institutions, regimes, and "clubs" are the armature around which transnational relations have grown. This takes us to the second part of the thesis – transnational collective action.

Transnational collective action

In his summary of the rapidly burgeoning literature on globalization, Robins claimed only that it erodes the boundaries of national *economies*; but others have seen it eroding the power of the national state. In the age of globalization, the thesis continues, not only are images of contentious politics transmitted rapidly from country to country, triggering diffusion and imitation; so are people and their claims and conflicts. Cheap airline tickets and porous national boundaries make it possible for movement missionaries and their local allies to diffuse movements as diverse as Muslim fundamentalism and Serbian nationalism around the world (Kane, 1997). Using fax machines, electronic mail, the collection of "charitable contributions" from well-meaning sympathizers, moving funds, arms, and terrorists across borders with ease, "diaspora nationalists" advance their causes in their home countries without moving from their comfortable Western havens (Anderson, 1992).

In part in response to global economic trends, international organizations have proliferated in the twentieth century and especially since World War II. Many, like the World Bank, have become targets for social protest (Kowalewski, 1989; Walton, 1989), while others, like the United Nations and the European Union, deliberately encourage transnational nongovernmental groups with subsidies, meetings, and opportunities for consultation. For example, the European Union's Directorate for the Environment, Nuclear Safety and Civil Protection subsidizes the European Environmental Bureau, an umbrella organization representing nearly all relevant environmental associations in the countries of the EU (Rucht, 1997: 202, 206).

Where international organizations can make decisions that are binding – or even semibinding – on member states, they offer domestic challengers institutional opportunities to transcend their national arenas for consultation, collective action, and contestation at an international level (Keck, 1995). Some of these efforts are bilateral and vertical: that is, between a particular domestic group and a particular international organization. But [. . .] challengers create opportunities for other challengers; over the past decades, a host of transnational nongovernmental organizations (TNGOs) have clustered around each major international institution (Smith, 1994, 1997). Like the national state in the eighteenth and nineteenth centuries, international organizations and institutions provide opportunities for collective action to a host of social actors. This takes us to what I call "the strong thesis" of transnational social movements.

The strong transnational thesis

The strong thesis of transnational social movements, which I have aggregated from a number of sources, grows out of these observations. Its proponents make the following five claims.

First, in the age of global television, whirring fax machines, and electronic mail, the national political opportunity structures that used to be needed to mount collective action may be giving way to transnational ones (Pagnucco and Atwood, 1994: 411).

Second, the national state may be losing its capacity to constrain and structure collective action. In part, this is because of the declining capacity of governments to disguise what is going on abroad from their own citizens. But, in part, it is because the integration of the international economy weakens states' capacity to cope with global economic trends (Tilly, 1991: 1; Badie, 1997).

Third, as the state's capacity to control global economic forces declines, individuals and groups have gained access to new kinds of resources to mount collective action across borders (Rosenau, 1990), as we saw in the Vilvoorde case. These are not different in kind from the types of resources analyzed by resource mobilization theorists in domestic politics (McCarthy, 1997; Keck and Sikkink, 1998b), but they include travel abroad, communication with like-minded others across national boundaries, and growing expertise at using transnational communication and international institutions.

Fourth, as economies globalize, cultures universalize, and institutions proliferate, "principled ideas" are increasingly adopted as international norms (Finnemore, 1996) and then become socialized into domestic understandings (Price, 1997; Risse et al., 1999).

Finally, growing out of a global economy and its attendant communications revolution, wound around the latticework of international organizations and institutions, drawing on the inequalities and abuses created by economic globalization and fortified by international norms, a web of new transnational organizations and movements is being formed.

Although the parameters she uses to identify transnational social movements (TSMOs) are broader than ours are (see subsequent discussion), Jackie Smith's compendium of TSMOs illustrates the tremendous growth in these ogranizations.[2] Smith found that "the transnational social movement sector is quite large and diverse and that it has grown dramatically in recent years – from just over 300 in 1983 to about 600 in 1993" (1997: 47). "Sixty-five percent of all TSMOs active in 1993," she writes, "were formed after 1970, and their average age declined over the two decades from 33 to 25 years" (1997: 46). There is a growing potential for contentious politics beyond the borders of national states as the world enters the twenty-first century. But how new is this new phenomenon? And how contentious is it likely to be?

WHAT HISTORY TEACHES

Before proposing a thesis that is not quite as strong as the one previously sketched – but which seems to fit better with many emerging trends in the world today – it is important to provide some historical background to the claim that it is new technologies and new forms of communication that are creating a world of transnational movements. [. . .]

For example, as Susanne Rudolf reminds us, the fluidity of religion across political boundaries is very old, both from West to East and from East to West (1997: 2). The most dramatic example was perhaps the transfer of organized Catholicism to Latin America on the swords of Spanish and Portuguese colonialism. In the eighteenth century, there was a close connection between the American Revolution, the Dutch Patriot movement, and the French Revolution (Markoff, 1996). Soon after, a relationship developed among antislavery advocates in Britain, the United States, and western Europe. The first modern slave rebellion – that of Haiti – was a direct response to the French Revolution (Drescher, 1987: ch. 2).

In the nineteenth century [. . .] every major revolution and many minor ones had reverberations in other countries. By the 1880s the loose ties that had linked the working-class movement across Europe crystallized into the Second International, whose parties built similar organizations and at least claimed to be working toward the same international goal. European strike waves and protest cycles responded to broad international trends too (Mikkelson, 1996). Transnational advocates of antislavery, nationalism, and women's emancipation were able to win converts and make modest progress against traditional or colonial governments (Hanagan, 1998; Keck and Sikkink, 1998a: ch. 2).

History also teaches that transnational contention takes many forms – not all of them easy to catalog as social movements. Although most of the campaigns studied by Margaret Keck and Kathryn Sikkink from the nineteenth century were based on religious belief, some, like the antifemale circumcision campaign in Kenya, involved only missionaries (Keck and Sikkink, 1998a: 66–72); others, like the campaign against Chinese foot binding, involved missionaries and secular nationalists (1998a: 60–6); still others, like antislavery, "built linkages largely on the basis of corresponding religious organizations" (1998a: 41–51). Of Keck and Sikkink's cases, only women's suffrage involved dedicated international movement organizations (1998a: 51–8).

Moreover, although the initial impetus for many movements came from the diffusion of advocacy across national boundaries, they often depended on the power of hegemonic states – like the British use of its powerful navy to impede the slave trade – and took root differently in different soils. Where they did so successfully, they produced increasingly differentiated national movements, parties, and unions. As Keck and Sikkink observe, "Advocacy campaigns take place in organizational contexts; not only must their ideas resonate and create allies, their organizations must also overcome opposition" (1998a: 74).

Consider the differences that grew up within the national parties of the Second International: under a common umbrella of internationalism, each was invested in different national cultures – cultures that became active forces for division when, in 1914, almost every socialist party in Europe supported its national government's "capitalist war." As John McCarthy points out, "national political opportunity structures affect the variable likelihood of transnational activism" (1997: 256).

History also casts a skeptical eye on the assumption that international norms can be socialized into domestic norms without concrete mechanisms to effect such transformations. In the more abstract formulations, civil society "generates" international norms, which somehow shape and redefine state interests (Price, 1997). But although new definitions of interest and identity are constantly being proposed by concrete actors, history provides few that are transformed into international norms and even fewer that are successfully socialized into domestic societies without the exercise of agency. Consider the spread of antislavery around the world; it had as much to do with the British navy protecting the economies of former British slave colonies as it did with the "norm" of human rights (Markoff, 1996: ch. 2). As Margaret Keck puts it, there are "limits to social construction" (1995: 420–1).

In summary, history not only teaches that transnational contention is nothing new under the sun; it shows that it takes a number of forms and integrates differently within domestic societies; and that it requires special conjunctures of incentives and opportunities to be mounted and transmit new norms and identities. Before concluding that the world is fast becoming a global civil society, we should examine these forms and levels of integration and ask where they are leading and which ones are likely to produce new norms and identities.

A Typology of Transnational Contention

Two empirical observations drawn from these brief historical examples can help us to unravel the complex strands in transnational politics in the world today. First, many of the phenomena that must have seemed structurally transnational at the time turned out to be part of processes that ended when political conditions changed. Second, many of the examples of transnational contention lacked solid bases in domestic social networks. Turned into analytical dimensions and intersected, these two observations help us to differentiate and describe the broad range of transnational contention that we see in the world today. This

**INTEGRATION IN
DOMESTIC SOCIAL NETWORKS**

TIME FRAME	Nonintegrated	Integrated
Temporary	Diffusion	Political Exchange
Sustained	Transnational Issue Networks	Transnational Social Movements

Figure 10.1   *A typology of transnational collective action*

intersection is represented graphically in the typology in figure 10.1. In what follows, I define each of these forms, provide a few examples from the literature on both social movements and transnational politics, and then speculate briefly about their major properties and dynamics.

Transnational social movements

By transnational social movements, I intend *sustained contentious interactions with opponents – national or nonnational – by connected networks of challengers organized across national boundaries.* The targets of transnational movements can change from time to time; they may be either international or national, private or public. What is important in our definition is that the challengers themselves be both rooted in domestic social networks and connected to one another more than episodically through common ways of seeing the world, or through informal or organizational ties, and that their challenges be contentious in deed as well as in word. Such a definition is tight enough to exclude some kinds of transnational interactions but broad enough to include those which – in terms of the typology in figure 10.1 – combine duration in time and integration within the domestic structures of more than one society.

Our definition is restrictive, but not so restrictive that it would be impossible to find real-world phenomena that match it. For example, Greenpeace is a transnational movement organization with the properties proposed in the foregoing definition. It claims millions of members in a number of countries, connected in a hierarchical way by a transnational organization; its members share a common world view; and it engages in confrontational actions with both governments and private firms that pollute or threaten to pollute the environment (Wapner, 1995, 1996). Greenpeace has also developed an action repertoire that allows it to oppose projects and opponents outside national boundaries – for example, in its opposition to French nuclear testing in the Pacific or against Shell Oil's plan to sink an oil platform in the North Sea, or against the overkill of ocean stocks by French and British trawlers (Imig and Tarrow, 1996).

The European and American peace movement of the 1980s was a second transnational movement, albeit one that lacked a single hierarchical organization (Rochon, 1988). Islamic fundamentalism is a third, even if it appears to take different forms in different parts of the world, from the Afghanistani Taliban to Iranian nationalism to the Algerian Islamic Salvation Front (Eickelman, 1997; Kane, 1997). The former movement was able to mobilize hundreds of thousands of demonstrators against nuclear missiles in the early 1980s, while the latter has seriously challenged or undermined numerous governments since the Iranian Revolution in 1979.[3]

The conditions necessary to produce a sustained social movement that is, at once, integrated within several societies, unified in its goals and organization, and capable of mounting contention against a variety of targets are hard to fulfill. Greenpeace grew out of a congeries of domestic movements that were similarly motivated and had a few highly visible targets whose activities crossed national boundaries. The peace movement of the 1980s was a response to an international issue that combined threat and opportunity – the policies of an American president who appeared to be threatening the planet with his administration's arms buildup. And Islamic fundamentalism grew up within one of the oldest transnational institutions in the world, with autonomous religious schools, mosques, and sects all over the world in which to root itself. These conditions are not reproduced each time a transnational interaction occurs among nongovernmental actors and, as Margaret Keck observes, "the international attention span is, after all, short" (1995: 421). Far more common are the conditions that permit the rapid cross-border diffusion of domestic contention.

Cross-border diffusion

By cross-border diffusion, I mean the communication of movement ideas, forms of organization, or challenges to similar targets from one center of contention to another. Such interaction can lead to strong movements – but not necessarily to movements with strong connective tissue in more than one society. Since it is uncontrolled by strong connective tissue across boundaries, diffusion leaves great scope for domestic opportunities and constraints to affect how challenges are transformed in their new settings (Ernst, 1997). Diffusion is a transnational phenomenon that is both temporary and unrooted as such in domestic social networks.

Diffusion is perhaps the oldest form of transnational politics we know of. We saw it first in the Reformation, when Calvinist "saints," Puritan immigrants, and exiled Catholic priests carried religious ideas and contentious practices from one country to another. We saw it again in the diffusion of the ideas of the American and French revolutions – although the movement of soldiers from Paris to the rest of Europe was one important vehicle for diffusion. By the nineteenth century social movements were less dependent on the movement of arms. [. . .] By the second half of the century, eastern and southern European immigrants were building workers' movements in the New World, from the lower east side of Manhattan to Chile and Argentina.[4] But once established, each national movement that struck indigenous roots and encountered local opportunity structures became largely independent of the others.

Contemporary collective action is diffused more rapidly than these nineteenth-century movements and is assisted in its diffusion both by the internationalization of the world economy and by mass communications. Consider the tactics linking the series of "fishing wars" that spread from the Bay of Biscay to the Grand Banks to the offshore North American salmon fisheries. In 1994, Spanish tuna fishermen sequestered a French trawler, accusing both British and French fishermen of using illegal nets to bag more than their share of tuna stocks. When the French government responded by taking one of the Spanish ships in tow, the Spaniards blocked the port of Hendaye. It took complicated negotiations among the three states and a decision by the European Union to resolve the dispute (Tarrow, 1998).

Six months later a different group of Spanish fishermen was in the news – this time taking fish from the Grand Banks that Canadian fishermen thought were rightly theirs. The Canadian navy sequestered a Spanish trawler and towed it into the harbor of St Johns, to the jeers and thrown tomatoes of the fishing port's citizens (Tarrow, 1998). The Canadian government resolved the issue, but only after the European Union intervened on behalf of the Spaniards. Finally, in 1997, it was Canadian and American sailors who were locked in conflict on the Pacific coast, when over a hundred Canadian salmon boats blocked an American ferry in the port of Prince Rupert in retaliation for the American's taking of Canadian salmon from international waters (*New York Times*, July 23, 1997; *Toronto Globe and Mail*, July 18, 1997). Six thousand miles apart, similar issues gave rise to a similar form of action and brought social actors and governments from five countries into international contention.

The diffusion of the tactics of the "fishing wars" was the result of unconnected emulation. But diffusion can also occur at the hands of purposive agents. The spread of nationalism in east central Europe after 1989 was, as Mark Beissinger shows, no automatic transfer of ideas from one country to another but a set of purposive events depending on opportunities, interests, and threats, real and anticipated, advanced by movement entrepreneurs, some of them in power and others seeking power in the vacuum created by the fall of communism (1996).

The eastern European nationalism studied by Beissinger was triggered by international opportunities but created *national* movements. Can *trans*national movements result from diffusion? Claire Ernst's work on French Act-Up suggests it can. She tells of how both emulation and informal contacts in New York led to the creation of an Act-Up branch in Paris, struggling to defend the interests of AIDS victims there (1997). But after showing how closely French activists emulated the tactics and the slogans of their New York friends, Ernst examines how the specifics of French politics affected the outcome of the movement – in particular, the French republican tradition that demands integration in place of difference (1997: 22–3).

Transnational political exchange

By transnational political exchange, I refer to temporary forms of cooperation among essentially national actors that identify a common interest or set of values in a particular political configuration. Like transnational diffusion, political exchange across boundaries generally involves actors from different countries with ideological affinities, each of whom has something to gain from the relationship and offers something to the other. Unlike diffusion, the actors on both sides of the exchange have a stable existence in their respective countries prior to the episode that brings them together, but their interaction is the product of a particular national and international conjuncture.

Needless to say, the terms "gains" and "losses" should not be interpreted narrowly and materially. For example, in the 1980s, a number of northern environmental organizations, based partly on contacts made through anthropologists with experience in the area, formed alliances with the representatives of Brazilian rubber tappers (Keck, 1995: 415–16). The original issue had been one of economic gains and losses, due to the hectic land rush in northeastern Brazil in the late 1970s. The environmental core group based in Washington, DC, linked the tappers' plight to the World Bank's Polonoroeste project in Rondónia and interested the American Congress in the case, giving Brazilian activists the leverage on the Brazilian government to create reserves for the tappers' activities. It was the combination of labor union and church pressure domestically and environmental pressure internationally that tipped the scales in favor of the tappers. As Margaret Keck concludes, "foreign environmentalists and representatives of the rubber tappers' movement in Acre finally met and established a relationship that filled important needs and provided important political resources for all for them" (1995: 415).

These were not permanent arrangements. Although the northern groups involved had strong ideological beliefs in both the environment and the rights of indigenous peoples, the alliances were organized around a specific issue, and when that issue was resolved or became irrelevant, the campaign ended. Because political exchange is issue-based and is not lodged in a permanent organization, it is hardly more stable than the diffusion of collective action across national boundaries. But it can create networks that survive after a particular issue is resolved.

Transnational advocacy networks

This takes us to the hundreds of nongovernmental associations that link citizens across the world in environmental, human rights, women's, peace, and indigenous peoples' networks. Do they not qualify for inclusion in the concept of "transnational social movements?" My answer is that, although they are the most rapidly growing sector of transnational politics today, we do not advance understanding by assimilating them to social movements. It seems more accurate to classify them, with Margaret Keck and Kathryn Sikkink, as parts of "transnational advocacy networks." To quote Keck and Sikkink, "a transnational advocacy network includes those relevant actors working internationally on an issue, who are bound together by shared values, a common discourse, and dense exchanges of information and services" (1998a: 2). Such networks, they continue, "are most prevalent in issue areas characterized by high value content and informational uncertainty" (1998a: 2). They involve actors from nongovernmental, governmental, and intergovernmental organizations, and are increasingly present in such issue areas as human rights, women's rights, and the environment (also see Keck and Sikkink, 1998b).

How do these networks differ from social movements and why are they often confused with them? Part of the confusion results from two different uses of the term "network:" connective structures and the social networks that are the building blocks for social movements and a number of other kinds of contentious politics. [. . .] While some scholars are coming to believe that electronic communications are providing groups with the resources to form social networks across wide bands of space (Wellman and Gulia, 1998), there is a clear difference between Keck and Sikkink's concept of *advocacy* networks and the interpersonal *social* networks that social movement researchers have detected at the foundation of domestic social movements.[5]

Keck and Sikkink's advocacy networks are primarily communicative in content; they are "distinguishable largely by the centrality of principled ideas or values in motivating their formation;" and "at the core of the relationship [among their components] is information exchange." "They mobilize information strategically so as to gain leverage over much more powerful organizations and governments" (Keck and Sikkink, 1995: 1). And, it should be added, they profit from financial support from international agencies and northern governments interested in the norms they try to advance (Risse et al., 1999).

Advocacy networks lack the categorical basis, the sustained interpersonal relations, and the exposure to similar opportunities and constraints that social movement scholars have found in domestic social networks. But they have working for them the enormous increase in the density of transnational communication and in the involvement of northern governments, foundations, and public interest groups in issues of equality, human rights, and the environment in other parts of the world. "Minding other people's business" is becoming an important spur to social and political change in the world today.

NETWORKING FOR CHANGE

Are transnational advocacy networks therefore *un*important, compared with what we know of transnational social movements? Certainly, because of their frequent dependency on foundation funding and the support of northern governments, they lack the drama, the deliberate contentiousness, and the broad goals of such transnational movements as Greenpeace, the 1980s peace movements, and fundamentalist Islam. But although transnational advocacy networks are analytically distinct from social movements, they are a powerful force for change in the world today, and this for at least three reasons. First, many of them are *biographically* and *thematically* in the debt of social movements. Second, given the undemocratic or semiauthoritarian conditions of many parts of the world today, they provide a second-best but a safer alternative to social movements for millions of people. Third, their most important role may be to provide a mechanism for the diffusion of collective action frames to resource-poor domestic actors that can help them construct their own social movements. Each of these arguments could be elaborated at great length and supported with numerous examples. But since Margaret Keck and Kathryn Sikkink have done exactly this in their recent book, *Activists beyond Borders* (1998a), we can content ourselves with brief summaries of their arguments.

Movement sources of network recruitment

In the fields of human rights, women's rights, and ecology, transnational advocacy networks do not resemble social movements, but recruit supporters whose domestic experience in movements provides skills and models of activism. Such movement activists may join transnational networks through casual contacts with activists like themselves from other countries; through experiences with Western foundations or international organizations; and in part because, as they get older, their willingness to engage in vigorous and possibly dangerous movement actions gives way to a desire for more routine activities.

One such area of activism involves the international conferences that have been held periodically for women activists under the auspices of the United Nations since the mid-1970s. They provide a venue in which personal and foundation contacts are made and ideas and experiences exchanged, and activists may find themselves invited to foreign countries. While continuing to think of themselves as movement activists, many become increasingly involved in such transnational networks, at times losing their contacts with the grass roots, but bringing much needed resources to where they can do the most good.

In western Europe, a similar process of transnational exchange and funding has seen a European environmental network created with the encouragement of the Environmental Directorate of the European Union. Russell Dalton's study of this "green network" demonstrates clearly how important networking at the European level has become for many of its members through membership in the transnational European Environmental Bureau (1994). But such external sources of support and networking also have a negative implication: in tending to attract the more moderate environmental groups, they can deepen the cleavage between them and the more radical ecological movement, stretching the bonds of the "green networks" that give activists their power in domestic politics.

The same danger appears in the women's movement in Third World countries. It appears increasingly divided between (largely urban and well-educated) former militants linked into transnational networks through their ties with foundations, northern governments, and "big sister" organizations in the North, and grass-roots activists struggling against female exploitation, abuse, and legal inequality on the ground. Without strong domestic connective structures, the women's movement of the South risks a split very similar to the gap between its internationally oriented export sector and its domestic economies.

Domestic blockages and transnational opportunities

"Advocacy networks," write Keck and Sikkink, "have been the most visible in situations where domestic access of claimants is blocked, or where those making claims are too weak politically for their voices to be heard" (1998b). In such cases, international or foreign venues may be the only ones in which claims can be legitimately or safely presented. By shifting venues, activists try to involve new and more sympathetic actors to their cause, hoping in this way to tilt the domestic power balance that has been skewed against them in their favor. This is what Keck and Sikkink mean by what they call "the boomerang effect" (1988a: 12–13): "attempting to produce it is one of the most common strategies of advocacy networks."

Keck and Sikkink use the human rights and indigenous rights networks activities in Latin America to illustrate the strategy of venue shopping (1998a: 18). They argue that, although stable domestic structures help to determine the outcome of transnational politics (Risse and Schmitz, 1995), domestic structures do not tell enough of the story. Like [some] domestic movements [. . .] it is more often "purely conjunctural, and sometimes even accidental aspects of political opportunity for which transnational networkers . . . watch ceaselessly" (Keck and Sikkink, 1998b).

Network sources of domestic movements

So much of the attention of scholars of transnational contention has been taken up with the image of a global civil society that a crucial implication of transnational advocacy is often forgotten – the socialization of new movements within national states (Risse et al., 1999; McAdam, 1998). [. . .] [B]uilding new collective action frames is an essential part of movements' work; in this respect, transnational advocacy networks resemble movements in their attempts to both place new issues on the agenda and make them resonant with indigenous cultural understandings (Keck and Sikkink, 1998b). But there is a special problem in doing so: "unlike domestic movements," observe Keck and Sikkink, "different parts of advocacy networks need to appeal to belief systems, lifeworlds, and stories, myths and folk tales in many different countries and cultures."

Two dangers result: first, the search for transnational common denominators that will resonate at some level with many cultures and traditions; second, following a variety of issues that take root in particular places, which can produce ideological divergence within the same transnational network, as activists adapt them to "their" cultures.

A good example of the former is the attempt to reproduce the success of such movements as the Brazilian rubber tappers in places, such as Sarawak, where the same conditions do not obtain. "Although the stories that make social problems resonate in the experience of people far from their situation can legitimately be said to have a life of their own," writes Margaret Keck, the tappers of northeastern Brazil had a strong tradition of labor organization, the support of domestic church and labor organizations, and the particular political opportunity of a democratizing government (Keck, 1995: 420–1).

On the other hand, with no overarching themes or organization, transnational networks can divide along ideological or political lines. This was clearly the case for the 1980s peace movements in western Europe and the United States, the former calling for complete nuclear disarmament and the latter for no more than a "nuclear freeze" (Meyer, 1990). It is no wonder that transnational movement organizations like Greenpeace maintain rigid control over the kinds of issues their militants become involved in.

In summary, the effects of transnational activism within domestic politics may be their most important function. Transnational advocacy networks can help resource-poor actors construct new *domestic* movements out of combinations of indigenous and imported materials. If nothing else, they can help to create "imagined commonalities" which provide otherwise isolated activists with the impression that they are part of broader, more cosmopolitan movements.

Skeptics may point out that the creation of such imagined commonalities is nothing new. After all, what else did Marx and Engels mean by the phrase "workers of the world, unite"? No doubt thousands of working-class militants struggled toward an imaginary goal because they were convinced that unseen hundreds of thousands like themselves were working toward the same goal around the world. What seems to be qualitatively new is that, unlike the international working-class movement of the past, transnational advocacy networks are not locked teleologically into a fixed social movement; their geographic mobility, loose organizational models, and access to communications provide the capacity to shift their campaigns and resources to venues in which they have the strongest chance to succeed; and they can draw upon the elements of common cultural framing that economic globalization and the communications revolution have brought to many corners of the world.

If this hypothesis is correct, rather than focusing on the abstraction of a global civil society and regarding every incident of transnational activism as evidence of its coming, we will learn more by seeing transnational networks as external actors providing resources and opportunities for domestic movements in formation. These movements may identify themselves ideologically – and financially – with their transnational collaborators; but unless we focus empirically on what happens within national political struggles, we may miss the true significance of transnational contention.

For example, when Doug Imig and the author began to investigate collective action surrounding the decisions of the European Union, our assumption was that a neat dividing line would separate national from transnational contention, with the latter taking the cross-border forms illustrated in the conflict that introduced this chapter (1996). But even a brief exposure to a large population of cases of European collective action showed that social actors aggrieved by European decisions are most likely to turn to the institutions with which they have the most familiarity, and which implement EU decisions – their own national states. Rather than the transnationalization of contention, Europeans may be creating a Europeanization *within* domestic conflict structures (Imig and Tarrow, 1997).

IS THERE A TRANSNATIONAL DYNAMIC?

The next research task in plotting the progress and the process of transnational contention is to look more closely at the *kinds* of linkages that are developing across national boundaries. Are they cumulative and dynamic or distinct and differentiating? And do they construct the most durable new realities at the transnational or at the domestic levels?

Consider, first, the spread of indigenous rights campaigns in Latin America and elsewhere over the past decade or so. Assisted by transnational advocacy networks and drawing on ecological activism, the emergence of Indian organizations in Ecuador, Bolivia, Colombia, Guatemala, and Mexico at roughly the same time may relate to a particular political moment – what Deborah Yashar calls "the twin emergence of delegative democracies and neo-liberal reforms" (1996: 87). If Yashar is right, then the co-occurrence of indigenous rights movements in so many countries at the same time is not due to anything so grand or world-systemic as "globalization" and may subside with the next phase of Latin American political struggle.

Next, consider the expanding web of e-mail networks that are traversing the world today, and which excite the attention of those with easy access to computers. They have an obvious capacity to reduce transaction costs and transmit information across national lines, as could be seen in their role in diffusing information about the dramatic Chiapas rebellion in Mexico around the world. They put those with access to computers into contact with others like themselves rapidly and with a sense of participation lacking in less personal forms of communication (Bob, 1997). But do such contacts promise the same crystallization of collective trust as, say, the lived experience of mounting a barricade in Parisian neighborhoods studied by Roger Gould (1995) or Mark Traugott (1995)? Or the creation of cross-organizational collective identities woven out of the coalitional campaigns of the

Italian environmental organizations studies by Mario Diani (1995)? As anyone who has caught the internet virus can attest, virtual activism may serve as a *substitute* – and not as a spur – to activism in the real world.

On the other hand, the trends that some have seen creating a world of transnational movements are only in their infancy and may be cumulative. As in the past, some forms of transnational exchange and diffusion may ultimately produce true transnational movements, but – as was more often true in the past – these processes may also generate separate national movements or dissipate in the face of indifference or repression. So I close this chapter not with a conclusion, but with five questions that we will need to confront about the dynamics of transnational contention.

First, is the new technology of global communication changing the forms of the diffusion of collective challenges or only the speed of their transmission? Before concluding that the world is entering an unprecedented age of global movements, we will need to follow some of the recent campaigns that have been assisted by electronic communication to find out whether it increases the movement's power or merely changes how it frames its message.

Second, can integrated social movements span continents in the absence of an integrated interpersonal community at both ends of the transnational chain? And, to question an even stronger claim, can such transnational communities be *created* with resources borrowed from abroad? Those who are convinced of the strong thesis will need to show that impersonal cyberspace networks or cheap air travel not only stimulate new national movements but can also maintain the transnational tie as part of their underlying connective structures. Evidence like that of Margaret Keck's about the rubber tapper's movement underscores the advantages of organization and opportunity that preceded their alliance with transnational activists (1995: 420).

Third, will the new forms of transnational exchange lead to benevolent forms of "people's power," as writers like O'Neil seem to think (1993: ch. 4)? Or will they lead to the violent forms that Anderson and others have seen in the potential of "long distance nationalism" (1992)? The most powerful global movement of the early 1990s was not made up of Western environmentalists or human rights activists linked benevolently to indigenous people's movements, but radical Islamic fundamentalists who slit the throats of folk singers and beat up women who dare to go unveiled.

Fourth, is there a cumulative movement from the two temporary forms of transnational politics sketched here – diffusion and political exchange – to the two stronger ones, and particularly toward true transnational movements? Although it might seem logical that transnational advocacy networks will evolve into unified transnational movements, they are actually seen as alternatives for many activists who come out of the risky world of domestic movements, and see transnational activism as an alternative to mobilization.

Finally, what of the role of the national state in all of this? Modern states developed in a strategic dialogue with social movements, ceding to them the autonomy and opportunity to organize when they had to and reclaiming that territory whenever these movements faded or became too dangerous. Why would states be any more supine today when faced by transnational diffusion, exchange, advocacy networks, or even social movements than they were against domestic movements in the late nineteenth or early twentieth centuries?

Some states play a role transnationally today that they seldom could in the past: intervening peacefully and publicly on behalf of domestic movements or groups in other countries whose claims are brought to their attention by groups in their own countries. For understandable reasons, transnational groups claim credit for such intervention – and often play a key role in publicizing the claims of their allies to governments in other countries. Trying to understand this relationship without reference to state power is just as deceptive, in its way, as the attempt to understand international politics as a world made up only of states.

Many states are evolving transnational strategies and creating transnational organizations responsive to their interests. States encourage some movements – like the European environmental movement – to take their claims to transnational institutions like the European Union, while inhibiting these institutions from dealing with others, such as the less welcome antinuclear movement. In the mid-nineteenth century, states like Austria, Russia, and Britain intervened in contentious episodes with cannon fire and bayonets; in the late twentieth century, states make more than war; they make transnational organizations and institutions to combat and pacify social movements. If this is the case, then both the national state and the national social movement will be with us for a long time to come.

ACKNOWLEDGMENTS

An earlier version of this chapter [was] published in M. Hanagan, L. Page Moch and W. te Brake (eds), *Challenging Authority: the Historical Study of Contentious Politics* (1998), ch. 15. Thanks to Matt Evangelista, Doug Imig, Margaret Keck and John Meyer for comments on a draft of this chapter.

NOTES

1   For a more detailed analysis of the strike, see Imig and Tarrow (1997).
2   Smith drew her analysis from the *Yearbook of International Organizations*, which uses "UN records on NGO's, self-reports, referrals, and the media to identify organizations." In [. . .] Smith et al. (1997: 45–6), she coded "every nongovernmental organization whose primary aims included some form of social change (broadly defined)."
3   While we have a number of good studies of the Western peace movement (see Rochon, 1988; Meyer, 1990; Kleidman, 1993; Meyer and Rochon, 1997), less work has been done on religion as a transnational movement. But see the impressive collection of work edited by Rudolf and Piscatori (1997), especially the contributions by Eickelman, Kane, and Levine and Stoll.
4   Three classic studies trace the transfer of the eastern European labor movement experience to the New World: for the United States, see Hourwich (1969); for the influence of immigrants on the Argentinean labor movement, see del Campo (1973); on the immigrant origins of the Chilean labor movement, see Ansell (1972).
5   I believe that this is so even though Keck and Sikkink derive their definition of the term "network" from the work of J. Clyde Mitchell, who was writing about domestic networks (1973: 23). For an excellent adaptation of social network analysis to the study of social movements, see Diani (1995, 1997).

REFERENCES

Anderson, Benedict (1992) *Long-distance Nationalism: World Capitalism and the Rise of Identity Politics*. Center for Asian Studies, Amsterdam, Netherlands.

Ansell, Alan (1972) *Politics and the Labour Movement in Chile*. New York: Oxford University Press.

Badie, Bertrand (1997) "Le jeu triangulaire," in Pierre Birnbaum (ed.), *Sociologie des nationalismes*, pp. 447–62. Paris: Presses Universitaires de France.

Beissinger, Mark (1996) "How nationalism spread: Eastern Europe adrift," *Social Research*, 63: 97–145.

Bob, Clifford (1997) "The marketing of rebellion in global civil society: political insurgencies, international media, and the growth of transnational support," PhD dissertation, Massachusetts Institute of Technology.

Brysk, Alison (1994) "Acting globally: Indian rights and international politics in Latin America," in Donna Lee Van Cott (ed.), *Indigenous Peoples and Democracy in Latin America*, pp. 29–51. New York: St Martin's Press.

Castells, Manuel (1994) "European cities, the informational society, and the global economy," *New Left Review*, 204: 18–32.

Castells, Manuel (1997) *The Information Age: Economy, Society, and Culture*, vol. 2: *The Power of Identity*. Oxford: Blackwell.

Cerny, Philip (1995) "Globalization and the changing logic of collective action," *International Organization*, 49: 595.

Dalton, Russell (1994) *The Green Rainbow: Environmental Groups in Western Europe*. New Haven, Conn.: Yale University Press.

del Campo, Hugo (1973) *Los origines del movimiento obrero argentino: historia del movimiento obrero 25*. Buenos Aires: Centro Editor de America Latina.

Diani, Mario (1995) *Green Networks: a Structural Analysis of the Italian Environmental Movement*. Edinburgh: Edinburgh University Press.

Diani, Mario (1997) "Social movements and social capital: a network perspective on social movement outcomes," unpublished paper, University of Strathclyde, Glasgow.

Drescher, Seymour (1987) *Capitalism and Antislavery: British Mobilization in Comparative Perspective*. New York: Oxford University Press.

Eickelman, Dale F. (1997) "Trans-state Islam and security," in Susanne Rudolf and James Piscatori (eds), *Transnational Religion and Fading States*, pp. 27–46. Boulder, Colo.: Westview Press.

Ernst, Claire (1997) "Americans in Paris: Act Up – Paris and identity politics," *French Politics and Society*, 15: 22–31.

Finnemore, Martha (1996) "Norms, culture, and world politics: insights from sociology's institutionalism," *International Organization*, 47: 565–98.

Ganley, Gladys (1992) *The Exploding Political Power of Personal Media*. Norwood, NJ: Ablex.

Garner, Roberta Ash (1994) "Transnational movements in postmodern society," *Peace Review*, 6: 427–33.

Gould, Roger (1995) *Insurgent Identities: Class, Community, and Protest in Paris from 1848 to the Commune*. Chicago: University of Chicago Press.

Hanagan, Michael (1998) "Transnational social movements, deterritorialized migrants, and the state system: a nineteenth-century case study," in Marco Giugni, Doug McAdam and Charles Tilly (eds), *How Movements Matter*. Minneapolis: University of Minnesota Press.

Hourwich, Isaac (1969) *Immigration and Labor: the Economic Aspects of European Immigration to the United States*. New York: Arno.

Imig, Doug, and Tarrow, Sidney (1996) "The Europeanization of movements? Contentious politics and the European Union, October 1983–March 1995," Institute for European Studies working paper No. 96.3. Ithaca, NY: Cornell University Press.

Imig, Doug, and Tarrow, Sidney (1997) "From strike to Eurostrike: the Europeanization of social movements and the development of a Euro-polity," Harvard University, Center for International Affairs working paper.

Kane, Ousmane (1997) "Muslim missionaries and African states," in Susanne Rudolf and James Piscatori (eds), *Transnational Religion and Fading States*, pp. 47–62. Boulder, Colo: Westview Press.

Keck, Margaret E. (1995) "Social equity and environmental politics in Brazil," *Comparative Politics*, 27: 409–24.

Keck, Margaret E. and Sikkink, Kathryn (1995) "Transnational issue networks in international politics," presented to the Annual Conference of the American Political Science Association, Chicago.

Keck, Margaret E. and Sikkink, Kathryn (1998a) *Activists beyond Borders: Transnational Advocacy Networks in International Politics.* Ithaca, NY: Cornell University Press.

Keck, Margaret E. and Sikkink, Kathryn (1998b) "Transnational advocacy networks in the movement society," in David Meyer and Sidney Tarrow (eds), *The Social Movement Society: Contentious Politics for a New Century,* ch. 10. Boulder, Colo.: Rowman and Littlefield.

Kleidman, Robert (1993) *Organizing for Peace: Neutrality, the Test Ban and the Freeze.* Syracuse: Syracuse University Press.

Kowalewski, David (1989) "Global debt crises in structural-cyclical perspective," in W. P. Avery and D. P. Rapkin (eds), *Markets, Politics and Change in the Global Political Economy,* pp. 357–84. Boulder, Colo.: Lynne Reiner.

McAdam, Doug (1998) "On the international origins of domestic political opportunities," in Anne N. Costain and Andrew McFarland (eds), *Social Movements and American Political Institutions,* ch. 14. Boulder, Colo.: Rowman and Littlefield.

McCarthy, John D. (1997) "The globalization of social movement theory," in J. Smith, C. Chatfield and R. Pagnucco (eds), *Transnational Social Movements and World Politics: Solidarity beyond the State,* ch. 14. Syracuse: Syracuse University Press.

Markoff, John (1996) *Waves of Democracy.* Thousand Oaks, CA: Pine Forge Press.

Meyer, David (1990) *A Winter of Discontent: the Nuclear Freeze and American Politics.* New York: Praeger.

Meyer, David, and Rochon, Tom (1997) "Towards a coalitional theory of social and political movements," in T. Rochon and D. Meyer (eds), *Coalitions and Political Movements: the Lessons of the Nuclear Freeze,* pp. 237–51. Boulder, Colo.: Lynne Rienner.

Meyer, John W., Boli, John, Thomas, George M. and Ramirez, Francisco O. (1996) "World societies and the nation-state," unpublished paper, Stanford University Department of Sociology.

Mikkelsen, Flemming (1996) "Contention and social movements in Denmark in a transnational perspective," presented at the Second European Conference on Social Movements, University of the Basque Country, Bilbao, July.

Mitchell, J. Clyde (1973) "Networks, norms and institutions," in Jeremy Boissevain and J. Clyde Mitchell (eds), *Network Analysis: Studies in Human Interaction,* pp. 15–36. The Hague: Mouton.

O'Neil, Michael (1993) *The Roar of the Crowd: How Television and People Power are Changing the World.* New York: Times Books.

Pagnucco, Ron and Atwood, David (1994) "Global strategies for peace and justice," *Peace Review,* 6: 411–18.

Pizzorno, Alessandro (1978) "Political exchange and collective identity in industrial conflict," in Colin Crouch and Alessandro Pizzorno (eds), *The Resurgence of Class Conflict in Western Europe since 1968,* vol. 2, pp. 277–98. London: Macmillan.

Price, Richard (1997) "Reversing the gunsights: transnational civil society takes aim at landmines," unpublished paper, University of Minnesota, Department of Political Science.

Risse, Thomas (1995) *Bringing Transnational Politics Back In: Non-state Actors, Domestic Structures and International Institutions*. Ithaca, NY: Cornell University Press.

Risse, Thomas and Schmitz, Hans Peter (1995) "Principled ideas, international institutions, and domestic political change in the human rights area: insights from African cases," presented to the Annual Meeting of the American Political Science Association, Chicago, September.

Risse, Thomas, Ropp, Stephen C. and Sikkink, Kathryn (1999) *Human Rights Norms and Domestic Politics*. New York: Cambridge University Press.

Robins, Kevin (1995) "Globalization," in Adam Kuper and Jessica Kuper (eds), *Social Science Encyclopedia*, pp. 345–6. London: Routledge.

Rochon, Thomas R. (1988) *Mobilizing for Peace: the Antinuclear Movements in Western Europe*. Princeton, NJ Princeton University Press.

Rosenau, James (1990) *Turbulence in World Politics: a Theory of Change and Continuity*. Princeton, NJ: Princeton University Press.

Rucht, Dieter (1997) "Limits to mobilization: environmental policy for the European Union," in J. Smith, C. Chatfield and R. Pagnucco (eds), *Transnational Social Movements and World Politics: Solidarity beyond the State*, ch. 11. Syracuse: Syracuse University Press.

Rudolf, Susanne Hoeber (1997) "Religion, states, and transnational civil society," in Susanne Rudolf and James Piscatori (eds), *Transnational Religion and Fading States*, pp. 1–26. Boulder, Colo.: Westview Press.

Rudolf, Susanne Hoeber and Piscatori, James (eds) (1997) *Transnational Religion and Fading States*. Boulder, Colo.: Westview Press.

Smith, Jackie (1994) "Organizing global action," *Peace Review*, 6: 419–26.

Smith, Jackie (1997) "Characteristics of the modern transnational social movement sector," in J. Smith, C. Chatfield and R. Pagnucco (eds), *Transnational Social Movements and World Politics: Solidarity beyond the State*, ch. 3. Syracuse: Syracuse University Press.

Smith, Jackie, Chatfield, Charles and Pagnucco, Ron (eds) (1997) *Transnational Social Movements and World Politics: Solidarity beyond the State*. Syracuse: Syracuse University Press.

Tarrow, Sidney (1998) "Fishnets, Internets, and catnets: globalization and transnational collective action," in Michael Hanagan, Leslie Page Moch and Wayne te Brake (eds), *Challenging Authority: the Historical Study of Contentious Politics*, ch. 15. Minneapolis: University of Minnesota Press.

Tilly, Charles (1991) "Prisoners of the state," Center for Studies of Social Change, working paper no. 129. New York: New School for Social Research.

Traugott, Marc (1995) "Barricades as repertoire: continuities and discontinuities in the history of French contention" in M. Traugott (ed.), *Repertoires and Cycles of Collective Action*, pp. 43–56. Durham, NC: Duke University Press.

Wade, Robert (1996) "Globalization and its limits: reports of the death of the national economy are greatly exaggerated," in Suzanne Berger and Ronald

Dore (eds), *National Diversity and Global Capitalism*, pp. 60–88. Ithaca, NY: Cornell University Press.

Walton, John (1989) "Debt, protest and the state in Latin America," in Susan Eckstein (ed.), *Power and Popular Protest: Latin American Social Movements*, pp. 299–328. Berkeley, CA: University of California Press.

Wapner, Paul (1995) "Bringing society back in: environmental activism and world civic politics," *World Politics*, 47: 311–40.

Wapner, Paul (1996) *Environmental Activism and World Civic Politics*. Albany, NY State University of New York Press.

Wellman, Barry and Gulia, Milena (1988) "Net surfers don't ride alone: virtual communities as communities," in Peter Kollock and Marc Smith (eds), *Communities in Cyberspace*. London: Routledge.

Yashar, Deborah J. (1996) "Indigenous protest and democracy in Latin America," in Jorge I. Dominguez and Abraham Lowenthal (eds), *Constructing Democratic Governance: Latin America and the Caribbean in the 1990s*, pp. 87–105. Baltimore, MD: Johns Hopkins University Press.

PART IV   CITIZENSHIP, EXCLUSION, AND DIFFERENCE

Introduction

The chapters in part IV deal with different aspects of citizenship. Chapter 11 by Maurice Roche is the most comprehensive, linking social movements and citizenship to changes in global political economy. Carole Pateman's chapter is exemplary of feminist analyses of the ways in which citizenship is gendered (chapter 12). This was overlooked in sociological theory until the women's movement became influential in universities, but it has always been a fundamental dimension of citizenship, and it is particularly prominent in the case of the social rights promised by the welfare state in the twentieth century. Yasemin Soysal, in chapter 13, is concerned with change in the modern form of citizenship rights: the growth of international human rights law is contributing to new forms of post-national membership of political communities. This is especially evident in countries belonging to the European Union.

Roche bases his discussion of citizenship on the model developed by T. H. Marshall which was dominant in the post-war period. Citizenship consists of civil, political, and social rights, with the latter provided by the welfare state. Like many other sociologists, Roche argues that the context assumed by Marshall – a growing capitalist economy based on Keynesian management by the nation-state and underpinned by a homogeneous culture – can no longer be taken for granted. We are now living through a transitional period to what is variously described as post-industrial, post-Fordist, or postmodern society, characterized by globalization, technical change, and the fragmentation of cultural norms accompanied by increased individualization. As a result, the nation-state no longer has the same degree of control over the economy, there is the prospect of permanently high structural unemployment, and women's unpaid care in the family – on which the welfare state actually relied – has become much more problematic.

The crisis of the welfare state is an important issue for social movements concerned with citizenship. Roche usefully distinguishes between different types of social movement in this respect. The most well-known and frequently studied are progressive social movements, including feminism, environmentalism, and anti-racism. As Roche points out, however, there are also "anti-progressive" counter-movements which are explicitly concerned to return women to the home, to deny ethnic minority groups full citizenship rights, and so on. Roche also identifies what he calls "non-progressive" social movements. These include "anti-political" movements among elites which mobilize to defend or extend their power and advantages, by-passing democratic accountability. More controversially, he includes in the category of non-progressive social movements, "anti-social" movements which engage in destructive or self-destructive behaviour such as gang warfare, drug addiction, and so on. Roche's idea here is that exclusion from full citizenship rights leads to anti-social behaviour and attitudes. It is, however, controversial to identify the black urban underclass in this way since "scientific" findings on this group may be as much a product of racial stereotyping as of good research. Finally, Roche identifies ideological movements which take place in popular and everyday culture or "discourse." His main example of a social movement, anti-progressive American neo-conservatism, is ideological. In fact, it would seem from studies of social movements that all social movements are bound up with cultural contestation and change, so that all social movements are, in Roche's terms, ideological (see Calhoun, chapter 8). Neo-conservatism is well chosen in the context of the relationship between social movements and the welfare state since, in the US and Britain at least, it has certainly been among the most effective.

Pateman (chapter 12) writes from a socialist feminist perspective. Her analysis is closely identified with the progressive women's movement discussed by Roche. In fact, Pateman's work has been an important influence on behalf of that movement within universities. First published in 1988, this chapter is mainly concerned with the historical construction of women's citizenship in relation to the welfare state. On the basis of the historical material, Pateman develops an analytical model of the patriarchal welfare state which is still relevant today.

Using statistics from the US, Britain, and Australia, she demonstrates how the welfare state contributes to, and exemplifies, men's power over women. Pateman shows how women are the main recipients of welfare; how the welfare state is the major source of employment for women; how it is assumed that women will provide the unpaid care on which the welfare state depends; and, despite the fact that it has been called "the women's branch of the state," how women are largely excluded from the administration and policy-making by which the welfare state is governed. The patriarchal welfare state is structured according to the assumption that male citizens will be employed, supporting female citizens who are their dependants in nuclear families. The growth in female employment in the labour market and the pluralization of family forms in recent years has exposed this assumption, but women continue to be excluded from full citizenship rights. The "feminization of poverty" is well documented as increasing numbers of female-headed households are forced to rely on low wages and/or inadequate welfare benefits.

As Pateman points out, however, there is no easy solution to women's situation as second-class citizens in patriarchal welfare states. She argues that the women's movement is currently faced with "Wollstonecraft's dilemma," which she has named after the eighteenth-century feminist, Mary Wollstonecraft. Women may claim equal citizenship with men, demanding an end to discrimination enforced by gender-neutral laws and policies. However, this means that women's differences from men, their historical role in the family, and their biological capacities must be ignored. Alternatively, women may claim citizenship *as* women, on the grounds that they make different contributions from men and have different needs. In the first case, genuine equality will be impossible, Pateman thinks, because women *are* different from men. In the second case, however, the risk is that women's traditional role will simply be reinforced, making equality impossible to achieve. Pateman's point is that the way in which the patriarchal welfare state has been structured allows only these two alternatives. However, the way in which it is currently being undermined, by changes in women's lives and also by changes in the global economy, may enable the complete transformation of the dichotomy between paid work in the public sphere and unpaid care in the private sphere on which it currently depends. Only then will full citizenship rights be enjoyed by both sexes.

Soysal (chapter 13) deals with a particular aspect of the changing social and political forms of citizenship – the way in which rights are becoming "post-national." While citizenship rights are formally universal – in principle they are granted to citizens on the grounds that they are human beings – in modernity they have, in fact, been guaranteed by nation-states. They have, therefore, been valid only for persons defined as members of the national community. With the growth of international human rights, however, rights are increasingly granted to human beings as such, regardless of their status as members of national communities. As a result, Soysal argues, there are now multiple statuses in Western liberal democracies in relation to citizenship rights; including, for example, those who have certain rights without citizenship, such as guest-workers and refugees, and others who have dual citizenship. Since the modern understanding of rights is that they *should* be universal, this multiplicity of statuses is controversial and encourages claims for rights which extend beyond those already secured. In the post-war period, the basic civil rights initially encoded in human rights conventions have been extended to incorporate social and cultural rights.

Soysal stresses that the development of post-national rights does not mean that the nation-state is now irrelevant. On the contrary, while it is the case that post-national rights are the direct consequence of the growth of international law and political institutions and their attempts to deal with transnational migration, rights are still secured and administered by individual states. There is, therefore, what Soysal calls a dialectic between post-national membership and the nation-state. States continually attempt to reaffirm control over their national boundaries and populations, by strictly regulating transnational migration, for example, so confirming the link between nationality and citizenship rights. On the other hand, they also administer rights according to human rights conventions. In this way, nation-states faced with transnational migration which they cannot actually control in a globalizing world are acting as the mechanisms for institutionalizing international human rights. In fact, Soysal notes that national self-determination is itself an individual human right, so that, paradoxically, the modern relation between nationality and citizenship has now been rearticulated as a post-national right. The institutionalization of post-national rights does not, therefore, signal the end of nationalism. On the contrary, as Soysal notes (in a point similar to that of Appadurai in chapter 6), nations are currently engaged in attempting to secure their own states and vice versa. Soysal's argument concerning post-national rights is also linked to that of David Held in chapter 16, where he discusses globalization and its consequences for national political communities.

CHAPTER 11

Rethinking Citizenship and Social Movements: Themes in Contemporary Sociology and Neoconservative Ideology

Maurice Roche

In this chapter I aim to explore the nature of citizenship, particularly social citizenship, in contemporary society. The chapter develops themes in the new sociology of citizenship (section II) and considers these themes in the context of a case study of the reconstruction of social citizenship proposed by American Neoconservatism since the early 1980s (section III). In addition, since Neoconservatism is viewed here as an ideological movement, it is necessary to begin by considering the general relationship between the sociological study of citizenship and of social movements in modernity (section I).

Social citizenship refers to those rights and duties of citizenship concerned with citizens' welfare, broadly understood to include work, income, education and health. In the mid-twentieth century, and certainly throughout much of the post-Second World War period, its meaning came to be intimately bound to the project and structures of the welfare state – particularly in Western Europe, but also in North America and elsewhere. In this chapter I refer to this meaning of social citizenship as the dominant paradigm. However, in the late twentieth century the welfare state is being significantly reconstructed in most Western societies, and the dominant paradigm is under assault from two sets of social forces: structural and ideological changes.

The structural changes involve globalization and technological transformation in the capitalist economy, together with the global and sub-

This chapter is an edited extract from *Social Movements and Social Classes: the Future of Collective Action*, edited by L. Mahen (London, Sage, 1995), pp. 186–219. Reprinted by permission of Sage Publications Ltd.

national political dynamics associated with these economic changes. The ideological changes involve the rise of various new social movements, especially ecology and feminism, and of various forms of New Right conservatism, particularly the traditionalistic Neoconservatism which we will consider at greater length later in this chapter, as well as pro-market libertarianism. These changes, both individually and in their confluence and conjuncture since the early 1980s, are restructuring the dominant paradigm of social citizenship in contemporary societies, whether intentionally or not.

[. . .]

I   CITIZENSHIP AND SOCIAL MOVEMENTS: SOCIOLOGICAL PERSPECTIVES

Background

[. . .]

Mainstream sociology, as we now realize in retrospect, had unwittingly allowed its thinking and its vision to become limited by the conventional wisdom of its traditional theoretical paradigms (e.g. liberal and Marxist functionalism) and its traditional empirical concerns. These simply failed to provide it with the tools needed to anticipate and explain the historical social changes which have overtaken Western societies since the late 1970s. There was clearly a need for the discipline to begin to address the emergent debates about the nature of and prospects for the social, the public, civil society, and the citizen community in the 1980s in both East and West. In particular, there was a need to understand the new politics of citizens' rights and duties against the background of new and renewed social problems of long-term poverty and unemployment – social problems particularly associated with structural changes and crises in the modern economy and in the role and powers of the modern state, especially the welfare state. The new sociology of citizenship, then, animated as it is by these sorts of issues, has developed as a leading aspect of sociology's more general attempt to reorient itself to the realities of social life, politics and history in the late twentieth century. As such, the new sociology of citizenship could be said to have much in common with the sociology of social movements. Although the latter pre-dates the sociology of citizenship by a decade or more, the former's interest in the theory and practice of the various forms of new social and political movements – which have developed outside conventional post-war parties and their social class bases and worldviews – is implicitly and explicitly connected with the social development and politics of contemporary citizenship [. . .].

Social movements and citizenship: diversity and commonality

From my perspective, and setting aside some of the more restrictive definitions of the field, the sociology of social movements consists of a collection of distinctive sociological projects. The main projects are as follows: (a) the long-established sociological attempt to understand the old working-class movements (the labour movement, trade unionism, etc.) and the growth of the welfare state and social citizenship rights in response to this; (b) the relatively long-established sociology of new social movements which, since the 1970s, has attempted to understand the nature of such movements as the anti-nuclear, ecological and anti-communist movements (such as Solidarity), and their significance for modernity; (c) feminist sociology and its concern with the women's movement, the critique of sexism and patriarchal power, and the affirmation of female rights and identity/difference; and (d) the sociology of ethnicity and its concern with movements oriented to ethnic politics and immigrants' problems, the critique of racism and dominant/host culture power, and the affirmation of ethnic/immigrant rights and identity/difference.

The Marxist theoretical voice of the old social movements – labour and trade unionism – tended to evaluate the notion of citizenship negatively as compared with conceptions of social membership and collective identity, such as comradeship in the movement, or worker in (the building of) the Communist state. From this point of view, citizenship in the allegedly liberal and democratic state – a state seen as run by and for capitalism – was little more than another weapon of mystification and falsification in the armoury of bourgeois/ruling-class ideology.

Nonetheless the waves of growth of civil, political and social rights in modern Western history, no doubt through long, divisive and discontinuous struggles, can be seen as the extension and intensification of citizens' rights and status. Sociologists of various theoretical persuasions have reasonably analysed old and, more recently, new social movements in terms of the historical development of citizenship (e.g. Marshall, 1964; Parsons, 1970; Turner, 1986; Scott, 1990). In addition, the sociology of social movements has always tried to retain a critical/normative dimension in its analysis, that is, it has always maintained an interest in assessing the social justice and progressiveness both of social movements and of the states and conditions which they oppose and try to transform. Given this, the universalistic notion and language of citizenship (together with its normatively laden implications for rights, duties and so on) is always likely to provide, explicitly or implicitly, a theoretical and normative conceptual foundation within the sociology of social movements.

Each of the new social movements noted above (ecology, feminism, ethnic movements) advocates, in one way or another, the creation or renewal of some set of citizen rights (whether against the state, against other citizens or both), and in some cases argues for the recognition and acceptance of new or renewed responsibilities for citizens as well. So, although it typically casts its net wider in the social and political theory of modernity than a focus on social movements alone would allow, the sociology of citizenship nonetheless must recognize and address the phenomena dealt with by the various social movement sociologies mentioned above.

There are, however, clear differences between the various new social movements with respect to self-understanding, aims, constituencies, and the nature of their struggles. Such fragmentation of the general social movement field, and of the salience within it of the old labour movement, seems to confound attempts at analysis in terms of any singular theme. Certainly the traditional Left's view that ecology and feminism could simply be included in its conception of the movement for the apparently unitary ideal of socialism was always artificial and questionable, given, for example, the trade union movement's traditional patriarchal and pro-industrial assumptions, and the effective absence of feminist and ecological themes in Marxist theory. The potential for dialogue between new social movements and the various sociologies that address them initially appears to be limited to the extent that the particularism and fragmentation of the movements is reflected in these sociologies.

However, contemporary post-communist Left thinking (e.g. Mouffe, 1992) attempts to take a more positive view of this kind of particularism and fragmentation, seeing it as exemplifying common themes and radical ideals of difference, pluralism and democracy. Taking a cue from this political approach to new social movements, sociologists might use the common theme of citizenship to explore and monitor social movements – by developing a "citizenship reading" or hermeneutic of individual social movements and of the social movement field in general. Such an approach would investigate intra-movement, inter-movement and extra-movement democratic and citizenship issues: it would explore (a) the nature of democracy and members' rights and responsibilities practised within each movement; (b) the tolerance for and linkages between each movement, and their conceptions of citizenship, rights and responsibilities; and (c) the democratic nature of the state and of the citizen community context in which they operate, as well as the ways of and prospects for furthering the development of democracy, citizenship empowerment and civil society autonomy. In each of these respects, social movement analysis could use common citizenship as a way to construct potential common ground, purpose and political language within the diversity of contemporary social movements.

Redefining the political: social movements, post-industrialism and post-nationalism

Post-war social movements, as is often noted, have stretched the boundaries of what can reasonably be deemed political (that is, a matter of public interest, of power struggle and of rights, and thus of potential concern to all citizens) beyond the sphere constructed by the nation-state – its decision-making apparatus, parties, laws and public institutions. The anti-nuclear movement and the ecology movement have addressed and politicized the problems of nature and history – the global and intergenerational scale of the human threat to plant, animal and human species survival. Traditionally, these problems were seen as outside the public sphere simply because they raised issues beyond the scope of the nation-state. New social movements, however, urge modern societies to treat these as political problems. Comparably, the women's movement addresses and politicizes problems in the most private and personal spheres – those of male power and violence in the spheres of sexuality, intimacy, parenting and domesticity; and it presses modern society to reconstruct the national public domain to include these sub-national dimensions also.

Conversely, on the one hand the anti-nuclear movement and the ecology movement have also pursued a highly particularist and sub-national politics of place – for example, neighbourhood cleaning and recycling initiatives, and NIMBY ('not in my back yard') opposition to the location of nuclear or waste sites in threatened neighbourhoods. On the other hand, the politics of the women's movement contains strong transnational themes, in that patriarchy is a global and historical phenomenon (albeit institutionalized in different ways and to different extents, and thus differently contested) in all societies. In these and other senses, while they undoubtedly continue to operate largely at a national level and in nationally constructed political spheres, these social movements are essentially post-national phenomena calling for a theory and a practice concerned with the trans- and sub-national levels in addition to the national level.

Social movements can thus be said to address the problems of politics in a post-national era. Indeed, new social movement sociology has engaged in a continuing dialogue with the self-understanding of the ecology movement, which has tended to present itself as a fundamental practical and philosophical critique of industrial society. Thus new social movement sociology has begun to analyse social movements in terms of the structural changes involved in the emergence of post-industrialism and post-industrial society (Touraine, 1977).

Social movement sociology, as much as the new citizenship sociology, can be said to address the problems of politics in a post-industrial stage of the development of the capitalist economy. This is a stage in which one of the central institutions of industrial capitalism – the welfare state – is in crisis; and states feel compelled to explore and experiment with moralistic, individualistic and market-based solutions to capitalism's problems of poverty, unemployment and welfare. In each of these respects, the sociology of social movements is concerned with the same problematics and forces of social-structural and societal change that interest writers and researchers in the contemporary sociology of citizenship. There is clearly a basis here for dialogue between these perspectives, and indeed the work of some notable contemporary sociologists overlaps both fields (e.g. Offe, 1985a: chs 9, 10, 1985b; Turner, 1986: ch. 4; Habermas, 1987: pt VIII, 1994).

[. . .]

Social and ideological movements: progressive and non-progressive types

[. . .]

Clearly, the sociology of citizenship must be concerned, along with the sociology of social movements, with what might be understood in critical/normative terms as progressive social movements (e.g. citizen-organized movements and/or movements promoting the extension of citizenship and the empowerment of citizens) together with their relationship to the state and to institutionalized political processes. However, as part of the task of understanding the political environment, and thus the field of obstacles and opportunities within which new and progressive movements operate, it is also necessary to study other types of socially and politically relevant movements of ideas, ideals and actions, movements and organizations. Whether they are recent or not, in critical/normative terms these other types may be regarded as non-progressive or, in some cases, as anti-progressive or reactionary. Furthermore, they may or may not be explicitly connected with the state and the formal political process; in many ways they may be based, as much as progressive social movements are, in civil society, albeit in the uncivil regions of that political territory.

In some cases, such movements may be identified by their antagonistic stance to new social movements. So it is necessary, when attempting to understand the nature and dynamics of ethnic and anti-racist movements and organizations, to address the problem of understanding both self-consciously racist organizations and racism as a general ideological movement (so-called institutionalized racism, racism as a form of collective consciousness and popular discourse). The same sort of observation could be made about explicitly sexist/patriarchal organizations, together with sexism/patriarchy as a general ideological movement in relation to understanding the obstacles and opportunities facing feminism. And the same thing could be said about explicitly polluting and animal/habitat-destroying industrial states and corporations, together with the wasteful and polluting aspects of mass consumerism seen as a popular ideological movement.

These examples illustrate the point that both the sociology of social movements and the sociology of citizenship need to conceptualize the political field they address as one which includes non- and anti-progressive movements as well as progressive social movements. Furthermore it is not helpful in attempting to understand the political field in which progressive movements operate to restrict unnecessarily what is to count as a movement. The examples indicate that it is wise to broaden the concept to include both formal or semi-formal organizations (often involving intellectuals and/or senior sectors within the media industries) attempting to influence and lead public opinion, and also what can be referred to as ideological movements, namely movements within the collective consciousness or popular and everyday culture, involving widely held sets of beliefs and forms of popular discourse.

This way of approaching social movements is to a certain extent illustrated in the case study of American Neoconservatism, together with its project to reconstruct the meaning and practice of social citizenship in contemporary American society and polity, which we consider in section III of this chapter. This is an ideological movement which is evidently non- or anti-progressive, which combines both a degree of formal organization through the activities of social policy analysts and intellectuals, and which is also resonant with themes in American popular culture, collective consciousness and public discourse.

Anti-political and anti-social movements

From the point of view of the new sociology of citizenship, then, the relevant sociological approach to the analysis of social movements needs to be fairly broadly based, open to non-progressive as well as progressive formations, and open to ideological and discursive as well as practical forms of collective action. With non-progressive movements, moreover, in order to be relevant to an understanding of the modern political field facing citizenship politics, the sociology of citizenship needs to be open to what might be called, provisionally and provocatively, anti-political and anti-social social movements.

The concept of an anti-political movement refers to organizations of common ideas, ideals and actions among the powerful (for example politicians and senior state officials at national, regional and urban levels; corporate owners and senior managers; media owners and senior managers) to defend and extend elite power and control, and at best to co-opt, and at worst to ignore, bypass and override democracy and accountability processes. Classic examples include traditional early and mid-twentieth-century forms of corporatism. Contemporary examples include the important wave of movements among elite groups in many North American and West European cities in the 1980s and early 1990s: new forms of urban corporatism involving formal or quasi-formal partnerships among private and public sector leaderships in order to promote economic growth and regeneration. These are as important for sociological study as movements among the relatively less powerful or the powerless, because they often use the language of citizenship and help to structure and constrain the ideological and material sites and contexts in which citizens live and citizens' movements emerge and operate (e.g. Jacobs, 1992; Roche, 1992b).

The concept of an anti-social movement refers to anomic and other-destructive and/or self-destructive patterns of collective attitudes and behaviour (such as violence, addiction or abuse). These may, unlike fully-fledged social movements, involve action which is recurrent but unpredictable. Activity may appear to be organized (via gang and criminal networks and subcultures) or disorganized and in the long term is usually demoralizing and demobilizing – in that it works against whatever potential for social movement organization a community may possess. Anti-social movements are typically connected to the structural situation of poverty and multiple deprivation, as in the urban black underclass in many cities in the US.

This kind of movement is important for the sociology of citizenship in that it indicates something of the exclusive (Lister, 1990; Brubaker, 1992) as well as the inclusive nature of full citizenship. The status and fate of those with second-class citizenship, or with little or no effective citizenship at all, is often that of mere denizenship (Hammar, 1990). Denizenship as a ground for anti-social movements represents an internal division and limit within a society's operational conception of its citizen community. It poses real threats to the quality of the civil society which can exist in that community, and it provides motivating interests and targets for anti-political movements among the powerful.
[. . .]

II CITIZENSHIP AND MODERNITY: THE DOMINANT PARADIGM AND STRUCTURAL CHANGE

The sociology of citizenship

The sociology of citizenship is derived, to a considerable extent, from the seminal formulations of British sociologist T. H. Marshall in his 1949 lecture 'Citizenship and social class' (Marshall, 1964). In the

1960s and 1970s, leading American sociologists used and developed Marshall's analysis in the context of their studies of nation-building (Bendix, 1964), of the modernization process (Parsons, 1970), and of the growth of welfare states (Rimlinger, 1971). In the 1970s, British social analysts applied Marshall's framework to the analysis of social policy (e.g. Parker, 1975; Room, 1979).

The sociology of citizenship really began to take shape in the 1980s, however, in response to structural and ideological changes during that period. British social and political theorists (e.g. Giddens, 1985; Turner, 1986; King, 1987; Hall and Held, 1989) began to review and reopen debates about the nature of modern citizenship, particularly in the context of the welfare state and social citizenship (e.g. Jordan, 1987; Plant, 1988). By the early 1990s the field had been revived in American sociology (e.g. Brubaker, 1992) and was developing in European sociology (e.g. Coenen and Leisink, 1993).

In my approach to the sociology of citizenship I have suggested (e.g. Roche, 1987, 1992a) that any substantial sociological analysis of citizenship needs in principle to give an account of at least three interlinked dimensions of citizenship. Briefly these are (1) the nature of the citizen and the citizen community; (2) the social-structural context underlying citizenship and the citizen community and influencing (both enabling and limiting) their capacities for development; and (3) the history of change in the nature of both citizenship and its structural context.

The first dimension requires attention to such things as the typical forms of experience, typical actor prerequisites, and the typical ideals and values of citizenship and of a community of citizens. These (respectively) phenomenological, ontological and moral aspects of citizenship I will refer to here as the citizen's world, for the sake of brevity. The second dimension requires sociological and political economic analysis of the relation between industrial capitalism and the nation-state as both enabler and disabler of the liberties and equalities, the rights and the duties of citizenship. Finally, the third dimension refers to the historicity of citizen ideologies, communities and structural contexts. It requires an account of the evolutionary or revolutionary character of citizenship's change and development in the modern period.

In the discussion that follows I will use these concepts as a framework for outlining and analysing social citizenship and the contemporary ideological and social forces pressing for its reconstruction. The rest of the chapter then deals with some of the main aspects and debates about the citizen's world and about citizenship's structural context in the dominant discourse on citizenship, in the implications of contemporary social-structural changes, and in an important, contemporary conservative discourse on social citizenship. [...]

Modernity and citizenship: the dominant paradigm and national functionalism

In much of the sociology of citizenship, and implicit in everyday commonsense understandings of citizenship in modern societies, there is a set of assumptions about the citizen's world, citizenship's structural context, and its history. This loose set of assumptions can be referred to as the dominant paradigm or discourse of citizenship. As an intellectual construct, it is probably most clearly expressed in T. H. Marshall's (1964) classic discussion. But in one form or another – and with due acknowledgement of the inevitable oversimplification of complex ideas involved in this claim – the paradigm underlines the consensus on post-war British social policy (Roche, 1992a: chs 1, 2). Moreover this paradigm, and the debate over it, permeates much of the sociology of citizenship (e.g. Turner, 1986; Barbalet, 1988; Lister, 1990; Coenen and Leisink, 1993).

In Marshall's (1964) analysis the citizen world consists of three types of rights – civil, political and social – with corresponding state institutions servicing rights claims (respectively the law, democracy and the welfare state). Social rights are distinct from civil and political rights, but they continue and complement such rights. Social rights enable participation in civilized society and include the rights to welfare, work and income, and to health and education. While the notion of citizens' social *duties* is noted in passing, the main emphasis is on their social *rights* and on the (welfare) state's duties to service the social dimension of citizenship (see also Marshall, 1981). This strong emphasis on rights has been characteristic of the dominant discourse on citizenship throughout the post-war period.

In addition, Marshall's relatively apolitical formulation of social citizenship as distinct from civil and political citizenship is characteristic not only of the dominant discourse but also, in modified form, of the recent Neoconservative alternative, as we shall see later. The main concern of the dominant discourse has been to use state power to overcome inequality in the distribution and realization of citizens' rights within a structural context which is, nonetheless, generative of multiple forms of inequality.

In Marshall's analysis the structural context of citizenship is generally modernity or modern society and, more specifically, what can be called "national functionalism" (Roche, 1992a: chs 1, 2). This is the complex formed by (1) the nation-state; (2) an industrial capitalist economy, in particular a national capitalism capable of management by Keynesian state economic policy; and (3) a common and functional culture and value system (containing ideological, familial and other such elements functional for the reproduction of the nation-state and national capitalism).

As far as social citizenship and welfare rights are concerned, Marshall and the subsequent dominant discourse tended to focus on one dimension of the modern social complex: the modern state and its welfare role and services. Such a focus tends to take for granted and to make hidden assumptions about modern culture and economic life. First there is the existential fact that in all human societies, including modernity, it is the culture, particularly the family system, which supplies the bulk of welfare services. Secondly there is the historical fact that, since the rise of industrial capitalism in the nineteenth century, a great and increasing share of welfare services have been provided through the economy – through capitalist markets, involving goods and services produced by capitalist producers, consumed by consumers using income derived from capitalist labour markets.

Marshall (1964, 1981: ch. 6) considered the conflicts over inequality which occur between the democratic polity and the economy, between the welfare state and capitalism (see also Titmuss, 1963: ch. 2). However, along with William Beveridge, Richard Titmuss and other proponents of the welfare state, he assumed that in practice a mixed economy (capitalism and state-controlled economic sectors) was viable and that welfare state relations with capitalism could be functional, mutually reinforcing and capable of supporting minimally unequal citizen relations. Many others have subsequently made similar but more explicit arguments from neo-Marxist and critical social theory perspectives (e.g. Gough, 1979; Doyal, 1983; Turner, 1986), albeit with varying *evaluations* of this functionality and of the possibilities for equality.

Overall, in its analysis of the politics of welfare and of social citizenship, the dominant paradigm has, on the one hand, tended to overemphasize the role and capacity of the state and its officials to produce and distribute welfare *per se*, and to do so on an egalitarian and citizen-respecting basis. On the other hand, the dominant paradigm has tended to underestimate the actual and potential role of markets, the family and voluntary organizations both to produce and to distribute welfare, and to do so not only on an egalitarian and citizen-respecting basis, but on a participative and mutual basis beyond the capacity of the state apparatus. Evidently, the possibilities available in the non-state sectors can be exaggerated, and Neoconservatism typically greatly exaggerates the role of labour markets in terms of welfare and citizenship. In the light of this the dominant paradigm tends, when it explicitly addresses them, to adopt a critical stance toward the inadequacies and inequities of the non-state sectors as welfare providers.

But there are important hidden assumptions in this stance. The dominant paradigm – usually reluctantly and *sotto voce* – is usually well aware that the non-state sectors are in actual fact providers of welfare both on a massive scale and in ways quite beyond the capacity and competence even of totalitarian states to take over or replicate as a whole. It may be that in some areas and on some occasions state welfare provision is superior in quantity or quality to that provided in non-state sectors. But it is important to understand the necessary condition for such welfare state success and superiority as there is: that the state explicitly or tacitly recognizes its *limits vis-à-vis* civil society and non-state sectors. So the resources necessary to support welfare state achievements and successes, such as they are, are only available because they are *not* required to be dispersed in pursuit of grandiose projects of substitution for non-state-sector provision. Ironically, in this analysis the condition of success of the welfare state is the conservation of resources which the effectiveness of the non-state welfare sectors allows it. The hidden assumption of the welfare state, and of the dominant paradigm which supports it, is that of the existence, persistence and success of a plurality of non-state welfare systems understood as functionally related to each other and to the national society as a functional whole, with the state largely in a regulatory as opposed to a provisory role (Jordan, 1987).

Finally, there is the question of the history of citizenship. Marshall offers a picture, based on Britain, of the successive growth of each of the three types of citizenship and relevant state institutions. Thus it is possible to assign the formative period in the life of each to a different century – civil rights to the eighteenth, political to the nineteenth and social to the twentieth (1964: 73). Bendix and Parsons took over this rough evolutionary account in their studies of nation-building in countries such as Japan, India, Germany and Russia (Bendix, 1964) and of Western modernization (Parsons, 1970). A related evolutionary/revolutionary image of successive waves in the growth of citizenship appears repeatedly in a recent study of the intimate relationship between citizenship and the modernization process and between citizenship and its capitalist structural context (Turner, 1986).

Overall, though, the dominant paradigm's conception of the history of citizenship in general is that of long-term growth, formation and coalescence between processes of nation-state democratization on the one hand and the development of industrial capitalism on the other, while its conception of the history of social citizenship is that of the long-term growth of a conflictual but contained and ultimately functional relationship between the welfare state and industrial capitalism.

Recent history and critical reflection give us many reasons to question the assumptions of the dominant paradigm and to rethink its conception of social citizenship. The following sections will examine some of the main contemporary incentives for doing so and their implications for social citizenship. We will look first at the incentives provided by changes in the structural context of citizenship, and then at ideological challenges, especially those of Neoconservatism.

Citizenship and structural change: the postmodern condition

The dominant paradigm of social citizenship – with its associated discourse of welfare rights, its politics of welfare state provision, and its relative silence on family-based and market-based welfare systems and provision – held sway throughout the early post-war period, the period of post-war reconstruction and the long boom from the 1950s to the mid-1970s. Since then, for a variety of reasons (see Roche, 1992a: pt III), the structural base of the dominant paradigm of citizenship has been subject to stresses and to significant change.

In particular, the welfare state and the concept of social citizenship it sustains have been subjected to two sorts of critique. First there is the economic critique that the growth of state welfare spending damages economic growth and thus the tax base on which it depends. Secondly there is the moral critique that the welfare state tends to perpetuate the dependency of its clients, that it disables rather than enables them, and even that it increases the poverty it was set up to abolish. We will consider the moralistic conservative criticisms later (section III).

The problems of the welfare state, whether real or perceived, are symptomatic of deeper problems in contemporary society. These problems are associated with social change and a period of historic transition away from the modern social formation of the nation-state, industrial capitalism and a common and functional culture and toward an unfamiliar, uncertain and unclear future. There can be little doubt that, certainly by the late 1980s, the advanced Western societies had begun to part company with the modern formation in many important respects. This drift (with some exceptions such as Japan) involved no clear vision of the likely shape or alternative profiles of a future social formation, even assuming that the pace of social change would never ease sufficiently for stable formations to develop in the early twenty-first century (Toffler, 1970, 1980, 1985).

Without any wish to get detoured into the Byzantine world of postmodernism, I will nonetheless use the terms "postmodern" and "postmodern problematic" to refer to this process of significantly unpredictable and apparently irresistible structural change in the main elements of the modern formation. This usage is consistent with other contemporary conceptualizations of the postmodern condition (e.g. Harvey, 1989) and postmodernization (e.g. Crook et al., 1992). It is also consistent with the view that postmodern institutional configurations are continuous with the dynamics of modernity and modernization and represent a new stage within a modernization process which has already gone through a number of qualitatively distinct stages since the pre-industrial period.

The postmodern condition involves the emergence of new orders of transnational and sub-national complexity in the politics, economics and cultures of modern societies. This complexity is potentially disorienting in ideological and normative cultural spheres, and disintegrative and disorganizational in economic and political economic terms (Urry and Lash, 1987) for modern formations. To counter its anomic effects requires a continuous labour of ideological reorientation and of restructuring (i.e. integrative institution-building) from all members, and from social organizations at all levels, in these formations.

The new complexity distinctive of the postmodern condition is clearly visible in the modern polity in the shape of (a) the emerging web of transnational political organizations managing global and world-regional affairs; (b) the emergence of continental/world-regional economic and political alliances, of which the European [Union] is the leading example; (c) the persistence and development of sub-national nationalist and regional autonomy claims; and (d) the persisting difficulties in realizing the claims of modern societies to be effectively multicultural rather than simply hopelessly politically fragmented along ethnic lines. The new postmodern complexity is equally clearly visible in the modern economy in the interconnected processes of globalization and flexibilization in contemporary capitalism.

Globalization (e.g. Hall and Jacques, 1989: pt III) refers to the rapid development of a multinational structure and role in large corporations and of a genuinely global level of capital movement, production organization and marketing. Flexibilization (e.g. Piore and Sabel, 1984; Hall and Jacques, 1989: pt I) refers to the introduction of computerization and automation into goods production and distribution and into financial and information services for producers and consumers. This is at the heart of the currently much debated shift from industrial to post-industrial or post-Fordist capitalism. Capital equipment and labour are having to become more flexible and skilled, capable of rapid adjustment to changing and segmented markets.

These two processes have operated to profoundly undermine conventional economic policy assumptions. First there is the notion that economies can be national and hence that their labour markets and general price levels can be significantly influenced by national governments. The breakdown of this assumption has profound consequences for the ability of states both to service social citizenship claims to (full) employment and to control inflationary tendencies in consumer (welfare) goods and services markets.

Secondly the flexibilized post-industrial/post-Fordist economy (unlike the mass production/mass consumption Fordist economy it replaces) continuously reduces the demand for labour relative to output (i.e. it increases labour productivity). This presents a permanent threat of structural unemployment (Gorz, 1982, 1985, 1989; Keane and Owen, 1986) as well as increasing pressures for national economic growth and for improvements in national labour supply and training systems to sustain employment (Robins and Webster, 1989; Freeman and Soete, 1987). This comes at the very time when the possibility of economic regulation at the national level is being seriously undermined by globalization. There are serious structural problems of either structural unemployment or at least of underemployment and of a labour market segmented between full-time and part-time or temporary workers. These problems challenge one of the hidden assumptions of the dominant paradigm of citizenship, namely that a great bulk of welfare can be distributed through the market system via consumption based on employment income (Dore, 1987).

Finally, there are significant trends in modern culture toward postmodern complexity. Among other things, these challenge the other hidden assumption of the dominant paradigm. This assumption, as noted earlier, is that the greatest bulk of welfare can be distributed through a standardized family system and mainly through women's labour as those who care for young children, the sick and the elderly. The main development relevant here is the long-term and accelerating breakdown of the standardized family pattern of patriarchally based gender roles and division of labour, and of commonly held and legitimized norms regarding such matters as divorce, incest, violence and illegitimate births (e.g. Wicks and Kiernan, 1990). Since this particular dysfunctionality of postmodern culture for the modern formation is one that greatly worries Neoconservatives, we will return to it again in the next section.

There are evidently many other cultural developments toward postmodern complexity which challenge the functionality of the modern cultural system for both the polity and the economy. Not least is the development of an individualistic, privatistic and hedonistic consumer culture (Lasch, 1979; Featherstone, 1991). As regards the polity, consumerism tends to contribute to ecological problems and to undermine politics based on the legitimacy of notions of the public sphere and the public good. As regards the economy, it has been argued that consumerism constitutes one of the basic cultural contradictions of capitalism (Bell, 1976) in that it tends to undermine both the work ethic and also the incentive to save, thereby also undermining labour productivity and investment resources.

Each of these late twentieth-century shifts away from the modern social formation toward the transitional postmodern condition outlined above carries problems and potential fuel for movements challenging the dominant paradigm of citizenship, particularly its assumed structural context and its welfare-state-based version of social citizen-ship. The next section will consider some of the main challenges to the dominant paradigm in the contemporary period from ideological movements, especially American Neoconservatism. These challenges respond to some of the social problems generated by the structural changes which have been reviewed in this section.

III CITIZENSHIP AND IDEOLOGY: THE DOMINANT PARADIGM AND NEOCONSERVATISM

Duty discourses: ideological and social movements in modernity

The dominant paradigm of citizenship, in addition to its structural and historical assumptions, contains assumptions about the nature of the citizen world, as suggested earlier. This latter sphere is the main focus of various ideological movements and challenges which have arisen in the late twentieth century. I have suggested that the paradigm's picture of the nature of citizenship and of the citizen community is one which emphasizes the priority of citizens' rights, together with the continuity and complementarity of social rights *vis-à-vis* civic and political rights. Certainly the struggle for rights has been a central and recurrent theme in nineteenth- and twentieth-century politics. But there is another side to citizenship which has been relatively neglected by the dominant paradigm: citizens' duties.

Duties have stimulated a considerable amount of political conflict in the post-war West (e.g. the anti-conscription/anti-Vietnam war move-ment, tax-payers' revolts against welfare state spending and recently the British anti-poll-tax movement). But it is notable that they have been relatively little analysed in the social and political theory of citizenship (for an exception, see Walzer, 1985). This neglect is all the worse in that late twentieth-century popular politics seems to be accumulating duty discourses, particularly in the field of new social movements, namely such areas as internationalism, environmentalism and the anti-nuclear-weapons movement. That is, there is a certain popular recog-nition in the West – albeit one which has yet to find expression through organized national and international politics and policy-making – that rich nations have duties to poor ones, and that all nations and indi-viduals have duties to nature and the environment, as well as to future generations regarding the conservation and transmission of humankind's environmental and sociohistorical heritage (Roche, 1992a: chs 2, 9).

Besides this radical new social movement wing of the new duty dis-course in contemporary society, there is also of course (as there traditionally always has been) a right-wing discourse about citizens' duties and responsibilities in Western politics. In the 1980s and 1990s in the US, Britain and elsewhere, interest groups, parties, movements and governments on the Right have developed and deployed a duty discourse, a repertoire of rhetorical and policy strategies focusing on individuals' personal responsibility for themselves and their (as against the community's, the public's, the state's) dependants (children, aged parents, unwaged partners, etc.), and generally upon the social obligations of citizenship. This discourse has been developed and deployed in particular with respect to the underclass, and more generally with respect to the poor and those dependent for some or all of their income and/or welfare services on the state, and thus indirectly on the employed and taxpaying sectors of any society's population. The discourse has achieved considerable popularity and support among skilled working-class and the lower middle-class sectors of societies like the US and Britain, and to a significant extent it authentically formulates and expresses important elements of their ethico-political worldview. Given its orchestration by politicians, parties and sectors of the media, its continuing popular appeal, and the challenges it raises to the welfare state and to the dominant paradigm of social citizenship, I will refer to the development and diffusion of this discourse as an ideological movement.

This ideological movement was most clearly expressed in the early and mid-1980s in the development of American Neoconservative social thinking (to be distinguished from other more economistic and neo-libertarian forms of New Right thinking) which dominated social policy debates and policy-making during the Reagan and Bush presidencies. However, before we consider American Neoconservatism further, it is worth underlining the point that this distinctive movement in the language and assumptions of everyday politics in the US in the 1980s has had a popular and intellectual appeal and resonance beyond the traditional spheres of right-wing politics and beyond the US. Aspects of it, predictably, have appeared on the Right in Britain, in the post-Thatcherite Conservative Party's and government's thinking and rhetoric on social issues and social policy. For instance, inspired by examples in the repertoire of American Neoconservative family policy measures, the Conservative government created the Family Support Agency in 1992 to enforce absent/divorced fathers' child-support duties. Inspired by comparable examples of American Neoconservative work policy, the Conservatives [began] the gradual introduction of workfare-oriented reforms to the state's provision of income for the unemployed. In addition, familist rhetoric and policy (pro-family values, pro-two-parent and anti-one-parent families, etc.) has become a popular theme in Conservative Party think-tanks and at the Conservatives' annual party conferences in recent years.

But these elements have also appeared in the discourses of Centrist and Leftist parties and movements in a number of Western countries, particularly Britain, in the late 1980s and 1990s. Many of the Neoconservative themes we will outline here are connected with a rethinking of social citizenship away from a pure focus on rights toward giving full weight to social obligations as well. These elements have also appeared in recent years in such Centrist and Leftist political spheres as American communitarianism (e.g. Etzioni, 1992); British ethical socialism (Dennis and Halsey, 1988); and President Clinton's social policy agenda. Such themes are evident, too, in the British Labour Party's, and associated Centre/Left think-tanks', continued rethinking of a range of issues bearing on the idea and ideal of citizenship, and of citizens' rights and responsibilities (issues such as the proper relation between the market and the state in welfare, the proper balance between individual freedom and the goal of equality, the nature and importance of the enabling state ideal and constitutional reform: e.g. Andrews, 1991; IPPR, 1993).

An ideological movement: American Neoconservatism and social citizenship

Neoconservatism is to be found in the pro-capitalism and pro-individual-liberty writings of a number of notable American sociologists and policy analysts, and also in journals such as *The Public Interest*. It is a loose label for a relatively diverse group ranging from sceptical liberals such as the sociologist Daniel Bell and the influential Democratic Senator Daniel P. Moynihan on its Left, to New Right anti-welfare state libertarians such as Charles Murray (Ehrenreich, 1987; King, 1987; also Karger, 1991; Lasch, 1991).

What are some of the main preoccupations of Neoconservatism relevant to understanding its conceptions of social citizenship? As far as the *structural context* of citizenship goes, Neoconservatism recognizes the importance of some structural changes comparable to those discussed above, particularly the changes in the cultural (family and value system). But in general (and with due recognition of the federalist subnationalism of some Neoconservatives, e.g. Murray, 1984; Butler and Kondratas, 1987), it tends to operate within the dominant paradigm's structural context assumptions of nation-statism, national (here US) capitalism and national functionalism.

But Neoconservatism's main contribution to the ideological challenge to the dominant paradigm of citizenship bears on the paradigm's conception of the nature of citizenship and of the citizen world. On this issue Neoconservatives are forthright and blunt, if also, as we shall see, self-contradictory and at odds with themselves. They set out to counter the dominant paradigm's arguably unjustified overemphasis on rights and on the role of the state in welfare provision and in social citizenship. So their emphasis (or rather their arguably equally unjustified overemphasis) is on duties and the role of the non-state sectors of employment and family in welfare and social citizenship. Neoconservatism undoubtedly makes a general case for the importance of having a conception of duty as a vital part of any conception of social citizenship. However, there are conflicts and contradictions at the heart of the perspective on the relative priority, and indeed the very compatibility, of family duties as against employment (capitalist labour market) duties. (For fuller accounts and critiques of Neoconservatism's approach to social citizenship, family and work policy, see Roche, 1992a: chs 4–6; Coenen and Leisink, 1993).

For the sake of this discussion we will assume that social policy helps to demarcate and constitute the political field in which the world of social citizenship exists. On social policy, then, Neoconservatives are united in a belief that the post-war state has failed, that (in the words attributed to Ronald Reagan) in the 1960s we fought a War on Poverty, and Poverty won. They are united also in going further and seeing the liberal welfare state as being the major contributor to the social problems it was ostensibly designed to solve, namely long-term poverty and unemployment. The persistence of these problems has, in the view of Neoconservatives (e.g. Mead, 1986; Murray, 1989) and many liberal commentators (e.g. Auletta, 1983; Wilson, 1987) led to the growth of an underclass of variously incompetent, disturbed and alienated people, often women, mainly in inner-city black ghettos, prone to crime and maintained in their marginalized position by the welfare benefits they usually depend upon (Roche, 1992a: ch. 3).

Neoconservative work policy and social citizenship

Beyond their shared diagnoses of the problems, Neoconservatives differ considerably among themselves about the best prescription for solving them. There is much agonizing and agnosticism about whether any solution exists, together with a distinct difference of view between a libertarian wing (e.g. Murray, 1984, 1988), which would abolish much of the welfare state and its custodial democracy, and an authoritative state wing (e.g. Mead, 1986), which would retain the welfare state but would seek to transform the alleged permissiveness of its professional culture and its effects on clients.

The main debate within American Neoconservative social policy, however, is one which is also often heard in current British conservatism. It concerns the relative priority to be given to distinct and possibly competing types of social obligations of citizenship. On the one hand there are the duties enjoined by the (once-Protestant) work ethic, while on the other there are the duties enjoined by traditional family values. The work ethic wing in the US (but also increasingly in Britain, for example current Restart employment policy) 'is most concerned with workfare policy. In the US it is represented particularly well in the writings of the policy analyst Lawrence Mead (1986; also Roche, 1992a: ch. 6) among others. The familist wing is most concerned with various pro-family policies. In the US it is represented by notable sociologists (e.g. Peter and Brigitte Berger, 1983; George Gilder, 1986) and policy-makers (e.g. Senator Daniel P. Moynihan, 1989). In the UK it is strongly represented in Prime Minister Major's government. We can now briefly look at the workfare and familist positions within Neoconservatism and at the issues they raise for social citizenship.

Workfare is the policy of making welfare benefits conditional upon employment or training and effectively treating benefits as a loan to be paid off by work. Its implementation has been patchy, covering many but by no means all US states. In practice it has taken a variety of forms ranging from the punitive to the supportive, few of which save public expenditure (rather the reverse), and with a variety of effects, none of them very spectacular in reducing welfare dependency, poverty or unemployment. While the policy threatened to take a more punitive and national (federal) form under the Reagan presidency, Congress was largely able to stall this line of development.

Lawrence Mead is probably the leading academic spokesman for workfare in American social policy and for the view that the importance of work duties is best communicated and legitimized in terms of the discourse of citizenship and its duties. His major study of workfare policy, significantly entitled *Beyond Entitlement* (1986), provided a thorough account and defence, in citizenship duty terms, of the drift toward the more authoritative form of workfare in the 1970s and 1980s. However, in recent years US workfare policy has begun to take on a more benign, even supportive, appearance. For instance, the biggest single group of able-bodied unemployed in the underclass consists of young single black mothers on welfare. In recent years Congress has acknowledged that involvement in workfare for these women requires the provision of child care and other support services, and that what they arguably need is skill training in preference to coercion into unskilled and low-paying jobs.

Nonetheless, with some qualifications, Mead has continued to argue for just such coercion (e.g. Mead, 1988a–d). He argues that the alleged barriers to the welfare poor finding employment such as racism and inner-city deindustrialization and economic decline are largely illusory. He points out that there is a strong and continuing demand for workers in urban areas, albeit in low-skilled and low-paid dirty and menial jobs. He concludes that much contemporary long-term unemployment must be seen as largely voluntary and the product of a lack of job skills and an unwillingness to accept employer authority, not to mention laziness. This produces a vicious circle of personal and social incompetence among the underclass, including a lack of self-respect as well as respectability in the eyes of mainstream American society. For Mead, the only hope to break such circles is through a virtual resocialization of underclass members into the social obligations of citizenship, particularly the work ethic, by an authoritative national workfare policy.

Neoconservative family policy and social citizenship

For other Neoconservatives, however, the primary social obligations of citizenship are family duties – duties to contain the satisfaction of sexual desire and also procreation within the space of legitimacy provided by the institution of marriage; to honour the parental role and to care for children; to honour the dutiful son or daughter role and to care for elderly parents. In the familist view, family duties and work duties are complementary only if traditional patriarchal assumptions are made (and maintained in reality) about the sexual division of labour. Work and family are complementary only if males seek employment and act as breadwinners while females provide child care, elderly relative care and care for the breadwinner (Gilder, 1986).

But, as noted earlier, the traditional institution of the family is clearly changing and is arguably in a deep long-term crisis in contemporary Western society (Berger and Berger, 1983; Wicks and Kiernan, 1990). Rising rates of divorce, male desertion of children, male unemployment and female employment, male violence in families, child neglect and abuse, and finally illegitimacy are all indicators of the severity of the problems here. The family is in crisis not only as a system of regulating gender relations but also as a system of intergenerational relations and as a (indeed *the*) basic non-state welfare system. In particular it is in crisis as the basic system of child care and of childrens' primary socialization. These social systems are changing and/or breaking down generally in contemporary societies, but especially among the poor and the underclass.

The familist wing of Neoconservatism is greatly exercised by these crises. From their perspective, the problems of poor families headed by women, of welfare mothers and their children, are not addressed but exacerbated by a tough workfare approach such as Mead's. Workfare encourages women to attempt to be breadwinners and undermines their mothering role and their performance of its duties. From this perspective, these women need a long-term stable relationship with a male breadwinner, ideally marriage, and their children need a father (Gilder, 1987).

Of course, familism does not suggest that the state can supply husbands and fathers to poor single mothers. But, on the one hand, the state can legitimately enforce the duty of poor unemployed fathers to support their families, by means of authoritative forms of workfare. It can also enforce the paternal duties of deserting fathers by determined efforts to establish paternity and arrange maintenance payments. On the other hand, the state should support motherhood and child care, without providing *incentives* to single parenting. For this familist wing of Neoconservatism, the tough Meadian approach to enforcing workfare on poor single mothers is, to say the least, not the obvious way to support motherhood and family values and may even be damaging to them (Gilder, 1986: ch. 8, 1987; Butler and Kondratas, 1987: ch. 5).

However, in the late 1980s Neoconservatives began to attempt to construct a new consensus of the family (Novak et al., 1987) and on social policy (Glazer, 1988) while Congress advocated a more supportive approach in workfare policy (Moynihan, 1989). It is possible that the underlying tensions between work and family duties will turn out to be relatively manageable for Neoconservatism at the political level and less divisive than they appear when considered at the level of principle.

In this section I have concentrated on outlining some of the internal inconsistencies, tensions and contradictions within Neoconservatism as an ideological movement. To conclude on this theme, we can now note some further problems within this political perspective. The work ethic wing of this ideological movement clearly has a number of major blind spots. For instance, despite appearances to the contrary (for instance the presence in their ranks of the doyen of post-industrial theory, Daniel Bell), proponents of the work ethic approach seem to have little grasp of the negative structural trends in the development of global and high-technology capitalism noted earlier. They wrongly underplay the implications of these trends for labour markets and employment opportunities, particularly for the underclass (e.g. Dore, 1987; Roche, 1992a). Neither do they appear to have grasped one of the messages of the women's movement: that there is more to work than employment (e.g. Oakley, 1974; Pahl, 1988: pts III, IV). They seem oblivious to the notion that child-care and other care work, so-called women's work, actually *is* work.

In the late twentieth century it is clear that the gendered division of labour implicit in and legitimized by the Protestant work ethic needs to be challenged and reorganized between men and women. Given this, in the agenda of the new politics of citizenship, care work obligations have as much, if not more, right to be understood as social duties of citizenship as have duties to participate in labour markets, particularly cheap labour markets.

By contrast, the familist wing of this ideological movement appears to grasp the latter point, but totally rejects any feminist interpretation of it. Thus it rejects the preceding point about the need to rethink the sexual division of labour, and the fact that the promotion of citizenship ideals requires a new politics of employment and care work distribution.

In this section we have reviewed some of the main contradictions in one of the main ideological movements currently pressing for a rethinking of social citizenship. From this case study we can now return to the broader picture of the theoretical and practical rethinking of social citizenship and social movements required by social change in Western societies in the late twentieth century.

Conclusion

This chapter has explored developments in the sociology of citizenship relevant to an understanding of the contested and changing nature of social citizenship in modernity. Its primary purpose has been to explore the research agenda of what can be called the new sociology of citizenship. As part of this inquiry it was necessary to consider the nature of the long-standing modern post-war rights-based and welfare-state-based paradigm of social citizenship, referred to here as the dominant paradigm, and also the articulation of this paradigm in the work of T. H. Marshall and others in the more traditional sociology of modern citizenship.

In section II we outlined this paradigm, together with the problems posed for the national functionalist societal configuration on which it rests, by structural change in Western society since the mid- to late 1970s. These changes involve post-industrialism, post-nationalism, and generally the development of a postmodern configuration within and between culture, economy and polity in modernity. In sections I and III we outlined something of the range of political responses to, and articulations of, this structural change and the postmodern condition. In various ways these political developments, from Left to Right, raise questions about the viability, effectiveness and legitimacy of national functionalism, the dominant paradigm of social citizenship and its institutionalization in the welfare state.

In section I we briefly surveyed the field of social movements and their sociological analysis. The latter has tended to prioritize the study of progressive (new) social movements such as the anti-nuclear, ecological and feminist movements. Progressive movements undoubtedly pose important challenges to the conventional structures and assumptions of post-war Western society and politics. It was suggested, however, that in order to understand how structural and ideological forces are currently conspiring to undermine and restructure the dominant paradigm of social citizenship, we must study and take full account of contemporary non- and anti-progressive organizations and movements.

In particular it was suggested that formal organizations, such as neo-corporatist projects among urban political and economic elites, and the entrenched potential for disorganization, such as that visible in the underclass and the urban ghetto, should equally come within the purview of social movements analysis. The former could be seen as anti-political movements, interested in the management of popular acquiescence and consent, and uninterested in the development of local democracy and governmental accountability, while the latter could be seen as anti-social movements parasitically draining the capacity of the communities which host them to develop even self-defensive and functional forms of organization, let alone more progressive types of collective action and social movement.

[. . .]

In addition, it was suggested that the national and transnational levels of citizenship formation and social movement operation required that a central position be given to actions and processes involving collective consciousness (and thus involving collective beliefs and commonsense knowledge, public discourse and communication), as well as collective behaviour. Thus it was proposed that social movements analysis, to be relevant to the interests of the new sociology of citizenship, needs to clarify the nature of its address to what might be termed ideological movements. Whether or not they are strongly linked to organizations and to social and political practice and behaviour, ideological movements contest the field of social values and ideals, and promote normative versions of collective social and political consciousness, at national, international and transnational levels.

In recent years American Neoconservatism has emerged as a particularly important non-progressive, indeed often explicitly anti-progressive, ideological movement which has been influential on British Conservative governments and on politics in other Western countries. In section III we reviewed some of the main themes in Neoconservatism bearing upon its critique of the welfare state and the dominant rights-based paradigm of social citizenship. Its own ideal of social citizenship involves prioritizing obligations over rights, and familial and market sources of welfare over the welfare state. We considered Neoconservative views on citizens' obligations, social ethics and government strategies in relation to the spheres of employment policy and family policy in particular. It was concluded that, among a number of intellectual weaknesses in Neoconservative ideology relating to its underemphasis on structurally generated conditions and problems, there is a fundamental weakness in the tension which exists between its supporters of family values and its supporters of the work ethic. These weaknesses and contradictions were argued to be especially evident in Neoconservative approaches to the various social problems experienced, and posed to the rest of society, by the poor and the underclass.

Nonetheless it was also observed that, to a certain extent, Neoconservatism is currently influential in Centre and Left parties and political movements, in setting the agenda for the reform of the welfare state and more generally for the future development of social citizenship. At the very least it is clear that the political problems caused by a recognition of the existential fact of citizens' individual responsibilities for their choices and for their own lives, and the social fact of citizens' responsibilities for their dependants (i.e. their children, elderly parents and unemployed partners), can no longer be avoided by, or submerged within, conventional Centrist and Left rights-based politics. Nor can they be ignored or avoided in the social and political thinking of the new social movements.

Indeed it is possible to argue that progressive social movements tend to operate in a moral and political discursive sphere which understands the limitations of purely rights-based politics and which promotes, whether explicitly or implicitly, important new conceptions of citizens' responsibilities. Ecology, for instance, promotes strong conceptions of personal, national and corporate-capitalist responsibilities for the environment, plant and animal life, and the quality of life of future generations. Feminism promotes equally strong conceptions of the responsibilities of men for making their rhetoric of equal opportunities a reality in the sphere of employment, for controlling their violence, and for parenting their children (Roche, 1992a: ch. 3).

However, the structural changes in the national functionalist context underpinning the welfare state and the dominant paradigm of social citizenship outlined in section II indicate the emergence of severe problems of social exclusion involving the poor and the underclass. Generally the post-industrial capitalist labour market, which is a market in increasingly flexibilized forms of labour, while it remains capable of generating aggregate economic growth, is becoming increasingly inefficient and inequitable as a distribution system for income, employment and market-based welfare, and as a servicing system for citizens' rights claims in these spheres.

These problems suggest that we need to work for a new generation of social rights, particularly rights to employment (e.g. Gorz, 1982, 1985, 1989; Keane and Owen, 1986; Coenen and Leisink, 1993; Pixley, 1993) and/or rights to income (Parker, 1989; Roche, 1992a: ch. 7; Van Parijs, 1992). But they also suggest that such rights are needed from the point of view of any reasonably objective sociological analysis. If nations and their market systems are to be sustained in the long term, albeit within new globalized and multinational settings and configurations, then some such new generation of citizens' social rights is likely to be produced by the working through of systemic imperatives, interpreted through the politics and power struggles, the collective consciousness and collective actions, of progressive and anti-progressive citizens' ideological and sociopolitical movements. In this respect it will be important to monitor the European Union, as a working model of a new transnational level of societal organization in modernity, in terms of the new levels of organization of new social movements it makes possible and also in terms of the new forms of transnational and social citizenship which come to be constructed within it (Roche, 1992a: ch. 8; Meehan, 1993).

The discussion in this chapter suggests that two important aspects of the practical agenda facing each of the progressive social movements in contemporary Western societies are intimately bound up with the problems of the meaning of citizenship in modernity. First there is the problem, which ecology, feminism and each of the movements needs to address, of how best to understand and to promote democratic citizenship, that is citizenship within and between social movements, within national civil societies and their states, and at all levels from the urban to the international. Secondly there is the problem faced by each movement – to understand and balance the social rights and obligations implicit in and/or relevant to their particular movement's overall goal and programme, together with the problem of how best to achieve that balance in their struggles to develop their vision of social citizenship. Finally the discussion suggests an important aspect of the new research agenda facing both the sociology of social movements and the sociology of citizenship. Both fields in contemporary sociology now need to set themselves the task of understanding social movements' struggles with these problems of democracy, rights and obligations seen as set within the new politics of citizenship which is developing in late twentieth-century society.

REFERENCES

Andrews, G. (ed.) (1991) Citizenship. London: Lawrence and Wishart.
Auletta, K. (1983) The Underclass. New York: Vintage.
Barbalet, J. (1988) Citizenship. Milton Keynes: Open University Press.
Bell, D. (1976) The Cultural Contradictions of Capitalism. London: Heinemann.
Bendix, R. (1964) Nation-building and Citizenship. New York: John Wiley.
Berger, B. and Berger, P. (1983) The War over the Family. London: Hutchinson.

Brubaker, R. (1992) *Citizenship and Nationhood in France and Germany*. Cambridge, MA: Harvard University Press.

Butler, S. and Kondratas, A. (1987) *Out of the Poverty Trap*. New York: Free Press.

Coenen, H. and Leisink, P. (eds) (1993) *Work and Citizenship in the New Europe*. Aldershot: Edward Elgar.

Crook, S., Pakulski, J. and Waters, M. (1992) *Postmodernization*. London: Sage.

Dennis, N. and Halsey, A. H. (1988) *English Ethical Socialism*. Oxford: Clarendon.

Dore, R. (1987) "Citizenship and employment in the age of high technology," *British Journal of Industrial Relations*, 25 (2): 201–25.

Doyal, L. (1983) *The Political Economy of Health*. London: Pluto.

Ehrenreich, B. (1987) "The New Right's attack on welfare," in F. Block, R. Cloward, B. Ehrenreich and F. Piven (eds), *The Mean Season*, pp. 161–96. New York: Pantheon.

Etzioni, A. (1992) *The Spirit of Community: Rights, Responsibilities and the Communitarian Agenda*. New York: Crown Publishers.

Featherstone, M. (1991) *Consumer Culture and Postmodernism*. London: Sage.

Freeman, C. and Soete, L. (eds) (1987) *Technical Change and Full Employment*. Oxford: Basil Blackwell.

Giddens, A. (1985) "Class sovereignty and citizenship," in *The Nation-state and Violence*, ch. 8. Cambridge: Polity Press.

Gilder, G. (1986) *Men and Marriage*. Gretna, LA: Pelican.

Gilder, G. (1987) "The collapse of the American family," *The Public Interest*, 89.

Glazer, N. (1988) *The Limits of Social Policy*. Cambridge, MA: Harvard University Press.

Gorz, A. (1982) *Farewell to the Working Class*. London: Pluto.

Gorz, A. (1985) *Paths to Paradise*. London: Pluto.

Gorz, A. (1989) *Critique of Economic Reason*. London: Verso.

Gough, I. (1979) *The Political Economy of the Welfare State*. London: Macmillan.

Habermas, J. (1987) *The Theory of Communicative Action*, vol. 2. London: Heinemann.

Habermas, J. (1994) "Citizenship and national identity," in B. Van Steenbergen (ed.), *The Condition of Citizenship*. London: Sage.

Hall, S. and Held, D. (1989) "Citizens and citizenship," in S. Hall and M. Jacques (eds), *New Times*. London: Lawrence and Wishart.

Hall, S. and Jacques, M. (eds) (1989) *New Times*. London: Lawrence and Wishart.

Hammar, T. (1990) *Democracy and the Nation-state: Aliens, Denizens and Citizens in a World of International Migration*. Aldershot: Gower.

Harvey, D. (1989) *The Postmodern Condition*. Oxford: Basil Blackwell.

IPPR (1993) *The Justice Gap*. London: Commission on Social Justice, Institute for Public Policy Research.

Jacobs, B. (1992) *Fractured Cities: Capitalism, Community and Empowerment in Britain and America*. London: Routledge.

Jordan, B. (1987) *Rethinking Welfare*. Oxford: Basil Blackwell.

Karger, H. (1991) "The radical right and welfare reform in the United States," in H. Glennerster and J. Midgley (eds), *The Radical Right and the Welfare State*, ch. 4. Hemel Hempstead: Harvester-Wheatsheaf.

Keane, J. and Owen, J. (1986) *After Full Employment*. London: Hutchinson.

King, E. (1987) *The New Right: Politics, Markets and Citizenship*. London: Macmillan.

Lasch, C. (1979) *The Culture of Narcissism*. London: Abacus.

Lasch, C. (1991) "Right-wing populism and the revolt against liberalism," in *The True and Only Heaven*, ch. 11. New York: W. W. Norton.

Lister, R. (1990) *The Exclusive Society: Citizenship and the Poor*. London: Child Poverty Action Group.

Marshall, T. H. (1964) "Citizenship and social class" (1949), in *Sociology at the Crossroads*. New York: Doubleday.

Marshall, T. H. (1981) *The Right to Welfare*. London: Heinemann.

Mead, L. (1986) *Beyond Entitlement: the Social Obligations of Citizenship*. New York: Free Press.

Mead, L. (1988a) "The new welfare debate," *Commentary*, 86: 44–52.

Mead, L. (1988b) "The potential for work enforcement," *Journal of Policy Analysis and Management*, 7 (2): 264–88.

Mead, L. (1988c) "Jobs for the welfare poor," *Policy Review*, Winter: 60–9.

Mead, L. (1988d) "The hidden jobs debate," *The Public Interest*, 91: 40–58.

Meehan, E. (1993) *Citizenship and the European Community*. London: Sage.

Mouffe, C. (ed.) (1992) *Dimensions of Radical Democracy: Pluralism, Citizenship, Community*. London: Verso.

Moynihan, P. (1989) "Towards a post-industrial social policy," *The Public Interest*, 96: 16–27.

Murray, C. (1984) *Losing Ground*. New York: Basic Books.

Murray, C. (1988) "The coming of custodial democracy," *Commentary*, 86: 19–24.

Murray, C. (1989) "The underclass," *Sunday Times Magazine*, 26 November: 26–45.

Novak, M. et al. (1987) *The New Consensus on Family and Welfare*. Washington, DC: American Enterprise Institute for Public Policy Research and Working Seminar on Family and American Welfare Policy (US).

Oakley, A. (1974) *The Sociology of Housework*. Oxford: Martin Robertson.

Offe, C. (1985a) *Disorganized Capitalism*. Cambridge: Polity Press.

Offe, C. (1985b) "New social movements: challenging the boundaries of institutional politics," *Social Research*, Winter: 817–68.

Pahl, R. (ed.) (1988) *On Work*. Oxford: Basil Blackwell.

Parker, H. (1989) *Instead of Dole*. London: Macmillan.

Parker, J. (1975) *Social Policy and Citizenship*. London: Macmillan.

Parsons, T. (1970) *The System of Modern Societies*. Englewood Cliffs, NJ: Prentice-Hall.

Piore, M. and Sabel, C. (1984) *The Second Industrial Divide*. New York: Basic Books.

Pixley, J. (1993) *Citizenship and Employment: Investigating Post-industrial Options*. Cambridge: Cambridge University Press.

Plant, R. (1988) *Citizenship, Rights and Socialism*. London: Fabian Society.

Rimlinger, G. (1971) *Welfare Policy and Industrialization in Europe, America and Russia*. New York: John Wiley.

Robins, K. and Webster, F. (1989) *The Technical Fix*. London: Macmillan.

Roche, M. (1987) "Citizenship, social theory and social change," *Theory and Society*, 16: 363–99.

Roche, M. (1992a) *Rethinking Citizenship: Welfare, Ideology and Change in Modern Society*. Cambridge: Polity Press.

Roche, M. (1992b) "Mega-event planning and citizenship (on the politics of urban cultural policy)," *Vrijetijd en Samenleving (Leisure and Society)* [The Hague], 10 (4): 47–67.

Room, G. (1979) *The Sociology of Welfare*. Oxford: Martin Robertson.

Scott, A. (1990) *Ideology and the New Social Movements*. London: Unwin Hyman.

Titmuss, R. (1963) *Essays on the Welfare State*. London: Allen and Unwin.

Toffler, A. (1970) *Future Shock*. London: Pan.

Toffler, A. (1980) *Third Wave*. London: Pan/Collins.

Toffler, A. (1985) *Previews and Premises*. London: Pan.

Touraine, A. (1977) *The Voice and the Eye: an Analysis of Social Movements*. Cambridge: Cambridge University Press.

Turner, B. (1986) *Citizenship and Capitalism*. London: Allen and Unwin.

Urry, J. and Lash, S. (1987) *The End of Organized Capitalism*. Cambridge: Polity Press.

Van Parijs, P. (ed.) (1992) *Arguing for Basic Income: Ethical Foundations for a Radical Reform*. London: Verso.

Walzer, M. (1985) *Spheres of Justice*. Oxford: Basil Blackwell.

Wicks, M. and Kiernan, K. (1990) *Family Change and Social Change*. London: Family Policy Studies Centre.

Wilson, W. J. (1987) *The Truly Disadvantaged*. Chicago: University of Chicago Press.

CHAPTER 12

The Patriarchal Welfare State

Carole Pateman

According to Raymond Williams's *Keywords*, "the Welfare State, in distinction from the Warfare State, was first named in 1939."[1] The welfare state was set apart from the fascist warfare state, defeated in the Second World War, and so the welfare state was identified with democracy at the christening. In the 1980s most Western welfare states are also warfare states, but this is not ordinarily seen as compromising their democratic character. Rather, the extent of democracy is usually taken to hinge on the *class* structure. Welfare provides a social wage for the working class, and the positive, social democratic view is that the welfare state gives social meaning and equal worth to the formal juridical and political rights of all citizens. A less positive view of the welfare state is that it provides governments with new means of exercising power over and controlling working-class citizens. But proponents of both views usually fail to acknowledge the sexually divided way in which the welfare state has been constructed. Nor do most democratic theorists recognize the *patriarchal* structure of the welfare state; the very different way that women and men have been incorporated as citizens is rarely seen to be of significance for democracy.[2] Even the fact that the earliest developments of the welfare state took place when women were still denied, or had only just won, citizenship in the national state is usually overlooked.[3]

I do not want to dispute the crucial importance of class in understanding the welfare state and democracy. To write about the welfare state is, in large part, to write about the working class. However, my discussion treats class in a manner unfamiliar to most democratic theorists, who usually assume that the welfare state, democracy and class can be discussed theoretically without any attention to the character of the relation between the sexes. I shall suggest some reasons why and how the patriarchal structure of the welfare state has been repressed from theoretical consciousness. I shall also consider the connection between employment and citizenship in the patriarchal welfare state, the manner in which "women" have been opposed to the "worker" and the "citizen", and a central paradox surrounding women, welfare and citizenship. By "the welfare state" here, I refer to the states of Britain (from which I shall draw a number of my empirical and historical examples), Australia and the United States. In the more developed welfare states of Scandinavia, women have moved nearer to, but have not yet achieved, full citizenship.[4]

For the past century, many welfare policies have been concerned with what are now called "women's issues". Moreover, much of the controversy about the welfare state has revolved and continues to revolve around the question of the respective social places and tasks of women and men, the structure of marriage and the power relationship between husband and wife. So it is not surprising that the Reagan administration's attack on the welfare state was seen as prompted by a desire to shore up the patriarchal structure of the state; the Reagan budgets, "in essence, . . . try to restabilize patriarchy . . . as much as they try to fight inflation and stabilize capitalism."[5] The difficulties of understanding the welfare state and citizenship today without taking the position of women into account are not hard to illustrate, because contemporary feminists have produced a large body of evidence and argument that reveals the importance of women in the welfare state and the importance of the welfare state for women.

Women are now the majority of recipients of many welfare benefits. In 1980 in the United States, for example, 64.8 per cent of the recipients of Medicare were women, while 70 per cent of housing subsidies went to women, either living alone or heading households;[6] and by 1979, 80 per cent of the families receiving Aid to Families with Dependent Children (AFDC) were headed by women (the number of such families having grown fourfold between 1961 and 1979).[7] A major reason why women are so prominent as welfare recipients is that women are more likely than men to be poor (a fact that has come to be known as "the feminization of poverty"). In the United States, between 1969 and 1979, there was a decline in the proportion of families headed by men that fell below the official poverty line while the proportion headed by women grew rapidly.[8] By 1982 about one-fifth of families with minor children were headed by women, but they constituted 53 per cent of all poor families,[9] and female heads were over three times as likely as male heads to have incomes below the poverty line.[10] By 1980 two out of every three adults whose incomes were below the poverty line were women. The National Advisory Council on Economic Opportunity reported in 1980 that, if these trends continued, the entire population of the poor in the United States would be composed of women and children by the year 2000.[11] In Australia women are also likely to be poor. A survey for the Commission of Inquiry into Poverty in 1973 found that, of the groups with "disabilities", fatherless families were poorest; 30 per cent of such families were below the poverty line, and another 20 per cent only marginally above it.[12] Nor had the situation improved by 1978–9: 41 per cent of women who were single parents were then below the poverty line.[13]

The welfare state is now a major source of employment for women. For instance, in Britain the National Health Service is the biggest single employer of women in the country; about three-quarters of NHS employees, and 90 per cent of NHS nurses, are women.[14] In 1981 there were more than five million jobs in the public health, education and welfare sector in Britain (an increase of two million from 1961) and three-fifths of these jobs were held by women.[15] In the United States in 1980 women occupied 70 per cent of the jobs at all levels of government concerned with social services, which was a quarter of all female employment and about half of all professional jobs occupied by women. Employment is provided largely at state and local levels in the United States. The federal government subsidizes the warfare state where there are few jobs for women; only 0.5 per cent of the female work force is employed on military contracts. One estimate is that, for each billion dollar increase in the military budget, 9,500 jobs are lost to women in social welfare or the private sector.[16]

Women are also involved in the welfare state in less obvious ways. Negotiations (and confrontations) with welfare state officials on a day-to-day basis are usually conducted by women; and it is mothers, not fathers, who typically pay the rent, deal with social workers, take children to welfare clinics and so forth. Women are also frequently in the forefront of political campaigns and actions to improve welfare services or the treatment of welfare claimants. The services and benefits provided by the welfare state are far from comprehensive and, in the absence of public provision, much of the work involved, for example, in caring for the aged in all three countries is undertaken by women in their homes (something to which I shall return).

Finally, to put the previous points into perspective, there is one area of the welfare state from which women have been largely excluded. The legislation, policy-making and higher-level administration of the welfare state have been and remain predominantly in men's hands. Some progress has been made; in Australia the Office of the Status of Women within the (Commonwealth) Department of Prime Minister and Cabinet monitors cabinet submissions, and the Women's Budget Program requires all departments to make a detailed assessment of the impact of their policies on women.

[. . .]

CITIZENSHIP AND EMPLOYMENT

Theoretically and historically, the central criterion for citizenship has been "independence", and the elements encompassed under the heading of independence have been based on masculine attributes and abilities. Men, but not women, have been seen as possessing the capacities required of "individuals", "workers" and "citizens". As a corollary, the meaning of "dependence" is associated with all that is womanly – and women's citizenship in the welfare state is full of paradoxes and contradictions. [. . .] Three elements of "independence" are particularly important for present purposes, all related to the masculine capacity for self-protection: the capacity to bear arms, the capacity to own property and the capacity for self-government.

First, women are held to lack the capacity for self-protection; they have been "unilaterally disarmed".[17] The protection of women is undertaken by men, but physical safety is a fundamental aspect of women's welfare that has been sadly neglected in the welfare state. From the nineteenth century, feminists (including J. S. Mill) have drawn attention to the impunity with which husbands could use physical force against their wives,[18] but women/wives still find it hard to obtain proper social and legal protection against violence from their male "protectors". Defence of the state (or the ability to protect your protection, as Hobbes put it), the ultimate test of citizenship, is also a masculine prerogative. The anti-suffragists in both America and Britain made a great deal of the alleged inability and unwillingness of women to use armed force, and the issue of women and combat duties in the military forces of the warfare state was also prominent in the recent campaign against the Equal Rights Amendment in the United States. Although women are now admitted into the armed force and so into training useful for later civilian employment, they are prohibited from combat duties in Britain, Australia and the United States. Moreover, past exclusion of women from the warfare state has meant that welfare provision for veterans has also benefited men. In Australia and the United States, because of their special "contribution" as citizens, veterans have had their own, separately administered welfare state, which has ranged from preference in university education (the GI bills in the United States) to their own medical benefits and hospital services, and (in Australia) preferential employment in the public service.

In the "democratic" welfare state, however, employment rather than military service is the key to citizenship. The masculine "protective" capacity now enters into citizenship primarily through the second and third dimensions of independence. Men, but not women, have also been seen as property-owners. Only some men own material property, but as "individuals", all men own (and can protect) the property they possess in their persons. Their status as "workers" depends on their capacity to contract out the property they own in their labour-power. Women are still not fully recognized socially as such property-owners. To be sure, our position has improved dramatically from the mid-nineteenth century when women as wives had a very "peculiar" position as the legal property of their husbands, and feminists compared wives to slaves. But today, a wife's person is still the property of her husband in one vital respect. Despite recent legal reform, in Britain and in some of the states of the United States and Australia, rape is still deemed legally impossible within marriage, and thus a wife's consent has no meaning. Yet women are now formally citizens in states held to be based on the necessary consent of self-governing individuals. The profound contradiction about women's consent is rarely if ever noticed and so is not seen as related to a sexually divided citizenship or as detracting from the claim of the welfare state to be democratic.

The third dimension of "independence" is self-government. Men have been constituted as the beings who can govern (or protect) themselves, and if a man can govern himself, then he also has the requisite capacity to govern others. Only a few men govern others in public life – but all men govern in private as husbands and heads of households. As the governor of a family, a man is also a "breadwinner". He has the capacity to sell his labour-power as a worker, or to buy labour-power with his capital, and provide for his wife and family. His wife is thus "protected." The category of "breadwinner" presupposes that wives are constituted as economic dependents or "housewives," which places them in a subordinate position. The dichotomy breadwinner/housewife, and the masculine meaning of independence, were established in Britain by the middle of the last century; in the earlier period of capitalist development, women (and children) were wage-labourers. A "worker" became a man who has an economically dependent wife to take care of his daily needs and look after his home and children. Moreover, "class," too, is constructed as a patriarchal category. "The working class" is the class of working *men*, who are also full citizens in the welfare state.

[. . .] The democratic implications of the right to work cannot be understood without attention to the connections between the public world of "work" and citizenship and the private world of conjugal relations. What it means to be a "worker" depends in part on men's status and power as husbands, and on their standing as citizens in the welfare state. The construction of the male worker as "breadwinner" and his wife as his "dependent" was expressed officially in the Census classifications in Britain and Australia. In the British Census of 1851, women engaged in unpaid domestic work were "placed ... in one of the productive classes along with paid work of a similar kind".[19] This classification changed after 1871, and by 1911 unpaid housewives had been completely removed from the economically active population. In Australia an initial conflict over the categories of classification was resolved in 1890 when the scheme devised in New South Wales was adopted. The Australians divided up the population more decisively than the British, and the 1891 Census was based on the two categories of "breadwinner and "dependent". Unless explicitly stated otherwise, women's occupation was classified as domestic, and domestic workers were put in the dependent category.

The position of men as breadwinner-workers has been built into the welfare state. The sexual divisions in the welfare state have received much less attention than the persistence of the old dichotomy between the deserving and undeserving poor, which predates the welfare state. This is particularly clear in the United States, where a sharp separation is maintained between "social security", or welfare-state policies directed at "deserving workers who have paid for them through 'contributions' over their working lifetimes", and "welfare" – seen as public "handouts" to "barely deserving poor people".[20] Although "welfare" does not have this stark meaning in Britain or Australia, where the welfare state encompasses much more than most Americans seem able to envisage, the old distinction between the deserving and undeserving poor is still alive and kicking, illustrated by the popular bogey-figures of the "scrounger" (Britain) and the "dole-bludger" (Australia). However, although the dichotomy of deserving/undeserving poor overlaps with the divisions between husband/wife and worker/housewife to some extent, it also obscures the patriarchal structure of the welfare state.

Feminist analyses have shown how many welfare provisions have been established within a two-tier system. First, there are the benefits available to individuals as "public" persons by virtue of their participation, and accidents of fortune, in the capitalist market. Benefits in this tier of the system are usually claimed by men. Second, benefits are available to the "dependents" of individuals in the first category, or to "private" persons, usually women. In the United States, for example, men are the majority of "deserving" workers who receive benefits through the insurance system to which they have "contributed" out of their earnings. On the other hand, the majority of claimants in means-tested programmes are women – women who are usually making their claims as wives or mothers. This is clearly the case with AFDC, where women are aided because they are mothers supporting children on their own, but the same is also true in other programmes: "46 per cent of the women receiving Social Security benefits make their claims as wives." In contrast: "men, even poor men, rarely make claims for benefits solely as husbands or fathers."[21] In Australia the division is perhaps even more sharply defined. In 1980–1, in the primary tier of the system, in which benefits are employment-related and claimed by those who are expected to be economically independent but are not earning an income because of unemployment or illness, women formed only 31.3 per cent of claimants. In contrast, in the "dependents group", 73.3 per cent of claimants were women, who were eligible for benefits because "they are dependent on a man who could not support them . . . [or] should have had a man support them if he had not died, divorced or deserted them."[22]

Such evidence of lack of "protection" raises an important question about *women's* standard of living in the welfare state. As dependents, married women should derive their subsistence from their husbands, so that wives are placed in the position of all dependent people before the establishment of the welfare state; they are reliant on the benevolence of another for their livelihood. The assumption is generally made that all husbands are benevolent. Wives are assumed to share equally in the standard of living of their husbands. The distribution of income *within* households has not usually been a subject of interest to economists, political theorists or protagonists in arguments about class and the welfare state – even though William Thompson drew attention to its importance as long ago as 1825[23] – but past and present evidence indicates that the belief that all husbands are benevolent is mistaken.[24] Nevertheless, women are likely to be better off married than if their marriage fails. One reason why women figure so prominently among the poor is that after divorce, as recent evidence from the United States reveals, a woman's standard of living can fall by nearly 75 per cent, whereas a man's can rise by nearly half.[25]

The conventional understanding of the "wage" also suggests that there is no need to investigate women's standard of living independently from men's. The concept of the wage has expressed and encapsulated the patriarchal separation and integration of the public world of employment and the private sphere of conjugal relations. In arguments about the welfare state and the social wage, the wage is usually treated as a return for the sale of *individuals'* labour-power. However, once the opposition breadwinner/housewife was consolidated, a "wage" had to provide subsistence for several people. The struggle between capital and labour and the controversy about the welfare state have been about the *family wage.* A "living wage" has been defined as what is required for a worker as breadwinner to support a wife and family, rather than what is needed to support himself; the wage is not what is sufficient to reproduce the worker's own labour power, but what is sufficient, in combination with the unpaid work of the housewife, to reproduce the labour-power of the present and future labour force.

The designer of the Australian Census classification system, T. A. Coghlan, discussed women's employment in his *Report* on the 1891 Census, and he argued that married women in the paid labour market depressed men's wages and thus lowered the general standard of living.[26] His line of argument about women's employment has been used by the trade union movement for the past century in support of bargaining to secure a family wage. In 1909 motions were put to the conferences of the Labour Party and Trades Union Congress in Britain to ban the employment of wives altogether, and as recently as 1982 a defence of the family wage was published arguing that it strengthens unions in wage negotiation.[27] In 1907 the family wage was enshrined in law in Australia in the famous Harvester judgement in the Commonwealth Arbitration Court. Justice Higgins ruled in favour of a legally guaranteed minimum wage – and laid down that a living wage should be sufficient to keep an unskilled worker, his (dependent) wife and three children in reasonable comfort.

Of course, a great deal has changed since 1907. Structural changes in capitalism have made it possible for large numbers of married women to enter paid employment, and equal-pay legislation in the 1970s, which in principle recognizes the wage as payment to an individual, may make it seem that the family wage has had its day. And it was always a myth for many, perhaps most, working-class families.[28] Despite the strength of the social ideal of the dependent wife, many working-class wives have always been engaged in paid work out of necessity. The family could not survive on the husband's wage, and the wife had to earn money, too, whether as a wage-worker, or at home doing outwork, or taking in laundry or lodgers or participating in other ways in the "informal" economy. In 1976 in Britain the wages and salaries of "heads of household" (not all of whom are men) formed only 51 per cent of household income.[29] The decline of manufacturing and the expansion of the service sector of capitalist economies since the Second World War have created jobs seen as "suitable" for women. Between 1970 and 1980 in the United States over thirteen million women entered the paid labour force.[30] In Britain, if present trends in male and female employment continue, women employees will outnumber men in less than ten years.[31] Nevertheless, even these dramatic shifts have not been sufficient to make women full members of the employment society. The civil right to "work" is still only half-heartedly acknowledged for women. Women in the workplace are still perceived primarily as wives and mothers, not workers.[32] The view is also widespread that women's wages are a "supplement" to those of the breadwinner. Women, it is held, do not need wages in the same way that men do – so they may legitimately be paid less than men.

When the Commonwealth Arbitration Court legislated for the family wage, 45 per cent of the male work force in Australia were single.[33] Yet in 1912 (in a case involving fruit pickers) Justice Higgins ruled that a job normally done by women could be paid at less than a man's rate because women were not responsible for dependents. On the contrary, while many men received a family wage and had no families, and breadwinners were given the power to determine whether their dependents should share in their standard of living, many women were struggling to provide for dependents on a "dependent's" wage. Eleanor Rathbone estimated that before and just after the Great War in Britain a third of women in paid employment were wholly or partially responsible for supporting dependents.[34] About the same proportion of women breadwinners was found in a survey of Victorian manufacturing industries in Australia in 1928.[35] Nevertheless, the classification of women as men's dependents was the basis for a living wage for women, granted in New South Wales in 1918; lower wages for women were enshrined in law and (until a national minimum wage for both sexes was granted in 1974) were set at 50–54 per cent of the male rate. Again in Britain, in the late 1960s and 1970s, the National Board for Prices and Incomes investigated low pay and argued that, as part-time workers, women did not depend on their own wage to support themselves.[36] In the United States, as recently as 1985, it was stated that "women have generally been paid less [than men] because they would work for lower wages, since they had no urgent need for more money. Either they were married, or single and living at home, or doubling up with friends."[37]

Women are prominent as welfare claimants because, today, it is usually women who are poor – and perhaps the major reason why women are poor is that it is very hard for most women to find a job that will pay a living wage. Equal-pay legislation cannot overcome the barrier of a sexually segregated occupational structure. Capitalist economies are patriarchal, divided into men's and women's occupations; the sexes do not usually work together, nor are they paid at the same rates for similar work. For example, in the United States, 80 per cent of women's jobs are located in only 20 of the 420 occupations listed by the Department of Labour.[38] More than half of employed women work in occupations that are 75 per cent female, and over 20 per cent work in occupations that are 95 per cent female.[39] In Australia in 1986, 59.5 per cent of women employees worked in the occupational categories "clerical, sales and services". In only 69 out of 267 occupational categories did the proportion of women reach a third or more.[40] The segregation is very stable; in Britain, for example, 84 per cent of women worked in occupations dominated by women in 1971, the same percentage as in 1951, and in 1901 the figure was 88 per cent.[41]

The economy is also vertically segregated. Most women's jobs are unskilled[42] and of low status; even in the professions women are clustered at the lower end of the occupational hierarchy. The British National Health Service provides a useful illustration. About one-third of employees are at the lowest level as ancillary workers, of whom around three-quarters are women. Their work is sex-segregated, so that the women workers perform catering and domestic tasks. As I noted previously, 90 per cent of NHS nurses are female but about one-quarter of senior nursing posts are held by men. At the prestigious levels, only about 10 per cent of consultants are female and they are segregated into certain specialities, notably those relating to children (in 1977, 32.7 per cent women).[43]

Many women also work part-time, either because of the requirements of their other (unpaid) work, or because they cannot find a full-time job. In Australia in 1986, 57.4 per cent of all part-time employees were married women.[44] In Britain two out of every five women in the work force are employed for thirty hours or less. However, the hourly rate for full-time women workers was only 75.1 per cent of men's in 1982 (and it is men who are likely to work overtime).[45] In 1980 women comprised 64 per cent of the employees in the six lowest paid occupations.[46] During the 1970s women's earnings edged slightly upward compared with men's in most countries, but not in the United States. In 1984 the median of women's earnings as full-time workers over a full year was $14,479, while men earned $23,218.[47] The growth in the service sector in the United States has largely been growth in part-time work; in 1980 almost a quarter of all jobs in the private sector were part-time. Almost all the new jobs appearing between 1970 and 1980 were in areas that paid less than average wages; in 1980 "51 per cent [of women] held jobs paying less than 66 per cent of a craft worker's wages."[48]

WOMEN'S WORK AND WELFARE

Although so many women, including married women, are now in paid employment, women's standing as "workers" is still of precarious legitimacy. So, therefore, is their standing as democratic citizens. If an individual can gain recognition from other citizens as an equally worthy citizen only through participation in the capitalist market, if self-respect and respect as a citizen are "achieved" in the public world of the employment society, then women still lack the means to be recognized as worthy citizens. Nor have the policies of the welfare state provided women with many of the resources to gain respect as citizens. Marshall's social rights of citizenship in the welfare state could be extended to men without difficulty. As participants in the market, men could be seen as making a public contribution, and were in a position to be levied by the state to make a contribution more directly, that *entitled* them to the benefits of the welfare state. But how could women, dependents of men, whose legitimate "work" is held to be located in the private sphere, be citizens of the welfare state? What could, or did, women contribute? The paradoxical answer is that women contributed – welfare.

The development of the welfare state has presupposed that certain aspects of welfare could and should continue to be provided by women (wives) in the home, and not primarily through public provision. The "work" of a housewife can include the care of an invalid husband and elderly, perhaps infirm, relatives. Welfare-state policies have ensured in various ways that wives/women provide welfare services gratis, disguised as part of their responsibility for the private sphere. A good deal has been written about the fiscal crisis of the welfare state, but it would have been more acute if certain areas of welfare had not been seen as a private, women's matter. It is not surprising that the attack on public spending in the welfare state by the Thatcher and Reagan governments goes hand-in-hand with praise for loving care within families, that is, with an attempt to obtain ever more unpaid welfare from (house)wives. The Invalid Care Allowance in Britain has been a particularly blatant example of the way in which the welfare state ensures that wives provide private welfare. The allowance was introduced in 1975 – when the Sex Discrimination Act was also passed – and it was paid to men or to single women who relinquished paid employment to look after a sick, disabled or elderly person (not necessarily a relative). Married women (or those cohabiting) were ineligible for the allowance.

The evidence indicates that it is likely to be married women who provide such care. In 1976 in Britain it was estimated that two million women were caring for adult relatives, and one survey in the north of England found that there were more people caring for adult relatives than mothers looking after children under 16.[49] A corollary of the assumption that women, but not men, care for others is that women must also care for themselves. Investigations show that women living by themselves in Britain have to be more infirm than men to obtain the services of home helps, and a study of an old people's home found that frail, elderly women admitted with their husbands faced hostility from the staff because they had failed in their job.[50] Again, women's citizenship is full of contradictions and paradoxes. Women must provide welfare, and care for themselves, and so must be assumed to have the capacities necessary for these tasks. Yet the development of the welfare state has also presupposed that women necessarily are in need of protection by and are dependent on men.

The welfare state has reinforced women's identity as men's dependents both directly and indirectly, and so confirmed rather than ameliorated our social exile. For example, in Britain and Australia the cohabitation rule explicitly expresses the presumption that women necessarily must be economically dependent on men if they live with them as sexual partners. If cohabitation is ruled to take place, the woman loses her entitlement to welfare benefits. The consequence of the cohabitation rule is not only sexually divided control of citizens, but an exacerbation of the poverty and other problems that the welfare state is designed to alleviate. In Britain today

> when a man lives in, a woman's independence – her own name on the weekly giro [welfare cheque] is automatically surrendered. The men become the claimants and the women their dependents. They lose control over both the revenue and the expenditure, often with catastrophic results: rent not paid, fuel bills missed, arrears mounting.[51]

It is important to ask what counts as part of the welfare state. In Australia and Britain the taxation system and transfer payments together form a tax-transfer system in the welfare state. In Australia a tax rebate is available for a dependent spouse (usually, of course, a wife), and in Britain the taxation system has always treated a wife's income as her husband's for taxation purposes. It is only relatively recently that it ceased to be the husband's prerogative to correspond with the Inland Revenue about his wife's earnings, or that he ceased to receive rebates due on her tax payments. Married men can still claim a tax allowance, based on the assumption that they support a dependent wife. Women's dependence is also enforced through the extremely limited public provision of child-care facilities in Australia, Britain and the United States, which creates a severe obstacle to women's full participation in the employment society. In all three countries, unlike Scandinavia, child-care outside the home is a very controversial issue.

Welfare-state legislation has also been framed on the assumption that women make their "contribution" by providing private welfare, and, from the beginning, women were denied full citizenship in the welfare state. In America "originally the purpose of ADC (now AFDC) was to keep mothers out of the paid labor force . . . In contrast, the Social Security retirement program was consciously structured to respond to the needs of white male workers."[52] In Britain the first national insurance, or contributory, scheme was set up in 1911, and one of its chief architects wrote later that women should have been completely excluded because "they want insurance for others, not themselves." Two years before before the scheme was introduced, William Beveridge, the father of the contemporary British welfare state, stated in a book on unemployment that the "ideal [social] unit is the household of man, wife and children maintained by the earnings of the first alone . . . Reasonable security of employment for the breadwinner is the basis of all private duties and all sound social action."[53] Nor had Beveridge changed his mind on this matter by the Second World War; his report, *Social Insurance and Allied Services*, appeared in 1942 and laid a major part of the foundation for the great reforms of the 1940s. In a passage now (in)famous among feminists, Beveridge wrote that "the great majority of married women must be regarded as occupied on work which is vital though unpaid, without which their husbands could not do their paid work and without which the nation could not continue."[54] In the National Insurance Act of 1946 wives were separated from their husbands for insurance purposes. (The significance of this procedure, along with Beveridge's statement, clearly was lost on T. H. Marshall when he was writing his essay on citizenship and the welfare state.)[55] Under the act, married women paid lesser contributions for reduced benefits, but they could also opt out of the scheme, and so from sickness, unemployment and maternity benefits, and they also lost entitlement to an old-age pension in their own right, being eligible only as their husband's dependent. By the time the legislation was amended in 1975, about three-quarters of married women workers had opted out.[56]

A different standard for men and women has also been applied in the operation of the insurance scheme. In 1911 some married women were insured in their own right. The scheme provided benefits in case of "incapacity to work", but given that wives had already been identified as "incapacitated" for the "work" in question, for paid employment, problems over the criteria for entitlement to sickness benefits were almost inevitable. In 1913 an inquiry was held to discover why married women were claiming benefits at a much greater rate than expected. One obvious reason was that the health of many working-class women was extremely poor. The extent of their ill health was revealed in 1915 when letters written by working women in 1913–14 to the Women's Cooperative Guild were published.[57] The national insurance scheme meant that for the first time women could afford to take time off work when ill – but from which "work"? Could they take time off from housework? What were the implications for the embryonic welfare state if they ceased to provide free welfare? From 1913 a dual standard of eligibility for benefits was established. For men the criterion was fitness for work. But the committee of inquiry decided that, if a woman could do her housework, she was not ill. So the criterion for eligibility for women was also fitness for work – but unpaid work in the private home, not paid work in the public market that was the basis for the contributory scheme under which the women were insured! This criterion for women was still being laid down in instructions issued by the Department of Health and Social Security in the 1970s.[58] The dual standard was further reinforced in 1975 when a non-contributory invalidity pension was introduced for those incapable of work but not qualified for the contributory scheme. Men and single women were entitled to the pension if they could not engage in paid employment; the criterion for married women was ability to perform "normal household duties".[59]

WOLLSTONECRAFT'S DILEMMA

So far, I have looked at the patriarchal structure of the welfare state, but this is only part of the picture; the development of the welfare state has also brought challenges to patriarchal power and helped provide a basis for women's autonomous citizenship. Women have seen the welfare state as one of their major means of support. Well before women won formal citizenship, they campaigned for the state to make provision for welfare, especially for the welfare of women and their children; and women's organizations and women activists have continued their political activities around welfare issues, not least in opposition to their status as "dependents". In 1953 the British feminist Vera Brittain wrote of the welfare state established through the legislation of the 1940s that "in it women have become ends in themselves and not merely means to the ends of men", and their "unique value as women was recognised".[60] In hindsight, Brittain was clearly overoptimistic in her assessment, but perhaps the opportunity now exists to begin to dismantle the patriarchal structure of the welfare state. In the 1980s the large changes in women's social position, technological and structural transformations within capitalism, and mass unemployment mean that much of the basis for the breadwinner/dependent dichotomy and for the employment society itself is being eroded (although both are still widely seen as social ideals). [. . .] As the current concern about the "feminization of poverty" reveals, there is now a very visible underclass of women who are directly connected to the state as claimants, rather than indirectly as men's dependents. [. . .] Social change has now made it much harder to gloss over the paradoxes and contradictions of women's status as citizens.

However, the question of how women might become full citizens of a democratic welfare state is more complex than may appear at first sight, because it is only in the current wave of the organized feminist movement that the division between the private and public spheres of social life has become seen as a major *political* problem. From the 1860s to the 1960s women were active in the public sphere: women fought not only for welfare measures and for measures to secure the private and public safety of women and girls, but for the vote and civil equality; middle-class women fought for entry into higher education, and the professions and women trade unionists fought for decent working conditions and wages and maternity leave. But the contemporary liberal-feminist view, particularly prominent in the United States, that what is required above all is "gender-neutral" laws and policies, was not widely shared.[61] In general, until the 1960s the focus of attention in the welfare state was on measures to ensure that women had proper social support, and hence proper social respect, in carrying out their responsibilities in the private sphere. The problem is whether and how such measures could assist women in their fight for full citizenship. In 1942 in Britain, for example, many women welcomed the passage in the Beveridge Report that I have cited because, it was argued, it gave official recognition to the value of women's unpaid work. However, an official nod of recognition to women's work as "vital" to "the nation" is easily given; *in practice*, the value of the work in bringing women into full membership in the welfare state was negligible. The equal worth of citizenship and the respect of fellow citizens still depended on participation as paid employees. "Citizenship" and "work" stood then and still stand opposed to "women".

The extremely difficult problem faced by women in their attempt to win full citizenship I shall call "Wollstonecraft's dilemma". The dilemma is that the two routes toward citizenship that women have pursued are mutually incompatible within the confines of the patriarchal welfare state, and within that context, they are impossible to achieve. For three centuries, since universal citizenship first appeared as a political ideal, women have continued to challenge their alleged natural subordination within private life. From at least the 1790s they have also struggled with the task of trying to become citizens within an ideal and practice that have gained universal meaning through their exclusion. Women's response has been complex. On the one hand, they have demanded that the ideal of citizenship be extended to them,[62] and the liberal-feminist agenda for a "gender-neutral" social world is the logical conclusion of one form of this demand. On the other hand, women have also insisted, often simultaneously, as did Mary Wollstonecraft, that *as women* they have specific capacities, talents, needs and concerns, so that the expression of their citizenship will be differentiated from that of men. Their unpaid work providing welfare could be seen, as Wollstonecraft saw women's tasks as mothers, as women's work *as citizens*, just as their husbands' paid work is central to men's citizenship.[63]

The patriarchal understanding of citizenship means that the two demands are incompatible because it allows two alternatives only: either women become (like) men, and so full citizens; or they continue at women's work, which is of no value for citizenship. Moreover, within a patriarchal welfare state neither demand can be met. To demand that citizenship, as it now exists, should be fully extended to women accepts the patriarchal meaning of "citizen", which is constructed from men's attributes, capacities and activities. Women cannot be full citizens in the present meaning of the term; at best, citizenship can be extended to women only as lesser men. At the same time, within the patriarchal welfare state, to demand proper social recognition and support for women's responsibilities is to condemn women to less than full citizenship and to continued incorporation into public life as "women", that is, as members of another sphere who cannot, therefore, earn the respect of fellow (male) citizens.

The example of child endowments on family allowances in Australia and Britain is instructive as a practical illustration of Wollstonecraft's dilemma. It reveals the great difficulties in trying to implement a policy that both aids women in their work and challenges patriarchal power while enhancing women's citizenship. In both countries there was opposition from the right and from laissez-faire economists on the ground that family allowances would undermine the father's obligation to support his children and undermine his "incentive" to sell his labour-power in the market. The feminist advocates of family allowances in the 1920s, most notably Eleanor Rathbone in Britain, saw the alleviation of poverty in families where the breadwinner's wage was inadequate to meet the family's basic needs as only one argument for this form of state provision. They were also greatly concerned with the questions of the wife's economic dependence and equal pay for men and women workers. If the upkeep of children (or a substantial contribution toward it) was met by the state outside of wage bargaining in the market, then there was no reason why men and women doing the same work should not receive the same pay. Rathbone wrote in 1924 that "nothing can justify the subordination of one group of producers – the mothers – to the rest and their deprivation of a share of their own in the wealth of a community."[64] She argued that family allowances would, "once and for all, cut away the maintenance of children and the reproduction of the race from the question of wages".[65]

But not all the advocates of child endowment were feminists – so that the policy could very easily be divorced from the public issue of wages and dependence and be seen only as a return for and recognition of women's private contributions. Supporters included the eugenicists and pronatalists, and family allowances appealed to capital and the state as a means of keeping wages down. Family allowances had many opponents in the British union movement, fearful that the consequence, were the measure introduced, would be to undermine the power of unions in wage bargaining. The opponents included women trade unionists who were suspicious of a policy that could be used to try to persuade women to leave paid employment. Some unionists also argued that social services, such as housing, education and health, should be developed first, and the TUC adopted this view in 1930. But were the men concerned, too, with their private, patriarchal privileges? Rathbone claimed that "the leaders of working men are themselves subsconsciously biased by prejudice of sex . . . Are they not influenced by a secret reluctance to see their wives and children recognised as separate personalities?"[66]

By 1941 the supporters of family allowances in the union movement had won the day, and family allowances were introduced in 1946, as part of the government's wartime plans for post-war reconstruction. The legislation proposed that the allowance would be paid to the father as "normal household head", but after lobbying by women's organizations, this was overturned in a free vote, and the allowance was paid directly to mothers. In Australia the union movement accepted child endowment in the 1920s (child endowment was introduced in New South Wales in 1927, and at the federal level in 1941). But union support there was based on wider redistributive policies, and the endowment was seen as a supplement to, not a way of breaking down, the family wage.[67] In the 1970s, in both countries, women's organizations again had to defend family allowances and the principle of redistribution from "the wallet to the purse".

The hope of Eleanor Rathbone and other feminists that family allowances would form part of a democratic restructuring of the wage system was not realized. Nevertheless, family allowances are paid to women as a benefit in their own right; in that sense they are an important (albeit financially very small) mark of recognition of married women as independent members of the welfare state. Yet the allowance is paid to women *as mothers*, and the key question is thus whether the payment to a mother – a private person – negates her standing as an independent citizen of the welfare state. More generally, the question is whether there can be a welfare policy that gives substantial assistance to women in their daily lives *and* helps create the conditions for a genuine democracy in which women are autonomous citizens, in which we can act *as women* and not as "woman" (protected/dependent/subordinate) constructed as the opposite to all that is meant by "man". That is to say, a resolution of Wollstonecraft's dilemma is necessary and, perhaps, possible.

The structure of the welfare state presupposes that women are men's dependents, but the benefits help to make it possible for women to be economically independent of men. In the countries with which I am concerned, women reliant on state benefits live poorly, but it is no longer so essential as it once was to marry or to cohabit with a man. A considerable moral panic has developed in recent years around "welfare mothers", a panic that obscures significant features of their position,

not least the extent to which the social basis for the ideal of breadwin-
ner/dependent has crumbled. Large numbers of young working-class
women have little or no hope of finding employment (or of finding a
young man who is employed). But there is a source of social identity
available to them that is out of the reach of their male counterparts.
The socially secure and acknowledged identity for women is still that
of a mother, and for many young women, motherhood, supported by
state benefits, provides "an alternative to aimless adolescence on the
dole" and "gives the appearance of self-determination". The price of
independence and "a rebellious motherhood that is not an uncritical
retreat into femininity"[68] is high, however; the welfare state provides a
minimal income and perhaps housing (often substandard), but child-
care services and other support are lacking, so that the young women
are often isolated, with no way out of their social exile. Moreover, even
if welfare state policies in Britain, Australia and the United States were
reformed so that generous benefits, adequate housing, health care, child-
care and other services were available to mothers, reliance on the state
could reinforce women's lesser citizenship in a new way.

Some feminists have enthusiastically endorsed the welfare state
as "the main recourse of women" and as the generator of "political
resources which, it seems fair to say, are mainly women's resources".[69]
They can point, in Australia for example, to "the creation over the
decade [1975–85] of a range of women's policy machinery and government subsidized women's services (delivered by women for women)
which is unrivalled elsewhere".[70] However, the enthusiasm is met with
the rejoinder from other feminists that for women to look to the welfare
state is merely to exchange dependence on individual men for dependence on the state. The power and capriciousness of husbands is being
replaced by the arbitrariness, bureaucracy and power of the state, the
very state that has upheld patriarchal power. The objection is cogent:
to make women directly dependent on the state will not in itself do anything to challenge patriarchal power relations. The direct dependence
of male workers on the welfare state and their indirect dependence when
their standard of living is derived from the vast system of state regulation of and subsidy to capitalism – and in Australia a national arbitration court – have done little to undermine class power. However, the
objection also misses an important point. There is one crucial difference
between the construction of women as men's dependents and dependence on the welfare state. In the former case, each woman lives with
the man on whose benevolence she depends; each woman is (in J. S.
Mill's extraordinarily apt phrase) in a "chronic state of bribery and
intimidation combined".[71] In the welfare state, each woman receives
what is hers by right, and she can, potentially, combine with other
citizens to enforce her rightful claim. The state has enormous powers of

intimidation, but political action takes place collectively in the public terrain and not behind the closed door of the home, where each woman has to rely on her own strength and resources.

Another new factor is that women are now involved in the welfare state on a large scale as employees, so that new possibilities for political action by women also exist. Women have been criticizing the welfare state in recent years not just as academics, as activists, or as beneficiaries and users of welfare services, but as the people on whom the daily operation of the welfare state to a large extent depends. The criticisms range from its patriarchal structure (and, on occasions, especially in health care, misogynist practices), to its bureaucratic and undemocratic policy-making processes and administration, to social work practices and education policy. Small beginnings have been made on changing the welfare state from within; for example, women have succeeded in establishing Well Women Clinics within the NHS in Britain and special units to deal with rape victims in public hospitals in Australia. Furthermore, the potential is now there for united action by women employees, women claimants and women citizens already politically active in the welfare state – not just to protect services against government cuts and efforts at "privatization" (which has absorbed much energy recently), but to transform the welfare state. Still, it is hard to see how women alone could succeed in the attempt. One necessary condition for the creation of a genuine democracy in which the welfare of *all* citizens is served is an alliance between a labour movement that acknowledges the problem of patriarchal power and an autonomous women's movement that recognizes the problem of class power. Whether such an alliance can be forged is an open question.

Despite the debates and the rethinking brought about by mass unemployment and attack on the union movement and welfare state by the Reagan and Thatcher governments, there are many barriers to be overcome. In Britain and Australia, with stronger welfare states, the women's movement has had a much closer relationship with working-class movements than in the United States, where the individualism of the predominant liberal feminism is an inhibiting factor, and where only about 17 per cent of the work force is now unionized. The major locus of criticism of authoritarian, hierarchical, undemocratic forms of organization for the last twenty years has been the women's movement. The practical example of democratic, decentralized organization provided by the women's movement has been largely ignored by the labour movement, as well as in academic discussions of democracy. After Marx defeated Bakunin in the First International, the prevailing form of organization in the labour movement, the nationalized industries in Britain and in the left sects has mimicked the hierarchy of the state – both the welfare and the warfare state. To be sure, there is a movement for industrial democracy and workers' control, but it has, by and large, accepted that the "worker" is a masculine figure and failed to question the separation of (public) industry and economic production from private life. The women's movement has rescued and put into practice the long-submerged idea that movements for, and experiments in, social change must "prefigure" the future form of social organization.[72]

If prefigurative forms of organization, such as the "alternative" women's welfare services set up by the women's movement, are not to remain isolated examples, or if attempts to set them up on a wider scale are not to be defeated, as in the past, very many accepted conceptions and practices have to be questioned. Recent debates over left alternatives to Thatcherite economics policies in Britain, and over the Accord between the state, capital and labour in Australia, suggest that the arguments and demands of the women's movement are still often unrecognized by labour's political spokesmen. For instance, one response to unemployment from male workers is to argue for a shorter working week and more leisure, or more time but the same money. However, in women's lives, time and money are not interchangeable in the same way.[73] Women, unlike men, do not have leisure after "work", but do unpaid work. Many women are arguing, rather, for a shorter working day. The point of the argument is to challenge the separation of part- and full-time paid employment and paid and unpaid "work". But the conception of citizenship needs thorough questioning, too, if Wollstonecraft's dilemma is to be resolved; neither the labour movement nor the women's movement (nor democratic theorists) has paid much attention to this. The patriarchal opposition between the private and public, women and citizen, dependent and breadwinner is less firmly based than it once was, and feminists have named it as a political problem. The ideal of full employment so central to the welfare state is also crumbling, so that some of the main props of the patriarchal understanding of citizenship are being undermined. The ideal of full employment appeared to have been achieved in the 1960s only because half the citizen body (and black men?) was denied legitimate membership in the employment society. Now that millions of men are excluded from the ideal (and the exclusion seems permanent), one possibility is that the ideal of universal citizenship will be abandoned, too, and full citizenship become the prerogative of capitalist, employed and armed men. Or can a genuine democracy be created?

The perception of democracy as a class problem and the influence of liberal feminism have combined to keep alive Engels's old solution to "the woman question" – to "bring the whole female sex back into public industry".[74] But the economy has a patriarchal structure. The Marxist hope that capitalism would create a labour force where ascriptive characteristics were irrelevant, and the liberal-feminist hope that antidiscrimination legislation will create a "gender-neutral" workforce, look utopian even without the collapse of the ideal of full employment. Engels's solution is out of reach – and so, too, is the generalization of masculine citizenship to women. In turn, the argument that the equal worth of citizenship, and the self-respect and mutual respect of citizens, depend upon sale of labour-power in the market and the provisions of the patriarchal welfare state is also undercut. The way is opening up for the formulation of conceptions of respect and equal worth adequate for democratic citizenship. Women could not "earn" respect or gain the self-respect that men obtain as workers; but what kind of respect do men "achieve" by selling their labour-power and becoming wage-slaves? Here the movement for workplace democracy and the feminist movement could join hands, but only if the conventional understanding of "work" is rethought. If women as well as men are to be full citizens, the separation of the welfare state and employment from the free welfare work contributed by women has to be broken down and new meanings and practices of "independence", "work" and "welfare" created.

For example, consider the implications were a broad, popular political movement to press for welfare policy to include a guaranteed social income to all adults, which would provide adequately for subsistence and also participation in social life.[75] For such a demand to be made, the old dichotomies must already have started to break down – the opposition between paid and unpaid work (for the first time all individuals could have a genuine choice whether to engage in paid work), between full- and part-time work, between public and private work, between independence and dependence, between work and welfare – which is to say, between men and women. If implemented, such a policy would at last recognize women as equal members of the welfare state, although it would not in itself ensure women's full citizenship. If a genuine democracy is to be created, the problem of the content and value of women's contribution as citizens and the meaning of citizenship has to be confronted.

[. . .]

The welfare state has been fought for and supported by the labour movement and the women's movement because only public or collective provision can maintain a proper standard of living and the means for meaningful social participation for all citizens in a democracy. The implication of this claim is that democratic citizens are both autonomous and interdependent; they are autonomous in that each enjoys the means to be an active citizen, but they are interdependent in that the welfare of each is the collective responsibility of all citizens. Critics of the class structure of the welfare state have often counterposed the fraternal interdependence (solidarity) signified by the welfare state to the bleak independence of isolated individuals in the market, but they have rarely noticed that both have been predicated upon the dependence (subordination) of women. In the patriarchal welfare state, independence has been constructed as a masculine prerogative. Men's "independence" as workers and citizens is their freedom from responsibility for welfare (except in so far as they "contribute" to the welfare state). Women have been seen as responsible for (private) welfare work, for relationships of dependence and interdependence. The paradox that welfare relies so largely on women, on dependents and social exiles whose "contribution" is not politically relevant to their citizenship in the welfare state, is heightened now that women's paid employment is also vital to the operation of the welfare state itself.

If women's knowledge of and expertise in welfare are to become part of their contribution as citizens, as women have demanded during the twentieth century, the opposition between men's independence and women's dependence has to be broken down, and a new understanding and practice of citizenship developed. The patriarchal dichotomy between women and independence–work–citizenship is under political challenge, and the social basis for the ideal of the full (male) employment society is crumbling. An opportunity has become visible to create a genuine democracy, to move from the welfare state to a welfare society without involuntary social exiles, in which women as well as men enjoy full social membership. Whether the opportunity can be realized is not easy to tell now that the warfare state is overshadowing the welfare state.

NOTES

1   R. Williams, *Keywords: a Vocabulary of Culture and Society*, rev. edn (New York, Oxford University Press, 1985), p. 333.
2   I have presented a theoretical elaboration of a modern conception of "patriarchy" as the systematic exercise by men of power over women in *The Sexual Contract* (Cambridge, Polity Press, 1988; Stanford CA, Stanford University Press, 1988). [. . .]
3   Women were formally enfranchised as citizens in 1902 in Australia, 1920 in the USA and 1928 in Britain (womanhood franchise in 1918 was limited to women over 30 years old).
4   On Scandinavia see, e.g., *Patriarchy in a Welfare Society*, ed. H. Holter (Oslo, Universitetsforlaget, 1984), esp. H. Hernes, "Women and the welfare state: the transition from private to public dependence"; and *Unfinished Democracy: Women in Nordic Politics* ed. E. Haavio-Mannila et al. (Oxford and New York, Pergamon Press, 1985).
5   Z. Eisenstein, *Feminism and Sexual Equality* (New York, Monthly Review Press, 1984), p. 125.
6   B. Nelson, "Women's poverty and women's citizenship: some political consequences of economic marginality," *Signs*, 10 (2) (1984), p. 221.

7   S. Erie, M. Rein and B. Wiget, "Women and the Reagan revolution: ther-
     midor for the social welfare economy," in *Families, Politics and Public
     Policy: a Feminist Dialogue on Women and the State*, ed. I. Diamond (New
     York, Longman, 1983), p. 96.
8   Ibid., p. 100.
9   S. Kamerman, "Women, children and poverty: public policies and female-
     Headed families in industrialized countries," *Signs*, 10 (2) (1984), p. 250.
10   J. Smith, "The paradox of women's poverty: wage-earning women and
     economic transformation," *Signs*, 10 (2) (1984), p. 291.
11   B. Ehrenreich and F. Fox Piven, "The feminization of poverty," *Dissent*
     (Spring 1984), p. 162.
12   L. Bryson, "Women as welfare recipients: women, poverty and the state,"
     in *Women, Social Welfare and the State*, ed. C. Baldock and B. Cass
     (Sydney, Allen and Unwin, 1983), p. 135.
13   B. Cass, "Rewards for women's work," in *Women, Social Science and
     Public Policy*, ed. J. Goodnow and C. Pateman (Sydney, Allen and Unwin,
     1985), p. 92. Cass also notes that women and their children were over-
     represented among the poor making claims on colonial and post-colonial
     charities in Australia (p. 70). Similarly, in Britain, from 1834 during the
     whole period of the New Poor Law, the majority of recipients of relief were
     women, and they were especially prominent among the very poor; see D.
     Groves, "Members and survivors: women and retirement pensions legis-
     lation," in *Women's Welfare Women's Rights*, ed. J. Lewis (London and
     Canberra, Croom Helm, 1983), p. 40.
14   L. Doval, "Women and the National Health Service: the carers and the
     careless," in *Women, Health and Healing*, ed. E. Lewin and V. Olesen
     (London, Tavistock, 1985), pp. 237, 253.
15   H. Land, "Beggars can't be choosers," *New Statesman* (17 May 1985),
     p. 8.
16   Ehrenreich and Fox Piven, "The feminization of poverty," p. 165; also Erie
     et al., "Women and the Reagan revolution," pp. 100–3.
17   The graphic phrase is Judith Stiehm's, in "Myths necessary to the pursuit
     of war" (unpublished paper), p. 11.
18   See especially F. Cobbe, "Wife torture in England," *The Contemporary
     Review*, 32 (1878), pp. 55–87. Also, for example, Mill's remarks when
     introducing the amendment to enfranchise women in the House of
     Commons in 1867, reprinted in *Women, the Family and Freedom: the
     Debate in Documents*, ed. S. Bell and K. Offen, vol. 1 (Stanford, CA, Stan-
     ford University Press, 1983), p. 487.
19   D. Deacon, "Political arithmetic: the nineteenth-century Australian census
     and the construction of the dependent woman," *Signs*, 11 (1) (1985), p.
     31 (my discussion draws on Deacon); also H. Land, "The family wage,"
     Feminist Review, 6 (1980), p. 60.
20   T. Skocpol, "The limits of the new deal system and the roots of contem-
     porary welfare dilemmas," in *The Politics of Social Policy in the United
     States*, ed. M. Weir, A. Orloff and T. Skocpol (Princeton, NJ, Princeton
     University Press, 1988).
21   Nelson, "Women's poverty and women's citizenship," pp. 222–3.

22 M. Owen, "Women – a wastefully exploited resource," *Search*, 15 (1984), pp. 271–2.

23 Thompson was a utilitarian, but also a feminist, cooperative socialist, so that he took his individualism more seriously than most utilitarians. In *Appeal of One Half the Human Race, Women, against the Pretensions of the Other Half, Men, to Retain Them in Political, and then in Civil and Domestic Slavery* (New York, Source Book Press, 1970 [first published 1825]), Thompson, writing of the importance of looking at the distribution of interests, or "the means of happiness," argues that the "division of interests" must proceed "until it is brought home to every *individual* of every family." Instead, under the despotism of husbands and fathers, "the interest of each of them is promoted, in as far only as it is coincident with, or subservient to, the master's interest" (pp. 46–7, 49).

24 As Beatrix Campbell has reminded us, "we protect men from the shame of their participation in women's poverty by keeping the secret. Family budgets are seen to be a *private* settlement of accounts between men and women, men's unequal distribution of working-class incomes within their households is a right they fought for within the working-class movement and it is not yet susceptible to *public* political pressure within the movement" (*Wigan Pier Revisited: Poverty and Politics in the 80s*, London, Virago Press, 1984, p. 57). Wives are usually responsible for making sure that the children are fed, the rent paid and so on, but this does not mean that they always decide how much money is allocated to take care of these basic needs. Moreover, in times of economic hardship women are often short of food as well as money; wives will make sure that the "breadwinner" and the children are fed before they are.

25 L. J. Weitzman, *The Divorce Revolution* (New York, The Free Press, 1985), ch. 10, esp. pp. 337–40.

26 Deacon, "Political arithmetic," p. 39.

27 Cited in A. Phillips, *Hidden Hands: Women and Economic Policies* (London, Pluto Press, 1983), p. 76.

28 See M. Barrett and M. McIntosh, "The family wage: some problems for socialists and feminists," *Capital and Class*, 11 (1980), pp. 56–9.

29 Ibid., p. 58.

30 Smith, "The paradox of women's poverty," p. 300.

31 Phillips, *Hidden Hands*, p. 21.

32 The perception is common to both women and men. (I would argue that women's perception of themselves is not, as is often suggested, a consequence of "socialization," but a realistic appraisal of their structural position at home and in the workplace.) For empirical evidence on this view of women workers, see, e.g., A. Pollert, *Girls, Wives, Factory Lives* (London, Macmillan, 1981); J. Wacjman, *Women in Control: Dilemmas of a Workers' Cooperative* (New York, St Martin's Press, 1983).

33 C. Baldock, "Public policies and the paid work of women," in Baldock and Cass, *Women, Social Welfare and the State*, pp. 34, 40.

34 Land, "The family wage," p. 62.

35   B. Cass, "Redistribution to children and to mothers: a history of child endowment and family allowances," in Baldock and Cass, *Women, Social Welfare and the State*, p. 62.
36   Campbell, *Wigan Pier Revisited*, pp. 130–1.
37   A. Hacker, "Welfare: the future of an illusion," *New York Review of Books*, 28 February 1985, p. 41.
38   Ehrenreich and Fox Piven, "The feminization of poverty," p. 163.
39   S. Hewlett, *A Lesser life: the Myth of Women's Liberation in America* (New York, William Morrow, 1986), p. 76.
40   Women's Bureau, Department of Employment and Industrial Relations, *Women At Work* (April 1986).
41   I. Bruegel, "Women's employment, legislation and the labour market," in Lewis, *Women's Welfare*, p. 133 and table 7.4.
42   "Skill" is another patriarchal category; it is men's work that counts as "skilled." See the discussion in C. Cockburn, *Brothers: Male Dominance and Technological Change* (London, Pluto Press, 1983), pp. 112–22.
43   Doyle, "Women and the National Health Service," pp. 250–4; and A. Oakley, "Women and health policy," in Lewis, *Women's Welfare*, p. 120 and table 6.3.
44   *Women at Work*, April 1986.
45   Phillips, *Hidden Hands*, p. 15.
46   Bruegel, "Women's employment," p. 135.
47   Hewlett, *A Lesser Life*, p. 72.
48   Smith, "The paradox of women's poverty," pp. 304, 307; quotation, p. 306.
49   J. Dale and P. Foster, *Feminists and the Welfare State* (London, Routledge and Kegan Paul, 1986), p. 112.
50   H. Land, "Who cares for the family?," *Journal of Social Policy*, 7 (3) (1978), pp. 268–9. Land notes that even under the old Poor Law twice as many women as men received outdoor relief, and there were many more old men than women in the workhouse wards for the ill or infirm; the women were deemed fit for the wards for the able-bodied.
51   Campbell, *Wigan Pier Revisted*, p. 76.
52   Nelson, "Woman's poverty and women's citizenship," pp. 229–30.
53   Both quotations are taken from Land, "The family wage," p. 72.
54   Cited in Dale and Foster, *Feminists and the Welfare State*, p. 17.
55   T. H. Marshall, "Citizenship and social class," reprinted in *States and Societies*, ed. D. Held et al. (New York University Press, New York, 1983).
56   H. Land, "Who still cares for the family?," in Lewis, *Women's Welfare*, p. 70.
57   M. Davis, *Maternity: Letters from Working Women* (New York, Norton, 1978) (first published 1915).
58   Information taken from Land, "Who cares for the family?," pp. 263–4.
59   Land, "Who still cares for the family?," p. 73.
60   Cited in Dale and Foster, *Feminists and the Welfare State*, p. 3.
61   There was considerable controversy within the women's movement between the wars over the question of protective legislation for women in industry. Did equal citizenship require the removal of such protection, so

that women worked under the same conditions as men; or did the legislation benefit women, and the real issue become proper health and safety
protection for both men and women workers?

62 I have discussed the earlier arguments in more detail in "Women and
    democratic citizenship," The Jefferson Memorial Lectures, University of
    California, Berkeley, 1985, lecture I.
63 For example, Wollstonecraft writes, "speaking of women at large, their
    first duty is to themselves as rational creatures, and the next, in point of
    importance, as citizens, is that, which includes so many, of a mother." She
    hopes that a time will come when a "man must necessarily fulfil the duties
    of a citizen, or be despised, and that while he was employed in any of the
    departments of civil life, his wife, also an active citizen, should be equally
    intent to manage her family, educate her children, and assist her neigh-
    bours:" A Vindication of the Rights of Woman (New York, Norton, 1975),
    pp. 145, 146.
64 Cited in Land, "The family wage", p. 63.
65 Cited in Cass, "Redistribution to children and to mothers," p. 57. My dis-
    cussion draws on Land and Cass. In the USA during the same period, fem-
    inists supported the movement for mothers' pensions. Unlike mothers
    eligible for family allowances, mothers eligible for pensions were without
    male breadwinners. The complexities of mothers' pensions are discussed
    by W. Sarvesy, "The contradictory legacy of the feminist welfare state
    founders," paper presented to the Annual Meeting of the American Politi-
    cal Science Association, Washington, DC, 1986.
66 Cited in Cass, "Redistribution to children and to mothers," p. 59.
67 Ibid., pp. 60–1.
68 Campbell, Wigan Pier Revisited, pp. 66, 78. 71.
69 F. Fox Piven, "Women and the state: ideology, power, and the welfare
    state," Socialist Review, 14 (2) (1984), pp. 14, 17.
70 M. Sawer, "The long march through the institutions: women's affairs under
    Fraser and Hawke," paper presented to the Annual Meeting of the Aus-
    tralasian Political Studies Association, Brisbane, 1986, p. 1.
71 J. S. Mill, "The subjection of women," in Essays on Sex Equality, ed. A.
    Rossi (Chicago, University of Chicago Press, 1970), p. 137.
72 See S. Rowbotham, L. Segal and H. Wainright, Beyond the Fragments:
    Feminism and the Making of Socialism (London, Merlin Press, 1979), a
    book that was instrumental in opening debate on the left and in the labour
    movement in Britain on this question.
73 See H. Hernes, Welfare State and Woman Power: Essays in State Feminism
    (Oslo, Norwegian University Press, 1987), ch. 5, for a discussion of the
    political implications of the different time-frames of men's and women's
    lives.
74 F. Engels, The Origin of the Family, Private Property and the State (New
    York, International Publishers, 1942), p. 66.
75 See also the discussion in J. Keane and J. Owens, After Full Employment
    (London, Hutchinson, 1986), pp. 175–7.

CHAPTER 13

Toward a Postnational Model of Membership [in Europe]

Yasemin Nuhoğlu Soysal

[. . .] In this chapter, reflecting upon guestworker membership, I analyze the changing structure and meaning of citizenship in the contemporary world. I introduce a new model of membership, the main thrust of which is that individual rights, historically defined on the basis of nationality, are increasingly codified into a different scheme that emphasizes universal personhood. I formalize the model by comparing it with the national model of citizenship and specifying its distinctive elements. The articulation of this model sets the stage for the further elaboration of dualities in the rules of the postwar global system, which, while insisting on the nation-state and its sovereignty, at the same time, legitimate a new form of membership that transcends the boundaries of the nation-state.

GUESTWORKERS AND CITIZENSHIP: OLD CONCEPTS, NEW FORMATIONS

The postwar era is characterized by a reconfiguration of citizenship from a more particularistic one based on nationhood to a more universalistic one based on personhood. Historically, citizenship and its rights and privileges have expanded in waves, with changes in how the national public is defined in relation to class, gender, and age (Marshall, 1964; Turner, 1986a,b; Ramirez, 1989). Each wave has represented the entry of a new segment of population into the national polity; workers, women, and children were eventually included in the definition of citizenship. This universalizing movement has made exclusions based on any criteria of ascribed status incompatible with the institution of citizenship (Turner, 1986a: 92–100). The expansion, however, was limited from within: the rights of men, women, and children, as individuals, were defined with respect to their membership in a particular nation-state. In that sense, the expansion of rights protracted and reinforced particularities ordained by national attributes. In contrast, in the postwar era, an intensified discourse of personhood and human rights has rent the bounded universality of national citizenship, generating contiguities beyond the limits of national citizenry. Accordingly, contemporary membership formations have superseded the dichotomy that opposes the national citizen and the alien, by including populations that were previously defined as outside the national polity. Rights that used to belong solely to nationals are now extended to foreign populations, thereby undermining the very basis of national citizenship. This transformation requires a new understanding of citizenship and its foundation.

[. . .] In acknowledging these deviations, [Brubacker (1989a,b)] offers a model of "dual membership" organized as concentric circles: an inner circle of citizenship, based on nationality, and an outer circle of denizenship, based on residency. [. . .]

Heisler and Heisler (1990) attribute the emergence of the denizenship status to the existence of a "mature" welfare state. They suggest that the elaborate redistribution machinery and the "ethos of equality" of the welfare state have led to the widening of the scope of citizenship in European societies [. . .] [S]tates of Europe have indeed expanded their comprehensive welfare apparatuses to guestworkers and their families. However, there is nothing inherent about the logic of the welfare state that would dictate the incorporation of foreigners into its system of privileges. Welfare states are also conceived as "compelled by their logic to be closed systems that seek to insulate themselves from external pressures and that restrict rights and benefits to members" (Freeman, 1986: 51; see also Leibfried, 1990). Not that this logic of closure is empirically realized in the world of welfare states. Many of the most advanced welfare states, especially those that are small in size and trade-dependent, have open economies that operate as part of an increasingly integrated global economy (Cameron, 1978; Katzenstein, 1985). Nevertheless, welfare states are expected to operate with the assumption of closure: the effective distribution of welfare among citizens and maintenance of high standards of benefits and services require the exclusion of noncitizens (see Walzer, 1983; Schuck and Smith, 1985). As such, the welfare state is universal only within national boundaries.

The denizenship model depicts changes in citizenship as an expansion of scope on a *territorial* basis: the principle of domicile augments the principle of nationality. Denizens acquire certain membership rights by virtue of living and working in host countries. Within this framework, denizenship becomes an irregularity for the nation-state and its citizenry, that should be corrected in the long-run (see Brubaker, 1989c; Heisler and Heisler, 1990; Layton-Henry, 1990).

In construing changes in citizenship as territorial, these studies remain within the confines of the nation-state model. They do not recognize the changing basis and legitimacy of membership or the recent, fundamental changes in the relationship between the individual, the nation-state, and the world order. As I see it, the incorporation of guestworkers is no mere expansion of the scope of national citizenship, nor is it an irregularity. Rather, it reveals a profound transformation in the institution of citizenship, both in its institutional logic and in the way it is legitimated. To locate the changes, we need to go beyond the nation-state.

A Model for Postnational Membership

This section introduces a model of membership that delineates the contemporary restructuring and reconfiguration of citizenship. The summary in table 13.1 compares this model, which I call *postnational*,

Table 13.1   *Comparison of national and postnational models of membership*

Dimension	Model I National citizenship	Model II Postnational membership
Time period	19th to mid-20th centuries	Postwar
Territorial	Nation-state bounded	Fluid boundaries
Congruence between membership and territory	Identical	Distinct
Rights/privileges	Single status	Multiple status
Basis of membership	Shared nationhood (national rights)	Universal personhood (human rights)
Source of legitimacy	Nation-state	Transnational community
Organization of membership	Nation-state	Nation-state

with the classical model of national citizenship as conceptualized in political sociology. The two models differ in various dimensions [. . .]. A comparative discussion, in terms of each dimension, follows.

Time period

The modern history of citizenship begins with the French Revolution. Although the idea of national citizenship emerged at the time of the Revolution, the realization of this particular form of membership occurred much later. Only quite recently has national citizenship become a powerful construct. The classical instruments for creating a national citizenry, the first compulsory education laws and universal (male) suffrage acts, were not enacted before the mid-nineteenth century (Ramirez and Soysal, 1989; Soysal and Strang, 1989). Moreover, construction of the dichotomy between national citizens and aliens, through the first immigration and alien acts, and made visible in the introduction of passports, identity cards, and visas, did not take place until as late as the First World War.

The reconfiguration of citizenship is mainly a postwar phenomenon. Even as the nation-state and its membership became authorized and taken-for-granted, its classificatory premises were beginning to be contested. By the 1960s, the classical model of nation-state membership was loosening its grip on the Western world, while consolidation of national polity and citizenship was an impassioned item on the agenda of many countries in Africa and Asia. The increasing flow of goods and persons and the large magnitude of labor migrations after World War II have facilitated this process.

Territorial dimension

The classical model is nation-state bounded. Citizenship entails a territorial relationship between the individual and the state (Bendix, 1977; Weber, 1978). It postulates well-defined, exclusionary boundaries and state jurisdiction over the national population within those boundaries. The model thus implies a congruence between membership and territory: only French nationals are entitled to the rights and privileges the French state affords – nobody else.

In the postnational model, the boundaries of membership are fluid; a Turkish guestworker can become a member of the French polity without French citizenship. By holding citizenship in one state while living and enjoying rights and privileges in a different state, guestworkers violate the presumed congruence between membership and territory. The growing number of dual nationality acquisitions further formalizes the fluidity of membership.

The fluid boundaries of membership do not necessarily mean that the boundaries of the nation-state are fluid. Neither does it imply that the nation-state is less predominant than before. Indeed, the nation-states, still acting upon the national model – since their existence is predicated on this model – constantly try to keep out foreigners by issuing new aliens laws and adopting restrictive immigration policies. However, these continued attempts testify that European states have not succeeded in controlling the influx of foreigners. In particular, such measures have failed to prevent migratory flows justified on humanitarian grounds – political asylum and family unification, two major sources of persisting immigration to European countries [. . .].

Rights and privileges

The classic order of nation-states expresses formal equality in the sense of uniform citizenship rights. Citizenship assumes a single status; all citizens are entitled to the same rights and privileges. The postnational model, on the other hand, implies multiplicity of membership – a principal organizational form for empires and city states. [. . .] [T]he distribution of rights among various groups and citizens is not even. In the emerging European system, certain groups of migrants are more privileged than others: legal permanent residents, political refugees, dual citizens, and nationals of common market countries.

In earlier polities, multiplicity of membership was also a given, but inequality was considered a "natural" characteristic of social order. Differential membership status, such as that of slaves, was thus constructed as part of the formal definition of the polity. Modern polities, however, claim a uniform and universal status for individuals. As Turner (1986a: 133) comments, in the modern polity "the particularistic criteria which define the person become increasingly irrelevant in the public sphere." What makes the case of the guestworker controversial is that it violates this claim for unitary status. Rendering differential status unjustifiable within the framework of universalistic personhood, the modern polity encourages a climate for diverse claims to and further expansion of rights.

Basis and legitimation of membership

In the classical model, shared nationality is the main source of equal treatment among members. Citizenship invests individuals with equal rights and obligations on the grounds of shared nationhood. In that sense, the basis of legitimacy for individual rights is located within the nation-state.

However, guestworker experience shows that membership and the rights it entails are not necessarily based on the criterion of nationality. In the postnational model, universal personhood replaces nationhood; and universal human rights replace national rights. The justification for the state's obligations to foreign populations goes beyond the nation-state itself. The rights and claims of individuals are legitimated by ideologies grounded in a transnational community, through international codes, conventions, and laws on human rights, independent of their citizenship in a nation-state. Hence, the individual transcends the citizen. This is the most elemental way that the postnational model differs from the national model.

Universal personhood as the basis of membership comes across most clearly in the case of political refugees, whose status in host polities rests exclusively on an appeal to human rights. Refugees are in essence stateless (some carry a United Nations passport) but are nonetheless still protected and granted rights as individuals. Similarly, the most universalized aspects of citizenship are those immediately related to the person – civil and social rights – which are often the subject of international conventions and discourse. These rights are more commonly secured in international codes and laws, and they permeate national boundaries more easily than universal political rights that still imply a referential proximity to national citizenship.

Organization of membership

While the basis and legitimation of membership rights have shifted to a transnational level, membership itself is not really organized in a new scheme. In both models, the responsibility of providing and implementing individual rights lies with national states. In other words, one still has to go through, for instance, the German, British, or French welfare system. The state is the immediate guarantor and provider, though now for "every person" living within its borders, noncitizen as well as citizen. Actually, the very transnational normative system that legitimizes universal personhood as the basis of membership also designates the nation-state as the primary unit for dispensing rights and privileges (Meyer, 1980).

This is critical to explaining why residency in a state is consequential in securing various rights. The world is still largely organized on the basis of spatially configured political units; and topographic matrixes still inform the models and praxis of national and international actors. Hence the nation-state remains the central structure regulating access to social distribution. The material realization of individual rights and privileges is primarily organized by the nation-state, although the legitimacy for these rights now lies in a transnational order.

TRANSNATIONAL SOURCES OF MEMBERSHIP

How can we account for the manifest changes in national citizenship, that celebrated and stubborn construction of the modern era? As it stands, postnational membership derives its force and legitimacy from changes in the transnational order that defines the rules and organization of the nation-state system. I regard two interrelated lines of development as crucial in explaining the reconfiguration of citizenship.

The first one concerns a transformation in the organization of the international state system: an increasing interdependence and connectedness, intensified world-level interaction and organizing, and the emergence of transnational political structures, which altogether confound and complicate nation-state sovereignty and jurisdiction (Meyer, 1980; Abu-Lughod, 1989a,b; Robertson, 1992; Boli, 1993). I refer not only to growth in the volume of transactions and interactions, which, in relative terms, has not changed significantly over the last century (Thomson and Krasner, 1989). More important are qualitative changes in the intensity of these interactions, and their perception by the parties involved.

In the postwar era, many aspects of the public domain that used to be the exclusive preserve of the nation-state have become legitimate concerns of international discourse and action. The case of guestworkers clearly demonstrates this shift. The host states no longer have sole control over migrant populations. The governments of the sending countries and extra-national organizations of various kinds also hold claims *vis-à-vis* these populations, in regard to their lives, education, welfare, family relations, and political activities. A dense set of interactions facilitated by inter- and transnational market and security arrangements (NATO, the EC, and the UN system) constrain the host states from dispensing with their migrant populations at will. In fact, this system not only delegitimizes host state actions that attempt to dispense with foreigners; it obliges the state to protect them.

[. . .]

The second major development is the emergence of universalistic rules and conceptions regarding the rights of the individual, which are formalized and legitimated by a multitude of international codes and laws. International conventions and charters ascribe universal rights to persons regardless of their membership status in a nation-state. They oblige nation-states *not* to make distinctions on the grounds of nationality in granting civil, social, and political rights. The Universal Declaration of Human Rights (1948) unequivocally asserts that "all beings are born free and equal in dignity and rights, independent of their race, color, national or ethnic origin." The International Covenant on Civil and Political Rights (1966) further imposes a responsibility on the state to respect and ensure the rights of "all individuals within its territory and subject to its jurisdiction" (Goodwin-Gill et al., 1985: 558). The European Convention on Human Rights (1950) expounds almost identical provisions, with further protection against the collective expulsion of aliens. Both the Universal Declaration of Human Rights and the European Convention have been incorporated into the constitutions and laws of many countries.

In addition to these principal codes of human rights, many aspects of international migration, including the status of migrant workers and their particular rights, have been elaborated and regularized through a complex of international treaties, conventions, charters, and recommendations. Some of these instruments originated in the early 1950s, at the onset of large-scale labor migration. Over time, their span has expanded to include entry and residence, the rights to choice and security of employment, working conditions, vocational training and guidance, trade-union and collective bargaining rights, social security, family reunification, education of migrant children, and associative and participatory rights, as well as individual and collective freedoms. These conventions differ in scope. Some have universal application; others are country-specific. Nonetheless, they all aim to set standards for the "equitable" treatment of migrants and the elimination of disparities between nationals and migrants of different categories.

[...]

Lastly, political refugees are protected by a set of international legal instruments designed to ensure their rights. According to the Geneva Convention on the Legal Status of Refugees (1951), persons shall not be forced to return to their country of origin if they have a "well-founded fear of persecution" for reasons of race, religion, nationality, membership of a particular social group or political opinion. The Convention further guarantees treatment in the country of asylum equal with that of nationals in regard to religious freedom, acquisition of property, rights of association, and access to courts and public education (Plender, 1985).

The multitude and scope of these instruments are impressive. The rights defined and codified assure not just the economic, civil, and social rights of individual migrants – membership rights, in Marshall's terms – but also the cultural rights of migrant groups as collectivities. Within this context, the collective rights of foreigners – the right to an ethnic identity, culture, and use of one's native tongue – emerge as a locus of international legal action. [...]

The most comprehensive legal enactment of a transnational status for migrants is encoded in European Communities law. Citizenship in one EC member state confers rights in all of the others, thereby breaking the link between the status attached to citizenship and national territory. The provisions specify a migrant regime under which European Community citizens are entitled to equal status and treatment with the nationals of the host country. The basic tenets of this regime are as follows:

- Citizens of member states have the right to free movement, gainful employment, and residence within the boundaries of the Community.
- Community law prohibits discrimination based on nationality among workers of the member states with regard to employment, social security, trade union rights, living and working conditions, and education and vocational training.
- Community law obliges host states to facilitate teaching of the language and culture of the countries of origin within the framework of normal education and in collaboration with those countries.
- The Commission of the European Community recommends full political rights in the long run for Community citizens living in other member states. Under current arrangements, they have the right to vote and stand as candidates in local and European elections.

These rights are protected by a growing body of directives, regulations, and laws that locates them within a human rights context (Commission of the European Communities, 1989). Moreover, the 1991 Maastricht treaty has created the status of citizen of the Community, to "strengthen the protection of the rights and interests of the nationals of its member states." The treaty foresees a multilevel citizenship structure that guarantees rights independently of membership in a particular state. Thus, the Community as a supranational organization establishes a direct relationship with individuals in the member nation-states. As such, "European citizenship" clearly embodies postnational membership in its most elaborate legal form. It is a citizenship whose legal and normative bases are located in the wider community, and whose actual implementation is assigned to the member states.

At the present, the new Community citizenship and the free-movement provision do not apply to nationals of non-EC countries, who constitute the majority of the migrant populations in Europe. For non-EC migrants, the Community has issued guidelines toward the equalization of their status with that of nationals of EC countries. In 1989, for example, the Community adopted the Charter of the Fundamental Rights of Workers, which requires the member states to guarantee workers and their families from non-member countries living and working conditions comparable to those of EC nationals. More directly, with its authority to engage in international treaties, the Community has made agreements with several non-EC sending countries. These bilateral agreements incorporate the rights of non-EC foreign workers into the legal framework of the Community with provisions in regard to social security, working conditions, and wages, under which workers and their families from signing countries can claim benefits on equal terms with community citizens (Callovi, 1992).

My intention in citing all of these instruments and regimes is to draw attention to the proliferation of transnational arrangements, grounded in human rights discourse, that address the rights and interests of migrants and refugees. These instruments and regimes provide guidelines as to the management of migrant affairs for national legislation, by standardizing and rationalizing the category and status of the international migrant. Like other transnational instruments, the charters and conventions regarding guestworkers do not for the most part entail formal obligations or enforceable rules. This does not mean that they do not effect binding dispositions. By setting norms, framing discourses, and engineering legal categories and legitimate models, they enjoin obligations on nation-states to take action. They define goals and levels of competence, and compel nation-states to achieve specific standards. They form a basis for the claims of migrants shaping the platforms of migrant organizations as well as other public interests. They generate transnational activity and stir up publicity regarding migrant issues.

[. . .]

Migrants themselves repeatedly urge the universalistic concept of personhood as the grounding principle for membership rights. Claims for membership become publicly coded as human rights, as is clearly discernible from the platforms and action programs of foreigners. In its sixth congress in Stockholm, the European Trade Union Confederation called for a more "humanitarian European unity," referring to the rights of migrant workers, especially those from the non-EC countries (*Ikibin'e Doğru*, 29 January 1989). Debates about local voting rights invariably center on the universal/humanistic versus national/particularistic controversy. The most notable argument put forth is that "the right to take part in the political process of one's country of residence is an essential aspect of human life" (Rath, 1990: 140). In their manifesto for local voting rights, the foreigners' organizations in Switzerland explicitly referred to humans' "natural right" of self-determination. The motto of the 1990 voting rights campaign of migrants in Austria was "Voting Rights Are Human Rights" (*Milliyet*, 10 October 1990). All these claims portray suffrage not only as a participatory right, but as an essential aspect of human personhood.

Human rights discourse dominates calls for cultural rights, as well. Multiculturalism, the right to be different and to foster one's own culture, is elementally asserted as the natural and inalienable right of all individuals. What is ironic is that the preservation of particularistic group characteristics – such as language, a customary marker of national identity – is justified by appealing to universalistic ideas of personhood. The Turkish Parents Association in Berlin demands mother-tongue instruction in schools on the grounds that "as a human being, one has certain natural rights. To learn and enrich one's own language and culture are the most crucial ones" (from the 1990 pamphlet of the association). In the same vein, the Initiative of Turkish Parents and Teachers in Stuttgart publicized its cause with the slogan "Mother Tongue is Human Right" (*Milliyet*, 4 October 1990).

Urging Islamic instruction in public schools, migrant associations also assert the natural right of individuals to their own cultures. During the 1987 national elections, Islamic associations in Britain justified their demands for the observance of Islamic rules in public schools and the recognition of Muslim family law by invoking the Declaration of Human Rights and the Declaration on the Elimination of All Forms of Intolerance based on Religion or Belief (Center for the Study of Islam and Christian-Muslim Relations, 1987). In May 1990, when the local authorities refused to permit the opening of another Islamic primary school, the Islamic Foundation in London decided to take the issue to the European Court of Human Rights. As part of the debate over the *foulard* affair in France, the head of the Great Mosque of Paris declared the rules preventing the wearing of scarves in school to be discriminatory. He emphasized personal rights, rather than religious duties: "If a girl asks to have her hair covered, I believe it is her most basic right" (*Washington Post*, 23 October 1989). Accordingly, the closing statement of the fourth European Muslims Conference made an appeal for the rights of Muslims as "human beings" and "equal members" of European societies (*Kirpi*, July 1990, p. 15).

In all of these examples, the prevalence of transnational discourse is evident. Membership rights are recast as human rights; governments, organizations, and individuals recurrently appeal to this "higher-order" principle. The changes I have delineated indicate, not only the empirical extension of rights, but the existence of legitimate grounds upon which new and more extensive demands can be made. The dominance of human rights discourse, and the definition of individuals and their rights as abstract universal categories, license even foreign populations to push for further elaboration of their rights. The fact that rights, and claims to rights, are no longer confined to national parameters, supports the premise of a postnational model of membership.

[. . .]

THE DIALECTICS OF POSTNATIONAL MEMBERSHIP AND THE NATION-STATE

Unfolding episodes of world politics in the 1990s may seem to contradict my assertions about postnational membership and the declining significance of national citizenship. Consider the reinventions and reassertions of national(ist) narratives throughout the world: fierce struggles for ethnic or national closure, in former Yugoslavia, Somalia, India, and Ireland; the violent vocalization of anti-foreigner groups throughout Europe, accompanied by demands for restrictive refugee and immigration policies.

How can we account for these seemingly contradictory propensities? In order to untangle such trends from the perspective of this [chapter], let me return to the dialectical dualities of the global system with which I began.

The apparent paradoxes reflected in postwar international migration emanate from the institutionalized duality between the two principles of the global system: national sovereignty and universal human rights. The same global-level processes and institutional frameworks that foster postnational membership also reify the nation-state and its sovereignty.

[. . .]

Incongruously, inasmuch as the ascription and codification of rights move beyond national frames of reference, postnational rights remain organized at the national level. The nation-state is still the repository of educational, welfare, and public health functions and the regulator of social distribution. Simply put, the exercise of universalistic rights is tied to specific states and their institutions. Even though its mode and scope of action are increasingly defined and constrained by the wider global system, the sovereign nation-state retains the formally and organizationally legitimate form venerated by the ideologies and conventions of transnational reference groups such as the UN, UNESCO, and the like.

Expressions of this duality between universalistic rights and the territorially confined nation-state abound. Faced with a growing flux of asylum seekers in 1990s, Western states have defensively reconsidered their immigration policies. Regulation of immigration is often articulated as indispensable to national sovereignty, and several host countries have initiated restrictions. On the other hand, the category of refugee has broadened to encompass new definitions of persecution. For example, Canada's Immigration and Refugee Board has begun to grant asylum to women persecuted because of their gender; cases involving rape, domestic violence, and states' restrictions on women's activities qualify for asylum (*New York Times*, 27 September 1993). France recognized "genital mutilation" as a form of persecution in granting asylum to a west African woman (*New York Times Magazine*, 19 September 1993). In the United States, an immigration judge in San Francisco granted asylum to a gay Brazilian man, as a member of a "persecuted social group" in his home country (*New York Times*, 12 August 1993). So, even as Western states attempt to maintain their boundaries through quantitative restrictions, the introduction of expanding categories and definitions of rights of personhood sets the stage for new patterns of asylum, making national boundaries more penetrable.

[. . .]

The European Community, as an emerging political entity, is not immune to the dualities of the global system either. The doctrine of human rights is frequently invoked in European Community texts and provisions. For instance, the Maastricht treaty and other EC conventions declare that immigration policies will comply with "international commitments" to human rights and the "humanitarian traditions" of EC states. Concurrently, the Community is engaged in boundary-maintaining activities through arrangements such as "European citizenship" and the Schengen agreement. While the latter aims at drawing the borders of a supranational entity through common visa and immigration procedures, the former reconstitutes an exclusionary membership scheme at a supranational level. However, constrained by its own discourse, conventions, and laws, the Community establishes, and compels its member states to provide, an expanding range of rights and privileges to migrants from both EC and non-EC countries.

These seemingly paradoxical affinities articulate an underlying dialectic of the postwar global system: while nation-states and their boundaries are reified through assertions of border controls and appeals to nationhood, a new mode of membership, anchored in the universalistic rights of personhood, transgresses the national order of things.

The duality embedded in the principles of the global system is further reflected in the incongruence between the two elements of modern citizenship: identity and rights. In the postwar era, these two elements of citizenship are decoupled. Rights increasingly assume universality, legal uniformity, and abstractness, and are defined at the global level. Identities, in contrast, still express particularity, and are conceived of as being territorially bounded. As an identity, national citizenship – as it is promoted, reinvented, and reified by states and other societal actors – still prevails. But in terms of its translation into rights and privileges, it is no longer a significant construction. Thus, the universalistic status of personhood and postnational membership coexist with assertive national identities and intense ethnic struggles.

Indeed, the explosion of nationalism can be construed as an exponent of the underlying dialectic of the postwar global system. More and more collectivities are asserting their "national identities" and alleging statehood on the basis of their acclaimed "nationness." These claims are fed and legitimated by the highly institutionalized principle of political sovereignty and self-determination, which promises each people an autonomous state of its own. As political practice, national sovereignty may be contested (as in the case of Kuwait and Iraq during the

Gulf war), but as a mode of organization, it is yet to have an alternative. Sovereignty provides a protected status in the international realm, authenticated by membership in the United Nations. Thus, even when previous nation-states are dissolving (e.g., the Soviet Union and Yugoslavia), the emerging units aspire to become territorial states with self-determination, and the world political community grants them this right. The new (or would-be) states immediately appropriate the language of nationhood, produce anthems and flags, and, of course, pledge allegiance to human rights.

The principle of self-determination further reinforces expressions of nationalism, since, for sovereign statehood, a nationally bounded and unified population is imperative. Therefore, collectivities that have been previously defined simply as ethnicities, religious minorities, or language groups reinvent their "nationness," accentuate the uniqueness of their cultures and histories, and cultivate particularisms to construct their "others" (see Hobsbawm, 1990).

At another level, the collective right to self-determination, and to political and cultural existence, is itself increasingly codified as a universal human right. Claims to particularistic identities, cultural distinctiveness, and self-determination are legitimated by reference to the essential, indisputable rights of persons, and, thus, are recast as world-level, postnational rights. This recodification is, in fact, what Roland Robertson (1992: 100) calls "the universalization of particularism and the particularization of universalism." What are considered particularistic characteristics of collectivities – culture, language, and standard ethnic traits – become variants of the universal core of humanness. In turn, as universal attributes and human rights, they are exercised in individual and collective actors' narratives and strategies.

[. . .]

All of these recontextualizations of "nationness" within the universalistic discourse of human rights blur the meanings and boundaries attached to the nation and the nation-state. The idea of the nation persists as an intense metaphor, at times an idiom of war. However, in a world within which rights, and identities as rights, derive their legitimacy from discourses of universalistic personhood, the limits of nationness, or of national citizenship, for that matter, become inventively irrelevant.

REFERENCES

Abu-Lughod, Janet L. (1989a) *Before European Hegemony: the World System, AD 1250–1350*. London: Oxford University Press.
Abu-Lughod, Janet L. (1989b) "Restructuring the premodern world system," paper presented at the Annual Meeting of the American Sociological Association, San Francisco.

Bendix, Reinhard (1977) *Nation-building and Citizenship: Studies of our Changing Social Order.* Berkeley and Los Angeles: University of California Press.

Boli, John (1993) "Sovereignty from a world polity perspective," paper presented at the Annual Meeting of the American Sociological Association, Miami.

Brubaker, William Rogers (1989a) "Introduction," in W. R. Brubacker (ed.), *Immigration and Politics of Citizenship in Europe and North America.* Lanham, MD: University Press of America.

Brubaker, William Rogers (1989b) "Membership without citizenship: the economic and social rights of noncitizens," in W. R. Brubaker (ed.), *Immigration and Politics of Citizenship in Europe and North America.* Lanham, MD: University Press of America.

Brubaker, William Rogers (ed.) (1989c) *Immigration and Politics of Citizenship in Europe and North America.* Lanham, MD: University Press of America.

Callovi, Giuseppe (1992) "Regulation of immigration in 1993: pieces of the European Community jig-saw puzzle," *International Migration Review,* 26: 353–72.

Cameron, David R. (1978) "The expansion of the public economy: a comparative analysis," *American Political Science Review,* 72: 1243–61.

Centre for the Study of Islam and Christian–Muslim Relations (1987) "Muslim demands of the British political parties," *News of Muslims in Europe,* 40: 6–7. Birmingham.

Commission of the European Communities (1989) "The European Community and human rights," *European File,* no. 5/89. Luxembourg: Office for Official Publications of the European Communities.

Freeman, Gary P. (1986) "Migration and the political economy of the welfare state," *Annals of the American Academy of Political and Social Science,* 485: 51–63.

Goodwin-Gill, Guy S., Jenny, R. K. and Perruchoud, Richard (1985) "Basic humanitarian principles applicable to non-nationals," *International Migration Review,* 19: 556–69.

Heisler, Martin O. and Heisler, Barbara Schmitter (1990) "Citizenship – old, new, and changing: inclusion, exclusion, and limbo for ethnic groups and migrants in the modern democratic state," in J. Fijalkowski, H. Merkens and F. Schmidt (eds), *Dominant National Cultures and Ethnic Identities.* Berlin: Free University.

Hobsbawm, Eric (1990) *Nations and Nationalism since 1780: Programme, Myth, Reality.* Cambridge: Cambridge University Press.

Katzenstein, Peter J. (1985) *Small States in World Markets: Industrial Policy in Europe.* Ithaca, NY: Cornell University Press.

Layton-Henry, Zig (1990) "Citizenship or denizenship for migrant workers?," in Z. Layton-Henry (ed.), *The Political Rights of Migrant Workers in Western Europe.* London: Sage.

Leibfried, Stephan (1990) "Sozialstaat Europa? Integrationsperspektiven europäischer Armutsregimes," *Nachrichtendienst des Deutschen Vereins für öffentliche und private Fürsorge (NDV),* 70: 296–305.

Marshall, T. H. (1964) *Class, Citizenship and Social Development.* Garden City, NY: Doubleday.

Meyer, John W. (1980) "The world polity and the authority of the nation-state," in A. Bergesen (ed.), *Studies of the Modern World System.* New York: Academic Press.

Plender, Richard (1985) "Migrant workers in Western Europe," *Contemporary Affairs Briefing,* 2 (14).

Ramirez, Francisco O. (1989) "Reconstituting, children: extension of personhood and citizenship," in D. Kertzer and K. W. Schaie (eds), *Age Structuring in Comparative Perspective.* Hillsdale, NJ: Lawrence Erlbaum.

Ramirez, Francisco O. and Soysal, Yasemin Nuhoğlu (1989) "Women's acquisition of the franchise: an event history analysis," paper presented at the Annual Meeting of the American Sociological Association, San Francisco.

Rath, Jan (1990) "Voting rights," in Z. Layton-Henry (ed.), *The Political Rights of Migrant Workers in Western Europe.* London: Sage.

Robertson, Roland (1992) *Globalization: Social Theory and Global Culture.* London: Sage.

Schuck, Peter H. and Smith Rogers, M. (1985) *Citizenship without Consent: Illegal Aliens in the American Polity.* New Haven, Conn.: Yale University Press.

Soysal, Yasemin Nuhoğlu and Strang, David (1989) "Construction of the first mass education systems in nineteenth-century Europe," *Sociology of Education,* 62: 277–88.

Thomson, Janice E. and Krasner, Stephen D. (1989) "Global transactions and the consolidation of sovereignty," in E. O. Czempiel and J. N. Rosenau (eds), *Global Changes and Theoretical Challenges: Approaches to World Politics for the 1990s.* Lexington, Mass.: Lexington Books.

Turner, Bryan S. (1986a) *Citizenship and Capitalism: the Debate over Reformism.* London: Allen and Unwin.

Turner, Bryan S. (1986b) "Personhood and citizenship," *Theory, Culture, and Society,* 3: 1–16.

Walzer, Michael (1983) *Spheres of Justice: a Defense of Pluralism and Equality.* New York: Basic Books.

Weber, Max (1978) *Economy and Society: an Outline of Interpretive Sociology,* vol. 1, ed. G. Roth and C. Wittich. Berkeley and Los Angeles: University of California Press.

PART V DEMOCRACY

Introduction

Part V reproduces a number of pieces which have been influential in democratic theory. The first is Jürgen Habermas's summary of *The Structural Transformation of the Public Sphere* (chapter 14). Chantal Mouffe's chapter comes from a post-Marxist perspective, influenced by post-structuralism (chapter 15). David Held's chapter on globalization and its consequences for democracy (chapter 16) represents an important challenge to models of democracy which see it as consent to rule since, as he argues, the conditions under which such models were elaborated are now much more problematic. Finally, William Connolly, in chapter 17, reflects on the encounter with "otherness" which is increasingly an issue in global politics.

Habermas's work on the development and degeneration of the public sphere has been enormously influential in political sociology and political theory. For Habermas, the public sphere is the domain of social life in which public opinion is formed. The ideal of the public sphere is that, by means of rational discussion, unconstrained by inequalities of power or money between the participants, citizens should be able to exercise influence on the state which has legitimate authority over them. This influence is, for the most part, informal; it only becomes formal periodically, during general elections. Habermas argues that this form of the public sphere – or, at least, a close approximation to it – was realized in bourgeois society. It was made possible by the separation of the state and the private sphere of economic and domestic life. The private individuals of the bourgeois public sphere, protected by basic civil rights, used meetings and newspapers to debate the rules which should govern economic life. In this way, Habermas claims, they changed the basis of state authority. Whereas, in feudalism, political power was based on tradition and force and represented to the people as public authority, in liberal society it was based on rational authority. The "general interest" was established by agreement between private persons in the public sphere and state power was legitimate only in so far as it protected this sphere and respected the opinion formed there.

In contemporary society, however, the public sphere no longer functions as the domain of rational debate. The liberal public sphere, although it presumed the participation of all, was actually limited to men with property. In the nineteenth century it expanded beyond these limits to include working-class men. At the same time, economic, social, and political forms became more complex and intertwined. With the growth of the welfare state, in particular, these changes mean that the public sphere is no longer the site of discussion between private individuals. It has now become that of conflicts of interests between groups and organizations. Furthermore, these interests are closely bound to those of the state; they are represented by political parties and institutionalized in public administration. Politics is no longer separated from society; large-scale social organizations are engaged in making important decisions behind closed doors. Habermas describes this as the "refeudalization of the state." As a result, "public opinion" no longer has the meaning it once had. It is now a matter for systematic manipulation rather than the outcome of rational debate. In this chapter, first published in 1973, Habermas suggests that democratization requires the opening up of organizations and institutions themselves to rational criticism. The public sphere must be instituted *internally* to social organizations, and re-instituted in relation to dealings with the state, if its ideal is to be realized in mass welfare-state societies.

From quite a different perspective, Mouffe (chapter 15) also considers the possibilities of the democratization of contemporary society. Like Habermas, she does not see democracy as confined to representation at the level of the state. On the contrary, democracy, according to Mouffe's understanding, is closer to the socialist ideal of equality for all, which, in this tradition, is seen as the only way of providing the conditions for genuine individual self-determination. In other respects, however, Mouffe is concerned to break with Marxism. She argues that it is mistaken to suppose that all conflicts should be understood in terms of economic class conflict. Individuals are made up of many identities, and this multiplicity is constructed in different contexts; it cannot be reduced to socio-economic class. At the same time, she is also opposed to the humanism on which much socialist thought has depended. It is not the case that human beings are naturally disposed to fight oppression and subordination. Democratic struggles are only possible where identities have been constructed in antagonisms. This requires a discourse of rights, which initially emerged in the French Revolution and was extended with the democratic movements of the nineteenth century.

Antagonism is possible where rights previously granted are ignored or removed, or where an identity is constructed as equal in some respects but not others. Mouffe mentions the example of Mary Wollstonecraft, who was "interpellated" by – that is, she identified with – the radicalism of the French Revolution and who was therefore able actively to resist the subordination which made equality for women impossible. (It is worth comparing Mouffe's use of this example with Pateman's discussion of "Wollstonecraft's dilemma" in chapter 12.)

For Mouffe, both identities and democratic rights are constructed in discourse. The main point here is that they are not structurally determined – by the economy – but are constructed in the situated understandings of social actors. At the level of society as a whole, when discourses support and reinforce each other in such a way that they become taken for granted, there is a hegemonic formation. According to Mouffe, a new hegemonic formation was constructed in the post-war period, which facilitated the emergence of social movements in the 1960s and which means that there is now the possibility for greater democracy. The commodification of social life in consumer society, the bureaucratization which results from state intervention, and the cultural uniformity produced by the mass media – all these are usually lamented on the left, and certainly by Habermas. As Mouffe sees it, however, they have provided the conditions for their own resistance on the part of social movements which see democratic rights curtailed, or, alternatively, opened up, by these changes. However, a hegemonic formation is never finally finished since discourses are always open to interpretation in different ways. Every democratic antagonism may be articulated in progressive or non-progressive ways, as Mouffe sees it. An example of the latter which she deals with is the neo-conservatism also discussed by Roche in chapter 11. According to Mouffe, it is necessary for progressive movements to join together in a counter-hegemonic project to defeat neo-conservatism and institute more democratic forms of social and political life.

As David Held points out in chapter 16, democratic theory has traditionally assumed a "national community of fate," a political community represented at the level of a sovereign state and consenting to be ruled by it. This model of the democratic society is, however, problematized by globalization. It is no longer the case – and, indeed, to some extent it never was the case – that the constituency affected by political decisions is the national community. Held gives the example of a government deciding to build a nuclear plant near another country's border. Furthermore, it is clear that processes of globalization mean that many decisions which would previously been taken by national governments are no longer effective. Where there are rapid and extensive global flows of capital, goods, and people, for example, the economy can no longer be managed at the national level with the same degree of confidence. Hence the growth of international and regional political institutions and organizations, like the European Union, the International Monetary Fund, the North Atlantic Treaty Organization, and so on. However, where the state's *autonomy* – its ability to act independently in the pursuit of domestic and international policies – is compromised by globalization, its *sovereignty* – its undisputed political authority within a given territory – is compromised by the growth of international law, agreements, organizations, and institutions set up to manage globalization. This does not mean, Held stresses, that the nation-state is now irrelevant. What it does mean, however, is that it no longer enjoys illimitable, indivisible sovereignty: sovereignty is now divided between international organizations, international law, and regional and global institutions.

These changes have important implications for democracy. While governance is no longer territorially bounded, democracy still tends to be seen as relevant only at the level of the nation-state. In the last few pages of his chapter, Held outlines a normative theory of global democracy, what he calls here a "federal model of democratic autonomy" and, more recently, "the cosmopolitan model of democracy," based on individual rights to self-determination. According to Held, it requires a "double democratization" of international political agencies and international civil society. He makes a number of suggestions for the democratization of political agencies: rules and principles to increase accountability; the enhancement of regional parliaments, like the European Parliament; referendums on issues which cut across national groups; the expansion of international courts to provide redress against undemocratic decisions and to uphold democratic rights. In relation to international civil society, Held suggests that democratization requires that the power of multinational corporations is curtailed, and experiments in other forms of economic and social life are encouraged. Although Held is not especially optimistic about the possibilities of global democratization, in so far as he sees it as rooted in changes already underway, he is concerned to analyze its real potential.

William Connolly's chapter is somewhat different from the others in part V in that it is not explicitly on democracy. However, it follows from Held's considerations in dealing with the confrontations between cultures that are a feature of global politics. In this respect, it is also linked to chapters 5 and 7, by Giddens and Hall respectively. Using Columbus's "discovery" of America as an example of an encounter with the "other," Connolly reflects on international relations and, by extension, global politics. He argues that "discovery" is not a suitable word to describe the encounter since this supposes a recognition of reality as it is in itself; nor is "invention," which suggests that the other was nothing before the encounter; nor is "dialogue" since this suggests too great a degree of mutuality; nor is "conquest" which suggests that the "discoverer" was left unaffected by the encounter. In this way he goes through the various epistemological possibilities of traditional, and more recent, sociological and political theory. He proposes instead the postmodern view that we should see the other as a text which needs to be interpreted and which changes our own identity – how we see ourselves – in the very act of interpretation.

Connolly draws a Foucauldian analogy between the encounter of self and other and that of international relations and postmodernism. He suggests that, as a normalizing discipline, international relations treats every encounter by containing it within the already known. In this way, it disciplines otherness. In particular, it attempts to discipline postmodernism, which is concerned to unsettle every identity, by containing it within the already known.

To develop his theme, Connolly uses Tvetzan Todorov's account of the encounter between Old and New Worlds in *The Conquest of America*. He sees it as exemplary of a postmodern approach to otherness. Todorov does not simply apply the supposedly universal terms of the Old – the discourse of man, rights, freedom, and truth – to understand the encounter. But nor does he try to see the world from the point of view of the New: to do so would be to assume that he has to access the truth of their authentic identity, of who they were before they were "discovered." This would not only be arrogant, it would also presume that the other, and oneself, had remained the same, unchanged by the encounter. What Todorov does instead is to show the self-doubt and creativity of some of the priests faced with the task of understanding the Aztecs they met. In Connolly's view, he shows the intertextuality of the encounter, the way in which it involved an interplay of identity and difference rather than a strict separation between self and other.

In this chapter, Connolly advocates a postmodern approach to the cultural confrontations of global politics. Those who take postmodernism seriously, he argues, do not see their identities as ultimately true. His counter-example here is Christians who believe that non-Christians are eternally damned, like some of those who arrived in America in the fifteenth century. He suggests that the desire for certainty is strong in the West because of this Christian tradition. Postmodernism, he argues, encourages greater tolerance, flexibility, and willingness to accommodate difference, all of which are necessary if we are to co-operate in a global democracy of the kind outlined by Held.

CHAPTER 14

The Public Sphere

Jürgen Habermas

CONCEPT

By "public sphere" we mean first of all a domain of our social life in which such a thing as public opinion can be formed. Access to the public sphere is open in principle to all citizens. A portion of the public sphere is constituted in every conversation in which private persons come together to form a public. They are then acting neither as business or professional people conducting their private affairs, nor as legal consociates subject to the legal regulations of a state bureaucracy and obligated to obedience. Citizens act as a public when they deal with matters of general interest without being subject to coercion; thus with the guarantee that they may assemble and unite freely, and express and publicize their opinions freely. When the public is large, this kind of communication requires certain means of dissemination and influence; today, newspapers and periodicals, radio and television are the media of the public sphere. We speak of a political public sphere (as distinguished from a literary one, for instance) when the public discussions concern objects connected with the practice of the state. The coercive power of the state is the counterpart, as it were, of the political public sphere, but it is not a part of it. State power is, to be sure, considered "public" power, but it owes the attribute of publicness to its task of caring for the public, that is, providing for the common good of all legal consociates. Only when the exercise of public authority has actually been subordinated to the requirement of democratic publicness does the

This chapter is taken from *Jürgen Habermas on Society and Politics*, edited by S. Seidman (Boston, Beacon Press, 1973), pp. 231–6. Reprinted by permission of Beacon Press, Boston.

political public sphere acquire an institutionalized influence on the government, by way of the legislative body. The term "public opinion" refers to the functions of criticism and control of organized state authority that the public exercises informally, as well as formally during periodic elections. Regulations concerning the publicness (or publicity [*Publizität*] in its original meaning) of state-related activities, as, for instance, the public accessibility required of legal proceedings, are also connected with this function of public opinion. To the public sphere as a sphere mediating between state and society, a sphere in which the public as the vehicle of public opinion is formed, there corresponds the principle of publicness – the publicness that once had to win out against the secret politics of monarchs and that since then has permitted democratic control of state activity.

It is no accident that these concepts of the public sphere and public opinion were not formed until the eighteenth century. They derive their specific meaning from a concrete historical situation. It was then that one learned to distinguish between opinion and public opinion, or *opinion publique*. Whereas mere opinions (things taken for granted as part of a culture, normative convictions, collective prejudices and judgments) seem to persist unchanged in their quasi-natural structure as a kind of sediment of history, public opinion, in terms of its very idea, can be formed only if a public that engages in rational discussion exists. Public discussions that are institutionally protected and that take, with critical intent, the exercise of political authority as their theme have not existed since time immemorial – they developed only in a specific phase of bourgeois society, and only by virtue of a specific constellation of interests could they be incorporated into the order of the bourgeois constitutional state.

HISTORY

It is not possible to demonstrate the existence of a public sphere in its own right, separate from the private sphere, in the European society of the High Middle Ages. At the same time, however, it is not a coincidence that the attributes of authority at that time were called "public." For a public representation of authority existed at that time. At all levels of the pyramid established by feudal law, the status of the feudal lord is neutral with respect to the categories "public" and "private;" but the person possessing that status represents it publicly; he displays himself, represents himself as the embodiment of a "higher" power, in whatever degree. This concept of representation has survived into recent constitutional history. Even today the power of political authority on its highest level, however much it has become detached from its former basis, requires representation through the head of state. But such elements derive from a pre-bourgeois social structure. Representation in the sense of the bourgeois public sphere, as in "representing" the nation or specific clients, has nothing to do with *representative publicness*, which inheres in the concrete existence of a lord. As long as the prince and the estates of his realm "are" the land, rather than merely "representing" it, they are capable of this kind of representation; they represent their authority "before" the people rather than for the people.

The feudal powers (the church, the prince, and the nobility) to which this representative publicness adheres disintegrated in the course of a long process of polarization; by the end of the eighteenth century they had decomposed into private elements on the one side and public on the other. The position of the church changed in connection with the Reformation; the tie to divine authority that the church represented, that is, religion, became a private matter. Historically, what is called the freedom of religion safe-guarded the first domain of private autonomy; the church itself continued its existence as one corporate body under public law among others. The corresponding polarization of princely power acquired visible form in the separation of the public budget from the private household property of the feudal lord. In the bureaucracy and the military (and in part also in the administration of justice), institutions of public power became autonomous *vis-à-vis* the privatized sphere of the princely court. In terms of the estates, finally, elements from the ruling groups developed into organs of public power, into parliament (and in part also into judicial organs); elements from the occupational status groups, in so far as they had become established in urban corporations and in certain differentiations within the estates of the land, developed into the sphere of bourgeois society, which would confront the state as a genuine domain of private autonomy.

Representative publicness gave way to the new sphere of "public power" that came into being with the national and territorial states. Ongoing state activity (permanent administration, a standing army) had its counterpart in the permanence of relationships that had developed in the meantime with the stock market and the press, through traffic in goods and news. Public power became consolidated as something tangible confronting those who were subject to it and who at first found themselves only negatively defined by it. These are the "private persons" who are excluded from public power because they hold no office. "Public" no longer refers to the representative court of a person vested with authority; instead, it now refers to the competence-regulated activity of an apparatus furnished with a monopoly on the legitimate use of force. As those to whom this public power is addressed, private persons subsumed under the state form the public.

As a private domain, society, which has come to confront the state, as it were, is on the one hand clearly differentiated from public power; on the other hand, society becomes a matter of public interest in so far as with the rise of a market economy the reproduction of life extends beyond the confines of private domestic power. The *bourgeois public sphere* can be understood as the sphere of private persons assembled to form a public. They soon began to make use of the public sphere of informational newspapers, which was officially regulated, against the public power itself, using those papers, along with the morally and critically oriented weeklies, to engage in debate about the general rules governing relations in their own essentially privatized but publicly relevant sphere of commodity exchange and labor.

THE LIBERAL MODEL OF THE PUBLIC SPHERE

The medium in which this debate takes place – public discussion – is unique and without historical prototype. Previously the estates had negotiated contracts with their princes in which claims to power were defined on a case-by-case basis. As we know, this development followed a different course in England, where princely power was relativized through parliament, than on the Continent, where the estates were mediatized by the monarch. The "third estate" then broke with this mode of equalizing power, for it could no longer establish itself as a ruling estate. Given a commercial economy, a division of authority accomplished through differentiation of the rights of those possessing feudal authority (liberties belonging to the estates) was no longer possible – the power under private law of disposition of capitalist property is nonpolitical. The bourgeois are private persons; as such, they do not "rule." Thus their claims to power in opposition to public power are directed not against a concentration of authority that should be "divided" but rather against the principle of established authority. The principle of control, namely publicness, that the bourgeois public opposes to the principle of established authority aims at a transformation of authority as such, not merely the exchange of one basis of legitimation for another.

In the first modern constitutions the sections listing basic rights provide an image of the liberal model of the public sphere: they guarantee society as a sphere of private autonomy; opposite it stands a public power limited to a few functions; between the two spheres, as it were, stands the domain of private persons who have come together to form a public and who, as citizens of the state, mediate the state with the needs of bourgeois society, in order, as the idea goes, to thus convert political authority to "rational" authority in the medium of this public sphere. Under the presuppositions of a society based on the free exchange of commodities, it seemed that the general interest, which served as the criterion by which this kind of rationality was to be evaluated, would be assured if the dealings of private persons in the marketplace were emancipated from social forces and their dealings in the public sphere were emancipated from political coercion.

The political daily press came to have an important role during this same period. In the second half of the eighteenth century, serious competition to the older form of news writing as the compiling of items of information arose in the form of literary journalism. Karl Bücher describes the main outlines of this development:

> From mere institutions for the publication of news, newspapers became the vehicles and guides of public opinion as well, weapons of party politics. The consequence of this for the internal organization of the newspaper enterprise was the insertion of a new function between the gathering of news and its publication: the editorial function. For the newspaper publisher, however, the significance of this development was that from a seller of new information he became a dealer in public opinion.

Publishers provided the commercial basis for the newspaper without, however, commercializing it as such. The press remained an institution of the public itself, operating to provide and intensify public discussion, no longer a mere organ for the conveyance of information, but not yet a medium of consumer culture.

This type of press can be observed especially in revolutionary periods, when papers associated with the tiniest political coalitions and groups spring up, as in Paris in 1789. In the Paris of 1848 every halfway prominent politician still formed his own club, and every other one founded his own *journal*: over 450 clubs and more than 200 papers came into being there between February and May alone. Until the permanent legalization of a public sphere that functioned politically, the appearance of a political newspaper was equivalent to engagement in the struggle for a zone of freedom for public opinion, for publicness as a principle. Not until the establishment of the bourgeois constitutional state was a press engaged in the public use of reason relieved of the pressure of ideological viewpoints. Since then it has been able to abandon its polemical stance and take advantage of the earning potential of commercial activity. The ground was cleared for this development from a press of viewpoints to a commercial press at about the same time in England, France, and the United States, during the 1830s. In the course of this transformation from the journalism of writers who were private persons to the consumer services of the mass media, the sphere of publicness was changed by an influx of private interests that achieved privileged representation within it.

THE PUBLIC SPHERE IN MASS WELFARE-STATE DEMOCRACIES

The liberal model of the public sphere remains instructive in regard to the normative claim embodied in institutionalized requirements of publicness; but it is not applicable to actual relationships within a mass democracy that is industrially advanced and constituted as a social-welfare state. In part, the liberal model had always contained ideological aspects; in part, the social presuppositions to which those aspects were linked have undergone fundamental changes. Even the forms in which the public sphere was manifested, forms which made its idea seem to a certain extent obvious, began to change with the Chartist movement in England and the February Revolution in France. With the spread of the press and propaganda, the public expanded beyond the confines of the bourgeoisie. Along with its social exclusivity the public lost the cohesion given it by institutions of convivial social intercourse and by a relatively high standard of education. Accordingly, conflicts which in the past were pushed off into the private sphere now enter the public sphere. Group needs, which cannot expect satisfaction from a self-regulating market, tend toward state regulation. The public sphere, which must now mediate these demands, becomes a field for competition among interests in the cruder form of forcible confrontation. Laws that have obviously originated under the "pressure of the streets" can scarcely continue to be understood in terms of a consensus achieved by private persons in public discussion; they correspond, in more or less undisguised form, to compromises between conflicting private interests. Today it is social organizations that act in relation to the state in the political public sphere, whether through the mediation of political parties or directly, in interplay with public administration. With the interlocking of the public and private domains, not only do political agencies take over certain functions in the sphere of commodity exchange and social labor; societal powers also take over political functions. This leads to a kind of "refeudalization" of the public sphere. Large-scale organizations strive for political compromises with the state and with one another, behind closed doors if possible; but at the same time they have to secure at least plebiscitarian approval from the mass of the population through the deployment of a staged form of publicity.

The political public sphere in the welfare state is characterized by a singular weakening of its critical functions. Whereas at one time publicness was intended to subject persons or things to the public use of reason and to make political decisions susceptible to revision before the tribunal of public opinion, today it has often enough already been enlisted in the aid of the secret policies of interest groups; in the form of "publicity" it now acquires public prestige for persons or things and renders them capable of acclamation in a climate of nonpublic opinion. The term "public relations" itself indicates how a public sphere that formerly emerged from the structure of society must now be produced circumstantially on a case-by-case basis. The central relationship of the public, political parties, and parliament is also affected by this change in function.

This existing trend toward the weakening of the public sphere, as a principle, is opposed, however, by a welfare-state transformation of the functioning of basic rights: the requirement of publicness is extended by state organs to all organizations acting in relation to the state. To the extent to which this becomes a reality, a no longer intact public of private persons acting as individuals would be replaced by a public of organized private persons. Under current circumstances, only the latter could participate effectively in a process of public communication using the channels of intra-party and intra-organizational public spheres, on the basis of a publicness enforced for the dealings of organizations with the state. It is in this process of public communication that the formation of political compromises would have to achieve legitimation. The idea of the public sphere itself, which signified a rationalization of authority in the medium of public discussions among private persons, and which has been preserved in mass welfare-state democracy, threatens to disintegrate with the structural transformation of the public sphere. Today it could be realized only on a different basis, as a rationalization of the exercise of social and political power under the mutual control of rival organizations committed to publicness in their internal structure as well as in their dealings with the state and with one another.

CHAPTER 15

Hegemony and New Political Subjects: Toward a New Concept of Democracy

Chantal Mouffe

Despite de Tocqueville's remarkable insight into the potential implications of the "democratic revolution," it is unlikely that he could have imagined its leading, today, to our questioning the totality of social relationships. He believed, in fact, as his reflections on women's equality testify, that the ineluctable drive toward equality must take into account certain real differences grounded in nature. It is precisely the permanent alterity based on such a conception of natural essences that is contested today by an important segment of the feminist movement. It is not merely that the democratic revolution has proven to be more radical than de Tocqueville foresaw; the revolution has taken forms that no one could have anticipated because it attacks forms of inequality that did not previously exist. Clearly, ecological, anti-nuclear, and antibureaucratic struggles, along with all the other commonly labeled "new social movements" – I would prefer to call them "new democratic struggles" – should be understood as resistances to new types of oppression emerging in advanced capitalist societies. This is the thesis my [chapter] will develop, and I shall try to answer the following questions: (1) What kind of antagonism do the new social movements express? (2) What is their link with the development of capitalism? (3) How should they be positioned in a socialist strategy? (4) What are the implications of these struggles for our conception of democracy?

This chapter is taken from *Marxism and the Interpretation of Culture*, edited by C. Nelson and L. Grossberg (Basingstoke, Macmillan, 1988), pp. 89–101. Reprinted by permission of Macmillan Press Ltd.

THEORETICAL POSITIONS

(1) Within every society, each social agent is inscribed in a multi-plicity of social relations – not only social relations of production but also the social relations, among others, of sex, race, nationality, and vicinity. All these social relations determine positionalities or subject positions, and every social agent is therefore the locus of many subject positions and cannot be reduced to only one. Thus, someone inscribed in the relations of production as a worker is also a man or a woman, white or black, Catholic or Protestant, French or German, and so on. A person's subjectivity is not constructed only on the basis of his or her position in the relations of production. Furthermore, each social pos-ition, each subject position, is itself the locus of multiple possible con-structions, according to the different discourses that can construct that position. Thus, the subjectivity of a given social agent is always pre-cariously and provisionally fixed or, to use the Lacanian term, sutured at the intersection of various discourses.

I am consequently opposed to the class reductionism of classical Marxism, in which all social subjects are necessarily class subjects (each social class having its own ideological paradigm, and every antagonism ultimately reducible to a class antagonism). I affirm, instead, the exis-tence in each individual of multiple subject positions corresponding both to the different social relations in which the individual is inserted and to the discourses that constitute these relations. There is no reason to privilege, a priori, a "class" position as the origin of the articulation of subjectivity. Furthermore, it is incorrect to attribute necessary paradig-matic forms to this class position. Consequently, a critique of the notion of "fundamental interests" is required, because this notion entails fixing necessary political and ideological forms within determined positions in the production process. But interests never exist prior to the discourses in which they are articulated and constituted; they cannot be the expres-sion of already existing positions on the economic level.

(2) I am opposed to the economic view of social evolution as gov-erned by a single economic logic, the view that conceives the unity of a social formation as the result of "necessary effects" produced in ideo-logical and political superstructures by the economic infrastructures. The distinction between infra- and superstructure needs to be ques-tioned because it implies a conception of economy as a world of objects and relations that exist prior to any ideological and political conditions of existence. This view assumes that the economy is able to function on its own and follow its own logic, a logic absolutely independent of the relations it would allegedly determine. Instead, I shall defend a concep-tion of society as a complex ensemble of heterogeneous social relations

possessing their own dynamism. Not all such relations are reducible to social relations of production or to their ideological and political conditions of reproduction. The unity of a social formation is the product of political articulations, which are, in turn, the result of the social practices that produce a hegemonic formation.

(3) By "hegemonic formation" I mean an ensemble of relatively stable social forms, the materialization of a social articulation in which different social relations react reciprocally either to provide each other with mutual conditions of existence, or at least to neutralize the potentially destructive effects of certain social relations on the reproduction of other such relations. A hegemonic formation is always centered around certain types of social relations. In capitalism, these are the relations of production, but this fact should not be explained as an effect of structure; it is, rather, that the centrality of production relations has been conferred by a hegemonic policy. However, hegemony is never established conclusively. A constant struggle must create the conditions necessary to validate capital and its accumulation. This implies a set of practices that are not merely economic but political and cultural as well. Thus, the development of capitalism is subject to an incessant political struggle, periodically modifying those social forms through which social relations of production are assured their centrality. In the history of capitalism we can see the rhythm of successive hegemonic formations.

(4) All social relations can become the locus of antagonism in so far as they are constructed as relations of subordination. Many different forms of subordination can become the origin of conflict and struggle. There exists, therefore, in society a multiplicity of potential antagonisms, and class antagonism is only one among many. It is not possible to reduce all those forms of subordination and struggle to the expression of a single logic located in the economy. Nor can this reduction be avoided by positing a complex mediation between social antagonisms and the economy. There are multiple forms of power in society that cannot be reduced to or deduced from one origin or source.

NEW ANTAGONISMS AND HEGEMONIC FORMATIONS

My thesis is that the new social movements express antagonisms that have emerged in response to the hegemonic formation that was fully installed in Western countries after World War II, a formation in crisis today. I say *fully* installed because the process did not begin at that time; these hegemonic forms were evolving, were being put into place since the beginning of this century. Thus, we also had social movements before the Second World War, but they really fully developed only after the war in response to a new social hegemonic formation.

The antagonisms that emerged after the war, however, have not derived from the imposition of forms of subordination that did not exist before. For instance, the struggles against racism and sexism resist forms of domination that existed not only before the new hegemonic formation but also before capitalism. We can see the emergence of those antagonisms in the context of the dissolution of all the social relations based on hierarchy, and that, of course, is linked to the development of capitalism, which destroys all those social relations and replaces them with commodity relations. So, it is with the development of capitalism that those forms of subordination can emerge as antagonisms. The relations may have existed previously, but they could not emerge as antagonisms before capitalism. Thus, we must be concerned with the structural transformations that have provided some of the objective conditions for the emergence of these new antagonisms. But you cannot automatically derive antagonism and struggle from the existence of these objective conditions – they are necessary but not sufficient – unless you assume people will necessarily struggle against subordination. Obviously I am against any such essentialist postulate. We need to ask under what conditions those relations of subordination could give birth to antagonisms, and what other conditions are needed for the emergence of struggles against these subordinations.

It is the hegemonic formation installed after the Second World War that, in fact, provides these conditions. We may characterize this formation as articulating: (a) a certain type of labor process based on the semiautomatic assembly line; (b) a certain type of state (the Keynesian interventionist state); and (c) new cultural forms that can be described as "mediating culture." The investiture of such a hegemonic formation involved a complex process, articulating a set of transformations, each of which derived from a different logic. It is impossible to derive any one of these from another in some automatic fashion, as in an economistic logic. In fact, the transformations of the labor process that led to Taylorization and finally to Fordism were governed by the need to destroy the autonomy that workers continued to exercise in the labor process and to end worker resistance to the valorization of capital. But the Fordist semiautomatic assembly line made possible a mass production for which, given the low salary level, there were insufficient outlets. Thus, the working class's mode of life had to change significantly in order to create the conditions necessary for accumulation to regain its ascendancy. However, the fact that certain conditions were necessary for the accumulation and reproduction of capitalist social relations to function in no way guaranteed that these conditions would come about. The solution was to use worker struggles, which were multiplying in response to the intensification of labor, to establish a connection between increased productivity and increased wages. But this required a state intervention with a double purpose: it was just as urgent to counter the capitalist's inclination to lower wages as it was to set up a political framework in which worker's demands could be made compatible with the reproduction of capitalism. This provides significant evidence that this new hegemonic formation resulted from a political intervention.

These changes in the labor process can also be defined as a transformation of an extensive regime of accumulation into an intensive regime of accumulation. The latter is characterized by the expansion of capitalist relations of production to the whole set of social activities, which are thereby subordinated to the logic of production for profit. A new mode of consumption has been created that expresses the domination of commodity relations over noncommodity relations. As a consequence, a profound transformation of the existing way of life has taken place. Western society has been transformed into a big marketplace where all the products of human labor have become commodities, where more and more needs must go through the market to be satisfied. Such a "commodification of social life" has destroyed a series of previous social relations and replaced them with commodity relations. This is what we know as the consumer society.

Today, it is not only through the sale of their labor power that individuals are submitted to the domination of capital but also through their participation in many other social relations. So many spheres of social life are now penetrated by capitalist relations that it is almost impossible to escape them. Culture, leisure, death, sex, everything is now a field of profit for capital. The destruction of the environment, the transformation of people into mere consumers – these are the results of that subordination of social life to the accumulation of capital. Those new forms of domination, of course, have been studied by many authors, but there has been a tendency, especially at the beginning of the sixties – you will remember Marcuse's *One Dimensional Man* – to believe that the power of capital was so overwhelming that no struggle, no resistance, could take place. Yet a few years later it became clear that those new forms of domination would not go unchallenged; they have given rise to many new antagonisms, which explains the widening of all forms of social conflict since the middle of the sixties. My thesis is that many of the new social movements are expressions of resistances against that commodification of social life and the new forms of subordination it has created.

But that is only one aspect of the problem; there is a second aspect that is extremely important. You remember that we have defined the new hegemonic formation not only in terms of Fordism but also in terms of the Keynesian welfare state. The new hegemonic formation has been characterized by growing state intervention in all aspects of social life, which is a key characteristic of the Keynesian state. The intervention of the state has led to a phenomenon of bureaucratization, which is also at the origin of new forms of subordination and resistance. It must be said that in many cases commodification and bureaucratization are articulated together, as when the state acts in favor of capital. Thus, while it might be difficult to distinguish between them, I think it is extremely important to do so and to analyze them as different systems of domination. There may be cases in which the state acts against the interests of capital to produce what Claus Offe has called "decommodification." At the same time, such interventions, because of their bureaucratic character, may produce new forms of subordination. This is the case, for example, when the state provides services in the fields of health, transportation, housing, and education.

A third aspect of the problem is that some new types of struggle must be seen as resistances to the growing uniformity of social life, a uniformity that is the result of the kind of mass culture imposed by the media. This imposition of a homogenized way of life, of a uniform cultural pattern, is being challenged by different groups that reaffirm their right to their difference, their specificity, be it through the exaltation of their regional identity or their specificity in the realm of fashion, music, or language.

The profound changes brought about by this construction of a new hegemonic formation gave rise to the resistances expressed in the new social movements. However, as I have said, one should not blame new forms of inequality for all the antagonisms that emerged in the sixties. Some, like the women's movement, concerned long-standing types of oppression that had not yet become antagonistic because they were located in a hierarchical society accepting certain inequalities as "natural."

Whether antagonism is produced by the commodification of all social needs, or by the intervention of state bureaucracy, or by cultural leveling and the destruction of traditional values (whether or not the latter are themselves oppressive) – what all these antagonisms have in common is that the problem is not caused by the individual's defined position in the production system; they are, therefore, not "class antagonisms." Obviously this does not mean that class antagonism has been eliminated. In fact, in so far as more and more areas of social life are converted into "services" provided by capitalism, the number of individuals subordinated to capitalist production relations increases. If you take the term "proletarian" in its strict sense, as a worker who sells his or her labor, it is quite legitimate to speak of a process of proletarianization. The fact that there are an increasing number of individuals who may suffer capitalist domination as a class does not signify a new form of subordination but rather the extension of an already existing one. What is new is the spread of social conflict to other areas and the politicization of all these social relations. When we recognize that we are dealing with resistances to forms of oppression developed by the postwar hegemonic formation, we begin to understand the importance of these struggles for a socialist program.

It is wrong, then, to affirm, as some do, that these movements emerged because of the crisis of the welfare state. No doubt that crisis exacerbated antagonisms, but it did not cause them; they are the expression of a triumphant hegemonic formation. It is, on the contrary, reasonable to suppose that the crisis was in part provoked by the growing resistance to the domination of society by capital and the state. Neoconservative theoreticians are, therefore, not wrong to insist on the problem of the ungovernability of Western countries, a problem they would solve by slowing down what they call the "democratic assault." To propose the crisis as the origin of the new social movements is, in addition, politically dangerous: it leads to thinking of them as irrational manifestations, as phenomena of social pathology. Thus, it obscures the important lessons these struggles provide for a reformulation of socialism.

NEW ANTAGONISMS AND DEMOCRATIC STRUGGLE

I have thus far limited my analysis to the transformations that have taken place in Western societies after World War II and to the resulting creation of new forms of subordination and inequality, which produced in turn the new social movements. But there is an entirely different aspect of the question that must now be developed. Pointing to the existence of inequalities is not sufficient to explain why they produce social unrest. If you reject, as I obviously do, the assumption that the essence of humankind is to struggle for equality and democracy, then there is an important problem to resolve. One must determine what conditions are necessary for specific forms of subordination to produce struggles that seek their abolishment. As I have said, the subordination of women is a very old phenomenon, which became the target of feminist struggles only when the social model based on hierarchy had collapsed. It is here that my opening reference to de Tocqueville is pertinent, for he was the first to grasp the importance of the democratic revolution on the symbolic level. As long as equality has not yet acquired (with the democratic revolution) its place of central significance in the social imagination of Western societies, struggles for this equality cannot exist. As soon as the principle of equality is admitted in one domain, however, the eventual questioning of all possible forms of inequality is an ineluctable consequence. Once begun, the democratic revolution has had, necessarily, to undermine all forms of power and domination, whatever they might be.

I would like to elaborate on the relationship between antagonism and struggle and to begin with the following thesis: an antagonism can emerge when a collective subject – of course, here I am interested in political antagonism at the level of the collective subject – that has been constructed in a specific way, to certain existing discourses, finds its subjectivity negated by other discourses or practices. That negation can happen in two basic ways. First, subjects constructed on the basis of certain rights can find themselves in a position in which those rights are denied by some practices or discourses. At that point there is a negation of subjectivity or identification, which can be the basis for an antagonism. I am not saying that this *necessarily* leads to an antagonism; it is a necessary but not sufficient condition. The second form in which antagonism emerges corresponds to that expressed by feminism and the black movement. It is a situation in which subjects constructed in subordination by a set of discourses are, at the same time, interpellated as equal by other discourses. Here we have a contradictory interpellation. Like the first form, it is a negation of a particular subject position, but, unlike the first, it is the subjectivity-in-subordination that is negated, which opens the possibility for its deconstruction and challenging.

For example, consider the case of the suffragist movement, or, more generally, the question of why it is that, although women's subordination has existed for so long, only at the end of the nineteenth century and the beginning of the twentieth century did subordination give rise to a feminist movement. That has lead some Marxist feminists to say that there was no real women's subordination before; women's subordination is a consequence of capitalism and that is why feminism emerged under capitalism. I think this is wrong. Imagine the way women were constructed, as women, in the Middle Ages. All the possible discourses – the church, the family – constructed women as subordinate subjects. There was absolutely no possibility, no play, in those subject positions for women to call that subordination into question. But with the democratic revolutions of the nineteenth century the assertion that "all men are equal" appears for the first time. Obviously "men" is ambiguous because it refers to both men and women, so women found themselves contradictorily interpellated. As citizens women are equal, or at least interpellated as equal, but that equality is negated by their being women. (It is no coincidence that Mary Wollstonecraft, one of the important English feminists, was living with William Godwin, who was an important radical; this demonstrates the influence of radicalism on the emergence of the suffragist movement.) So that is what I understand by contradictory interpellation – the emergence of a section of equality at a point of new subjectivity, which contradicts the subordination in all other subject positions. That is what allows women to extend the democratic revolution, to question all their subordinate subject positions. The same analysis could be given for the emergence of the black liberation movement.

I should emphasize here the importance of actually existing discourse in the emergence and construction of antagonisms. Antagonisms are always discursively constructed; the forms they take depend on existing discourses and their hegemonic role at a given moment. Thus, different positions in sexual relations do not necessarily construct the concept of woman or femininity in different ways. It depends on the way the antagonism is constructed, and the enemy is defined by the existing discourses. We must also take into account the role of the democratic discourse that became predominant in the Western world with the "democratic revolution." I refer to the transformation, at the level of the symbolic, that deconstructed the theological-political-cosmological vision of the Middle Ages, a vision in which people were born into a specific place in a structured and hierarchical society for which the idea of equality did not exist.

People struggle for equality not because of some ontological postulate but because they have been constructed as subjects in a democratic tradition that puts those values at the center of social life. We can see the widening of social conflict as the extension of the democratic revolution into more and more spheres of social life, into more social relations. All positions that have been constructed as relations of domination/subordination will be deconstructed because of the subversive character of democratic discourse. Democratic discourse extends its field of influence from a starting point, the equality of citizens in a political democracy, to socialism, which extends equality to the level of the economy and then into other social relations, such as sexual, racial, generational, and regional. Democratic discourse questions all forms of inequality and subordination. That is why I propose to call those new social movements "new democratic struggles," because they are extensions of the democratic revolution to new forms of subordination. Democracy is our most subversive idea because it interrupts all existing discourses and practices of subordination.

Now I want to make a distinction between democratic antagonism and democratic struggle. Democratic antagonisms do not necessarily lead to democratic struggles. Democratic antagonism refers to resistance to subordination and inequality; democratic struggle is directed toward a wide democratization of social life. I am hinting here at the possibility that democratic antagonism can be articulated into different kinds of discourse, even into right-wing discourse, because antagonisms are polysemic. There is no one paradigmatic form in which resistance against domination is expressed. Its articulation depends on the discourses and relations of forces in the present struggle for hegemony.

Stuart Hall's analysis of Thatcherism enables us to understand the way popular consciousness can be articulated to the Right. Indeed, any democratic antagonism can be articulated in many different ways. Consider the case of unemployment. A worker who loses his or her job is in a situation – the first one described above – in which, having been defined on the basis of the right to have a job, he or she now finds that right denied. This can be the locus of an antagonism, although there are ways of reacting to unemployment that do not lead to any kind of struggle. The worker can commit suicide, drink enormously, or batter his or her spouse; there are many ways people react against that negation of their subjectivity. But consider now the more political forms that reaction can take. There is no reason to believe the unemployed person is going to construct an antagonism in which Thatcherism or capitalism is the enemy. In England, for example, the discourse of Thatcherism says, "You have lost your job because women are taking men's jobs." It constructs an antagonism in which feminism is the enemy. Or it can say, "You have lost your job because all those immigrants are taking the jobs of good English workers." Or it can say, "You have lost your job because the trade unions maintain such high wages that there are not enough jobs for the working class." In all these cases, democratic antagonism is articulated to the Right rather than giving birth to democratic struggle.

Only if the struggle of the unemployed is articulated with the struggle of blacks, of women, of all the oppressed, can we speak of the creation of a democratic struggle. As I have said, the ground for new struggles has been the production of new inequalities attributable to the postwar hegemonic formation. That the objective of these struggles is autonomy and not power has often been remarked. It would, in fact, be wrong to oppose radically the struggles of workers to the struggles of the new social movements; both are efforts to obtain new rights or to defend endangered ones. Their common element is thus a fundamental one.

Once we have abandoned the idea of a paradigmatic form, which the workers' struggles would be obliged to express, we cannot affirm that the essential aim of these struggles is the conquest of political power. What is needed is an examination of the different forms that democratic struggles for equality may take, according to the type of adversary they oppose and the strategy they imply. In the case of resistances that seek to defend existing rights against growing state intervention, it is obvious that the matter of autonomy will be more important than for those resistances that seek to obtain state action in order to redress inequalities originating in civil society. This does not change the fact that they are of the same nature by virtue of their common aim: the reduction of inequalities and of various forms of subordination. That the vast extension of social conflict we are living through is the work of the democratic revolution is better understood by the New Right than by the Left. This is why the Right strives to halt the progress of equality. Starting from different viewpoints, both neoliberal theoreticians of the market economy and those who are called, in the United States, "neoconservatives" are variously seeking to transform dominant ideological parameters so as to reduce the central role played in these by the idea of democracy, or else to redefine democracy in a restrictive way to reduce its subversive power.

For neoliberals like Hayek, the idea of democracy is subordinated to the idea of individual liberty, so that a defense of economic liberty and private property replaces a defense of equality as the privileged value in a liberal society. Naturally, Hayek does not attack democratic values frontally, but he does make them into an arm for the defense of individual liberty. It is clear that, in his thinking, should a conflict arise between the two, democracy should be sacrificed.

Another way to stop the democratic revolution is offered by the neoconservatives, whose objective is to redefine the notion of democracy itself so that it no longer centrally implies the pursuit of equality and the importance of political participation. Democracy is thus emptied of all of its substance, on the pretext that it is being defended against its excesses, which have led it to the edge of the egalitarian abyss.

To this purpose, Brzezinski, when he was director of the Trilateral Commission, proposed a plan to "increasingly separate the political systems from society and to begin to conceive of the two as separate entities." The idea was to remove as many decisions as possible from political control and to give their responsibility exclusively to experts. Such a measure seeks to depoliticize the most fundamental decisions, not only in the economic but also in the social and political spheres, in order to achieve, in the words of Huntington, "a greater degree of moderation in democracy."

The attempt is to transform the predominant shared meanings in contemporary democratic liberal societies in order to rearticulate them in a conservative direction, justifying inequality. If it succeeds, if the New Right's project manages to prevail, a great step backward will have been taken in the movement of the democratic revolution. We shall witness the establishment of a dualistic society, deeply divided between a sector of the privileged, those in a strong position to defend their rights, and a sector of all those who are excluded from the dominant system, whose demands cannot be recognized as legitimate because they will be inadmissible by definition.

It is extremely important to recognize that, in their antiegalitarian crusade, the various formations of the New Right are trying to take advantage of the new antagonisms born of commodification, bureaucratization, and the uniformization of society. Margaret Thatcher's success in Great Britain and Ronald Reagan's in the United States are unmistakable signs: the populist Right has been able to articulate a whole set of resistances countering the increase in state intervention and the destruction of traditional values and to express them in the language of neoliberalism. It is thus possible for the Right to exploit struggles that express resistance to the new forms of subordination stemming from the hegemonic formation of the Keynesian welfare state.

This is why it is both dangerous and mistaken to see a "privileged revolutionary subject" constituted in the new social movements, a subject who would take the place formerly occupied by the now fallen worker class. I think this is the current thinking represented by Alain Touraine in France and by some of the people linked with the peace movement in Germany. They tend to see new social movements in a much too simplistic way. Like those of the workers, these struggles are not necessarily socialist or even progressive. Their articulation depends on discourses existing at a given moment and on the type of subject the resistances construct. They can, therefore, be as easily assimilated by the discourses of the anti-status quo Right as by those of the Left, or be simply absorbed into the dominant system, which thereby neutralizes them or even utilizes them for its own modernization.

It is, in fact, evident that we must give up the whole problematic of the privileged revolutionary subject, which, thanks to this or that characteristic, granted a priori by virtue of its position in social relations, was presumed to have some universal status and the historical mission of liberating society. On the contrary, if every antagonism is necessarily specific and limited, and there is no single source for all social antagonisms, then the transition to socialism will come about only through political construction articulating all the struggles against different forms of inequality. If, in certain cases, a particular group plays a central role in this transition, it is for reasons that have to do with its political capacity to effect this articulation in specific historical conditions, not for a priori ontological reasons. We must move beyond the sterile dichotomy opposing the working class to the social movements, a dichotomy that cannot in any case correspond to sociological separation, since the workers cannot be reduced to their class position and are inserted into other types of social relations that form other subject positions. We must recognize that the development of capitalism and of increasing state intervention has enlarged the scope of the political struggle and extended the effect of the democratic revolution to the whole of social relations. This opens the possibility of a war for position at all levels of society, which may, therefore, open up the way for a radical transformation.

The New Antagonisms and Socialism

This war for position is already underway, and it has hitherto been waged more effectively by the Right than by the Left. Yet the success of the New Right's current offensive is not definitive. Everything depends on the Left's ability to set up a true hegemonic counteroffensive to integrate current struggles into an overall socialist transformation. It must create what Gramsci called an "expansive hegemony," a chain of equivalences between all the democratic demands to produce the collective will of all those people struggling against subordination. It must create an "organic ideology" that articulates all those movements together. Clearly, this project cannot limit itself to questioning the structural relations of capitalist production. It must also question the mode of development of those forces endemic to the rationale of capitalist production. Capitalism as a way of life is, in fact, responsible for the numerous forms of subordination and inequality attacked by new social movements.

The traditional socialist model, in so far as it accepts an assembly-line productivity of the Fordist type, cannot provide an alternative within the current social crisis and must be profoundly modified. We need an alternative to the logic that promotes the maximum production of material goods and the consequent incessant creation of new material needs, leading in turn to the progressive destruction of natural resources and the environment. A socialist program that does not include the ecological and antinuclear movements cannot hope to solve current problems. The same objection applies to a socialism tolerant of the disproportionate role given to the state. State intervention has, in fact, been proposed as a remedy for the capitalist anarchy. But with the triumph of the Keynesian state, the bourgeoisie has in large part realized this objective. Yet it is just this increase in state intervention that has given rise to the new struggles against the bureaucratization of social life. A program wishing to utilize this potential cannot, therefore, propose increased state intervention but must encourage increased self-determination and self-government for both individuals and citizens. This does not mean accepting the arguments of the New Right, or falling back into the trap of renewed privatization. The state ought to have charge of key sectors of the economy, including control of welfare services. But all these domains should be organized and controlled by workers and consumers rather than the bureaucratic apparatus. Otherwise, the potential of this antistate resistance will simply be used by the Right for its own ends.

As for the women's movement, it is apparent that it needs an even more thoroughgoing transformation. Such a transformation is not utopian. We are beginning to see how a society in which the development of science and technology is directed toward the liberation of the individual rather than toward his or her servitude could also bring about a true equality of the sexes. The consequences of automation – the reduction of the workday and the change in the very notion of work that implies – make possible a far-reaching transformation of everyday life and of the sexual division of labor that plays such an important role in women's subordination. But for this to occur, the Left would have to abandon its conservative attitude toward technological development and make an effort to bring these important changes under its control.

We hear, all too often, as a reaction to the apologists of postindustrial society, that we are still in a capitalist society and that nothing has changed. Though it is quite true that capitalism still prevails, many things have changed since Marx. We are, today, in the midst of an important restructuring. Whether the outcome will strengthen capitalism or move us ahead in the construction of a more democratic society depends on the ability of existing forces to articulate the struggles taking place for the creation of a new hegemonic formation.

What is specific to the present situation is the proliferation of democratic struggles. The struggle for equality is no longer limited to the political and economic arenas. Many new rights are being defined and demanded: those of women, of homosexuals, of various regional and ethnic minorities. All inequalities existing in our society are now at issue. To understand this profound transformation of the political field we must rethink and reformulate the notion of democracy itself, for the view we have inherited does not enable us to grasp the amplitude of the democratic revolution. To this end, it is not enough to improve upon the liberal parliamentary conception of democracy by creating a number of basic democratic forms through which citizens could participate in the management of public affairs, or workers in the management of industries. In addition to these traditional social subjects we must recognize the existence of others and their political characters: women and the various minorities also have a right to equality and to self-determination. If we wish to articulate all these democratic struggles, we must respect their specificity and their autonomy, which is to say that we must institutionalize a true pluralism, a *pluralism of subjects*.

A new conception of democracy also requires that we transcend a certain individualistic conception of rights and that we elaborate a central notion of *solidarity*. This can only be achieved if the rights of certain subjects are not defended to the detriment of the rights of other subjects. Now it is obvious that, in many cases, the rights of some entail the subordination of the rights of others. The defense of acquired rights is therefore a serious obstacle to the establishment of true equality for all. It is precisely here that one sees the line of demarcation separating the Left's articulation of the resistances of the new social movements from the utilization of these same by the New Right. Whereas the Left's program seeks to set up a system of equivalences among the greatest possible number of democratic demands and thus strives to reduce all inequalities, the Right's solution, as a form of populism, satisfies the needs of certain groups by creating new inequalities. This is why the politics of the latter, instead of extending democracy, necessarily widens an already deep social split between the privileged and the nonprivileged.

The progressive character of a struggle does not depend on its place of origin – we have said that all workers' struggles are not progressive – but rather on its link to other struggles. The longer the chain of equivalences set up between the defense of the rights of one group and those of other groups, the deeper will be the democratization process and the more difficult it will be to neutralize certain struggles or make them serve the ends of the Right. The concept of solidarity can be used to form such a chain of democratic equivalences. It is urgent that we establish this new democratic theory, with the concept of solidarity playing the central role, to counter the New Right's offensive in the field of political philosophy.

Faced with an effort like Hayek's to redefine freedom individualistically, what the Left needs is a postindividualist concept of freedom, for it is still over questions of freedom and equality that the decisive ideological battles are being waged. What is at stake is the redefinition of those fundamental notions; and it is the nature of these relations that will determine the kinds of political subjects who will emerge and the new hegemonic block that will take shape.

To combine equality and liberty successfully in a new vision of democracy, one that recognizes the multiplicity of social relations and their corresponding subject positions, requires that we achieve a task conceived at the beginning of the democratic revolution, one that defines the kind of politics required for the advent of modernity. If to speak of socialism still means anything, it should be to designate an extension of the democratic revolution to the entirety of social relations and the attainment of a *radical, libertarian, and plural democracy*. Our objective, in other words, is none other than the goal de Tocqueville perceived as that of democratic peoples, that ultimate point where freedom and equality meet and fuse, where people "will be perfectly free because they are entirely equal, and where they will all be perfectly equal because they are entirely free."

CHAPTER 16

Democracy, the Nation-state and the Global System

David Held

Democracy has only occasionally enjoyed the acclaim it receives today; and its widespread popularity and appeal are little more than one hundred years old. The revolutions which swept across Central and Eastern Europe at the end of 1989 and the beginnings of 1990 have stimulated an atmosphere of celebration. Liberal democracy has been proclaimed as the agent of "the end of history": ideological conflict, it has been said, is being displaced by universal democratic reason. More and more political causes are being fought in the name of democracy, and increasing numbers of states are being recast in a democratic mould. But not far beneath the surface of democracy's triumph there is an apparent paradox: while the idea of "the rule of the people" is championed anew, the very efficacy of democracy as a national form of political organization is open to doubt. Nations are heralding democracy at the very moment at which changes in the international order are compromising the viability of the independent democratic nation-state. As vast areas of human endeavour are progressively organized on a global level, the fate of democracy is fraught with uncertainty.

[. . .]

This chapter is an edited extract from *Political Theory Today*, edited by D. Held (Cambridge, Polity Press, 1991), pp. 197–235. Reprinted by permission of Blackwell Publishers, the US publishers Stanford University Press and the author. Original collection © 1991 Polity Press. Each chapter copyright the author.

SOVEREIGNTY, NATIONAL POLITICS AND GLOBAL INTERCONNECTEDNESS

At the centre of the debate about liberal democracy is a taken-for-granted conception of "sovereignty". The sovereignty of the nation-state has generally not been questioned. It has been assumed that the state has control over its own fate, subject only to compromises it must make and limits imposed upon it by actors, agencies and forces operating within its territorial boundaries. [. . .] Leading perspectives on social and political change have assumed that the origins of societal transformation are to be found in processes internal to society. Change is presumed to occur via mechanisms "built in", as it were, to the very structure of a given society, and governing its development. The world putatively "outside" the nation-state – the dynamics of the world economy, the rapid growth of transnational links and major changes to the nature of international law, for example – is barely theorized, and its implications for democracy are not thought out at all.

The limits of a theory of politics that derives its terms of reference exclusively from the nation-state become apparent from a consideration of the scope and efficacy of the principle of "majority rule". The application of this principle is at the centre of Western democracy: it is at the root of the claim of political decisions to be regarded as worthy or legitimate. Problems arise, however, not only because decisions made by nation-states, or by quasi-regional or quasi-supranational organizations such as the European Community (EC), the North Atlantic Treaty Organization (NATO) or the World Bank, diminish the range of decisions open to a given "majority," but also because decisions of a majority affect (or potentially affect) not only its own citizens.

For example, a decision made against the siting of an international airport near a capital city for fear of upsetting the local rural vote may have disadvantageous consequences for airline passengers throughout the world who are without direct means of representation (Offe, 1985: 283–4). Similarly, a decision to build a nuclear plant near the borders of a neighbouring country is likely to be a decision taken without consulting those in the nearby country (or countries). The decision to permit the building of a chemical factory or manufacturing unit producing toxic or other noxious substances (perhaps as by-products) may contribute to ecological damage – whether in terms of pollution, threats to the ozone layer or the "greenhouse effect" – which does not acknowledge the national boundaries or frontiers which demarcate the formal limits of authority and responsibility of political decision-makers. A decision by a government to save resources by suspending food aid to a country may stimulate the sudden escalation of food prices in that country and contribute directly to an outbreak of famine among the urban and rural poor. Or a decision by a government in West or East to suspend or step up military aid to a political faction in a distant country may decisively influence the outcome of conflict in that country, or fan it into a further vortex of violence.

The modern theory of the sovereign democratic state presupposes the idea of a "national community of fate" – a community which rightly governs itself and determines its own future. This idea is challenged fundamentally by the nature of the pattern of global interconnections and the issues that have to be confronted by a modern state. National communities by no means exclusively "programme" the actions, decisions and policies of their governments and the latter by no means simply determine what is right or appropriate for their own citizens alone (Offe, 1985: 286ff). Any simple assumption in democratic theory that political relations are now or could be "symmetrical" or "congruent" is wholly unjustified.

The examples given above of the global interconnectedness of political decisions and outcomes raise questions which go to the heart of the categories of classical democratic theory and its contemporary variants. The idea that *consent* legitimates government and the state system more generally was central to both seventeeth- and eighteenth-century liberals as well as to nineteenth- and twentieth-century liberal democrats. While the former regarded the social contract as the original mechanism of individual consent, the latter focused on the ballot box as the mechanism whereby the citizen periodically conferred authority on government to enact laws and regulate economic and social life. In more radical accounts of democracy (among others, the republican and participatory models) consent was conceived as conditional on a process ideally involving citizens in the direct creation of the laws by which their lives are regulated; for in these arguments, citizens are only obligated to a system of rules, laws and decisions which they have prescribed for themselves (Held, 1987: 3–8, 254–6, 267–89).

Although many liberals stopped far short of proclaiming that for individuals to be "free and equal" in their communities they must themselves be sovereign, their work was preoccupied with, and affirmed the overwhelming importance of, uncovering the conditions under which individuals can determine and regulate the structure of their own association. And although the conditions of the possibility of consent were interpreted quite differently by particular traditions of liberal and democratic thinking, these traditions have none the less been united by an acceptance of the idea that "government" is upheld by the voluntary consent of free and equal persons. From the outset, consent has for democrats been the undisputed principle of legitimate rule.

But the very idea of consent, and the particular notion that the relevant constituencies of voluntary agreement are the communities of a bounded territory or a state, become deeply problematic as soon as the issue of national, regional and global interconnectedness is considered and the nature of a so-called "relevant community" is contested. Whose consent is necessary, whose agreement is required, whose participation is justified in decisions concerning, for instance, the location of an airport or nuclear plant? What is the relevant constituency? Local? National? Regional? International? To whom do decision-makers have to justify their decisions, and to whom should they? To whom are decision-makers accountable, and to whom should they be? What is the fate of the idea of legitimate rule when decisions, often with potentially life-and-death consequences, are taken in polities in which large numbers of the affected individuals have no democratic stake? What is the fate of legitimacy when the process of governance, both routine and extraordinary, has consequences for individuals and citizens within and beyond a particular nation-state and when only some of these people's consent is regarded as pertinent for the justification of rule and policy? Territorial boundaries demarcate the basis on which individuals are included in and excluded from participation in decisions affecting their lives (however limited the latter might be), but the outcomes of these decisions frequently "stretch" beyond national frontiers.

Regional and global interconnectedness contests the traditional national resolutions of the central questions of democratic theory and practice. The very process of governance seems to be "escaping the categories" of the nation-state. The implications of this are profound, not only for the categories of consent and legitimacy but for all the key ideas of democratic thought: the nature of a constituency, the meaning of accountability, the proper form and scope of political participation, and the relevance of the nation-state, faced with unsettling patterns of national and international relations and processes, as the guarantor of the rights and duties of subjects.

STATES, BORDERS AND GLOBAL POLITICS

It could be objected that there is nothing new about global interconnections, and that the significance of global interconnections for democratic theory has in principle been plain for people to see for a long time. Such an objection could be developed by stressing that a dense pattern of global interconnections began to emerge with the initial expansion of the world economy and the rise of the modern state (Wallerstein, 1974). Four centuries ago, as one commentator succinctly put it, "trade and war were already shaping every conceivable aspect of both domestic politics and the international system" (Gourevitch, 1978: 908). Domestic and international politics are interwoven throughout the modern era: domestic politics has always to be understood against the background of international politics; and the former is often the source of the latter. Whether one is reflecting on the monarchical politics of the sixteenth or seventeenth centuries (the question of whether, for instance, the King of France should be a Catholic or a Protestant), or seeking to understand the changing pattern of trade routes from East to West in the fifteenth and sixteenth centuries (and the way these changed the structure of towns, urban environments and the social balance), the examination of patterns of local and international interdependence and interpenetration seems inescapable (Gourevitch, 1978: 908–11).

[. . .]

But it is one thing to claim elements of continuity in the formation and structure of modern states and societies, quite another to claim that there is nothing new about aspects of their form and dynamics. For there is a fundamental difference between the development of a trade route which has an impact on particular towns and/or rural centres on the one hand and, on the other, an international order involving the emergence of a global economic system which outreaches the control of any single state (even dominant states); the expansion of vast networks of transnational relations and communications over which particular states have limited influence; the enormous growth in international organizations and regimes, and the intensification of multilateral diplomacy and transgovernmental interaction, which can check and limit the scope of the most powerful states; and the development of a global military order and the build-up of the means of "total" warfare as a "stable feature" of the contemporary world which can reduce the range of policies available to governments and their citizens. While trade routes may link distant populations together in long loops of cause and effect, modern developments in the international order link and integrate peoples through multiple networks of transaction and co-ordination, reordering the very notion of distance itself.

These international developments are often referred to as part of a process of "globalization" – or, more accurately put, of "Western globalization". Globalization in this context implies at least two distinct phenomena. First, it suggests that political, economic and social activity is becoming worldwide in scope. And secondly, it suggests that there has been an intensification of levels of interaction and interconnectedness among the states and societies which make up international society (McGrew, 1988: 19–20). What is new about the modern global system is the chronic intensification of patterns of interconnectedness, mediated by such phenomena as the modern communications industry and new information technology, and the spread of globalization in and through new dimensions of interconnectedness: technological, organizational, administrative and legal, among others, each with its own logic and dynamic of change. Politics unfolds today, with all its customary uncertainty, contingency and indeterminateness, against the background of a world "permeated and transcended by the flow of goods and capital, the passage of people, communication through airways, airborne traffic, and space satellites" (Kegley and Wittkopf, 1989: 511).

The significance of these developments for the form and structure of national and international politics can be explored further by examination of an argument found in the literature on globalization – often referred to as the "transformationalist" or "modernist" view – which offers an account of the way growing global interconnectedness can lead to a decline or "crisis" of state autonomy, and the requirement of nation-states to co-operate and collaborate intensively with one another (Keohane and Nye, 1972; Morse, 1976; Rosenau, 1980). In setting out the argument, I by no means intend simply to endorse it; rather, I intend to sketch issues and concerns with which, at the very least, democratic theory must engage. For the sake of brevity, the argument is set out in schematic form.

(1) With the increase in global interconnectedness, the number of political instruments available to governments and the effectiveness of particular instruments shows a marked tendency to decline (Keohane and Nye, 1972: 392–5). This tendency occurs, in the first instance, because of the loss of a wide range of border controls which formerly served to restrict transactions in goods and services, production factors and technology, ideas and cultural interchange (Morse, 1976: chs 2–3). The result is a decrease in policy instruments which enable the state to control activities within and beyond its borders.

(2) States can experience a further diminution in options because of the expansion in transnational forces and interactions which reduce and restrict the influence particular governments can exercise over the activities of their citizens. The impact, for example, of the flow of private capital across borders can threaten anti-inflation measures, exchange rates and other government policies.

(3) In the context of a highly interconnected global order, many of the traditional domains of state activity and responsibility (defence, economic management, communications, administrative and legal systems) cannot be fulfilled without resort to international forms of collaboration. As demands on the state have increased in the postwar years, the state has been faced with a whole series of policy problems which cannot be adequately resolved without co-operating with other states and non-state actors (Keohane, 1984a).

(4)   Accordingly, states have had to increase the level of their political integration with other states (for example, in the EC, Comecon and the Organization of American States) and/or increase multilateral negotiations, arrangements and institutions to control the destabilizing effects that accompany interconnectedness (for example, through the International Monetary Fund (IMF) and the General Agreement on Tariffs and Trade (GATT) which, along with other international agencies, generated an organizational environment for economic management and intergovernmental consultation in the immediate postwar years).

(5)   The result has been a vast growth of institutions, organizations and regimes which have laid a basis for global governance. (Of course, to say this is by no means to confuse such developments with the emergence of an integrated world government. There is a crucial difference between an international society which contains the possibility of political co-operation and order, and a supranational state which has a monopoly of coercive and legislative power.) The new global politics – involving, among other things, multibureaucratic decision-making within and between governmental and international bureaucracies, politics triggered by transnational forces and agencies and new forms of multinational integration between states (Kaiser, 1972: 358–60) – has created a framework in and through which the rights and obligations, powers and capacities of states have been redefined. The state's capacities have been both curtailed and expanded, allowing it to continue to perform a range of functions which cannot be sustained any longer in isolation from global or regional relations and processes. [...]

What these arguments suggest is that the meaning of national democratic decision-making today has to be explored in the context of a complex multinational, multilogic international society, and a huge range of actual and nascent regional and global institutions which transcend and mediate national boundaries.

[...]

GLOBAL INTERCONNECTEDNESS IN THE FACE OF THE STATES SYSTEM

From the perspective of globalization, the modern liberal democratic state is often portrayed as increasingly trapped within webs of global interconnectedness permeated by quasi-supranational, intergovernmental and transnational forces, and unable to determine its own fate. Globalization is frequently portrayed as a homogenizing force, eroding "difference" and the capacity of nation-states to act independently in the articulation and pursuit of domestic and international policy objectives: the democratic territorial nation-state seems to face decline or crisis (Morse, 1976). Yet, while there has been rapid expansion of inter-governmental and transnational links, among other things, the age of the nation-state is by no means exhausted. If the territorial nation-state has suffered decline, this is an uneven process, particularly restricted to the power and reach of dominant Western and Eastern nation-states. European global society reached a pinnacle of influence at the close of the nineteenth century and the beginning of the twentieth, and American hegemony was above all a feature of the immediate postwar decades. Their respective decline should not be taken to indicate the decline of the states system itself. Further, the recent transformation of the political regimes of Eastern Europe has regenerated a cluster of states, all asserting their independence and autonomy. While the "classical empires" of the British, French, Dutch etc. are now largely eradicated, the "new empires" created in the aftermath of the Second World War face the severest challenges.

The "nationalization" of global politics is a very recent phenomenon and, in all likelihood, it is a process which has by no means fully run its course. The importance of the nation-state and nationalism, territorial independence and the desire to establish or regain or maintain "sovereignty" does not seem to have diminished. Some of the world's most seemingly intractable regional crises do not escape the pull of sovereignty. The problem of the West Bank, for instance, can scarcely be thought through without reference to the idea of sovereign autonomy (Krasner, 1988). Moreover, the "nuclear balance" or "stalemate" achieved by the superpowers has created a paradoxical situation which has been referred to as the "unavailability of force"; that is, new spaces offering opportunities for non-nuclear powers and peoples to assert themselves in the knowledge that the great powers' nuclear option is barely feasible and the cost of conventional military intervention makes it a colossal political, military and economic gamble (Herz, 1976: 234ff). Vietnam and Afghanistan are obvious cases in point. These developments constitute powerful pressures in the direction of a "multipolar world" and a fragmented international order.

In addition, globalization in the domains of communication and information, far from creating a sense of common human purpose, interest and value, has arguably served to reinforce the sense of the significance of identity and difference, further stimulating the "nationalization" of politics. As one commentator has aptly noted: "awareness of other societies, even where it is perfect, does not merely help to remove imagined conflicts of interest or ideology that do not exist; it also reveals conflicts of interest and ideology that do exist" (Bull, 1977: 280).

One consequence of this is the elevation in many international forums of non-Western views of rights, authority and legitimacy. The meaning of some of the core concepts of the international system are subject to the deepest conflicts of interpretation (Bozeman, 1984). Attempts to create "a new cosmopolitan law" of international co-operation and conduct, inspired in large part by the UN Charter, have not succeeded in general terms (Vincent, 1986). Despite the enshrinement of rights in a battery of international and regional treaties, the attempts to enact human rights in and through the operation of the global system have achieved at best very limited success. Human rights discourse today may indicate aspirations for the entrenchment of certain liberties and entitlements across the globe but it by no means reflects common agreement on rights questions. If the global system is marked today by significant change, this is best conceived less as an end of the era of the nation-state and more as a challenge to the era of "hegemonic states" – a challenge which is as yet, of course, far from complete.

Another clear testimony of the durability of the states system is the reluctance of states, on the whole, to submit their disputes with other states to arbitration by a "superior authority", be it the UN, an international court or any other international body. At the heart of this "great refusal" is the protection of the right of states to go to war (Hinsley, 1986: 229–35). The modern state is still able in principle to determine the most fundamental aspect of people's life-chances – the question of life and death.

Those who herald the end of the nation-state all too often assume the erosion of state power in the face of globalizing pressures and fail to recognize the enduring capacity of the state apparatus to shape the direction of domestic and international politics. The degree to which the modern state enjoys "autonomy" under various conditions is underexplored and, therefore, a key basis for a systematic and rigorous account of the form and limits of modern democracies is too hastily put aside. The impact of global processes is clearly likely to vary under different international and national conditions – for instance, a nation-state's location in the international division of labour, its place in particular power blocs, its position with respect to the international legal system, its relation to major international organizations. Not all states, for example, are equally integrated into the world economy; thus, while national political outcomes will be heavily influenced by global processes in some countries, in others regional or national forces might well remain supreme.

POWERS AND DISJUNCTURES

While the nation-state manifests continuing vitality, this does not mean that the sovereign structure of individual nation-states remains unaffected by the intersection of national and international forces and relations: rather, it signals, in all probability, shifting patterns of powers and constraints. The precise scope and nature of the sovereign authority of individual nation-states can be mapped by looking at a number of "internal" and "external" disjunctures between, on the one hand, the formal domain of political authority they claim for themselves and, on the other, the actual practices and structures of the state and economic system at the national, regional and global levels.

The powers of political parties, bureaucratic organizations, corporations and networks of corporatist influence are among a variety of forces which put pressure on the range and scope of decisions that can be made within a nation-state. At the international level, there are disjunctures between the idea of the state as in principle capable of determining its own future, and the world economy, international organizations, regional and global institutions, international law and military alliances which operate to shape and constrain the options of individual nation-states. In the discussion that follows the focus will be on such "external" disjunctures; the question of "internal" disjunctures opens up many issues which cannot be explored within the confines of this [chapter]. Even the enumeration of external disjunctures, it should be stressed, is simply illustrative; it is neither complete nor systematic. It is intended simply to indicate to what extent globalization in a number of key domains can be said to constitute constraints or limits on political agency; and to what extent the possibility of a democratic polity has been transformed and altered.

When assessing the impact of disjunctures, it is important to bear in mind that sovereignty is eroded only when it is displaced by forms of "higher" and/or independent authority which curtail the rightful basis of decision-making within a national framework. For I take sovereignty to mean the political authority within a community which has the undisputed right to determine the framework of rules, regulations and policies within a given territory and to govern accordingly (Held, 1989: 215). Sovereignty should be distinguished from state "autonomy", or the state's actual capacity to act independently in the articulation and pursuit of domestic and international policy objectives. In effect, autonomy refers to the ability of nation-states to act free of international and transnational constraints, and to achieve goals once they have been set (for in an interconnected world all instruments of national policy may be less effective). Bearing these distinctions in mind, it can be shown that external disjunctures map a series of processes which alter the range and nature of the decisions open to political decision-makers within a delimited terrain. The central question to pose is: has sovereignty remained intact while the autonomy of the state has diminished, or has the modern state actually faced a loss of sovereignty? In addressing this question, I shall draw most of my examples from the processes and relations which impinge most directly on the states of Europe. It is the fate of the states of Europe which will be uppermost.

Disjuncture 1: the world economy

There is a disjuncture between the formal authority of the state and the actual system of production, distribution and exchange which in many ways serves to limit the power or scope of national political authorities (Keohane and Nye, 1977).

(1)   Two aspects of international economic processes are central: the internationalization of production and the internationalization of financial transactions, organized in part by fast-growing multinational companies. Multinational corporations (MNCs) plan and execute their production, marketing and distribution with the world economy firmly in mind. Even when MNCs have a clear national base, their interest is above all in global profitability, and their country of origin may count little in their overall corporate strategy. Financial organizations such as banks are also progressively more global in scale and orientation; they are able to monitor and respond to developments, be they in London, Tokyo or New York, almost instantaneously. New information technology has radically increased the mobility of economic units – currencies, stocks, shares, "futures" and so on – for financial and commercial organizations of all kinds.

(2)   There is considerable evidence to support the claim that technological advances in communication and transportation are eroding the boundaries between hitherto separate markets – boundaries which were a necessary condition for independent national economic policies (Keohane and Nye, 1972: 392–5). Markets, and societies, are becoming more sensitive to one another even when their distinctive identities are preserved: the October stock-market crash of 1987 is one obvious example of this. The very possibility of a national economic policy is, accordingly, reduced. The monetary and fiscal policies of individual national governments are frequently dominated by movements in the international financial markets. Likewise, the levels of employment, investment and revenue within a country are often subordinated to the decisions of MNCs about such matters as where they will locate their production and administrative facilities (Smith, 1987).

(3)   The globalization of economic relationships has altered the possibility of deploying whole ranges of economic policies. For instance, although there are many reasons why Keynesianism may no longer work today, one fundamental such reason is that it is much harder for individual governments to intervene and manage their economies faced with a global division of labour and monetary system (Ruggie, 1982; Cox, 1987: chs 8, 9; Gilpin, 1987: 354ff). Keynesianism functioned well in

the context of the system of "embedded liberalism" which existed in the postwar years; it was the operating framework of both international and national economic agreements across the Western world (Keohane, 1984b). But with the breakdown of the postwar "liberal consensus" in the wake of the 1973 oil crisis, among other events, the possibility of managing an economy and "bucking" international economic trends became more difficult. The forces and constraints of the international economy – including, for example, the mechanisms which transmitted inflation and recession, the changing terms of trade, and the steady expansion of industrial capitalism at the so-called "periphery" of the international economy (in South Korea, Taiwan and the other newly industrializing countries) – became more apparent. The increasing inter-connectedness of the world's economies was, accordingly, more readily accepted, especially by those governments which made much of the market as a, if not the, leading standard of rational decision-making.

(4) The loss of control of national economic programmes is, of course, not uniform across economic sectors or societies more generally: some markets and some countries can isolate themselves from transna-tional economic networks by such measures as attempts to restore the boundaries or "separateness" of markets and/or to extend national laws to cover internationally mobile factors and/or to adopt co-operative policies with other countries for the co-ordination of policy (Gilpin, 1987: 397ff). In addition, the regionalization of sections of the world economy, with economic activity clustering around a number of poles (among them the European market, the United States and the Pacific Basin, and Japan), provides scope for some regulation of market trends. The particular tensions between political and economic structures are likely to be different in different spheres, and between them: West–West, North–South, East–West. It cannot, therefore, simply be said that the very idea of a national economy is superseded. However, the interna-tionalization of production, finance and other economic resources is unquestionably eroding the capacity of an individual state to control its own economic future. At the very least, there appears to be a diminu-tion of state autonomy, and a disjuncture between the idea of a sover-eign state determining its own future and the conditions of modern economies, marked as they are by the intersection of national and inter-national economic forces.

Disjuncture 2: international organizations

A second major area of disjuncture between the theory of the sovereign state and the contemporary global system lies in the vast array of inter-national regimes and organizations that have been established to manage whole areas of transnational activity (trade, the oceans, space) and collective policy problems. The growth in the number of these new forms of political association reflects the rapid expansion of transnational links (Luard, 1977).

(1) The development of international and transnational organizations has led to important changes in the decision-making structure of world politics. New forms of multinational politics have been established and with them new forms of collective decision-making involving states, intergovernmental organizations and a whole variety of transnational pressure groups.

(2) Among the spectrum of international agencies and organizations are those whose primary concerns have been technical: the Universal Postal Union, the International Telecommunications Union, the World Meteorological Organization and a host of other bodies. These agencies have tended to work effectively and uncontroversially – providing, in most cases, extensions to the services offered by individual nation-states (Burnheim, 1986: 222). To the extent that their tasks have been sharply delimited, they have been politically unexceptional. At the opposite pole lie organizations like the World Bank, the IMF, UNESCO and the UN. Preoccupied with more central questions of the management and allocation of rules and resources, these bodies have been highly controversial and politicized. Unlike the smaller, technically based agencies, these organizations are at the centre of continual conflict over the control of policy (Burnheim, 1986: 222ff). While the mode of operation of these agencies tends to vary, they have all benefited over the years from a certain "entrenchment of authority" which has bestowed on some decisive powers of intervention.

(3) The operations of the IMF provide an interesting case. In pursuing a particular line of economic policy, the IMF may insist as a condition of its loan to a government that the latter cut public expenditure, devalue its currency and cut back on subsidized welfare programmes. In a Third World country, for instance, this may trigger bread riots and perhaps the fall of a government, or it might contribute directly to the imposition of martial law. It has to be borne in mind that IMF intervention routinely takes place at the request of governmental authorities or particular political factions within a state, and is often the result of the recognition that there is minimal scope for independent national policies; it cannot straightforwardly be interpreted, therefore, as a threat to sovereignty. None the less, a striking tension has emerged between the idea of the sovereign state – centred on national politics and political institutions – and the nature of decision-making at the international level. The latter raises serious questions about the conditions under which a community is able to determine its own policies and directions, given the constraints of the international economic order and the operating rules of agencies like the IMF.

(4) The European Community provides an important additional illustration of the issues posed by international organizations. Its significance, however, reaches perhaps further than that of any other kind of international organization by virtue of its right to make laws which can be imposed on member states; more than any other international agency, it justifies the label "quasi-supranational". Within Community institutions, the Council of Ministers has a unique position, for it has at its disposal powerful legal instruments (above all, "regulations", "directions" and "decisions") which allow it to make and enact policy. Of all these instruments "regulations" are the most notable because they have the status of law independently of any further negotiation or action on the part of member states. Accordingly, the member states of the European Community are no longer the sole centres of power within their own borders (Wickham, 1984). On the other hand, it is important to bear in mind that the Community's powers were gained by the "willing surrender" of aspects of sovereignty by member states – a "surrender" which, arguably, has actually helped the survival of the European nation-state faced with the dominance of the USA in the first three decades after the Second World War and the rise of the Japanese economic challenge. In short, like many other international organizations, the European Community provides both opportunities and constraints. The states of the Community retain the final and most general power in many areas of their domestic and foreign affairs – and the Community itself seems to have strengthened their options in some of these domains. However, within the Community sovereignty is now also clearly divided: any conception of sovereignty which assumes that it is an indivisible, illimitable, exclusive and perpetual form of public power – embodied within an individual state – is defunct.

Disjuncture 3: international law

The development of international law has subjected individuals, governments and non-governmental organizations to new systems of legal regulation. International law has recognized powers and constraints, and rights and duties, which transcend the claims of nation-states and which, while they may not be backed by institutions with coercive powers of enforcement, none the less have far-reaching consequences.

(1) There are two legal rules which, since the very beginnings of the international community, have been taken to uphold national sovereignty: "immunity from jurisdiction" and "immunity of state agencies". The former prescribes that "no state can be sued in courts of another state for acts performed in its sovereign capacity"; and the latter stipulates that "should an individual break the law of another state while acting as an agent for his country of origin and be brought before that

state's courts, he is not held guilty because he did not act as a private individual but as the representative of the state" (Cassese, 1988: 150–1). The underlying purpose of these rules is to protect a government's autonomy in all matters of foreign policy and to prevent domestic courts from ruling on the behaviour of foreign states (on the understanding that all domestic courts everywhere will be so prevented). And the upshot has traditionally been that governments have been left free to pursue their interests subject only to the constraints of the "art of politics". It is notable, however, that these internationally recognized legal mainstays of sovereignty have been progressively questioned by Western courts. And while it is the case that national sovereignty has most often been the victor when put to the test, the tension between national sovereignty and international law is now marked, and it is by no means clear how it will be resolved. Within the framework of EC law, this tension has developed into a "crisis"; with the passing of the Single European Act, with replaces unanimity by "qualified majority voting" within the Council of Ministers for a significant number of issue areas, the place of national sovereignty is no longer ensured (Noel, 1989: 10–11).

(2) Of all the international declarations of rights which were made in the postwar years, the European Convention for the Protection of Human Rights and Fundamental Freedoms (1950) is especially noteworthy (Negro, 1986). In marked contrast to the United Nations' Universal Declaration of Human Rights (1947) and subsequent UN charters of rights, the European Convention was concerned, as its preamble indicates, "to take the first steps for the *collective enforcement* of certain of the Rights of the UN Declaration" (emphasis added). The European initiative was committed to a most remarkable and radical legal innovation: an innovation which in principle would allow individual citizens to initiate proceedings against their own governments. European countries have now accepted an (optional) clause of the Convention which permits citizens to petition directly the European Commission on Human Rights, which can take cases to the Committee of Ministers of the Council of Europe and then (given a two-thirds majority on the Council) to the European Court of Human Rights. While the system is far from straightforward and is problematic in many respects, it has been claimed that, alongside legal changes introduced by the European Community, it no longer leaves the state "free to treat its own citizens as it thinks fit" (Capotorti, 1983).

(3) The gap between the idea of membership of a national community, i.e. citizenship, which traditionally bestows upon individuals both rights and duties, and the creation in international law of new forms of liberties and obligations is exemplified further by the results of the International Tribunal at Nuremberg. The Tribunal laid down, for

the first time in history, that when *international rules* that protect basic humanitarian values are in conflict with *state laws*, every individual must transgress the state laws (except where there is no room for "moral choice") (Cassese, 1988: 132). The legal framework of the Nuremberg Tribunal marked a highly significant change in the legal direction of the modern state, for the new rules challenged the principle of military discipline and subverted national sovereignty at one of its most sensitive points: the hierarchical relations within the military.

(4)   International law is a "vast and changing corpus of rules and quasi-rules" which set out the basis of co-existence and co-operation in the international order. Traditionally, international law has identified and upheld the idea of a society of sovereign states as "the supreme normative principle" of the political organization of humankind (Bull, 1977: 140ff). In recent decades, the subject, scope and source of international law have all been contested; and opinion has shifted against the doctrine that international law is and should be a "law between states only and exclusively" (Oppenheim, 1905: ch. 1). At the heart of this shift lies a conflict between claims made on behalf of the states system and those made on behalf of an alternative organizing principle of world order: ultimately, a cosmopolitan community. This conflict is, however, far from settled, and the recent resurgence of movements like Islam, and the renewed intensity of many nationalist struggles, indicate that claims mobilized on behalf of a cosmopolitan community look, at the very least, hastily arranged.

Disjuncture 4: hegemonic powers and power blocs

There is a further disjuncture involving the idea of the state as an autonomous strategic, military actor and the development of the global system of states, characterized by the existence of great powers and power blocs, which sometimes operates to undercut a state's authority and integrity.

(1)   The dominance of the USA and USSR as world powers, and the operation of alliances like the North Atlantic Treaty Organization (NATO) and the Warsaw Pact, has constrained decision-making for many states in the postwar years. A state's capacity to initiate particular foreign policies, pursue certain strategic concerns, choose between alternative military technologies and control certain weapon systems located on its own territory may be restricted by its place in the international system of power relations (Herz, 1976: 230–3).

(2)   Within NATO, for example, clear evidence of what might be called the "internationalization of security" can be found in its joint and integrated military command structure. Ever since NATO was established in the late 1940s, its concern with collective security has trodden

a fine line between, on the one hand, maintaining an organization of sovereign states (which permits, in principle, an individual member state *not* to act if it judges this appropriate) and, on the other, developing an international organization which *de facto*, if not *de jure*, operates according to its own logic and decision-making procedures. The existence of an integrated supranational command structure – headed by the Supreme Allied Commander in Europe, who has always been an American General appointed by the US President – ensures that, in a situation of war, NATO's "national armies" would operate within the framework of NATO's strategies and decisions (Smith, 1984: 131). The sovereignty of a national state is decisively qualified once its armed forces are committed to a NATO conflict.

(3) Even without a commitment to a NATO armed conflict, state autonomy as well as sovereignty can be limited and checked, for the routine conduct of NATO affairs involves the integration of national defence bureaucracies into international defence organizations; these, in turn, create transgovernmental decision-making systems which can escape the control of any single member state. Such systems can lead, moreover, to the establishment of informal, but none the less powerful, transgovernmental personnel networks or coalitions which are difficult to monitor by national mechanisms of accountability and control.

(4) Membership of NATO does not annul sovereignty; rather, it qualifies sovereignty for each state in different ways. No account of NATO (however brief) would be complete without emphasizing that its members are also rivals competing for scarce resources, arms contracts, international prestige and other means of national enhancement. Aspects of sovereignty are negotiated and renegotiated through the NATO alliance. [. . .]

DEMOCRACY AND THE GLOBAL SYSTEM

The international order, and with it the role of the nation-state, is changing. While a complex pattern of global interconnections has been evident for a long time, there is little doubt that there has recently been a further "internationalization" of domestic activities and an intensification of decision-making in international frameworks (Kaiser, 1972: 370). The evidence that international and transnational relations have eroded the powers of the modern sovereign state is certainly strong. Global processes have moved politics a long way from activity which simply crystallizes first and foremost around state and interstate concerns.
    [. . .]
How can democracy be understood in a world of independent and interdependent political authorities? Does not a system of interlocking

authority structures, creating diverse and potentially conflicting demands, pose a threat to the very basis of the modern state as an impersonal and privileged legal or constitutional order – a circumscribed structure of power with supreme jurisdiction over a territory accountable to a determinate citizen body? Can the very idea of a democratic polity or state persist, especially if the areas of interconnectedness grow between, say, the government of the UK, the EC, international governmental organizations and international legal structures?

[. . .]

It is part of the argument of this [chapter] that the international order today is characterized by both the persistence of the sovereign states system and the development of plural authority structures. The objections to such a hybrid system are severe. It is open to question whether it offers any solutions to the fundamental problems of modern political thought, among the most prominent of which have been the rationale and basis of order and toleration, of democracy and accountability, and of legitimate rule. But it is my view, to be sketched in the remainder of the [chapter], that these objections can be met, and the dangers they signal coherently addressed, within the framework of constitutional and democratic thought. For the dangers may in principle be surmounted if a multiple system of authority is bound by fundamental ordering principles and rules. The potentially fragmentary and undemocratic nature of these developments can be overcome if they are part of a common order committed to close collaboration and similar principles and constitutional guidelines. [. . .] I refer to this as the "federal model of democratic autonomy".[1]

SOVEREIGNTY, SELF-DETERMINATION AND DEMOCRATIC AUTONOMY

(1)   Historically, the idea of sovereignty offered a new way of thinking about an old problem: the nature of power and rule. It provided a fresh link between political power and rulership, and offered an alternative mode of conceiving the legitimacy of claims to power – an alternative, that is, to the theocratic conceptions of authority which dominated mediaeval Europe. The theory of sovereignty became a theory of the rightful use of power. It had two overriding preoccupations: a concern with where sovereign authority properly lay; and a concern with the proper form and limits – the legitimate scope – of state action. Hence, as the theory of sovereignty developed from Jean Bodin onwards, it became a theory of the possibility of, and the conditions of, the rightful exercise of political power. It became, thus, the theory of legitimate power or authority.

(2)   Within the debates about sovereighty two poles became clearly established: state sovereignty and popular sovereignty. Whereas advocates of the former tended to grant the state ultimate authority to define public right, advocates of the latter tended to see the state as a mere "commission" for the enactment of the people's will and, therefore, as open to direct determination by "the public" (Held, 1989: 212–25). Both positions, however, face a common objection; for both project conceptions of political power with tyrannical implications. The thesis of state sovereignty placed the state in an all-powerful position with respect to the community; and the thesis of popular sovereignty placed the community (or a majority thereof) in a wholly dominant position over individual citizens – the community is all-powerful and, therefore, the sovereignty of the people could easily destroy the liberty of individuals. Conceptions of sovereignty which fail to demarcate the limits or legitimate scope of political action need to be treated with the utmost caution.

(3)   An alternative to the thesis of the sovereignty of the state and the sovereignty of the people is implicit in the Lockean conception of an independent political community, and is essential to the traditions of political analysis which neither locate sovereignty exclusively in, nor reduce sovereignty to, either state or society (Dunn, 1984: esp. 44–57). This tradition – one, above all, of constitutional thinking – sought to provide ways of mediating, balancing and checking the relationship between state and society such that some protection existed for both public and private right. Ultimately, only a principle of sovereighty which places at its centre scepticism about both state and popular sovereignty can be an acceptable principle. Such a principle must insist, *contra* state sovereignty, on "the people" determining the conditions which govern their lives and insist, *contra* popular sovereignty, on the specification of limits to the power of the public – on a regulatory structure which is both enabling and constraining. The "principle of autonomy" marks out this terrain.

(4)   The principle of autonomy can be stated as follows:

persons should enjoy equal rights (and, accordingly, equal obligations) in the framework which generates and limits the opportunities available to them; that is, they should be free and equal in the determination of the conditions of their own lives, so long as they do not deploy this framework to negate the rights of others.[2]

Several notions require clarification:

(a)   The principle of autonomy seeks to articulate the foundations for the possibility of consent; it is a principle of legitimate power.

(b)   The notion that persons should enjoy equal rights and obligations in the framework which shapes their lives and opportunities means that they should enjoy a "common structure of action" in order that they may be able to pursue their projects – both individual and collective – as free and equal agents.

(c)   The concept of "rights" connotes, in the first instance, entitlements: entitlements to pursue action and activity without the risk of arbitrary or unjust interference. Rights define legitimate spheres of independent action (or inaction). While the benefits of rights are defined for particular individuals (or groups or agencies), they are a public or social phenomenon because they circumscribe networks of relationships between the individual, or right-holder, and others, or the community and its representatives. Rights are entitlements within the constraints of community, enabling – that is, creating spaces for action – and constraining – that is, specifying limits on independent action so that the latter does not curtail and infringe the liberty of others. Hence, rights have a structural dimension, bestowing both opportunities and duties. Further rights, if they are to specify the ability of people to enjoy a range of liberties not only in principle but also in practice, must be both formal and concrete. This entails the specification of a broad range of rights, with a profound "cutting edge", in the realms of both state and civil society.

(d)   The idea that people should be free and equal in the determination of the conditions of their own lives means that they should be able to participate in a process of deliberation, open to all on a free and equal basis, about matters of pressing public concern. A legitimate decision, within this framework, is not one that follows from the "will of all", but rather one that results from "the deliberation of all" (Manin, 1987: 352). The process of deliberation is, accordingly, compatible with the procedures and mechanisms of majority rule.

(e)   The qualification stated in the principle – that individual rights require explicit protection – represents a familiar call for constitutional government. The principle of autonomy specifies both that individuals must be "free and equal" and that "majorities" should not be able to impose themselves on others. There must always be institutional arrangements to protect the individuals' or minorities' position, i.e. constitutional rules and safeguards.

(5)   The rationale of the principle of autonomy, its ultimate grounding, is, to borrow a phrase from John Rawls (1985), "political not metaphysical". It is a principle at the heart of the modern liberal democratic project, preoccupied with the capability of persons to determine and

justify their own actions, with their ability to enter into self-chosen obligations, and with the underlying conditions for them to be free and equal. The actual pursuit of equal membership in political communities reconstituted the shape of modern Western politics. It did so because the struggle for rights re-formed earlier understandings of legitimate realms of independent action. If the early attempts to achieve rights involved struggles for autonomy or independence from the locale in which one was born, and from prescribed occupations, later struggles involved such things as freedom of speech, expression, belief and association, and freedom for women in and beyond marriage. The autonomy of the citizen can be represented by that bundle of rights which individuals can enjoy as a result of their status as free and equal members of society.

(6)   The principle of autonomy has both a normative and an empirical basis. The empirical basis derives from unfolding the different conditions and sites which have become the focus of struggle for membership of, and potentially full participation in, the political community; the normative basis from a reflection on the conditions under which autonomy is possible. The normative basis of the principle of autonomy is demarcated by the attempt to elaborate and project a conception of autonomy based on a "thought experiment" – an experiment into how people would interpret their capacities and needs, and which rules, laws and institutions they would consider justified, if they had access to a fuller account of their position in the political system and of the conditions of participation. This thought experiment is guided by an interest in examining the ways in which the practices, institutions and structures of social life might be transformed to enable citizens more effectively to understand, shape and organize their lives. It is concerned at its centre with an assessment of the conditions and rules that it would be necessary for people to enjoy if they were to be free and equal. It is my view that such a thought experiment reveals that five categories of rights are crucial in enabling people to participate on free and equal terms in the regulation of their own association: the civil, political, economic, social and reproductive. Together, these bundles of rights constitute the interrelated spaces within which the principle of autonomy can be pursued – and enacted.

(7)   The principle of autonomy can guide an account of the nature and meaning of legitimate power. But such an account would be incomplete without an enquiry into the organizational and institutional basis of the principle. For abstract reasoning about principles has to be supplemented with detailed analyses of the conditions under which such principles can be realized: without such an analysis the very meaning of a principle can barely be spelt out at all. Elsewhere, I have referred to the "conditions of enactment" of the principle of autonomy as requir-

ing ultimately, on the one hand, the reform of state power and, on the other hand, the restructuring of civil society (Held, 1987: ch. 9). This involves recognizing the indispensability of a process of "double democratization": the interdependent transformation of both state and civil society. The nature of this transformation is elaborated in the model of what I call "democratic autonomy", with its emphasis on: the enshrinement of the principle of autonomy in a constitution and bill of rights; the reform of state power to maximize accountability (within the terms of the constitution) to elected representatives and, ultimately, to the citizen body; and the experimentation in civil society with different democratic mechanisms and procedures.

(8)   In an interconnected world, however, the conditions of enactment of the principle of autonomy have to be thought through in relation to the international networks of states and organizations and the international networks of civil society. The international form and structure of politics and civil society must be built into the foundations of democratic theory. The problem of democracy in our times is to specify how the principle of autonomy can be enshrined and secured in a series of interconnected power and authority centres. For if one chooses democracy today, one must choose not only to operationalize a radical system of rights but also to do this in a complex, intergovernmental and transnational power structure. Democratic autonomy can only be fully sustained in and through the agencies and organizations which form an element in the life of, and yet cut across the territorial boundaries of, the nation-state. Democratic autonomy will be the result, and only the result, of a nucleus of, or federation of, democratic states and agencies. The principles and requirments of democratic autonomy have to be enshrined in, and enacted within, national and international power centres, if democratic autonomy is to be possible even within a delimited area alone. Democracy within a nation-state requires democracy within a network of intersecting international forces and relations. This is the meaning of democratization today.

(9)   The structure of interlocking political decisions and outcomes, which leaves a large variety of resources and forces beyond the control of nation-states, and which places nation-states themselves in a position to impinge and impose upon others, requires that the notion of a relevant constituency be expanded to incorporate the domains and groups of people significantly affected by such interconnectedness. Democratic autonomy requires, in principle, an expanding framework or federation of democratic states and agencies to embrace the ramifications of decisions and to render them accountable. There are two separate issues here. The first concerns changes in the territorial boundaries of systems of accountability so that those issues which escape the control of a nation-state – e.g. aspects of monetary management, environmental

questions, health, new forms of communication – can be brought under better control (a change that would imply, for instance, the shifting of some decisions from a nation-state to an enlarged regional or global framework). The second concerns the need to articulate territorially delimited polities with the key agencies, associations and organizations of the international system in such a way that the latter become part of a democratic process – adopting, within their very *modus operandi*, a structure of rules and principles compatible with those of democratic autonomy. In the face of the global system democracy requires both the nature and scope of territorially delimited polities, and the form and structure of the central forces and agencies of international civil society, to be recast. What is at stake, in sum, is the democratization of both the states system and the interlocking frameworks of the international civil order.

(10) The institutional basis of the federal model of democratic autonomy presupposes, in the first instance, an enhancement of the role of regional parliaments (for example, the European Parliament) so that decisions of such bodies become recognized, in principle, as legitimate independent sources of international law. Alongside such developments, the model anticipates the possibility of general referenda of groups cutting across nations and nation-states, with constituencies defined according to the nature and scope of controversial transnational issues. In addition, the opening of international governmental organizations to public scrutiny and the democratization of international "functional" bodies (on the basis perhaps of the creation of elected supervisory boards which are statistically representative of their constituencies) would be significant. Hand in hand with these changes the model assumes the entrenchment of the principle of autonomy (and its related cluster of rights) in order to provide shape, and limits, to democratic decision-making. This requires the enshrinement of the principle within the constitutions of parliaments and assemblies (at the international and national level) and the expansion of the influence of international courts so that groups and individuals have an effective means of suing political authorities for the enactment and enforcement of key rights both within and beyond political associations. In the final analysis, the formation of an authoritative assembly of all democratic states (a reformed General Assembly of the United Nations, or a complement to it) would be an objective. Such an assembly, if its terms of reference could ever be agreed upon in practice, might provide an international centre for the consideration and examination of pressing global issues such as food supply and distribution, the debt burden of the Third World, ozone depletion and the reduction of the risks of nuclear war.

(11) The implications for civil society are in part clear. A democratic federation of states and civil societies is incompatible with the exis-

tence of powerful sets of social relations and organizations which can – by virtue of the very bases of their operations – systematically distort democratic processes and hence outcomes. At issue here are such matters as the curtailment of the power of multinational corporations to constrain and influence the political agenda (through such diverse measures as the use of "golden shares", citizen directors, the public funding of elections) and the restriction of the activities of powerful transnational interest groups to pursue unchecked their interests, through, for example, the regulation of bargaining procedures to minimize the use of "strong-arm tactics" within and between public and private associations, and the enactment of rules preventing the sponsorship of political representatives by sectional interests, whether the latter be particular industries or trade unions. If individuals and peoples are to be free and equal in the determination of the conditions of their own existence there must be an array of social spheres – for instance, privately and co-operatively owned enterprises, independent communications media and health centres – which allow their members control of the resources at their disposal without direct interference from political agencies or other third parties. At issue is a civil society that is neither simply planned nor merely market-orientated but, rather, that is open to organizations, associations and agencies pursuing their own projects, subject to the constraints of a common structure of action and democratic processes.

(12)   A theory of legitimate power is inescapably a theory of democracy in the interlocking processes and structures of the global system. It is the theory of the democratic state within the global order and the theory of the impact of the global order on the democratic state. Such a theory need not assume a harmonious cosmopolitan international order – it would be absurd to do so – but it must assume that democratic processes and practices have to be articulated with the complex arena of national and international politics. The fate of democracy in the late twentieth century is inextricably bound up to the outcome of this process. There are good reasons for being optimistic about the results – and equally good ones for being pessimistic.

ACKNOWLEDGEMENTS

I would like to acknowledge the advice and comments offered on an earlier draft of this [chapter] by Tony McGrew, Michelle Stanworth, John Thompson and Anthony Giddens. Tony McGrew has been a constant guide through the voluminous literature of international relations; his constructive criticism has been especially helpful. The themes and arguments of this [chapter are] amplified further in Democracy and the Global Order: from the Modern State to Cosmopolitan Governance (Cambridge, Polity Press, 1995).

NOTES

1 The idea of "democratic autonomy" is set out in Held, *Models of Democracy* (1987: ch. 9), and *Political Theory and the Modern State* (1989: ch. 6). [Instead of the "federal model of democratic autonomy", in his more recent work David Held refers to this as the "cosmopolitan model of democracy". See, for example, his *Democracy and the Global Order* (1995). *Editor's note.*]

2 I have modified my earlier conception of this principle, to be found in Held, *Models of Democracy* (1987: 270–1).

REFERENCES

Bozeman, A. B. (1984) "The international order in a multicultural world," in H. Bull and A. Watson (eds), *The Expansion of International Society*. Oxford: Oxford University Press.

Bull, H. (1977) *The Anarchical Society*. London: Macmillan.

Burnheim, J. (1986) "Democracy, nation-states and the world system," in D. Held and C. Pollitt (eds), *New Forms of Democracy*. London: Sage.

Capotorti, F. (1983) "Human rights: the hard road toward universality," in R. St J. Macdonald and D. M. Johnson (eds), *The Structure and Process of International Law*. The Hague: Martinus Nijhoff.

Cassese, A. (1988) *Violence and Law in the Modern Age*. Cambridge: Polity Press.

Cox, R. W. (1987) *Production, Power and World Order*. New York: Columbia University Press.

Dunn, J. (1984) *Locke*. Oxford: Oxford University Press.

Gilpin, R. (1987) *The Political Economy of International Relations*. Princeton, NJ: Princeton University Press.

Gourevitch, P. (1978) "The second image reversed: the international sources of domestic politics," *International Organization*, 32 (4).

Held, D. (1987) *Models of Democracy*. Cambridge: Polity Press.

Held, D. (1989) *Political Theory and the Modern State*. Cambridge: Polity Press.

Held, D. (1995) *Democracy and the Global Order: from the Modern State to Cosmopolitan Governance*. Cambridge: Polity Press.

Herz, J. (1976) *The Nation-state and the Crisis of World Politics*. New York: McKay.

Hinsley, F. H. (1986) *Sovereignty*, 2nd edn. Cambridge: Cambridge University Press.

Kaiser, K. (1972) "Transnational relations as a threat to the democratic process," in R. O. Keohane and J. S. Nye (eds), *Transnational Relations and World Politics*. Cambridge, Mass.: Harvard University Press.

Kegley, C. W. and Wittkopf, E. R. (1989) *World Politics*. London: Macmillan.

Keohane, R. O. (1984a) *After Hegemony*. Princeton, NJ: Princeton University Press.

Keohane, R. O. (1984b) "The world political economy and the crisis of embedded liberalism," in J. H. Goldthorpe (ed.), *Order and Conflict in Contemporary Capitalism*. Oxford: Oxford University Press.

Keohane, R. O. and Nye, J. S. (eds) (1972) *Transnational Relations and World Politics*. Cambridge, Mass.: Harvard University Press.

Keohane, R. O. and Nye, J. S. (1977) *Power and Interdependence*. Boston: Little, Brown.

Krasner, S. D. (1988) "Sovereignty: an institutional approach," *Comparative Political Studies*, 21 (1): 40.

Luard, E. (1977) *International Agencies: the Emerging Framework of Interdependence*. London: Macmillan.

McGrew, A. (1988) "Conceptualizing global politics," in *Global Politics*. Milton Keynes: Open University Press.

Manin, B. (1987) "On legitimacy and political deliberation," *Political Theory*, 15 (3): 351–62.

Morse, E. (1976) *Modernization and the Transformation of International Relations*. New York: Free Press.

Negro, J. (1986) "International institutions," in *Democratic Government and Politics*. Milton Keynes: Open University Press.

Noel, E. (1989) "The Single European Act," *Government and Opposition*, 24 (1).

Offe, C. (1985) *Disorganized Capitalism*. Cambridge: Polity Press.

Oppenheim, L. (1905) *International Law*, vol. 1. London: Longman.

Rawls, J. (1985) "Justice as fairness: political not metaphysical," *Philosophy and Public Affairs*, 14 (3).

Rosenau, J. N. (1980) *The Study of Global Interdependence*. London: Pinter.

Ruggie, J. (1982) "International regimes, transactions and change: embedded liberalism in the post-war economic order," *International Organization*, 36.

Smith, D. (1984) *States and Military Blocs: Nato*. Milton Keynes: Open University Press.

Smith, R. (1987) "Political economy and Britain's external position," in *Britain in the World*. ESRC compilation, London.

Vincent, R. J. (1986) *Human Rights and International Relations*. Cambridge: Cambridge University Press.

Wallerstein, I. (1974) *The Modern World-System*. New York: Academic Press.

Wickham, A. (1984) "States and political blocs: the EEC," in D. Held and S. Hall (eds), *The State and Society*. Milton Keynes: Open University Press.

CHAPTER 17

Identity and Difference in Global Politics

William E. Connolly

DISCOVERY OF THE OTHER

In 1492 Columbus sailed the ocean blue. Then he discovered America. He did not discover a world as it existed in itself. Nor could he have. He discovered a world of otherness, a world of promise and danger, utopian bliss and barbaric cruelty, innocence and corruption, simplicity and mystery, all filtered through a late-medieval culture of perceptions, conceptions, aspirations, faiths, anxieties, and demands. His discovery was a creation; his creation was formed out of a clash between his cultural predispositions and unfamiliar materials – strange words, alien acts, surprising appearances, and uncanny responses.

The discovery by Columbus was essentially ambiguous, neither the recognition of a new world as it was in itself, nor the pure creation of a world out of nothing (in the manner of one of the stranger gods ever invented), nor a preliminary map to be filled out gradually and unproblematically with the collection of more information. The most compelling discovery Columbus made was that of an enigma, an enigma resisting straightforward formulation while persistently demanding recognition: the enigma of otherness and knowledge of it, of otherness and the constitution of personal identity, of otherness and estrangement from it, of otherness and the consolidation of collective identity, of otherness and dependence upon it, of otherness and the paradoxes of ethical integrity.

This chapter is an edited extract from *International/Intertextual Relations*, edited by J. Der Derian and M. J. Shapiro (New York, Lexington Books, 1989), pp. 323–42. Reprinted by permission of Lexington Books.

The simple word *discovery*, then, does not capture the relation between Columbus and the world he encountered. Neither does any other single word in English. Words such as *invention* and *constitution* give too much impetus to the initiating side; words such as *dialogue* and *discourse* give too much to a mutual task of decipherment to promote common understanding; words such as *conquest* and *colonization* underplay the effects of the encounter upon the self-identities of the initiating power. All these words, in their common ranges of signification, reflect one or another of the epistemologies of purity; each projects a "regulative ideal" that seems to me not only to be unattainable but dangerous to invoke in any simple or unambiguous way. I will stick with *discovery*, though, allowing its internal composition to shift as we proceed.

Columbus's discovery was not only more than a simple discovery (in the sense of finding what was there in itself before arrival); it was also a rediscovery. Christians before him had made similar discoveries, and explorers before him had landed on the American continent. It was also, like those before it, an incomplete rediscovery subject to self-erasure. Augustine (and he too was not the first to follow this path) encountered the enigma of otherness when he found it necessary to invent the shallow, egocentric, conceited self of paganism to promote the deep, confessing, interior self of christianity. He required this perception of the other to enable creation of the christian self. The Columbus discovery of the enigma of otherness was both a rediscovery and a partial discovery because, like most of his predecessors and successors, he protected and refined his own cultural identity by concealing the enigma he had begun to encounter. The enigma was subjected to erasure even as it was being read. If this is a familiar tactic of western, christian culture, with roots in the Bible, the church, medieval political thought, and early-modern thinkers, there are also counterpoints to it in these same traditions.

Perhaps the word *discovery* – retaining its established sense of adventure, newness, encounter with strangeness, promise of untapped riches, the initiation of ownership and entitlements, the suggestion of advance and progress – may now be infused with the idea of irony – an irony crafted from insight into how forgetting, denial, self-conceit, and erasure enter into the very relation between the discoverer and that which he discovers. Columbus discovered America out of the blue in 1492. But this blue now acquires depth beneath its pure, glistening, innocent surface. The surface and the depth, in this discovery out of the blue, now compromise and confound one another.

It is useful to think of the discovery of the New World as the discovery of a text – not because the text consisted only of words, not because a single author had written it, not because it could be reshaped or reconstituted at will by erasing some words and installing others, not because it lacked real things, natural powers, actual bodies, unexpected events, dwellings, and modes of power. But because the early explorers, once they decided to establish entitlements over their discoveries, had no recourse but to read what was there as a strange text that did not mesh well with presumptions, concepts, expectations, and demands they brought to their reading. And because there was no neutral place from which they could cognize the New World itself separate from the cultural text that permeated it. And because there was no master code into which they could translate both their codes and the codes of the New World without violence. And because the New World was susceptible to multiple readings, only some of which were immediately available to them. And because the New World provided a pretext that functioned eventually to redefine elements in the world from which they had come. The New World is a text, and it too is compounded from earlier texts. It is text all the way down and all the way to the top. "International relations," as we know them, were compounded at this time out of the intertext between the Old World and the New. This is a world historical moment in the history of western intertextuality.

Where is the god who promises to transcend the double edge of intertextuality so that one true account can in principle be given of the world? What should be done with or to those who refuse to believe in this god (and others like him or her) on the contestable grounds that this belief itself embodies conceit, cruelty, and danger? Must those who locate incorrigible contingency, contestability, and intertextuality in the most fundamental texts of international relations also be defined as others who lack the "discipline" (the self-control and the support of an academic field) appropriate for the study of international relations? What is the status of this "must"? Does it reflect ontological, epistemological, ethical, political, or security imperatives? Or does it contain a politically potent combination of them? Certainly this disciplinary "must," proposed variously and repeatedly in the late-modern academy, follows a line of time-honored practices in christianity when it encounters the other who deviates from the faith that grounds the rest of its faith. There may be something to learn by attending to this line of continuity amid discontinuity.

There are, indeed, parallels between the history of christian definitions and treatment of otherness and the range of contemporary orientations to academic otherness among secular social scientists. There have been shifts in the locus of faith, in the degree to which faithfulness is demanded, and in the treatment of the new heretics, but the range of discursive strategies by which the core elements of faith are protected reflect a certain consistency. Today, too, the academic other is often constituted as the innocent to be converted, the amoralist to be excommunicated, or the indispensable Jew to be enclosed in a ghetto and used occasionally as a counter to consolidate consensus within the canon. These microstrategies of academic containment, like their world historical predecessors, reveal how fragile the established structure of faith is, how compelling its maintenance is to the identities of the faithful, how impossible it is to keep the faith by demonstration, reason, and evidence alone, how indispensable this field of contrasts, threats, and accusations is to its internal organization. They disclose, as their reversal does too, some elements in the enigma of identity in its relation to the other.

We have here another intertext, filtering old christian dualities of faith and heresy, purity and sin, monotheism and paganism, conquest and conversion into the structure of secular academic life through the vehicle of the ambiguous "must": "You *must* presuppose truth in calling it into question; you *must* presuppose morality in accusing it of immorality; you *must* presuppose the deep subject in the act of criticizing it; you *must* presuppose the purity of freedom in opposing it. You *must* . . . or else we *must* define you accordingly!" Again, what is the necessity that governs this must today? And why should anyone, yesterday or today, refuse to conform to it?

We might learn something pertinent to today about the power of intertextuality and the enigma of otherness by pondering those questions as they emerged during encounters between the Old World and New World in the sixteenth century. These can only be indirect lessons, contestable lessons, lessons containing riddles in them. That, indeed, is one of the lessons – the one (particularly, perhaps, in international relations) that is the hardest to learn, the easiest to erase, and the most difficult to translate into practical precepts for global politics.

The first lesson may now be given a preliminary statement: to deny the enigma of external otherness – to treat it as the innocent, primitive, terrorist, oriental, evil-empire, savage, communist, underdeveloped, or pagan whose intrinsic defects demand that it be conquered or converted – is also to treat radical difference within one's own church or academy as otherness (as amoralism, evil, or irrationalism) to be neutralized, converted, or defeated. The definition of the internal other and the external other compound one another, and both of these seep into the definition given to the other within the interior of the self.

THE ENIGMA OF OTHERNESS

Tzvetan Todorov, in *The Conquest of America*, illuminates the enigma of otherness as it emerges in those early encounters of the Old World with the New World.[1] Todorov does not try to transcend the enigma by enclosing the relations conquistadors and priests established with the

Aztecs inside a universal discourse. He does not invoke the discourse of man, reason, rights, freedom, and truth in their universality to transcend simultaneously the parochial perspectives of the discoverers and those of the discovered. That would subject a previously hegemonic set of discourses – the discourses of the Old World – to another, later set evolving out of them. For the early discoverers themselves thought they brought a universal truth to bear on parochial, primitive, savage, pagan prejudices and superstitions.

Nor does he try, at least not persistently or single-mindedly, to transcend the early code of the West by "entering into" the internal perspective of the discovered peoples. For that strategy provides a mirror image of the first one. It supposes that if we cannot fashion a pure universalism (a pure rationalism or a pure empiricism) uncontaminated by the particular culture in which we are located, we must be able to fashion a pure contextualism (a pure understanding, a pure interpretation) that draws us into the perspective of the other as it was prior to its discovery. These two familiar and contending modalities complement each other as well. Each is governed by a quest for purity of understanding, either as pure particularity or pure universality; each is driven by the impulse to transparency that impels its competitor. And the common quest for purity erases (while leaving marks and smudges behind) the very enigma of otherness it began to render legible. Universalism subjugates the particularity of the other to its own particular code with universalist pretensions; and internal contextualism subjugates the particularity of the other to the myth of universal transparency through intellectual sympathy emanating from a superior culture.

Those critics of Todorov, then, who chastise him for not examining the conquest of the Aztecs from within the vantage point of the conquered people do not see that he already refuses the grounds upon which their objections rest. Indeed, as we shall see, versions of both the universalist and particularist strategies were pursued in the early encounters between the Old World and the New. These two modalities can support complementary strategies of domination, one supporting conquest of the other in the name of the universal superiority of the conqueror's own identity and the other neutralizing resistance to colonization by understanding the customs of the other well enough to launch a campaign of conversion.

Since Todorov contests the sufficiency and political implications of these two codes of inquiry, since he suggests how they function together in the encounters he charts, he himself adopts neither unambiguously. Yet, since he cannot avoid opting into both of them partially and provisionally, his text functions best if it adopts an ironic and problematizing stance to its own mode of inquiry. In place of trying to understand the other (the Aztecs) within a universal code or as they understood themselves, he explores how fixed patterns of encounter available to the Western invaders forced some priests into moments of self-doubt, confusion, and creative thinking. He treats Western texts of conquest and conversion – the two dominant patterns consistent with the cultural universalism of the West – as if they were the decipherable other to the late-modern West, both because similar texts are still inscribed in us today and because other things in these early texts possess the power to disturb us about the terms of similarity. That is, these texts – situated on a cusp between the late-medieval age and the early-modern age – remain close enough for discomfort, a discomfort that foments thought today about orientations to otherness in the present.

Todorov treats Aztec culture, on the other hand, mostly as if it were an undecipherable, resistant, and inexhaustible text upon which representatives of the West reinscribed their own stories and, when pushed to the limits of their own cultural resources, encountered the enigma of otherness in the other and themselves.

Todorov introduces a zone of intertextuality between late-medieval christianity and modern secular inter-nationality to open the present to an interrogation of its past and present.

Christianity posits a *single* god, enjoining a *universalist* religion applicable to human beings *equally*. It thus stands permanently above any religion with multiple gods making claims of allegiance to a select people. This medieval christian groundwork creates its other and constitutes them as pagans, savages, primitives, innocents, or barbarians. Once this basic orientation is secure, two stances toward otherness can contend for primacy within it. It might be deemed necessary to conquer or destroy those who worship other gods and who engage in practices alien to christian doctrine (such as human sacrifice, polygamy, cannibalism, and sodomy) on the grounds that they are a fallen people who defile god and contaminate the purity sought by christians. Or it might be thought necessary to convert them because they too have souls and they too can come to acknowledge christian faith. Columbus, Cortez, and the priest Sepulveda embody, in different ways, the first alternative. Las Casas, in his early writings, joins other priests in pressing the second. In general, the conquistadors press the first claim while the priests reactively seek to install the second. It is difficult to wander far outside this field of debate (as it is to wander outside the realist–idealist debate in international relations discourse today) because the conjunction of universalism, singularity, and equality clamps down upon any christian effort to do so.

The premises of singularity and universality press against affirming a plurality of gods appropriate to the other in the name of cultural pluralism, while the premise of equality before the christian god makes it sinful to practice benign neglect or indifference toward these pagan beliefs and practices. If innocent, they must be converted; if hopelessly corrupted, they must be conquered or eliminated so the corruption will not spread. Perhaps tolerance can be added to the list of possible stances within this field, but it must become, as tolerance usually is, a circumscribed and tactical tolerance. Tolerance, in this context, becomes forbearance toward cultural practices thought to be intrinsically wrong, but also thought to contain a glimmer of the truth within them, that might evolve, with proper prodding, into realization of christian truth. Tolerance emerges as a tactic of conversion, as the practice of christian charity toward the other because the christian, too, is a sinner.

If conquest and conversion are the two authorized orientations to otherness, neither engages the enigma of otherness. Both operate as contending and complementary strategies by which a superior people maintains its self-assurance by bringing an inferior people under its domination or tutelage. These two modes function together as premises and signs of superiority; each supports the other in the effort to erase the threat of difference to self-identity.

But conversion contains an interior dialectic that can push it to the edge of this field of discourse. The priests Las Casas and Sahugan represent two different exemplars of this possibility. Las Casas seeks to learn more about the other to convert them, but this deep engagement throws his initial confidence of superiority into doubt. For instance, christians charge the pagans with the sins of idolatry and human sacrifice, but Las Casas eventually concludes that the "idols" stand for a principle of divinity in a manner that makes them not totally unlike Christian representations of Christ and Mary. Or, while the Aztecs practice sacrifice, it also occurs in the Old Testament, and even Christ himself was once sacrificed so that we could be saved. The lines of differentiation now become blurred and temporalized. Las Casas slides from a simple model of christian conversion to a distributive model of multiple routes to the experience of divinity all heading broadly in the same vague direction. Both christians and pagans need to progress further along this uncharted path.

But this new posture is precarious and ambiguous. Las Casas clears a little more potential space for the other to be in its difference by losing a clear voice for himself as a bearer of christian conscience. His voice is no longer heard in Spain. The logic by which he falls into silence while continuing to write and speak may disclose an element within the enigma of otherness: when you remain within the established field of identity and difference, you become a bearer of strategies to protect identity through devaluation of the other; but if you transcend the field of identities through which the other is constituted, you lose the identity and standing needed to communicate with those you sought to inform. Identity and difference are bound together. It is impossible to reconstitute the relation to the second without confounding the experience of the first.

Sahugan plows further into the culture of the other than Las Casas (but not as far as other priests who simply become "renegades"). His voluminous *Historia general de Nueva Espana* is an encyclopedia of Aztec culture. He tries to give voice to the other without losing his own identity as a christian. But no appropriate vocabulary is available to him. The key terms embody judgments affirming christian ontology, reflecting Aztec ontology, or, at the edge of discursive possibility, giving birth to some perspective inside neither.

Sahugan must negotiate this field of possibilities and limitations in an effort to respect the identity of the other without forsaking his identity as a christian. So sometimes he alternates, using the term *god* in one sentence and *idol* in another; sometimes he adopts (or invents) the language of estrangement, describing acts of sacrifice in behavioral terms that neutralize cultural judgment at the cost of betraying alienation from the interpretive systems available in either culture. But these microtextual strategies are contained within an architectural organization that places God at the top and stones at the bottom of the cosmological hierarchy. Sahugan concludes that christianity is a superior religion but that the attempt to impose it upon the Aztecs has only destroyed one internally coherent system without enabling the emergence of another. His text becomes an inventory of the cultural devastation created by Spanish policies of conquest and conversion. But the inventory, by the very terms of its articulation, becomes one that his contemporaries in Spain can find reasons to avoid or condemn. By 1577, Philip II has cut off all of Sahugan's funding and forbidden the circulation of this texts.

Sahugan and Las Casas invent voices that enable critical reflection into the relation to the other, but each loses the ground inside his own culture from which such a dialogue can proceed.

While Las Casas and Sahugan help to bring out the enigma of otherness, there are differences between their circumstances and ours that might operate to create openings today unavailable to them. First, we have access to the history they helped to create. Second, we reside in a setting where the ontological closure of christian culture, partly through the self-critical history inaugurated by thinkers such as Las Casas and Sahugan, has been fractured and where it is now possible to question some of the parameters of the secular culture it helped to spawn. It is perhaps more possible today to expose and combat strategies through which contemporary practices of identity and difference conquer, convert, or degrade the external other while neutralizing internal others who interrogate this first relationship. Moreover, (and third), we live in a time of recognizable *global* danger that, while it presses in exactly the opposite direction too, provides cultural impetus to rethink the field of identity and difference through which contemporary states define and cope with otherness.

Todorov concludes his own foray into the issue of otherness with a gesture aimed at the present: "We want equality without its compelling to accept identity, but also difference without its degenerating into superiority/inferiority."[2] The aura shines brightly here, but it is not yet clear what it illuminates.

It is not immediately pertinent to question Todorov on the material means by which this goal could be advanced. Before that question can be raised, the goal itself must be made more credible as an alternative worthy of materialization. At this crucial level of intellectual imagination, Todorov leaves much to be desired. What could be the ontological status of an identity that established such a relation to other, foreign identities? Would this mean a culture without governing identities for the individual and the collectivity? What, then, could provide the pull for equality? What would provide the basis from which difference could be identified before it was accepted as difference? Todorov lapses into silence here, perhaps because he thinks he has reached the point within our culture that Las Casas and Sahugan reached in theirs, the point where the attempt to elaborate a new idea sounds inside it either like noise or collaboration with the enemy.

We (the "we" here is an invitation) might make progress on these issues by considering how an identity contains at least two dimensions. First, it might be tightly or loosely demarcated in the dimension of its breadth. Thus, christianity could restrict itself to catholicism, extend itself to include protestantism, extend itself further to include the judeo-christian tradition, or extend itself in another way to incorporate secular humanism and secular scientism on the grounds that they too draw their ethic from this tradition.

An identity, second, can also vary along the dimension of depth. An identity might have ontological depth because it construes itself to be the bearer of a fundamental truth that it knows to be true; it might have faith in its truth and look forward to a day when the faith is translated into knowledge; it might conclude that it must always be founded on a contestable faith in its truth; or it might conclude that it is both crucial to its individual and collective bearers but historically contingent in its formation and ungrounded ontologically in its truth – ungrounded, not because it alone in the world of identities has no ground, but because it treats as true the proposition that no identity is grounded in onto-logical truth; no identity is the true identity because every identity is particular and contingent.

Now this last position accepts the indispensability of identity and lives within the medium of identity while *refusing* (while struggling vigorously to refuse) to live its own identity as the truth.[3] Its bearers may acknowledge a drive within themselves and their culture to ontologize the identity given to them, a drive discernible in the history of their previous relationships to external, internal, and interior forms of otherness. But its bearers also struggle to overcome this drive because they think it is ungrounded in any truth they can prove and because they find it ethically compelling to revise their relation to otherness in the absence of such a proof.

Such a shift in orientation to individual and collective identity would be highly significant, but it does not lack precursors and premonitions within Western culture. It is far enough away from modern understandings to be distinctive, but close enough to currents within modern culture prefigured by Las Casas and Sahugan to be a development of it. Perhaps it stands in that ambiguous space between internal possibility and external challenge best described as "postmodern."

A postmodern identity assumes an ironic stance toward what it is even while affirming itself in its identity. And this changes both the experience of identity and its *possible* range of relationships with other identities. It would not rule out, of course, particular historical circumstances that spawn or intensify conflicts between opposing identities, but it would support new *possibilities* that establish new terms of comparison and debate and that place new pressures upon the established field of actualities and possibilities. It would put new pressure on the dominant field of actualities by forcing them to defend themselves against new possibilities not previously enunciated.

The basic strategy here is well articulated by Nietzsche: "Even the thought of a possibility can shake and transform us; it is not merely sensations or particular expectations that do that! Note how effective the possibility of eternal damnation was!"[4]

I think we might interpret Nietzsche's saying as follows: the possibility of eternal damnation shook and transformed thought once it was elaborated. For this possibility, once it is known as a possibility, can by the pressure of its own weight become transmuted into faith. "I had better believe this, for if it is true and I do not, the penalty is infinitely high." And once this thought becomes fixed in belief, the thought about what "eternal salvation" or "heaven" could mean becomes immunized against self-critical thought. Suppose, for instance, the promise of eternal life were instead juxtaposed against the threat of eternal oblivion. Since that is not quite so threatening, some might be led to ponder more carefully and critically just what the eternal life of a disembodied soul could mean. Once one ponders that, one might even conclude that the difference between eternal oblivion and eternal life is not that great. What would freedom be like, for instance, where there was no temporal dimension to the experience of choice? The essence of the christian promise might have been thrown into doubt a few centuries earlier if the possibility of eternal damnation had been left unstated.

The power of the possibility of damnation, then, was that it stilled this process of critical exploration before it could gather momentum. The power of the articulation of alternative possibilities is that they open up thinking into the restricted range of possibilities within which late-modern discourse about identity and global danger proceed.

Such an orientation to identity appears strange within the christian tradition, maybe within the judeo-christian tradition, probably within the secular tradition that has grown out of these first two, and perhaps within any culture that has yet acquired hegemony on the face of the earth. It may stand as far from late-modern conceptions of identity as the thought of Las Casas about divinity did from sixteenth-century christianity – that is, outside the normal range of discussion, but not so far as to be incomprehensible. It is the only position, as far as I can see, compatible with the Todorov aspiration even to *imagine* a world in which a given field of identities might hope to recognize differences without being *internally* compelled to define many of them as forms of otherness to be conquered, assimilated, or defiled. In this place (this world), I would strive to live my identity as a contingency that has become branded into me and we would strive to live ours in a similar way. Another identity would not pose a threat to me or us simply because it deviated significantly from the structure governing mine and ours. It would pose a threat if its definition of the goodness of its own identity required it to define ours as intrinsically evil or if its cultural priorities required it to infringe significantly upon resources essential to the maintenance of our identity in its nonhegemonic bearing.

If one thinks, to put the point starkly, that conflicts of *identity* sometimes create and often inflame international conflicts of *interest*, then this reconstitution of the lived politics of identity in late-modern states might have salutary effects on the structure of global politics. I want to say that some postmodern thinkers today stand in a productively problematic relation to modern advocates of realist and idealist theories of international politics (with their assumptions of strong identity). We have trouble breaking out of the molds in which contemporary thought is set and they have difficulty comprehending what it is we are saying. We threaten identities that sustain the nation and the academy in their realisms and idealisms and they define us according to the terms of discourse we are striving to interrogate. We charge them with contributing to global cruelties and dangers and these charges seem imaginary or contrived from within the assumptions governing their thought. But just as it is possible today to discern the discursive rules that both enabled the creativity of Las Casas and Sahugan and drove their contemporaries to defame and silence them, it may become possible for a generation of young thinkers to problematize the assumptions that confine established debates between realists, neorealists, and idealists. Time itself moves faster than it used to.

These last judgments are immodest and contestable; so too are the judgments that oppose them. No stance is modest or uncontestable when it comes to questions over assumptions and demands grounding a general field of theoretical discourse. That this condition must be so is itself part of the theoretical stance elaborated here.

[. . .]

NOTES

1 Tzvetan Todorov, *The Conquest of America: the Question of the Other*, trans. Richard Howard (New York, Harper and Row, 1985).
2 Ibid., p. 249.
3 The background to this elaboration of identity is developed in my book *Politics and Ambiguity* (Madison, University of Wisconsin Press, 1987), esp. chs 1, 7, 9 and 10.
4 Quoted from Nietzsche's *Nachlass* in Martin Heidegger, *Nietzsche, vol. II: The Eternal Recurrence of the Same*, trans. David Farrell Krell (San Francisco, Harper and Row, 1984), p. 129. The interpretation of its meaning that follows is mine.

INDEX

bureaucratization, 285, 300, 306–7
Byron, Lord, 144

Cady Stanton, E., 143
Calhoun, C., 125–6
Campbell, A., 144
capital accumulation, 52, 70, 299
  see also flexible accumulation
capitalism
  and citizenship, 214, 217–21, 230, 239
  "disorganized," 75, 101, 108
  and globalization, 66, 69–82 passim, 84, 87, 94, 95, 97, 101, 103
  international capital, 102
  organized, 46
  and radical democracy, 306–8
  and social movements, 149, 150, 214, 295
  see also global economy
capitalist economy, 90–2, 205, 209
capitalists, 46, 51, 66
care, 205–7, 223, 229–31, 248–52, 257
Castells, M., 172n
Chartism, 138, 144, 293
Christianity, 13–14, 337–9, 341–6
citizenship, xiii, 205–79 passim
  and capitalism, 214, 217–21, 230, 239
  and class, 238–9, 255, 258–9
  and culture, 218–19, 226–7
  and democracy, 212, 216, 218, 232, 234, 238, 251, 254, 256–9
  dominant paradigm of, 218–21, 224–5, 227, 231
  dual, 207, 267, 268
  duties/responsibilities, 210, 212, 217, 218, 226–30, 233–4
  and education, 209, 218, 254, 267, 271–2
  and employment, 227, 229–31, 233, 239, 240, 242, 245–8, 250, 252, 255–7, 259, 271–2
  European, 271–3, 276
  national, 59, 264–70, 275–77, 324

post-national, 207–8, 264–77 passim
  social, 209–34 passim
  women's, 207, 238–59 passim, 264–5
citizenship identity, see national identity
civil rights movement, 125, 138, 146
civil society, 126, 127, 185, 212, 214, 216, 220, 234
  global, 128, 179, 185, 193–4
  international, 286, 331–3
class, xi, 31, 43–60 passim, 92, 126, 129, 133, 135, 138–9, 296–7, 300–1
  and citizenship, 238–9, 255, 258–9
  middle class, 54, 107
  "new middle class," 48, 53
  ruling class, 51
  service class, 6, 48
  working class, 53, 54, 111, 245
  see also collective action; conflict; identity; interests; state
class actor (Touraine), 159
class conflict, 44, 51, 178, 284
class identity, xiii, 6, 44, 54, 135
class politics, see labor movement; political parties
class structure, 6, 43–6, 50, 51
Clinton, B., 178, 226
Club of Rome, 94
Cohen, J., 147
Cold War, 95–6
collective action, 166, 170, 190, 194, 215, 232, 234
  of classes, 44, 51, 81; see also labor movement
  consciousness, 215, 232, 234
  of social movements, 125, 127, 131, 149, 156, 159, 160, 162–5, 168
  transnational, 182–3
collective behavior approach, 126, 156–7, 165
collective identity, 5, 126, 127, 195, 336
collective will (Gramsci), 307